CLYMER®

YAMAHA

RAPTOR 660R • 2001-2005

The world;s finest publisher of mechanical how-to manuals

CLYMER®

P.O. Box 12901, Overland Park, Kansas 66282-2901

Copyright ©2005 Penton Business Media, Inc.

FIRST EDITION
First Printing October, 2003

SECOND EDITION
Updated to include 2004-2005 models
First Printing May, 2005
Second Printing December, 2006
Third Printing March, 2012

Printed in U.S.A.

CLYMER and colophon are registered trademarks of Penton Business Media, Inc.

ISBN-10: 0-89287-934-3

ISBN-13: 978-0-89287-934-2

Library of Congress: 2005925507

AUTHOR: Jay Bogart.

TECHNICAL PHOTOGRAPHY: Jay Bogart. Machine courtesy of Bryan Allen.

TECHNICAL ASSISTANCE: Jim Stuhr and Jerry Nicholson at Shawnee Cycle Plaza, Shawnee, KS.

TECHNICAL ILLUSTRATIONS: Errol McCarthy.

WIRING DIAGRAMS: Bob Meyer.

EDITOR: James Grooms.

PRODUCTION: Sarah Van Goethen.

TOOLS AND EQUIPMENT: K & L Supply Co. at www.klsupply.com.

COVER: Mark Clifford Photography at www.markclifford.com.

CLYMER®

Publisher Ron Rogers

EDITORIAL

Editorial Director
James Grooms

Editor
Steven Thomas

Associate Editor
Rick Arens

Authors
Ed Scott
Ron Wright
Michael Morlan
George Parise
Jay Bogart

Illustrators
Bob Meyer
Steve Amos
Errol McCarthy
Mitzi McCarthy

SALES

Sales Manager–Marine/I&T
Jay Lipton

Sales Manager–Powersport
Matt Tusken

CUSTOMER SERVICE

Customer Service Manager
Terri Cannon

Customer Service Representatives
Dinah Bunnell
Suzanne Johnson
April LeBlond
Sherry Rudkin

PRODUCTION

Director of Production
Dylan Goodwin

Production Manager
Greg Araujo

Senior Production Editors
Darin Watson
Adriane Wineinger

Associate Production Editors
Ashley Bally
Samantha Collins

Penton

P.O. Box 12901, Overland Park, KS 66282-2901 • 800-262-1954 • 913-967-1719

More information available at *clymer.com*

CONTENTS

QUICK REFERENCE DATA

ATV INFORMATION

MODEL:_____YEAR:_____

VIN NUMBER:_____

ENGINE SERIAL NUMBER:_____

CARBURETOR SERIAL NUMBER OR I.D. MARK:_____

ROUTINE ADJUSTMENT SPECIFICATIONS

Brake pad lining minimum thickness	1.0 mm (0.040 in.)
Brake pedal height	4.0 mm (0.16 in.)
Choke plunger stroke	15 mm (0.60 in.)
Clutch lever free play (at lever end)	5-10 mm (0.20-0.40 in.)
Drive chain	
Free play	30-45 mm (1.2-1.8 in.)
Length wear limit (10 pitch/11 pins)	150.1 mm (5.91 in.)
Parking brake	
Cable end length	64-68 mm (2.5-2.7 in.)
Lever free play	0 mm (0 in.)
Radiator cap relief pressure	95-125 kPa (13.8-18.1 psi)
Reverse cable length	135 mm (5.3 in.)
Reverse knob free play	0 mm (0 in.)
Rim runout (radial and lateral)	2.0 mm (0.08 in.)
Shift pedal height	22 mm (0.9 in.)
Speed limiter length (standard)	12 mm (0.47 in.)
Throttle lever free play	3-5 mm (0.12-0.20 in.)
Tire pressure (cold)	
Standard	27.5 kPa (4.0 psi) for maximum 100 kg (220 lb.) load
Mimimum	24.5 kPa (3.5 psi)
Maximum	30.5 kPa (4.4 psi)
Tire wear limit	3 mm (0.12 in.)
Tire toe-in	0-10 mm (0-0.40 in.)

FUEL, LUBRICANTS AND FLUIDS

Air filter	Foam air filter oil
Brake fluid type	DOT 4
Control cables	Cable lube
Cooling system	
Capacity	1.3 liters (1.4 U.S. qt.)
Radiator capacity	0.55 liter (0.58 U.S. qt.)
Reservoir capacity	0.29 liter (0.31 U.S. qt.)
Antifreeze type	Ethylene glycol containing anti-corrosion inhibitors for aluminum engines
Coolant mixture	50/50 (antifreeze/distilled water)
Drive chain	O-ring type chain lubricant
Engine oil	SG rated, four-stroke engine oil SAE 5W-30, 10W-30 or 20W-40

(continued)

FUEL, LUBRICANTS AND FLUIDS (continued)

Engine oil	
Capacity	2.3 liters (2.43 U.S. qt.)
Without filter change	1.9 liters (2.01 U.S. qt.)
With filter change	1.95 liters (2.06 U.S. qt.)
Fuel type	Unleaded gasoline
Octane rating (minimum)	86 (R+M/2) or 91 RON
Fuel tank capacity	12 liters (3.17 U.S. gal.)
Reserve amount	2.6 liters (0.69 U.S. gal.)

TUNE-UP SPECIFICATIONS

Battery	12 volt, 12 amp-hour
Battery type	YTX14-BS
Compression	
Standard	1250 kPa (181 psi)
Minimum	1050 kPa (152 psi)
Maximum	1350 kPa (196 psi)
Compression ratio	9.2:1
Idle speed	1450-1550 rpm
Ignition timing	12 BTDC° at 1500 rpm
Pilot mixture screw (initial setting)	
Left carburetor	3 turns out
Right carburetor	2 turns out
Spark plug	
Type	NGK DPR8EA-9
Gap	0.8-0.9 mm (0.031-0.035 in.)
Valve clearance (cold)	
Intake	0.10-0.15 mm (0.004-0.006 in.)
Exhaust	0.15-0.20 mm (0.006-0.008 in.)

MAINTENANCE TORQUE SPECIFICATIONS

Item	N•m	in.-lb.	ft.-lb.
Axle hub nuts	90	–	66
Chain adjuster locknuts	16	–	12
Coolant drain plug	10	88	–
Crankcase drain plug	30	–	22
Oil filter	17	–	13
Oil tank drain plug	25	–	18
Spark plug	18	–	13
Valve cover bolts			
Intake	12	106	–
Exhaust	10	88	–
Wheel lug nuts	45	–	33

CHAPTER ONE

GENERAL INFORMATION

This detailed and comprehensive manual covers the 2001-2005 Yamaha Raptor.

The text provides complete information on maintenance, tune-up, repair and overhaul. Hundreds of original photographs and illustrations created during the complete disassembly of ATV guide the reader through every job. All procedures are in step-by-step form and designed for the reader who may be working on the machine for the first time.

MANUAL ORGANIZATION

A shop manual is a tool and as in all Clymer manuals, the chapters are thumb tabbed for easy reference. Main headings are listed in the table of contents and the index. Frequently used specifications and capacities from the tables at the end of each individual chapter are listed in the *Quick Reference Data* section at the front of the manual. Specifications and capacities are provided in metric and U.S. Standard units of measure.

During some of the procedures there will be references to headings in other chapters or sections of the manual. When a specific heading is called out it in a step it will be *italicized* as it appears in the manual. If a sub-heading is indicated as being "in this section" it is located within the same main heading.

For example, the sub-heading ***Handling Gasoline Safely*** is located within the main heading ***SAFETY***.

This chapter provides general information on shop safety, tools and their usage, service fundamentals and shop supplies. **Tables 1-7**, at the end of the chapter, provide the following:

Table 1 lists the model code numbers covered in this manual.

Table 2 lists general dimensions and weight.

Table 3 lists technical abbreviations.

Table 4 lists general torque specifications.

Table 5 lists conversion formulas.

Table 6 lists metric tap and drill sizes.

Table 7 lists metric, inch and fractional equivalents.

Chapter Two provides methods for quick and accurate diagnosis of problems. Troubleshooting procedures present typical symptoms and logical methods to pinpoint and repair the problem.

Chapter Three explains all routine maintenance and recommended tune-up procedures necessary to keep the machine running well.

Subsequent chapters describe specific systems such as engine, transmission, clutch, drive system, fuel and exhaust systems, suspension and brakes. Each disassembly, repair and assembly procedure is discussed in step-by-step form.

WARNINGS, CAUTIONS AND NOTES

The terms WARNING, CAUTION and NOTE have specific meanings in this manual.

A WARNING emphasizes areas where injury or even death could result from negligence. Mechanical damage may also occur. WARNINGS *are to be taken seriously*.

A CAUTION emphasizes areas where equipment damage could result. Disregarding a CAUTION could cause permanent mechanical damage, though injury is unlikely.

A NOTE provides additional information to make a step or procedure easier or clearer. Disregarding a NOTE could cause inconvenience, but would not cause equipment damage or personal injury.

SAFETY

Follow these guidelines and practice common sense to safely service the machine:

1. Do not operate the machine in an enclosed area. The exhaust gasses contain carbon monoxide, an odorless, colorless and tasteless poisonous gas. Carbon monoxide levels build quickly in small enclosed areas and can cause unconsciousness and death in a short time. Properly ventilate the work area, or operate the machine outside.

2. *Never* use gasoline or any extremely flammable liquid to clean parts. Refer to *Cleaning Parts* and *Handling Gasoline Safely* in this section.

3. *Never* smoke or use a torch in the vicinity of flammable liquids, such as gasoline or cleaning solvent.

4. If welding or brazing on the machine, move the fuel tank a safe distance away from the work area.

5. Use the correct type and size of tools to avoid damaging fasteners.

6. Keep tools clean and in good condition. Replace or repair worn or damaged equipment.

7. When loosening a tight fastener, be guided by what would happen if the tool slips.

8. When replacing fasteners, check that the new fasteners are of the same size and strength as the original ones.

9. Keep the work area clean and organized.

10. Wear eye protection *anytime* eye injury is possible. This includes procedures involving drilling, grinding, hammering, compressed air and chemicals.

11. Wear the correct clothing for the job. Tie up or cover long hair so it cannot get caught in moving equipment.

12. Do not carry sharp tools in clothing pockets.

13. Always have an approved fire extinguisher available. Check that it is rated for gasoline (Class B) and electrical (Class C) fires.

14. Do not use compressed air to clean clothes, the machine or the work area. Debris may be blown into the eyes or skin. *Never* direct compressed air at yourself or others. Do not allow children to use or play with any compressed air equipment.

15. When using compressed air to dry rotating parts, hold the part so it cannot rotate. Do not allow the force of the air to spin the part. The air jet is capable of rotating parts at extreme speed. The part may be damaged or disintegrate, causing serious injury.

16. Do not inhale the dust created by brake pad and clutch wear. In most cases these particles contain asbestos. In addition, some types of insulating materials and gaskets may contain asbestos. Inhaling asbestos particles is hazardous to health.

17. Never work on the machine while someone is working under it.

18. When placing the machine on a stand, check that it is secure.

Handling Gasoline Safely

Gasoline is a volatile, flammable liquid and is one of the most dangerous items in the shop. Keep in mind, when working on a machine, gasoline is always present in the fuel tank, fuel line and carburetor. To avoid an accident when working around the fuel system, carefully observe the following precautions:

1. *Never* use gasoline to clean parts. See *Cleaning Parts* in this chapter.

2. When working on the fuel system, work outside or in a well-ventilated area. Turn off the fuel valve.

3. Do not add fuel to the fuel tank or service the fuel system while the machine is near open flames, sparks or where someone is smoking. Gasoline vapor is heavier than air, it collects in low areas and is more easily ignited than liquid gasoline.

4. Allow the engine to cool completely before working on any fuel system component.

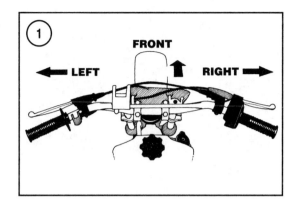

5. When draining the carburetor, catch the fuel in a plastic container and then pour it into an approved gasoline storage device.

6. Do not store gasoline in glass containers. If the glass breaks, a serious explosion or fire may occur.

7. Immediately wipe up spilled gasoline. Store the contaminated shop cloths in a metal container with a lid until they can be properly disposed, or place them outside in a safe place for the fuel to evaporate.

8. Do not pour water onto a gasoline fire. Water spreads the fire and makes it more difficult to put out. Use a class B, BC or ABC fire extinguisher to extinguish the fire.

9. Always turn off the engine before refueling. Avoid spilling fuel onto the engine or exhaust system. Do not overfill the fuel tank. Leave an air space at the top of the tank to allow room for the fuel to expand due to temperature fluctuations.

Cleaning Parts

Cleaning parts is one of the more time consuming jobs performed in the home shop. There are many types of chemical cleaners and solvents available for shop use. Most are poisonous and extremely flammable. To prevent chemical exposure, vapor buildup, fire and serious injury, observe each product warning label and note the following:

1. Read and observe the entire product label before using any chemical. Always know what type of chemical is being used and whether it is poisonous and/or flammable.

2. Do not use more than one type of cleaning solvent at a time. If mixing chemicals is called for, measure the proper amounts according to the manufacturer.

3. Work in a well-ventilated area.

4. Wear chemical-resistant gloves.

5. Wear safety glasses.

6. Wear a vapor respirator when necessary.

7. Wash hands and arms thoroughly after cleaning parts.

8. Keep chemical products away from children and pets.

9. Thoroughly clean all oil, grease and cleaner residue from any part that must be heated.

10. Use a nylon brush when cleaning parts. Wire brushes may cause a spark.

11. When using a parts washer, only use the solvent recommended by the manufacturer. Check that the parts washer is equipped with a metal lid that will lower in case of fire.

Warning Labels

Most manufacturers attach information and warning labels to the machine. These labels contain instructions that are important to personal safety when operating, servicing, transporting and storing the machine. Refer to the owner's manual for the description and location of labels. Order replacement labels from the manufacturer if they are missing or damaged.

BASIC SERVICE METHODS

Most of the procedures in this manual are straightforward and can be performed by anyone reasonably competent with tools. However, consider personal capabilities carefully before attempting any operation involving major disassembly of the engine.

1. *Front*, in this manual, refers to the front of the machine. The front of any component is the end closest to the front of the machine. The left and right sides refer to the position of the parts as viewed by the rider sitting on the seat facing forward (**Figure 1**).

2. Whenever servicing an engine or suspension component, secure the machine in a safe manner.

3. Tag all similar parts for location and mark all mating parts for position. Record the number and thickness of any shims as they are removed. Identify parts by placing them in sealed and labeled plastic bags.

4. Tag disconnected wires and connectors with masking tape and a marking pen.

5. Protect finished surfaces from physical damage or corrosion. Keep gasoline and other chemicals off painted surfaces.

6. Use penetrating oil on frozen or tight bolts. Avoid using heat where possible. Heat can warp, melt or affect the temper of parts. Heat also damages the finish of paint and plastics.

7. When a part is a press-fit or requires a special tool for removal, the information or type of tool is identified in the text. Otherwise, if a part is difficult to remove or install, determine the cause before proceeding.

8. Cover all openings to prevent objects or debris from falling into the engine.

9. Read each procedure thoroughly and compare the illustrations to the actual components before starting the procedure. Perform the procedure in sequence.

10. Recommendations are occasionally made to refer service to a dealership or specialist. In these cases, the work can be performed more economically by the specialist than by the home mechanic.

11. The term *replace* means to discard a defective part and replace it with a new part. *Overhaul* means to remove, disassemble, inspect, measure, repair and/or replace parts as required to recondition an assembly.

12. Some operations require the use of a hydraulic press. If a press is not available, have these operations performed by a shop equipped with the necessary equipment. Do not use makeshift equipment that may damage the machine.

13. Repairs are much faster and easier if the machine is clean before starting work. Degrease the machine with a commercial degreaser; follow the directions on the container for the best results. Clean all parts with cleaning solvent as they are removed.

CAUTION
Do not apply a chemical degreaser to an O-ring drive chain. These chemicals will damage the O-rings. Use kerosene to clean O-ring type chains.

CAUTION
Do not direct high-pressure water at steering bearings, carburetor hoses, wheel bearings, suspension and electrical components, or O-ring drive chains. The water will force the

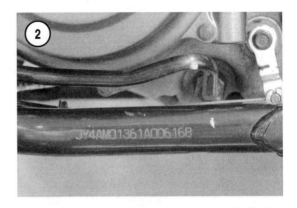

grease out of the bearings and possibly damage the seals.

14. If special tools are required, have them available before starting the procedure. When special tools are required, they will be described in the procedure.

15. Make diagrams of similar-appearing parts. For instance, crankcase bolts are often not the same lengths. Do not rely on memory alone. It is possible that carefully laid out parts will become disturbed, making it difficult to reassemble the components correctly without a diagram.

16. Check that all shims and washers are reinstalled in the same location and position.

17. Whenever rotating parts contact a stationary part, look for a shim or washer.

18. Use new gaskets if there is any doubt about the condition of old ones.

19. If self-locking fasteners are used, replace them with new ones. Do not install standard fasteners in place of self-locking ones.

20. Use grease to hold small parts in place if they tend to fall out during assembly. Do not apply grease to electrical or brake components.

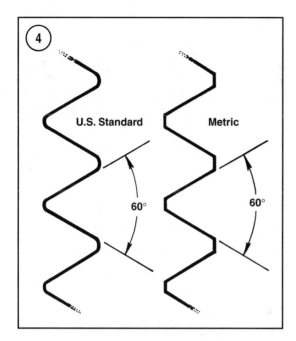

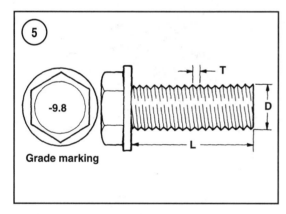

SERIAL NUMBERS

Serial numbers are stamped on the frame and air filter housing cover. Record these numbers in the *Quick Reference Data* section at the front of the manual. Have these numbers available when ordering parts.

The vehicle identification number (VIN) is stamped on the left frame tube, below the left engine cover (**Figure 2**).

The model code and engine family information are on stickers adhered to the top of the air filter housing cover (**Figure 3**).

Table 1 lists model code years and VIN numbers, if available.

FASTENERS

Proper fastener selection and installation is important to ensure the machine operates as designed, and can be serviced efficiently. Check that replacement fasteners meet all the same requirements as the originals.

Threaded Fasteners

Threaded fasteners secure most of the components on the machine. Most are tightened by turning them clockwise (right-hand threads). If the normal rotation of the component being tightened would loosen the fastener, it may have left-hand threads. If a left-hand threaded fastener is used, it is noted in the text.

Two dimensions are required to match the thread size of the fastener: the number of threads in a given distance and the outside diameter of the threads.

Two systems are currently used to specify threaded fastener dimensions: the U.S. Standard system and the metric system (**Figure 4**). Pay particular attention when working with unidentified fasteners; mismatching thread types can damage threads.

NOTE
To ensure that fastener threads are not mismatched or become cross-threaded, start all fasteners by hand. If a fastener is hard to start or turn, determine the cause before tightening with a wrench.

The length (L), diameter (D) and distance between thread crests (pitch) (T) (**Figure 5**) classify metric screws and bolts. A typical bolt may be identified by the numbers, 8-1.25×130. This indicates the bolt has diameter of 8 mm, the distance between thread crests is 1.25 mm and the length is 130 mm. Always measure bolt length as shown in **Figure 6** to avoid purchasing replacements of the wrong length.

The numbers located on the top of the fastener (**Figure 5**) indicate the strength of metric screws and bolts. The higher the number, the stronger the fastener. Unnumbered fasteners are the weakest.

Many screws, bolts and studs are combined with nuts to secure particular components. To indicate the size of a nut, manufacturers specify the internal diameter and the thread pitch.

The measurement across two flats on a nut or bolt indicates the wrench size.

> *WARNING*
> *Do not install fasteners with a strength classification lower than what was originally installed by the manufacturer. Doing so may cause equipment failure and/or damage.*

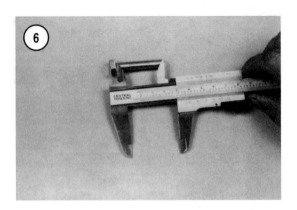

Torque Specifications

The materials used in the manufacture of the machine may be subjected to uneven stresses if the fasteners of the various subassemblies are not installed and tightened correctly. Fasteners that are improperly installed or work loose can cause extensive damage. It is essential to use an accurate torque wrench, described in this chapter, with the torque specifications in this manual.

Specifications for torque are provided in Newton-meters (N•m), foot-pounds (ft.-lb.) and inch-pounds (in.-lb.). Refer to **Table 5** for torque conversions and **Table 4** for general specifications. To use **Table 4**, first determine the size of the fastener as described in *Fasteners* in this chapter. Torque specifications for specific components are at the end of the appropriate chapters. Torque wrenches are covered in the *Basic Tools* section.

Self-Locking Fasteners

Several types of bolts, screws and nuts incorporate a system that creates interference between the two fasteners. Interference is achieved in various ways. The most common type is the nylon insert nut and a dry adhesive coating on the threads of a bolt.

Self-locking fasteners offer greater holding strength than standard fasteners, which improves their resistance to vibration. Most self-locking fasteners cannot be reused. The materials used to form the lock become distorted after the initial installation and removal. It is a good practice to discard and replace self-locking fasteners after their removal. Do not replace self-locking fasteners with standard fasteners.

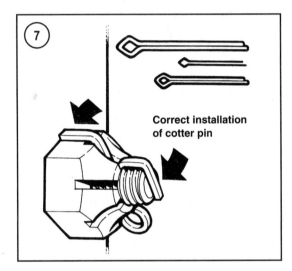

Correct installation of cotter pin

Washers

There are two basic types of washers: flat washers and lockwashers. Flat washers are simple discs with a hole to fit a screw or bolt. Lockwashers are used to prevent a fastener from working loose. Washers can be used as spacers and seals, or to help distribute fastener load and to prevent the fastener from damaging the component.

As with fasteners, when replacing washers check that the replacement washers are of the same design and quality.

Cotter Pins

A cotter pin is a split metal pin inserted into a hole or slot to prevent a fastener from loosening. In certain applications, such as the rear axle on an ATV or motorcycle, the fastener must be secured in this

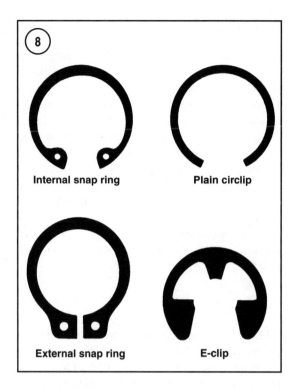

8

Internal snap ring   Plain circlip

External snap ring   E-clip

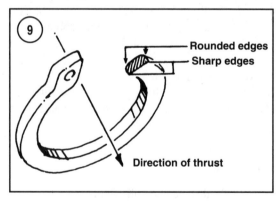

9

Rounded edges
Sharp edges

Direction of thrust

Snap Rings and E-clips

Snap rings (**Figure 8**) are circular-shaped metal retaining clips. They are required to secure parts and gears in place on parts such as shafts, pins or rods. External type snap rings are used to retain items on shafts. Internal type snap rings secure parts within housing bores. In some applications, in addition to securing the component(s), snap rings of varying thickness also determine end play. These are usually called selective snap rings.

Two basic types of snap rings are used: machined and stamped snap rings. Machined snap rings can be installed in either direction, since both faces have sharp edges. Stamped snap rings (**Figure 9**) are manufactured with a sharp edge and a round edge. When installing stamped snap rings in a thrust application, install the sharp edge facing away from the part producing the thrust.

Observe the following when installing snap rings:

1. Remove and install snap rings with snap ring pliers. See *Snap Ring Pliers* in this chapter.

2. In some applications, it may be necessary to replace snap rings after removing them.

3. Compress or expand snap rings only enough to install them. If overly expanded, they lose their retaining ability.

4. After installing a snap ring, check that it seats completely.

5. Wear eye protection when removing and installing snap rings.

E-clips are used when it is not practical to use a snap ring. Remove E-clips with a flat blade screwdriver by prying between the shaft and E-clip. To install an E-clip, center it over the shaft groove and push or tap it into place.

SHOP SUPPLIES

Lubricants and Fluids

Periodic lubrication helps ensure long service-life for any type of equipment. Using the correct type of lubricant or fluid is as important as performing the service. The following section describes the types of lubricants most often required. Follow the manufacturer's recommendations for lubricant and fluid types.

way. For these applications, a cotter pin and castellated (slotted) nut is used.

To use a cotter pin, first make sure the diameter is correct for the hole in the fastener. After correctly tightening the fastener and aligning the holes, insert the cotter pin through the hole and bend the ends over the fastener (**Figure 7**). Unless instructed to do so, never loosen a torqued fastener to align the holes. If the holes do not align, tighten the fastener just enough to achieve alignment.

Cotter pins are available in various diameters and lengths. Measure length from the bottom of the head to the tip of the shortest pin.

Engine oil

Engine oil is classified by two standards: the American Petroleum Institute (API) service classification and the Society of Automotive Engineers (SAE) viscosity rating. This information is on the oil container label. Two letters indicate the API service classification. The number or sequence of numbers and letter (10W-40 for example) is the oil's viscosity rating. The API service classification and the SAE viscosity index are not indications of oil quality.

The service classification indicates that the oil meets specific lubrication standards. The first letter in the classification (*S*) indicates the oil is for gasoline engines. The second letter indicates the standard the oil satisfies. The classification started with the letter *A* and is currently at the letter *L*. Most motorcycle/ATV oils are specifically made to the *G* classification, which is recommended by most motorcycle/ATV manufacturers.

Always use an oil with a classification recommended by the manufacturer. Using an oil with a classification different than that recommended can cause engine damage.

Viscosity is an indication of the oil's ability to lubricate and circulate at specific temperatures. Light oils have a lower number while heavy oils have a higher number. Engine oils fall into the 5- to 50-weight range for single-grade oils.

Most manufacturers recommend multigrade oil. These oils perform efficiently across a wide range of operating conditions. Multigrade oils are identified by a *W* after the first number, which indicates the low-temperature viscosity.

Engine oils are most commonly mineral (petroleum) based; however synthetic and semi-synthetic types are frequently used. When selecting engine oil, follow the manufacturer's recommendation for type, classification and viscosity.

Grease

Grease is lubricating oil with thickening agents. The National Lubricating Grease Institute (NLGI) grades grease. Grades range from No. 000 to No. 6, with No. 6 being the thickest. Typical multipurpose grease is NLGI No. 2. For specific applications, manufacturers may recommend water-resistant type grease or one with an additive such as molybdenum disulfide (MoS_2).

Chain lubricant

There are many types of chain lubricants available. Which type of chain lubricant to use depends on the type of chain.

On O-ring (sealed) chains, the lubricant keeps the O-rings pliable and prevents corrosion. The actual chain lubricant is enclosed in the chain by the O-rings. Recommended types include aerosol sprays specifically designed for O-ring chains, and conventional engine or gear oils. When using a spray lubricant, check that it is suitable for O-ring chains.

Do not use a high-pressure washer, solvents or gasoline to clean an O-ring chain. Clean O-rings with kerosene only.

Foam air filter oil

Filter oil is specifically designed for use on foam air filters. The oil is blended with additives, making it easy to pour and apply evenly to the filter. Some filter oils include additives that evaporate quickly, making the filter oil very tacky. This allows the oil to remain suspended within the foam pores, trapping dirt and preventing it from being drawn into the engine.

Do not use engine oil as a substitute for foam filter oil. Engine oils will not remain in the filter. Instead, they will be drawn into the engine, leaving the filter ineffective.

Brake fluid

Brake fluid is the hydraulic fluid used to transmit hydraulic pressure (force) to the wheel brakes. Brake fluid is classified by the Department of Transportation (DOT). Current designations for brake fluid are DOT 3, DOT 4 and DOT 5. This classification appears on the fluid container.

Each type of brake fluid has its own definite characteristics. Do not intermix different types of brake fluid. DOT 5 fluid is silicone-based. DOT 5 is not compatible with other fluids or in systems for which it was not designed. Mixing DOT 5 fluid with other fluids may cause brake system failure. When adding brake fluid, *only* use the fluid recommended by the manufacturer.

Brake fluid will damage any plastic, painted or plated surface it contacts. Use extreme care when working with brake fluid and remove any spills immediately with soap and water.

Hydraulic brake systems require clean and moisture-free brake fluid. Never reuse brake fluid. Keep containers and reservoirs sealed.

> *WARNING*
> *Never put a mineral-based (petroleum) oil into the brake system. Mineral oil will cause rubber parts in the system to swell and break apart, resulting in complete brake failure.*

Coolant

Coolant is a mixture of water and antifreeze used to dissipate engine heat. Ethylene glycol is the most common form of antifreeze. Check the manufacturer's recommendations when selecting an antifreeze; most require one specifically designed for use in aluminum engines. These types of antifreezes have additives that inhibit corrosion.

Only mix distilled water with antifreeze. Impurities in tap water may damage internal cooling system passages.

Cleaners, Degreasers and Solvents

Many chemicals are available to remove oil, grease and other residue from the machine.

Before using cleaning solvents, consider how they will be used and disposed of, particularly if they are not water-soluble. Local ordinances may require special procedures for the disposal of many types of cleaning chemicals. Refer to *Safety* and *Cleaning Parts* in this chapter for more information on their use.

Use brake parts cleaner to clean brake system components when contact with petroleum-based products will damage seals. Brake parts cleaner leaves no residue. Use electrical contact cleaner to clean electrical connections and components without leaving any residue. Carburetor cleaner is a strong solvent used to remove fuel deposits and varnish from fuel system components. Use this cleaner carefully, as it may damage finishes.

Generally, degreasers are strong cleaners used to remove heavy accumulations of grease from engine and frame components.

Most solvents are designed to be used in a parts washing cabinet for individual component cleaning.

For safety, use only nonflammable or high flash-point solvents.

Gasket Sealant

Sealants are used in combination with a gasket or seal and are occasionally alone. Follow the manufacturer's recommendation when using sealants. Use extreme care when choosing a sealant. Choose sealants based on their resistance to heat, various fluids and their sealing capabilities.

One of the most common sealants is RTV, or room temperature vulcanizing sealant. This sealant cures at room temperature over a specific time period. This allows the repositioning of components without damaging gaskets.

Moisture in the air causes the RTV sealant to cure. Always install the tube cap as soon as possible after applying RTV sealant. RTV sealant has a limited shelf life and will not cure properly if the shelf life has expired. Keep partial tubes sealed and discard them if they have surpassed the expiration date.

Applying RTV sealant

Clean all old gasket residue from the mating surfaces. Remove all gasket material from blind threaded holes; it can cause inaccurate bolt torque. Spray the mating surfaces with aerosol parts cleaner and then wipe with a lint-free cloth. The area must be clean for the sealant to adhere.

Apply RTV sealant in a continuous bead 2-3 mm (0.08-0.12 in.) thick. Circle all the fastener holes unless otherwise specified. Do not allow any sealant to enter these holes. Assemble and tighten the fasteners to the specified torque within the time frame recommended by the RTV sealant manufacturer.

Gasket Remover

Aerosol gasket remover can help remove stubborn gaskets. This product can speed up the removal process and prevent damage to the mating surface that may be caused by using a scraping tool. Most of these types of products are very caustic. Follow the manufacturer's instructions for use.

Threadlocking Compound

Threadlocking compound is a fluid applied to the threads of fasteners. After tightening the fastener, the fluid sets and becomes a solid filler between the threads. This makes it difficult for the fastener to work loose from vibration, or heat expansion and contraction. Some threadlocking compounds also provide a seal against fluid leakage.

Before applying threadlocking compound, remove any old compound from both thread areas and clean them with aerosol parts cleaner. Use the compound sparingly. Excess fluid can run into adjoining parts.

Threadlocking compounds are available in different strengths. Follow the manufacturer's recommendations regarding compound selection. Two manufacturers of threadlocking compound are ThreeBond and Loctite. They both offer a wide range of compounds for various strength, temperature and repair applications.

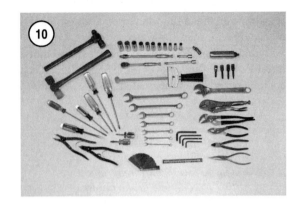

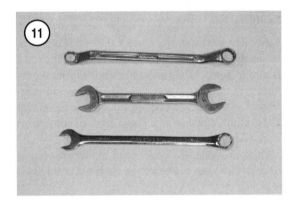

BASIC TOOLS

Most of the procedures in this manual can be carried out with simple hand tools and test equipment familiar to the home mechanic. Always use the correct tools for the job at hand. Keep tools organized and clean. Store them in a tool chest with related tools organized together.

Quality tools are essential. The best are constructed of high-strength alloy steel. These tools are light, easy to use and resistant to wear. Their working surface is devoid of sharp edges and the tool is carefully polished. They have an easy-to-clean finish and are comfortable to use. Quality tools are a good investment.

When purchasing tools to perform the procedures covered in this manual, consider the tools' potential frequency of use. If just starting a tool kit, consider purchasing a basic tool set (**Figure 10**) from a large tool supplier. These sets are available in many tool combinations and offer substantial savings when compared to individually purchased tools. As work experience grows and tasks become more complicated, specialized tools can be added.

Some of the procedures in this manual specify special tools. In most cases, the tool is illustrated in use. Well-equipped mechanics may be able to substitute similar tools or fabricate a suitable replacement. However, in some cases, the specialized equipment or expertise may make it impractical for the home mechanic to attempt the procedure. When necessary, such operations are identified in the text with the recommendation to have a dealership or specialist perform the task. It may be less expensive to have a professional perform these jobs, especially when considering the cost of the equipment.

Screwdrivers

Screwdrivers of various lengths and types are mandatory for the simplest tool kit. The two basic types are the slotted tip (flat blade) and the Phillips tip. These are available in sets that often include an assortment of tip sizes and shaft lengths.

As with all tools, use a screwdriver designed for the job. Check that the size of the tip conforms to the size and shape of the fastener. Use them only for driving screws. Never use a screwdriver for prying or chiseling metal. Repair or replace worn or damaged screwdrivers. A worn tip may damage the fastener, making it difficult to remove.

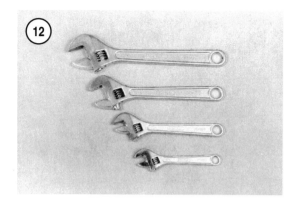

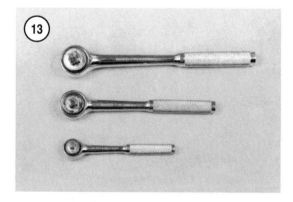

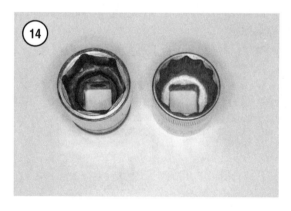

ers, the 6-point provides superior holding ability by contacting the fastener across a wider area at all six edges. For general use, the 12-point works well. It allows the wrench to be removed and reinstalled without moving the handle over such a wide arc.

An open-end wrench is fast and works best in areas with limited overhead access. It contacts the fastener at only two points, and is subject to slipping under heavy force, or if the tool or fastener is worn. A box-end wrench is preferred in most instances, especially when breaking loose and applying the final tightness to a fastener.

The combination wrench has a box-end on one end, and an open-end on the other. This combination makes it a very convenient tool.

Adjustable Wrenches

An adjustable wrench or Crescent wrench (**Figure 12**) can fit nearly any nut or bolt head that has clear access around its entire perimeter. Adjustable wrenches are best used as a backup wrench to keep a large nut or bolt from turning while the other end is being loosened or tightened with a box-end or socket wrench.

Adjustable wrenches contact the fastener at only two points, which makes them more subject to slipping off the fastener. The fact that one jaw is adjustable and may loosen only aggravates this shortcoming. Make certain the solid jaw is the one transmitting the force.

Socket Wrenches, Ratchets and Handles

Sockets that attach to a ratchet handle (**Figure 13**) are available with 6-point or 12-point openings (**Figure 14**) and different drive sizes. The drive size indicates the size of the square hole that accepts the ratchet handle. The number stamped on the socket is the size of the work area and must match the fastener head.

As with wrenches, a 6-point socket provides superior holding ability, while a 12-point socket needs to be moved only half as far to reposition it on the fastener.

Sockets are designated for either hand or impact use. Impact sockets are made of thicker material for more durability. Compare the size and wall thickness of a 19 mm hand socket (A, **Figure 15**) and the 19 mm impact socket (B). Use impact sockets when

Wrenches

Open-end, box-end and combinations wrenches (**Figure 11**) are available in a variety of types and sizes.

The number stamped on the wrench refers to the distance between the work areas. This size must match the size of the fastener head.

The box-end wrench grips the fastener on all sides. This reduces the chance of the tool slipping. The box-end wrench is designed with either a 6- or 12-point opening. For stubborn or damaged fasten-

using an impact driver or air tools. Use hand sockets with hand-driven attachments.

> *WARNING*
> *Do not use hand sockets with air or impact tools, as they may shatter and cause injury. Always wear eye protection when using impact or air tools.*

Various handles are available for sockets. The speed handle is used for fast operation. Flexible ratchet heads in varying lengths allow the socket to be turned with varying force, and at odd angles. Extension bars allow the socket setup to reach difficult areas. The ratchet is the most versatile. It allows the user to install or remove the nut without removing the socket.

Sockets combined with any number of drivers make them undoubtedly the fastest, safest and most convenient tool for fastener removal and installation.

Impact Driver

An impact driver provides extra force for removing fasteners by converting the impact of a hammer into a turning motion. This makes it possible to remove stubborn fasteners without damaging them. Impact drivers and interchangeable bits (**Figure 16**) are available from most tool suppliers. When using a socket with an impact driver, check that the socket is designed for impact use. Refer to *Socket Wrenches, Ratchets and Handles* in this chapter.

> *WARNING*
> *Do not use hand sockets with air or impact tools as they may shatter and cause injury. Always wear eye protection when using impact or air tools.*

Allen Wrenches

Allen or set screw wrenches (**Figure 17**) are used on fasteners with hexagonal recesses in the fastener head. These wrenches are available in L-shaped bar, socket and T-handle types. A metric set is required when working on most machines. Allen bolts are sometimes called socket bolts.

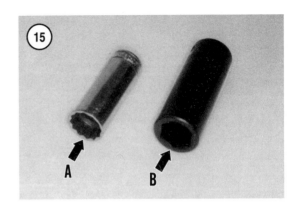

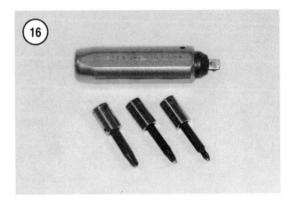

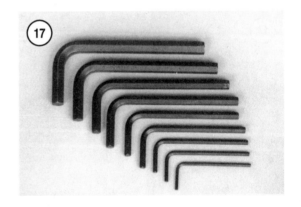

Torque Wrenches

A torque wrench is used with a socket, torque adapter or similar extension to tighten a fastener to a measured torque. Torque wrenches come in several drive sizes (1/4, 3/8, 1/2 and 3/4 in.) and have various methods of reading the torque value. The drive size indicates the size of the square drive that accepts the socket, adapter or extension. Common types of torque wrenches are the deflecting beam, dial indicator and audible click (**Figure 18**).

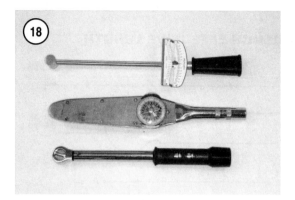

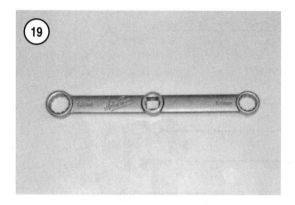

When choosing a torque wrench, consider the torque range, drive size and accuracy. The torque specifications in this manual provide an indication of the range required.

A torque wrench is a precision tool that must be properly cared for to remain accurate. Store torque wrenches in cases or separate padded drawers within a toolbox. Follow the manufacturer's instructions for their care and calibration.

Torque Adapters

Torque adapters or extensions extend or reduce the reach of a torque wrench. The torque adapter shown in **Figure 19** is used to tighten a fastener that cannot be reached due to the size of the torque wrench head, drive, and socket. If a torque adapter changes the effective lever length (**Figure 20**), the torque reading on the wrench will not equal the actual torque applied to the fastener. It is necessary to recalibrate the torque setting on the wrench to compensate for the change of lever length. When using a torque adapter at a right angle to the drive head, cal-

ibration is not required, since the effective length has not changed.

To recalculate a torque reading when using a torque adapter, use the following formula, and refer to **Figure 20**.

$$TW = \frac{TA \times L}{L + A}$$

TW is the torque setting or dial reading on the wrench.

TA is the torque specification and the actual amount of torque that will be applied to the fastener.

A is the amount that the adapter increases (or in some cases reduces) the effective lever length as measured along the centerline of the torque wrench.

L is the lever length of the wrench as measured from the center of the drive to the center of the grip.

The effective length of the torque wrench measured along the centerline of the torque wrench is the sum of L and A.

Example:

TA = 20 ft.-lb.

A = 3 in.

L = 14 in.

$$TW = \frac{20 \times 14}{14 + 3} = \frac{280}{17} = 16.5 \text{ ft. lb.}$$

In this example, a click-type torque wrench would be set to the recalculated torque value (TW = 16.5 ft.-lb.). When using a dial or beam-type wrench, tighten the fastener until the pointer aligns with 16.5 ft.-lb. In either case, although the torque wrench indicates 16.5 ft.-lb., the actual torque applied to the fastener is 20 ft.-lb.

Pliers

Pliers come in a wide range of types and sizes. Pliers are useful for holding, cutting, bending and crimping. Do not use them to turn fasteners. **Figure 21** and **Figure 22** show several types of useful pliers. Each design has a specialized function. Slip-joint pliers are general-purpose pliers used for gripping and bending. Diagonal cutting pliers are needed to cut wire and can be used to remove cotter pins. Needlenose pliers are used to hold or bend small objects. Locking pliers (**Figure 22**), sometimes called Vise Grips, are used to hold objects very tightly. They have many uses, ranging from holding two parts together to gripping the end of a broken stud. Use caution when using locking pliers, as the sharp jaws will damage the objects they hold.

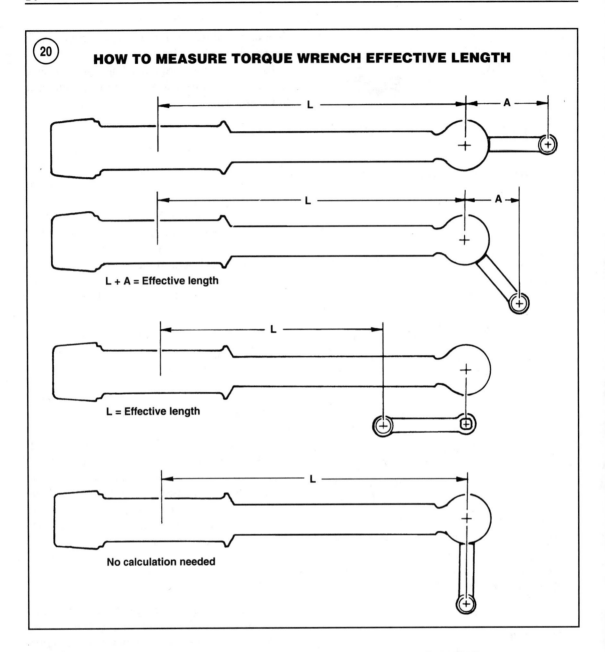

(20) HOW TO MEASURE TORQUE WRENCH EFFECTIVE LENGTH

L + A = Effective length

L = Effective length

No calculation needed

Snap Ring Pliers

Snap ring pliers (**Figure 23**) are specialized pliers with tips that fit into the ends of snap rings to remove and install them.

Snap ring pliers are available with a fixed action (either internal or external) or convertible (one tool works on both internal and external snap rings). They may have fixed tips or interchangeable ones of various sizes and angles. For general use, select a convertible type plier with interchangeable tips.

> *WARNING*
> *Snap rings can spring from the pliers during removal or installation. also, the snap rings plier tips may break. Always wear eye protection when using snap rings pliers.*

Hammers

Various types of hammers (**Figure 24**) are available to fit a number of applications. A ball-peen hammer is used to strike another tool, such as a

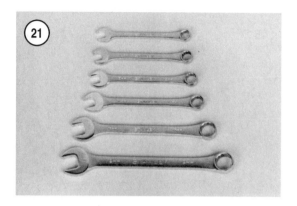

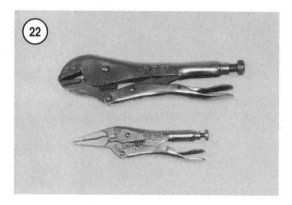

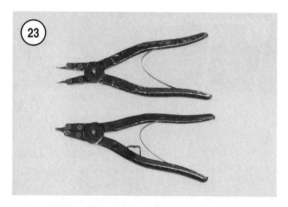

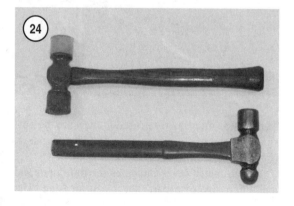

punch or chisel. Soft-faced hammers are required when a metal object must be struck without damaging it. *Never* use a metal-faced hammer on engine and suspension components, as damage will occur in most cases.

Always wear eye protection when using hammers. Check that the hammer face is in good condition and the handle is not cracked. Select the correct hammer for the job and strike the object squarely. Do not use the handle or the side of the hammer to strike an object.

PRECISION MEASURING TOOLS

The ability to accurately measure components is essential to successfully inspect and rebuild an engine. Equipment is manufactured to close tolerances, and obtaining consistently accurate measurements is essential to determining which components require replacement or further service.

Each type of measuring instrument is designed to measure a dimension with a certain degree of accuracy and within a certain range. Always use a measuring tool that is designed for the task.

As with all tools, measuring tools provide the best results if cared for properly. Improper use can damage the tool and result in inaccurate results. If any measurement is questionable, verify the measurement using another tool. A standard gauge is usually provided with measuring tools to check accuracy and calibrate the tool if necessary.

Precision measurements can vary according to the experience of the person performing the procedure. Accurate results are only possible if the mechanic possesses a feel for using the tool. Heavy-handed use of measuring tools will produce less accurate results than if the tool is grasped gently by the fingertips so the point at which the tool contacts the object is easily felt. This feel for the equipment will produce more accurate measurements and reduce the risk of damaging the tool or component. Refer to the following sections for specific measuring tools.

Feeler Gauge

The feeler or thickness gauge (**Figure 25**) is used for measuring the distance between two surfaces.

A feeler gauge set consists of an assortment of steel strips of graduated thickness. Each blade is marked with its thickness. Blades can be of various lengths and angles for different procedures.

A common use for a feeler gauge is to measure valve clearance. Wire (round) type gauges are used to measure spark plug gap.

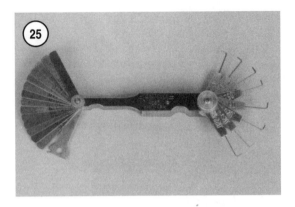

Calipers

Calipers (**Figure 26**) are used to determine outside, inside and depth measurements. Although not as precise as a micrometer, they allow reasonable precision, typically to within 0.05 mm (0.001 in.). Most calipers have a range up to 150 mm (6 in.).

Calipers are available in dial, vernier or digital versions. Dial calipers have a dial readout that provides convenient reading. Vernier calipers have marked scales that must be compared to determine the measurement. The digital caliper uses an LCD to show the measurement.

Properly maintain the measuring surfaces of the caliper. There must not be any dirt or burrs between the tool and the object being measured. Never force the caliper closed around an object; close the caliper around the highest point so it can be removed with a slight drag. Some calipers require calibration. Always refer to the manufacturer's instructions when using a new or unfamiliar caliper.

To read a vernier caliper, refer to **Figure 27**. The fixed scale is marked in 1 mm increments. Ten individual lines on the fixed scale equal 1 cm. The moveable scale is marked in 0.05 mm (hundredth) increments. To obtain a reading, establish the first number by the location of the 0 line on the movable scale in relation to the first line to the left on the fixed scale. In this example, the number is 10 mm. To determine the next number, note which of the lines on the movable scale align with a mark on the fixed scale. A number of lines will appear close, but only one will align exactly. In this case, 0.50 mm is the reading to add to the first number. The result of adding 10 mm and 0.50 mm is a measurement of 10.50 mm.

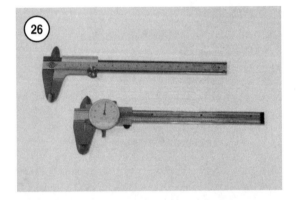

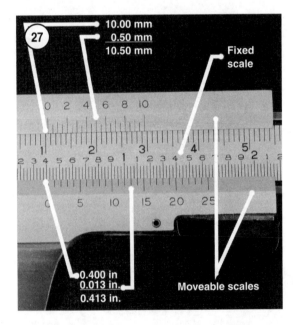

Micrometers

A micrometer (**Figure 28**) is an instrument designed for linear measurement using the decimal divisions of the inch or meter. While there are many types and styles of micrometers, most of the procedures in this manual call for an outside micrometer.

The outside micrometer is used to measure the outside diameter of cylindrical forms and the thickness of materials.

A micrometer's size indicates the minimum and maximum size of a part that it can measure. The

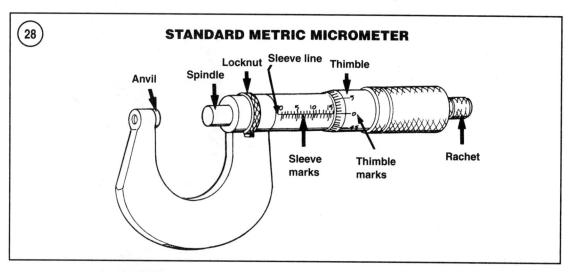

STANDARD METRIC MICROMETER

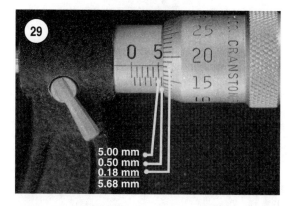

5.00 mm
0.50 mm
0.18 mm
5.68 mm

usual sizes are 0-1 in. (0-25 mm), 1-2 in. (25-50 mm), 2-3 in. (50-75 mm) and 3-4 in. (75-100 mm).

Micrometers that cover a wider range of measurement are available. These use a large frame with interchangeable anvils of various lengths. This type of micrometer offers a cost savings; however, its overall size may make it less convenient.

Reading a micrometer

When reading a micrometer, numbers are taken from different scales and added together. For accurate results, properly maintain the measuring surfaces of the micrometer. There must not be any dirt or burrs between the tool and the measured object. Never force the micrometer closed around an object. Close the micrometer around the highest point so it can be removed with a slight drag.

The standard metric micrometer is accurate to one one-hundredth of a millimeter (0.01-mm). The sleeve line is graduated in millimeter and half millimeter increments. The marks on the upper half of the sleeve line equal 1.00 mm. Every fifth mark above the sleeve line is identified with a number. The number sequence depends on the size of the micrometer. A 0-25 mm micrometer, for example, has sleeve marks numbered 0 through 25 in 5 mm increments. This numbering sequence continues with larger micrometers. On all metric micrometers, each mark on the lower half of the sleeve equals 0.50 mm.

The tapered end of the thimble has fifty lines marked around it. Each mark equals 0.01 mm. One complete turn of the thimble aligns its 0 mark with the first line on the lower half of the sleeve line or 0.50 mm.

When reading a metric micrometer, add the number of millimeters and half-millimeters on the sleeve line to the hundredths of a millimeter shown on the thimble. Perform the following steps while referring to **Figure 29.**

1. Read the upper half of the sleeve line and count the number of lines visible. Each upper line equals 1 mm.
2. See if the half-millimeter line is visible on the lower sleeve line. If so, add 0.50 to the reading in Step 1.
3. Read the thimble mark that aligns with the sleeve line. Each thimble mark equals 0.01 mm.

NOTE
If a thimble mark does not align exactly with the sleeve line, estimate the amount between the lines. For accu-

rate readings to two-thousandths of a millimeter (0.002 mm), use a metric vernier micrometer.

4. Add the readings from Steps 1-3.

Micrometer adjustment

Before using a micrometer, check its adjustment as follows:

1. Clean the anvil and spindle faces.

2A. To check a 0-1 in. or 0-25 mm micrometer:

  a. Turn the thimble until the spindle contacts the anvil. If the micrometer has a ratchet stop, use it to ensure that the proper amount of pressure is applied.

  b. The adjustment is correct if the 0 mark on the thimble aligns exactly with the 0 mark on the sleeve line. If the marks do not align, the micrometer is out of adjustment.

  c. Follow the manufacturer's instructions to adjust the micrometer.

2B. To check a micrometer larger than 1 in. or 25 mm, use the standard gauge supplied by the manufacturer. A standard gauge is a steel block, disc or rod that is machined to an exact size.

  a. Place the standard gauge between the spindle and anvil, and measure its outside diameter or length. If the micrometer has a ratchet stop, use it to ensure that the proper amount of pressure is applied.

  b. The adjustment is correct if the 0 mark on the thimble aligns exactly with the 0 mark on the sleeve line. If the marks do not align, the micrometer is out of adjustment.

  c. Follow the manufacturer's instructions to adjust the micrometer.

Micrometer care

Micrometers are precision instruments. They must be used and maintained with great care. Note the following:

1. Store micrometers in protective cases or separate padded drawers in a toolbox.

2. When in storage, make sure the spindle and anvil faces do not contact each other or another object. If they do, temperature changes and corrosion may damage the contact faces.

3. Do not clean a micrometer with compressed air. Dirt forced into the tool will cause wear.

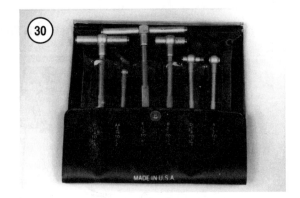

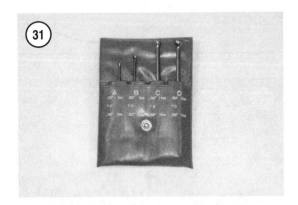

4. Lubricate micrometers with WD-40 to prevent corrosion.

Telescoping and Small-Bore Gauges

Use telescoping gauges (**Figure 30**) and small-bore gauges (**Figure 31**) to measure bores. Neither gauge has a scale for direct readings. An outside micrometer must be used to determine the reading.

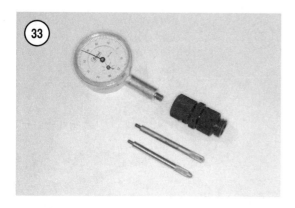

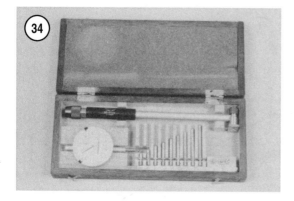

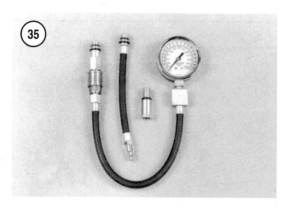

To use a telescoping gauge, select the correct size gauge for the bore. Compress the movable post and carefully insert the gauge into the bore. Carefully move the gauge in the bore to check that it is centered. Tighten the knurled end of the gauge to hold the movable post in position. Remove the gauge and measure the length of the posts. Telescoping gauges are typically used to measure cylinder bores.

To use a small-bore gauge, select the correct size gauge for the bore. Carefully insert the gauge into the bore. Tighten the knurled end of the gauge to

carefully expand the gauge fingers to the limit within the bore. Do not overtighten the gauge, as there is no built-in release. Excessive tightening can damage the bore surface and damage the tool. Remove the gauge and measure the outside dimension (**Figure 32**). Small-hole gauges are typically used to measure valve guides.

Dial Indicator

A dial indicator (**Figure 33**) is a gauge with a dial face and needle used to measure variations in dimensions and movements. Measuring brake rotor runout is a typical use for a dial indicator.

Dial indicators are available in various ranges and graduations and with three basic types of mounting bases: magnetic, clamp, or screw-in stud. When purchasing a dial indicator, select the magnetic stand type, with a continuous dial.

Cylinder Bore Gauge

A cylinder bore gauge is similar to a dial indicator. The gauge set shown in **Figure 34** consists of a dial indicator, handle and different length adapters (anvils) to fit the gauge to various bore sizes. The bore gauge is used to measure bore size, taper and out-of-round. When using a bore gauge, follow the manufacturer's instructions.

Compression Gauge

A compression gauge (**Figure 35**) measures combustion chamber (cylinder) pressure, usually in psi or kPa. The gauge adapter is either inserted or screwed into the spark plug hole to obtain the reading. Disable the engine so it will not start and hold the throttle in the wide-open position when performing a compression test. An engine that does not have adequate compression cannot be properly tuned. See Chapter Three.

Multimeter

A multimeter (**Figure 36**) is an essential tool for electrical system diagnosis. The voltage function indicates the voltage applied or available to various electrical components. The ohmmeter function tests circuits for continuity, or lack of continuity, and measures the resistance of a circuit.

Some manufacturer's specifications for electrical components are based on results using a specific test meter. Results may vary if using a meter not recommend by the manufacturer. Such requirements are noted when applicable.

Removing Frozen Fasteners

If a fastener cannot be removed, several methods may be used to loosen it. First, apply penetrating oil such as Liquid Wrench or WD-40. Apply it liberally and let it penetrate for 10-15 minutes. Strike the fastener several times with a small hammer. Do not hit it so hard as to cause damage. Reapply the penetrating oil if necessary.

For frozen screws, apply penetrating oil as described, then insert a screwdriver in the slot and strike the top of the screwdriver with a hammer. This loosens the rust so the screw can be backed out. If the screw head is too damaged to use this method, grip the head with locking pliers and twist the screw out.

Avoid applying heat, unless specifically instructed, as it may melt, warp or remove the temper from parts.

> *CAUTION*
> *Cases made of magnesium alloy can ignite if heated with a flame.*

Removing Broken Fasteners

If the head breaks off a screw or bolt, several methods are available for removing the remaining portion. If a large portion of the remainder projects out, try gripping it with locking pliers. If the projecting portion is too small, file it to fit a wrench or cut a slot in it to fit a screwdriver (**Figure 37**).

If the head breaks off flush, use a screw extractor. To do this, center-punch the remaining portion of the screw or bolt. Drill a small hole in the screw and tap the extractor into the hole. Back the screw out with a wrench on the extractor (**Figure 38**).

Repairing Damaged Threads

Occasionally, threads are stripped through carelessness or impact damage. Often the threads can be repaired by running a tap (for internal threads on

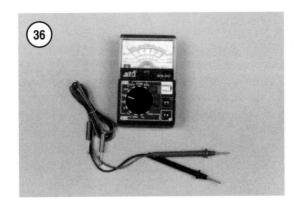

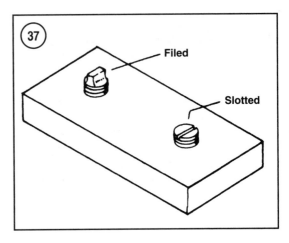

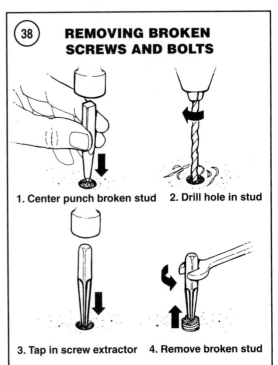

REMOVING BROKEN SCREWS AND BOLTS

1. Center punch broken stud   2. Drill hole in stud

3. Tap in screw extractor   4. Remove broken stud

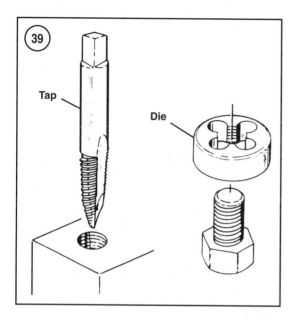

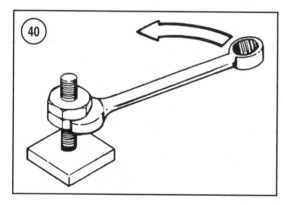

1. Measure the height of the stud above the surface.
2. Thread the stud removal tool onto the stud and tighten it, or thread two nuts onto the stud.
3. Remove the stud by turning the stud remover or the lower nut.
4. Remove any threadlocking compound from the threaded hole. Clean the threads with an aerosol parts cleaner.
5. Install the stud removal tool onto the new stud or thread two nuts onto the stud.
6. Apply threadlocking compound to the threads of the stud.
7. Install the stud and tighten with the stud removal tool or the top nut.
8. Install the stud to the height noted in Step 1 or its torque specification.
9. Remove the stud removal tool or the two nuts.

Removing Hoses

When removing stubborn hoses, do not exert excessive force on the hose or fitting. Remove the hose clamp and carefully insert a small screwdriver or pick tool between the fitting and hose. Apply a spray lubricant under the hose and carefully twist the hose off the fitting. Clean the fitting of any corrosion or rubber hose material with a wire brush. Clean the inside of the hose thoroughly. Do not use any lubricant when installing the hose (new or old). The lubricant may allow the hose to come off the fitting, even with the clamp secure.

Bearings

Bearings are used in the engine and transmission assembly to reduce power loss, heat and noise resulting from friction. Because bearings are precision parts, they must be maintained by proper lubrication and maintenance. If a bearing is damaged, replace it immediately. When installing a new bearing, take care to prevent damaging the part. Many bearing replacement procedures are included in the individual chapters where applicable; however, use the following sections as a guideline.

> *NOTE*
> *Unless otherwise specified, install bearings with the manufacturer's mark or number facing outward.*

nuts) or die (for external threads on bolts) through the threads (**Figure 39**). To clean or repair spark plug threads, use a spark plug tap.

If an internal thread is damaged, it may be necessary to install a Helicoil or some other type of thread insert. Follow the manufacturer's instructions when installing their insert.

If it is necessary to drill and tap a hole, refer to **Table 6** for metric tap and drill sizes.

Stud Removal/Installation

A stud removal tool is available from most tool suppliers. This tool makes the removal and installation of studs easier. If one is not available, thread two nuts onto the stud and tighten them against each other. Remove the stud by turning the lower nut (**Figure 40**).

Removal

While bearings are normally removed only when damaged, there may be times when it is necessary to remove a bearing that is in good condition. However, improper bearing removal will damage the bearing and maybe the shaft or case half. Note the following when removing bearings:

1. When using a puller to remove a bearing from a shaft, take care that the shaft is not damaged. Always place a piece of metal between the end of the shaft and the puller screw. In addition, place the puller arms next to the inner bearing race. See **Figure 41**.

2. When using a hammer to remove a bearing from a shaft, do not strike the hammer directly against the shaft. Instead, use a brass or aluminum rod between the hammer and shaft (**Figure 42**) and be sure to support both bearing races with wooden blocks, as shown.

3. The ideal method of bearing removal is with a hydraulic press. Note the following when using a press:

   a. Always support the inner and outer bearing races with a suitable size wooden or aluminum ring (**Figure 43**). If only the outer race is supported, pressure applied against the balls and/or the inner race will damage them.

   b. Always check that the press arm (**Figure 43**) aligns with the center of the shaft. If the arm is not centered, it may damage the bearing and/or shaft.

   c. The moment the shaft is free of the bearing, it will drop to the floor. Secure or hold the shaft to prevent it from falling.

Installation

1. When installing a bearing in a housing, apply pressure to the *outer* bearing race (**Figure 44**). When installing a bearing on a shaft, apply pressure to the *inner* bearing race (**Figure 45**).

2. When installing a bearing as described in Step 1, some type of driver is required. Never strike the bearing directly with a hammer or the bearing will be damaged. When installing a bearing, use a length of pipe or a driver with a diameter that matches the bearing race. **Figure 46** shows the correct way to use a driver and hammer to install a bearing.

3. Step 1 describes how to install a bearing in a case or over a shaft. However, when installing a bearing

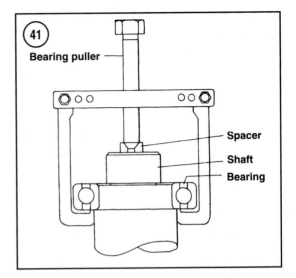

(41) Bearing puller — Spacer, Shaft, Bearing

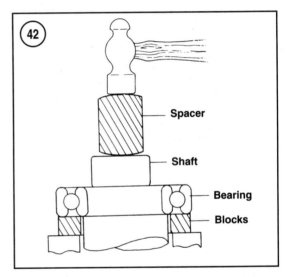

(42) Spacer, Shaft, Bearing, Blocks

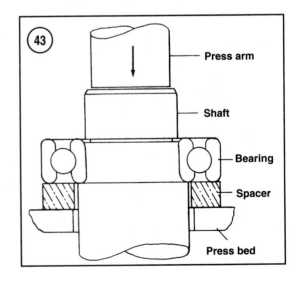

(43) Press arm, Shaft, Bearing, Spacer, Press bed

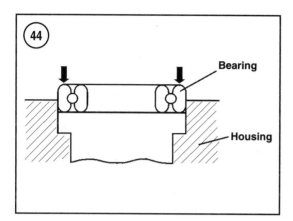

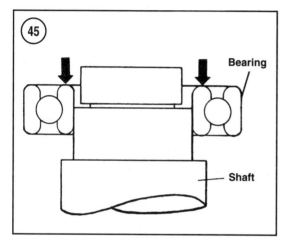

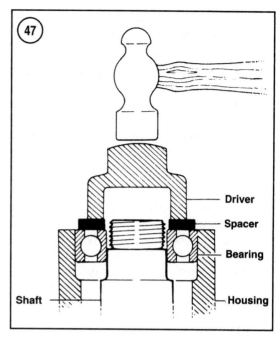

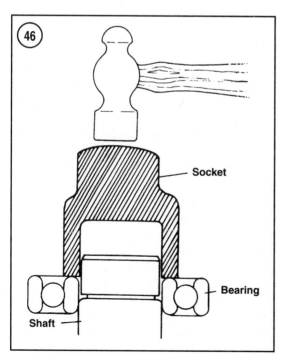

over a shaft and into a housing at the same time, a tight fit will be required for both outer and inner bearing races. In this situation, install a spacer under the driver tool so pressure is applied evenly across both races (**Figure 47**). If the outer race is not supported, the balls will push against the outer bearing race and damage it.

Interference fit

1. Follow this procedure when installing a bearing over a shaft. When a tight fit is required, the bearing inside diameter will be smaller than the shaft. In this case, driving the bearing on the shaft using normal methods may cause bearing damage. Instead, heat the bearing before installation. Note the following:

   a. Secure the shaft so it is ready for bearing installation.

   b. Clean all residues from the bearing surface of the shaft. Remove burrs with a file or sandpaper.

   c. Fill a suitable container with clean mineral oil. Place a thermometer rated above 120° C (248° F) in the oil. Support the thermometer so that it does not rest on the bottom or side of the container.

   d. Remove the bearing from its wrapper and secure it with a piece of heavy wire bent to hold it in the container. Hang the bearing so it does not touch the bottom or sides.

e. Turn the heat on and monitor the thermometer. When the oil temperature rises to approximately 120° C (248° F), remove the bearing and quickly install it. If necessary, place a socket on the inner bearing race and tap the bearing into place. As the bearing chills, it will tighten on the shaft, so installation must be done quickly. Check that the bearing is installed completely.

2. Follow this step when installing a bearing in a housing. Bearings are generally installed in a housing with a slight interference fit. Driving the bearing into the housing using normal methods may damage the housing or cause bearing damage. Instead, heat the housing before the bearing is installed. Note the following:

> *CAUTION*
> *Before heating the housing in this procedure, wash the housing thoroughly with detergent and water. Rinse and rewash the cases as required to remove all traces of oil and other chemical deposits.*

a. Heat the housing to approximately 100° C (212° F) in an oven, or use a heat gun to warm the immediate area around the bearing bore. An easy way to check that it is at the proper temperature is to place tiny drops of water on the housing; if they sizzle and evaporate immediately, the temperature is correct. Heat only one housing at a time.

> *CAUTION*
> *Do not heat the housing or bearing with a propane or acetylene torch. The direct heat will destroy the case hardening of the bearing and will likely warp the housing. Cases made of magnesium alloy can ignite.*

b. Handle the heated housing with insulated gloves or kitchen pot holders.

> *NOTE*
> *Remove and install the bearings with a suitable-size socket and extension.*

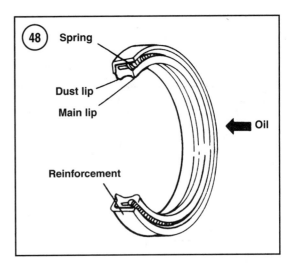

c. Hold the housing with the bearing side down and tap the bearing out. Repeat for all bearings in the housing.

d. Before heating the bearing housing, place the new bearing in a freezer if possible. Chilling a bearing slightly reduces its outside diameter while the heated bearing housing assembly is slightly larger due to heat expansion. This will make bearing installation easier.

> *NOTE*
> *Always install bearings with the manufacturer's mark or number facing outward.*

e. While the housing is still hot, install the new bearing(s) into the housing. Install the bearings by hand, if possible. If necessary, lightly tap the bearing(s) into the housing with a socket placed on the outer bearing race (**Figure 44**). Do not install new bearings by driving on the inner bearing race. Install the bearing(s) until it seats completely.

Seal Replacement

Seals (**Figure 48**) are used to contain oil, water, grease or combustion gasses in a housing or shaft. Improper removal of a seal can damage the housing or shaft. Improper installation of the seal can damage the seal. Note the following:

1. Prying is generally the easiest and most effective method of removing a seal from a housing. However, always place a shop cloth under the pry tool (**Figure 49**) to prevent damage to the housing.

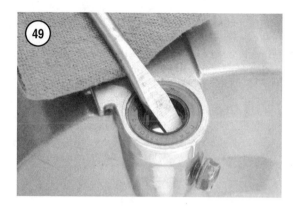

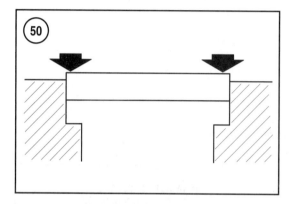

2. Pack waterproof grease in the seal lips before the seal is installed.

3. Install seals with the manufacturer's numbers or marks face out.

4. Install seals with a socket placed on the outside of the seal as shown in **Figure 50**. Drive the seal squarely into the housing. Never install a seal by hitting the top of the seal with a hammer.

STORAGE

Several months of non-use can cause a general deterioration of the machine. This is especially true in areas of extreme temperature variations. This deterioration can be minimized with careful preparation for storage. A properly stored machine will be much easier to return to service.

Storage Area Selection

When selecting a storage area, consider the following:

1. The storage area must be dry. A heated area is best, but not necessary. It should be insulated to minimize extreme temperature variation.

2. If the building has large window areas, cover them to keep sunlight off the machine.

3. Avoid areas close to saltwater.

4. Consider the area's risk of fire, theft or vandalism. Check with an insurer regarding coverage while the machine is in storage.

Preparing the Machine for Storage

The amount of preparation a machine should undergo before storage depends on the expected length of non-use, storage area conditions and personal preference. Consider the following list the minimum requirement:

1. Wash the engine and bodywork. Remove all dirt, mud and road debris.

2. Check the cooling system for proper level and mix ratio.

3. Start the engine and allow it to reach operating temperature. Drain the engine oil regardless of the riding time since the last service. Fill the engine with the recommended type of oil.

4. Drain all fuel from the fuel tank and carburetors. Run the engine until all the fuel is consumed from the lines and carburetors.

5. Remove the spark plug and pour a teaspoon of engine oil into the cylinder. Place a shop cloth over the opening and slowly turn the engine over to distribute the oil. Reinstall the spark plug.

6. Remove the battery. Store the battery in a cool, dry location.

7. Cover the exhaust and intake openings.

8. Inflate the tires to their normal pressure.

9. Apply a commercial protectant to the plastic and rubber components, including the tires. Follow the manufacturer's instructions for each type of product being used.

10. Place the machine on stands so the tires are off the ground. If this is not possible, place a piece of plywood between the tires and the ground.

11. Cover the machine with a drop cloth or similar cover. Do not use plastic covers; these will trap moisture and promote corrosion.

Returning the Machine to Service

The amount of service required to return a machine to operating condition depends on the length of non-use and storage conditions. Follow the above procedure and install/check each area that was prepared at time of storage. Also check that the brakes, clutch, throttle and engine stop switch work properly before operating the machine. Refer to the maintenance and lubrication schedule in Chapter Three and determine which areas require additional service.

Table 1 MODEL CODE NUMBERS

Year and model	Model code	Starting VIN numbers
2001		
YFM660RN	5LP1	JY4AM013 1A000052-on
YFM660RNC (California)	5LP3	JY4AM01Y 1A000002-on
2002		
YFM660RP	5LP5	JY4AM01Y 2C003061-on
YFM660RPB (limited edition)	5LP8	JY4AM01Y 2C015340-on
2003		
YFM660RR	5LP9	JYA4AM01Y 23C022872-on
YFM660RLER (limited edition)	5LPC	JYAAM01Y 53C027578-on
2004		
YFM660RS	5LPF	JY4AM01Y 4C045660-on
YFM6600RLES (limited edition)	5LPJ	JY4AM01Y 64C047906-on
2005		
YFM6600RT	5FUF	JY4AM01Y 85C064904-on
YFM660RSET (limted edition)	5LPT	–

Table 2 GENERAL DIMENSIONS AND WEIGHT

	mm	in.
Ground clearance		
Below skid plate	265	10.4
Below rear brake disc	114.3	4.5
Minimum turning radius	3300	129.9
Overall length	1830	72.0
Overall width	1100	43.3
Overall height	1150	45.3
Seat height	860	33.9
Wheelbase	1245	49.0
Weight		
Dry	180 kg	398 lb.
With oil and full fuel tank	193 kg	426 lb.

Table 3 TECHNICAL ABBREVIATIONS

ABDC	After bottom dead center
ATDC	After top dead center
BBDC	Before bottom dead center
BDC	Bottom dead center
BTDC	Before top dead center
C	Celsius (centigrade)
cc	Cubic centimeters
cid	Cubic inch displacement
CDI	Capacitor discharge ignition
cu. in.	Cubic inches
F	Fahrenheit
ft.	Feet
ft.-lb.	Foot-pounds
gal.	Gallons
H/A	High altitude
hp	Horsepower
in.	Inches
in.-lb.	Inch-pounds
I.D.	Inside diameter
kg	Kilograms
kgm	Kilogram meters
km	Kilometer
kPa	Kilopascals
L	Liter
m	Meter
MAG	Magneto
ml	Milliliter
mm	Millimeter
N•m	Newton-meters
O.D.	Outside diameter
oz.	Ounces
psi	Pounds per square inch
PTO	Power take off
pt.	Pint
qt.	Quart
rpm	Revolutions per minute
SOHC	Single overhead cam

Table 4 GENERAL TORQUE SPECIFICATIONS

Thread diameter (mm)	N•m	in.-lb.	ft.-lb.
6	6	53	–
8	15	–	11
10	30	–	22
12	55	–	41
14	85	–	63
16	130	–	96

Table 5 CONVERSION FORMULAS

Multiply:	By:	To get the equivalent of:
Length		
Inches	25.4	Millimeter
Inches	2.54	Centimeter
Miles	1.609	Kilometer
Feet	0.3048	Meter
Millimeter	0.03937	Inches
Centimeter	0.3937	Inches
Kilometer	0.6214	Mile
Meter	3.281	Feet
Fluid volume		
U.S. quarts	0.9463	Liters
U.S. gallons	3.785	Liters
U.S. ounces	29.573529	Milliliters
Imperial gallons	4.54609	Liters
Imperial quarts	1.1365	Liters
Liters	0.2641721	U.S. gallons
Liters	1.0566882	U.S. quarts
Liters	33.814023	U.S. ounces
Liters	0.22	Imperial gallons
Liters	0.8799	Imperial quarts
Milliliters	0.033814	U.S. ounces
Milliliters	1.0	Cubic centimeters
Milliliters	0.001	Liters
Torque		
Foot-pounds	1.3558	Newton-meters
Foot-pounds	0.138255	Meters-kilograms
Inch-pounds	0.11299	Newton-meters
Newton-meters	0.7375622	Foot-pounds
Newton-meters	8.8507	Inch-pounds
Meters-kilograms	7.2330139	Foot-pounds
Volume		
Cubic inches	16.387064	Cubic centimeters
Cubic centimeters	0.0610237	Cubic inches
Temperature		
Fahrenheit	$(°F - 32) \times 0.556$	Centigrade
Centigrade	$(°C \times 1.8) + 32$	Fahrenheit
Weight		
Ounces	28.3495	Grams
Pounds	0.4535924	Kilograms
Grams	0.035274	Ounces
Kilograms	2.2046224	Pounds
Pressure		
Pounds per square inch	0.070307	Kilograms per square centimeter
Kilograms per square centimeter	14.223343	Pounds per square inch
Kilopascals	0.1450	Pounds per square inch
Pounds per square inch	6.895	Kilopascals
Speed		
Miles per hour	1.609344	Kilometers per hour
Kilometers per hour	0.6213712	Miles per hour

Table 6 METRIC TAP AND DRILL SIZES

Metric size	Drill equivalent	Decimal fraction	Nearest fraction
3 × 0.50	No. 39	0.0995	3/32
3 × 0.60	3/32	0.0937	3/32
4 × 0.70	No. 30	0.1285	1/8
4 × 0.75	1/8	0.125	1/8
5 × 0.80	No. 19	0.166	11/64
5 × 0.90	No. 20	0.161	5/32
6 × 1.00	No. 9	0.196	13/64
7 × 1.00	16/64	0.234	15/64
8 × 1.00	J	0.277	9/32
8 × 1.25	17/64	0.265	17/64
9 × 1.00	5/16	0.3125	5/16
9 × 1.25	5/16	0.3125	5/16
10 × 1.25	11/32	0.3437	11/32
10 × 1.50	R	0.339	11/32
11 × 1.50	3/8	0.375	3/8
12 × 1.50	13/32	0.406	13/32
12 × 1.75	13/32	0.406	13/32

Table 7 METRIC, INCH AND FRACTIONAL EQUIVALENTS

mm	in.	Nearest fraction	mm	in.	Nearest fraction
1	0.0394	1/32	26	1.0236	1 1/32
2	0.0787	3/32	27	1.0630	1 1/16
3	0.1181	1/8	28	1.1024	1 3/32
4	0.1575	5/32	29	1.1417	1 5/32
5	0.1969	3/16	30	1.1811	1 3/16
6	0.2362	1/4	31	1.2205	1 7/32
7	0.2756	9/32	32	1.2598	1 1/4
8	0.3150	5/16	33	1.2992	1 5/16
9	0.3543	11/32	34	1.3386	1 11/32
10	0.3937	13/32	35	1.3780	1 3/8
11	0.4331	7/16	36	1.4173	1 13/32
12	0.4724	15/32	37	1.4567	1 15/32
13	0.5118	1/2	38	1.4961	1 1/2
14	0.5512	9/16	39	1.5354	1 17/32
15	0.5906	19/32	40	1.5748	1 9/16
16	0.6299	5/8	41	1.6142	1 5/8
17	0.6693	21/32	42	1.6535	1 21/32
18	0.7087	23/32	43	1.6929	1 11/16
19	0.7480	3/4	44	1.7323	1 23/32
20	0.7874	25/32	45	1.7717	1 25/32
21	0.8268	13/16	46	1.8110	1 13/16
22	0.8661	7/8	47	1.8504	1 27/32
23	0.9055	29/32	48	1.8898	1 7/8
24	0.9449	15/16	49	1.9291	1 15/16
25	0.9843	31/32	50	1.9685	1 31/32

CHAPTER TWO

TROUBLESHOOTING

Diagnosing problems with the machine, either mechanical or electrical, can be relatively easy if the fundamental operating requirements are kept in mind. By doing so, problems can be approached in a logical and methodical manner. The first steps are to:

1. Define the symptoms of the problem.

2. Determine which areas could exhibit those symptoms.

3. Test and analyze the suspect area.

4. Isolate the problem.

Being quick to assume a particular area is at fault can lead to increased problems, lost time and unnecessary parts replacement. The easiest way to keep troubleshooting simple, is to perform the lubrication, maintenance and tune-up procedures described in Chapter Three. The rider will gain a better understanding of the condition and functions of the machine.

Always start with the simple and obvious checks when troubleshooting. This would include: engine stop switch operation, fuel level, fuel valve position and spark plug cap tightness. If the problem cannot be solved, stop and evaluate all conditions prior to the problem.

For removal, installation and test procedures for some components, refer to the specific chapter in the manual. When applicable, tables at the end of each chapter provide specifications and service limits.

OPERATING REQUIREMENTS

There are three requirements for an engine to run properly. These are: correct air/fuel mixture, compression and properly timed spark. If one of these requirements is not correct, the engine will not run or will run poorly. A four-stroke engine performs these functions as shown in **Figure 1**.

STARTING THE ENGINE

Before starting the engine, always perform a pre-ride inspection of the machine (Chapter Three).

Engine is Cold

1. The machine is equipped with the following safety switches that prevent the engine from starting or running if certain conditions occur.

  a. Neutral switch. With the transmission in any position except neutral, with the clutch engaged (clutch lever out), the engine will not start.

  b. Clutch switch. With the transmission in gear, the engine will not start if the clutch is engaged (clutch lever out). If the clutch is disengaged with the transmission in gear, the engine will start.

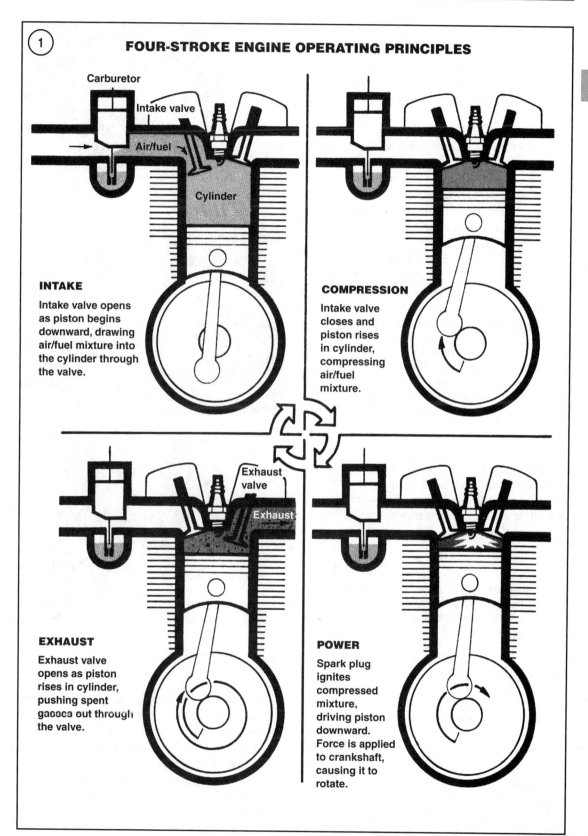

① **FOUR-STROKE ENGINE OPERATING PRINCIPLES**

Carburetor

Intake valve

Air/fuel

Cylinder

INTAKE

Intake valve opens
as piston begins
downward, drawing
air/fuel mixture into
the cylinder through
the valve.

COMPRESSION

Intake valve
closes and
piston rises
in cylinder,
compressing
air/fuel
mixture.

Exhaust
valve

Exhaust

EXHAUST

Exhaust valve
opens as piston
rises in cylinder,
pushing spent
gasses out through
the valve.

POWER

Spark plug
ignites
compressed
mixture,
driving piston
downward.
Force is applied
to crankshaft,
causing it to
rotate.

c. Engine stop switch (A, **Figure 2**). When moved to the off position (left), the switch will prevent the engine from starting, or, will stop the engine when it is running. The engine will start and run only when the switch is in the run position.

2. Shift the transmission into neutral.

3. Switch the engine stop switch to the run position.

4. Turn the fuel valve lever (**Figure 3**) from the off position to the on (down) position.

5. Move the choke lever fully to the left (**Figure 4**) to richen the air/fuel mixture.

6. Turn the ignition switch on.

7. Check that the neutral light (**Figure 5**) comes on.

8. Press the starter button (B, **Figure 2**) while keeping the throttle closed. The type of choke system used on the Raptor is most effective if the throttle remains completely closed during startup.

> *CAUTION*
> *Keep the starter button depressed until the engine is definitely started. Releasing the button too soon can cause engine kick back, which can potentially damage the starter clutch assembly.*

9. When the engine starts, gradually move the choke lever to the right as the engine warms up. Allow the engine to warm up at an idle for one minute, or until the engine responds smoothly and does not require the choke.

> *CAUTION*
> *Do not race the engine during the warm-up period. Excessive wear and potential engine damage can occur when the engine is not up to operating temperature.*

Engine is Warm or Hot

1. Shift the transmission into neutral.

2. Check that the engine stop switch is in the run position.

3. Turn the fuel valve lever from the off position (**Figure 3**) to the on (down) position.

4. Turn the ignition switch on.

5. Check that the neutral light (**Figure 5**) comes on.

6. Press the starter button (B, **Figure 2**) while keeping the throttle closed.

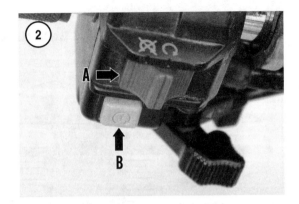

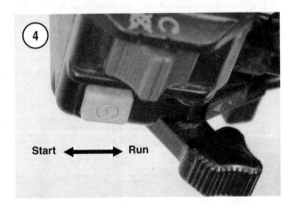

Engine is Flooded

If the engine fails to start after several tries (particularly if the choke has been used), it is probably flooded. This occurs when too much fuel is drawn into the engine and the spark plug fails to ignite the air/fuel mixture. The smell of gasoline is often evident when the engine is flooded. If there are no obvious signs of fuel overflow from the carburetor, attempt to start the engine by fully opening the throttle (no choke) and operating the starter. If the

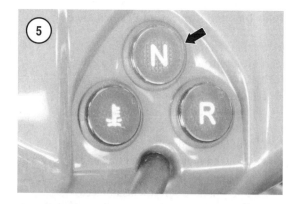

4. Remove the spark plug and dry the electrodes. Reinstall the plug and attempt to start the engine as described in this section.

5. Perform an engine spark test.

ENGINE SPARK TEST

An engine spark test will indicate whether the ignition system is providing power to the spark plug. It is a quick way to determine if a problem is in the electrical system or fuel system.

> *CAUTION*
> *When performing this test, the spark plug lead must be grounded before cranking the engine. If it is not, it is possible to damage the CDI circuitry. A spark plug can be used for this test, but a spark tester (**Figure 6**) will clearly show if spark is occurring, as well as the strength of the spark. This tester can be purchased at parts supply stores or suppliers of ignition test equipment.*

1. Remove the spark plug. Inspect the spark plug by comparing its condition to the plugs shown in Chapter Three.

2. Connect the spark plug lead to the spark plug, or to a spark tester.

3. Ground the plug/tester to bare metal on the engine (**Figure 7**). Position the plug/tester so the firing end can be viewed.

4. Crank the engine and observe the spark. A fat, blue spark should appear at the firing end. The spark should fire consistently as the engine is cranked.

5. If the spark appears weak, or fires inconsistently, check the following areas for the possible cause:

   a. Fouled/improperly gapped spark plug.

   b. Damaged/shorted spark plug lead and cap.

   c. Loose connection in ignition system.

   d. Damaged coil.

   e. Damaged ignition switch.

   f. Dirty/shorted engine stop switch.

   g. Broken Woodruff key on rotor shaft.

   h. Damaged ignition pickup coil (check ignition timing).

   i. Damaged CDI unit.

engine starts, keep the engine running at a fast idle until it has burned the excess fuel from the engine.

If the engine will not start, perform the following troubleshooting steps before making other checks.

1. Check that the choke lever is fully to the right.

2. Look for gasoline overflowing from the carburetors or overflow hoses. If gasoline is evident, the float in the carburetor bowl is stuck or adjusted too high. Remove and repair the float assembly (Chapter Eight).

3. Check the air filter for excessive buildup.

ENGINE PERFORMANCE

If the engine does not operate at peak performance, the following lists of possible causes may help isolate the problem. The easier checks for each area are listed first. These checks represent what is *commonly* responsible for poor engine performance.

It is recommended to review Chapter Eight and Chapter Nine to gain a working knowledge of the fuel and electrical systems. Throughout the chapters, explanations, drawings and photos are provided to aid in learning the function of the major components that make up each system.

Engine will Not Start or Starts and Dies

1. Fuel system:
   a. Fuel valve off.
   b. Fuel tank near empty.
   c. Improper operation of choke lever.
   d. Choke plunger stuck open.
   e. Idle speed too low.
   f. Engine flooded.
   g. Clogged fuel tank cap vent.
   h. Contaminated fuel.
   i. Clogged fuel valve, fuel line or carburetors.
   j. Clogged air filter.
   k. Pilot mixture screws misadjusted.
   l. Float valve clogged or sticking.
   m. Air leaks at intake duct.
   n. Wrong pilot jets for altitude.
2. Ignition:
   a. Loose, fouled, or improperly gapped spark plug.
   b. Damaged/shorted spark plug lead and cap.
   c. Loose connection in ignition system.
   d. Damaged coil.
   e. Damaged ignition switch.
   f. Dirty/shorted engine stop switch.
   g. Damaged ignition pickup coil (check ignition timing).
   h. Damaged CDI unit.
3. Engine:
   a. Compression release malfunctioning.
   b. No valve clearance.
   c. Leaking cylinder head gasket.
   d. Stuck/seized valve.
   e. Worn piston and/or cylinder.

Poor Idle and Low Speed Performance

1. Fuel system:
   a. Improper operation of choke lever.
   b. Choke plunger stuck open.
   c. Idle speed too low.
   d. Engine flooded.
   e. Clogged fuel tank cap vent.
   f. Contaminated fuel.
   g. Clogged fuel valve, fuel line or carburetor.
   h. Clogged air filter.
   i. Pilot mixture screws misadjusted.
   j. Float valve clogged or sticking.
   k. Air leaks at intake duct.
   l. Loose carburetor diaphragm cover.
   m. Torn or damaged slide diaphragm.
   n. Dragging carburetor slide.
   o. Wrong pilot jet for altitude.
   p. Clogged muffler.
2. Ignition:
   a. Loose, fouled or improperly gapped spark plug.
   b. Damaged/shorted spark plug lead and cap.
   c. Loose connection in ignition system.
   d. Damaged coil.
   e. Damaged ignition switch.
   f. Dirty/shorted engine stop switch.
   g. Damaged ignition pickup coil (check ignition timing).
   h. Damaged CDI unit.
3. Engine:
   a. Compression release malfunctioning.
   b. Improper valve clearance.
   c. Low compression.
   d. Improper valve/camshaft timing.

Engine Lacks Power and Acceleration

1. Fuel system:
   a. Improper operation of choke lever.
   b. Choke plunger stuck open.
   c. Contaminated fuel.
   d. Clogged fuel valve, fuel line or carburetor jets.
   e. Clogged air filter.
   f. Float valve clogged or sticking.
   g. Air leaks at intake duct.
   h. Loose carburetor diaphragm cover.
   i. Torn or damaged slide diaphragm.
   j. Dragging carburetor slide.

    k. Wrong pilot or main jet for altitude.
    l. Wrong clip position on jet needle.
    m. Clogged muffler.
2. Ignition:
    a. Fouled/improperly gapped spark plug.
    b. Damaged/shorted spark plug lead and cap.
    c. Loose connection in ignition system.
    d. Damaged coil.
    e. Damaged ignition pickup coil (check ignition timing).
    f. Damaged CDI unit.
3. Engine:
    a. Compression release malfunctioning.
    b. Improper valve clearance.
    c. Low compression.
    d. Improper valve/camshaft timing.
4. Brakes and wheels:
    a. Brake pads dragging on brake disc.
    b. Worn/seized wheel bearings.
    c. Drive chain too tight.
5. Clutch:
    a. Clutch incorrectly adjusted.
    b. Weak clutch springs.
    c. Worn clutch plates and discs.

Poor High Speed Performance

1. Fuel system:
    a. Improper operation of choke lever.
    b. Choke plunger stuck open.
    c. Contaminated fuel.
    d. Clogged fuel valve, fuel line or carburetor jets.
    e. Clogged air filter.
    f. Air leaks at intake duct.
    g. Float valve too high.
    h. Loose carburetor diaphragm cover.
    i. Torn or damaged slide diaphragm.
    j. Dragging carburetor slide.
    k. Worn needle and jet.
    l. Wrong main jet for altitude.
    m. Wrong clip position on jet needle.
    n. Clogged muffler.
2. Ignition:
    a. Damaged ignition pickup coil (check ignition timing).
    b. Damaged CDI unit.
3. Engine:
    a. Incorrect valve clearance.
    b. Weak/broken valve spring(s).

Engine Backfires

1. Pilot mixture screws adjusted too lean.
2. Air leaks into exhaust system.
3. Inoperative air cut-off valve (backfiring during deceleration).
4. Damaged ignition pickup coil (check ignition timing).

Engine Overheating

CAUTION
Engine overheating can occur when the machine is operated at slow speed at high rpm. This can occur in severe off-road riding conditions. Even though the fan turns on, excessive heat buildup can cause the engine to overheat. When this occurs, stop and allow the engine to cool. If overheating continues after the machine is ridden at moderate speeds and lower rpm, check and determine the cause of overheating.

1. Cooling system:
    a. Coolant level low.
    b. Water in system; no coolant mix.
    c. Air in system.
    d. Radiator clogged.
    e. Radiator cap damaged.
    f. Thermostat damaged.
    g. Water temperature sending unit faulty.
    h. Fan sending unit faulty.
    i. Fan shaft seized.
    j. Water pump impeller loose.
    k. Water pump impeller damaged.
2. Engine:
    a. Excessive idling.
    b. Insufficient oil level or viscosity.
    c. Incorrect spark plug heat range.
    d. Clogged crankcase oil strainer.
    e. Excessive carbon buildup on piston/cylinder head.
3. Fuel system (causing lean fuel mixture):
    a. Clogged/pinched fuel tank cap vent hose.
    b. Air leaks at intake duct.
    c. Wrong pilot or main jet for altitude.
    d. Clogged carburetor jets.
    e. Float level too low.
4. Ignition:
    a. Improper spark plug heat range.

2

b. Damaged ignition pickup coil (check ignition timing).

ELECTRICAL TESTING

Refer to Chapter Nine for testing the starting system, ignition system, charging system, fan system and switches. Refer to the procedures in *Engine Starting System* in this chapter for troubleshooting typical problems with the starting system. These checks should be made before disassembling and bench testing components. When doing electrical tests, refer to the diagram at the back of the manual.

Before testing a component, check the electrical connections related to that component. Check for corrosion and bent or loose connectors. Most of the connectors have a lock mechanism molded into the connector body. If these are not fully locked, a connection may not be made. If connectors are not locked, pull the connector apart and clean the fittings before reassembling.

ELECTRICAL COMPONENT REPLACEMENT

Most motorcycle dealerships and parts suppliers will not accept the return of any electrical part. If you cannot determine the *exact* cause of any electrical system malfunction, have a Yamaha dealership retest that specific system to verify your test results. If you purchase a new electrical component(s), install it, and then find that the system still does not work properly, you will probably be unable to return the unit for a refund.

Consider any test results carefully before replacing a component that tests only *slightly* out of specification, especially resistance. A number of variables can affect test results dramatically. These include: the testing meter's internal circuitry, ambient temperature and conditions under which the machine has been operated. All instructions and specifications have been checked for accuracy; however, successful test results depend to a great degree upon individual accuracy.

ENGINE STARTING SYSTEM

Starter Turns Slowly

1. Weak battery.
2. Poorly connected/corroded battery terminals and cables.
3. Loose starter cable.
4. Worn or damaged starter.

Starter Turns, But Does Not Crank Engine

1. Worn or damaged starter clutch.
2. Damaged teeth on starter gear or idle gears.

Starter Does Not Operate

When the starter does not operate, refer to *Starting System* (Chapter Nine) to begin testing at the starter relay.

ENGINE NOISE

Noise is often the first indicator that something is wrong with the engine. In many cases, damage can be avoided or minimized if the rider immediately stops the machine and diagnoses the source of the noise. Anytime engine noise is ignored, even when the machine seems to be running correctly, the rider risks causing more damage and personal injury.

Pinging During Acceleration

1. Poor quality or contaminated fuel.
2. Lean fuel mixture.
3. Excessive carbon buildup in combustion chamber.
4. Damaged ignition pickup coil (check ignition timing).

Knocks, Ticks or Rattles

1. Engine top end:
   a. Incorrect valve clearance.
   b. Broken or weak valve spring.
   c. Damaged compression release.
   d. Loose cam chain/damaged tensioner.
   e. Worn piston pin or piston pin bore.
   f. Worn connecting rod small end.

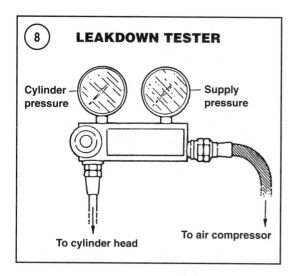

LEAKDOWN TESTER

Cylinder pressure

Supply pressure

To cylinder head

To air compressor

g. Worn piston, rings and/or cylinder.
2. Engine bottom end:
    a. Worn connecting rod bearings.
    b. Worn crankshaft bearings.
    c. Worn balancer bearings.
    d. Worn transmission bearings.
    e. Worn or damaged transmission gears.

MACHINE NOISE

The following possible causes of noise will likely occur only when the machine is in motion:
1. Excessively loose drive chain.
2. Worn chain slider or rollers.
3. Loose exhaust system.
4. Loose/missing body fasteners.
5. Loose skid plate.
6. Loose shock absorber.
7. Loose engine mounting bolts.
8. Brake pads dragging on brake disc.
9. Worn/seized wheel bearings.

ENGINE LEAKDOWN TEST

The condition of the piston rings and valves can accurately be checked with a leakdown tester (**Figure 8**). With all valves in the closed position, the tester is screwed into the spark plug hole and air pressure is applied to the combustion chamber. The gauge on the tester is then observed to determine the rate of leakage from the combustion chamber. An air compressor is required to use the leakdown tester.
1. Start the engine and allow it to warm up.

2. Shut off the engine and remove the carburetors and exhaust pipe.
3. Remove the spark plug.
4. Set the piston to TDC on the compression stroke.
5. Install the leakdown tester, following the manufacturer's instructions. The tester must not leak around the spark plug threads.
6. Perform the test, following the manufacturer's instructions for the tester. When pressure is applied to the cylinder, check that the engine remains at TDC. If necessary, put the transmission in gear.
7. While the cylinder is under pressure, listen for air leakage at the following areas:
    a. Exhaust port. If leakage is detected, the exhaust valves are leaking.
    b. Intake port. If leakage is detected, the intake valves are leaking.
    c. Crankcase breather tube. If leakage is detected, the piston rings are leaking.
8. A cylinder with a leakdown of five percent or less is ideal. A cylinder with over ten percent leakage should be inspected to determine if leakage is caused by normal wear or damage. Inspection of the parts will then indicate what action should be taken.

CLUTCH

The two main clutch problems are clutch slip (clutch does not fully engage) and clutch drag (clutch does not fully disengage). These problems are often caused by incorrect clutch adjustment or a damaged/unlubricated cable. Perform the following checks before removing the right crankcase cover to troubleshoot the clutch:
1. Check the clutch cable routing from the handlebar to the engine. Check that the cable is free when the handlebar is turned lock to lock and that the cable ends are installed correctly.
2. With the engine off, pull and release the clutch lever. If the lever is hard to pull, or the action is rough, check for the following:
    a. Damaged/kinked cable.
    b. Incorrect cable routing.
    c. Cable not lubricated.
    d. Worn/unlubricated lever at the handlebar.
    e. Damaged release lever at the engine.
3. If no damage was detected in the previous steps, and the lever moves without excessive roughness or binding, check the clutch adjustment (Chapter Three). Note the following:

a. If the clutch cannot be adjusted to the specifications in Chapter Three, the clutch cable is stretched or damaged.
b. If the clutch cable is in good condition and adjustment is correct, the clutch plates may be worn or warped.

Clutch Slipping

When the clutch slips, the engine accelerates faster than what the actual forward speed indicates. When continuous slipping occurs between the clutch plates, excessive heat quickly builds up in the assembly. This causes plate wear, warp and spring fatigue. One or more of the following can cause the clutch to slip:
1. Clutch wear or damage:
    a. Incorrect clutch adjustment.
    b. Weak or damaged clutch springs.
    c. Loose clutch springs.
    d. Worn friction plates.
    e. Warped clutch (steel) plates.
    f. Worn/damaged release lever assembly.
    g. Damaged pressure plate.
    h. Clutch housing and hub unevenly worn.
2. Clutch/engine oil:
    a. Incorrect oil viscosity.
    b. Oil additives.

Clutch Dragging

When the clutch drags, the plates are not completely separating. This will cause the machine to creep or lurch forward when the transmission is put into gear. Once underway, shifting is difficult. If this condition is not corrected, it can cause transmission gear and shift fork damage, due to the abnormal grinding and impacts on the parts. One or more of the following can cause the clutch to drag:
1. Clutch wear or damage:
    a. Worn/damaged release lever assembly.
    b. Warped clutch (steel) plates.
    c. Swollen friction plates.
    d. Warped pressure plate.
    e. Incorrect clutch spring tension.
    f. Galled clutch housing bushing.
    g. Uneven wear on clutch housing grooves or clutch hub splines.
    h. Incorrectly assembled clutch.
2. Clutch/engine oil:

a. Low oil level.
b. Incorrect viscosity oil.
c. Oil additives.

Clutch Noise

Clutch noise is usually caused by worn or damaged parts, and is more noticeable at idle or low engine speeds. Clutch noise can be caused by the following conditions:
1. Wear in the clutch pull rod bearing.
2. Excessive axial play in the clutch housing.
3. Excessive friction plate to clutch housing clearance.
4. Excessive wear between the clutch housing and primary drive gear.
5. Worn or damaged clutch housing and primary drive gear teeth.

GEAR SHIFT LINKAGE AND TRANSMISSION

Transmission problems are often difficult to distinguish from problems with the clutch and gear shift linkage. Often, the problem is symptomatic of one area, while the actual problem is in another area. For example, if the gears grind during shifting, the problem may be caused by a dragging clutch or a component of the shift linkage, not a damaged transmission. Of course, if the damaged part is not repaired, the transmission will eventually become damaged, too. Therefore, evaluate all of the variables that exist when the problem occurs, and always start with the easiest checks before disassembling the engine.

When the transmission exhibits abnormal noise or operation, drain the engine oil and check it for contamination or metal particles. Examine a small quantity of oil under bright light. If a metallic cast or pieces of metal are seen, excessive wear and/or part failure is occurring.

Difficult Shifting

1. Clutch:
    a. Improper clutch operation.
    b. Incorrect clutch adjustment.
    c. Incorrect oil viscosity.
2. Shift shaft:
    a. Loose/stripped shift lever.

b. Bent/damaged shift shaft.

c. Worn engagement points between lever and roller.

d. Damaged return spring or loose spring post.

3. Lever:
   a. Damaged lever or pawls.
   b. Broken pawl spring.
   c. Loose lever bolt.
   d. Damaged shift guide.

4. Shift drum and shift forks:
   a. Worn shift drum grooves.
   b. Worn shift forks/guide pins.
   c. Worn shift drum bearing.

Gears Do Not Stay Engaged

1. Lever:
   a. Damaged lever.
   b. Broken return spring.
   c. Worn shift drum bearing.

2. Shift drum and shift forks:
   a. Worn shift drum grooves.
   b. Worn shift forks/guide pins.

3. Transmission:
   a. Worn gear dogs and mating recesses.
   b. Worn gear grooves for shift forks.
   c. Worn/damaged shaft snap rings or thrust washers.

BRAKES

The brakes are critical to riding performance and safety. Inspect the brakes frequently and replace worn or damaged parts immediately. The brake system uses DOT 4 brake fluid. Always use new fluid from a sealed and closed container. The troubleshooting checks in **Figure 9** assist in isolating the majority of brake problems.

When checking brake pad wear, check that the pads in each caliper squarely contact the disc. Uneven pad wear on one side of the disc can indicate a warped or bent disc, damaged caliper or pad pins.

STEERING AND HANDLING

Correct poor steering and handling immediately after it is detected, because loss of control is possible. Check the following areas:

1. Excessive handlebar vibration:
   a. Incorrect tire pressure.
   b. Damaged rim (excessive runout).
   c. Bent tie rod.
   d. Incorrect toe-in.
   e. Loose or damaged handlebar clamps.
   f. Loose steering shaft nut or bearings.
   g. Worn or damaged front wheel bearings.
   h. Bent or loose axle.

2. Handlebar is hard to turn:
   a. Tire pressure too low.
   b. Incorrect cable routing.
   c. Steering shaft too tight.
   d. Improperly lubricated or damaged steering shaft bearing.

3. Handlebar pulls to one side:
   a. Uneven tire pressure.
   b. Bent tie rod.
   c. Dragging brake.

Figure 9 is on the following page.

⑨   **BRAKE TROUBLESHOOTING**

Brake fluid leakage

Check:
- Loose or damaged line fittings
- Worn caliper piston seals
- Scored caliper piston or bore
- Loose banjo bolts
- Damaged oil line washers
- Leaking master cylinder diaphragm
- Leaking master cylinder secondary seal
- Cracked master cylinder housing

Brake overheating

Check:
- Warped brake disc
- Incorrect brake fluid

Brake chatter

Check:
- Warped brake disc
- Incorrect caliper alignment
- Loose caliper mounting bolts
- Loose front axle nut and/or clamps
- Worn wheel bearings
- Damaged hub
- Restricted brake hydraulic line

Brake locking

Check:
- Incorrect brake fluid
- Plugged passages in master cylinder
- Caliper piston and/or brake pads hanging up
- Warped brake disc

Insufficient brakes

Check:
- Air in brake lines
- Worn brake pads
- Low brake fluid
- Incorrect brake fluid
- Worn brake disc
- Worn caliper piston seals
- Glazed brake pads

Brake squeal

Check:
- Contaminated brake pads and/or disc
- Dust or dirt collected behind brake pads

LUBRICATION, MAINTENANCE AND TUNE-UP

This chapter provides information and procedures for properly lubricating, fueling and adjusting the machine. Refer to **Table 1** for the recommended service intervals and those components that require inspection, lubrication or adjustment.

Refer to the sections in this chapter for performing many of the maintenance procedures described in **Table 1**. For services that require extensive disassembly of a component, refer to the appropriate chapter(s) in the manual for inspection and repair.

When performing maintenance procedures on the machine, refer to *Safety* in Chapter One.

PRE-RIDE INSPECTION

Routinely perform the following checks before riding the machine. When riding over rough terrain, perform the checks at least once daily. Perform the checks when the engine is *cold*. Refer to the procedures and tables in this chapter for information concerning fuel, lubricants, tire pressure and component adjustments. Start the machine as described in *Starting the Engine* (Chapter Two). Check the following:

1. Fuel lines and fittings for leakage.
2. Fuel level.
3. Engine oil level.
4. Coolant level.
5. Brake operation and lever/pedal free play.
6. Throttle operation and free play.
7. Clutch operation and free play.
8. Steering for smooth operation and no cable binding.
9. Tire condition and air pressure.
10. Wheel condition and tightness.
11. Nuts and bolts for tightness.
12. Exhaust system tightness.
13. Drive chain condition and adjustment.
14. Rear sprocket tightness.
15. Air filter for dirt/debris buildup.
16. Suspension for leakage and proper settings for riding conditions.
17. Engine stop switch for proper operation.
18. Lights for proper operation.
19. Coolant temperature light for proper operation.

ENGINE BREAK-IN

A proper break-in period must be observed for new and reconditioned engines. The performance and service life of the engine depends greatly on a careful and sensible break-in. Observe the following when breaking in a reconditioned engine:

1. Fill the engine with the correct amount and weight of engine oil.

2. Install a new spark plug.

3. Check that the air filter is clean.

4. For the first 10 hours of operation, use no more than 1/2 throttle. Vary the speed as much as possible within this throttle range. Avoid running the machine at a steady speed. Avoid hard acceleration.

5. For the next 10 hours of operation, use no more than 3/4 throttle. Vary the speed as much as possible within this throttle range. Intermittent use of full throttle is permissible, but do not maintain the engine at full throttle.

6. At the end of the break-in period, adjust the valves and change the engine oil and filter. This oil change is important to remove the metallic particles that result as the parts seat to one another.

TUNE-UP AND SERVICE INTERVALS

The service intervals in **Table 1** are recommended by Yamaha. If the machine is regularly operated in extreme weather conditions, or subjected to water or sand, perform the service procedures more frequently.

Record when each service is performed in the maintenance log at the end of this manual. With a detailed history it will be easier to plan maintenance and have the necessary parts on hand.

BATTERY

When new, the machine is equipped with a 12 volt, 12 amp-hour, maintenance-free battery. If the machine has not been used for at least two weeks, the battery should be charged to prevent sulfation of the battery plates.

If necessary refer to *Charging System* (Chapter Nine) for additional battery and charging system tests.

Removal and Installation

1. Remove the seat (Chapter Fourteen).

2. Remove the battery hold down bracket (A, **Figure 1**).

3. Disconnect the negative cable from the battery (B, **Figure 1**).

4. Remove the insulator cover (C, **Figure 1**) from the positive cable, then remove the cable from the battery.

5. Clean and check the battery and cables.

6. Reverse this procedure to install the battery. Note the following:

   a. To prevent corrosion, apply a thin coat of dielectric grease to the battery terminals and cable ends.

   b. Tighten the cables firmly. Do not apply excessive force.

Voltage Test

For a maintenance-free battery (original equipment), check the unloaded voltage using a voltmeter. An unloaded test will indicate the basic state of charge. If necessary, refer to Chapter Nine for performing a battery load test.

1. Disconnect the battery cables and allow the battery to remain undisturbed for at least 4 hours.

2. Connect a voltmeter to the negative and positive terminals as shown in **Figure 2**.

3. Measure the voltage.

   a. A fully charged battery will have a minimum of 12.8 volts.

   b. A battery that is approximately 75 percent charged will have a minimum of 12.5 volts.

   c. A battery that is approximately 50 percent charged will have a minimum of 12.0 volts.

Charging

When recharging the battery, do not use a charger that is rated higher than 1.2 amps output. Also, do not use an automotive-type charger. The charge

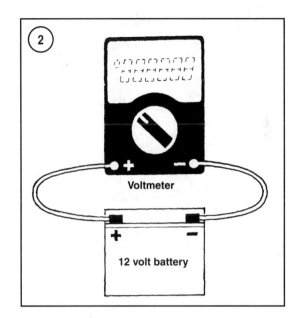

rates are too high and will overheat the battery and damage the plates.

CAUTION
To prevent possible electrical system damage, always remove the cables from the battery before charging the battery.

1. Remove the battery from the machine as described in this section.

2. Connect the positive and negative leads of the charger to the positive and negative terminals on the battery.

3. Set the charger to 12 volts. If the charger has a variable charge rate, select a low setting. Using a 1 amp, constant-current charger, the suggested charge rates for a maintenance-free battery are:

   a. 75 percent charge: 1 amp for 3-6 hours.

   b. 50 percent charge: 1 amp for 5-11 hours.

4. Turn on the charger and allow the battery to charge for the specified time.

5. After the battery is charged, turn off the charger and remove the leads from the terminals. Allow the battery to stabilize for at least 30 minutes.

6. Check battery voltage as described in this section. If the battery voltage does not remain stable for at least one hour, or continues to be undercharged, the battery should be replaced.

FUEL AND LUBRICANTS

Fuel Requirements

The engine is designed to operate on unleaded pump-grade gasoline, with an octane rating of 86 (R + M/2) or 91 RON (Research Octane Number). Gasoline containing up to 10 percent alcohol (gasohol) can be used. Gasoline containing methanol is not recommended.

Engine Oil

The engine requires a multigrade oil with an SAE viscosity of 5W-30, 10W-30 or 20W-40. The oil should have a service classification of SG. The oil viscosity and classification are indicated on the oil container.

Since multigrade oil is blended with chemical polymers that change the characteristics of the oil as it is heated or cooled, the SAE numerical ratings indicate the equivalent *weight* of the oil at 0° F (-18° C) and 210° F (99° C). The numbers do not indicate an actual thickness, but rather the oils' ability to circulate and lubricate at these extremes.

For this engine, the engine oil is also used to lubricate the transmission. Over time, the transmission will *shear* the polymers in the oil, reducing its lubrication abilities. Therefore, always change the oil and filter at the intervals indicated in **Table 1**. If possible, use the same brand of oil at each oil change.

CAUTION
Do not use oils or oil additives that contain graphite or molybdenum. These additives can cause clutch slippage and erratic operation.

Grease

Use a good quality, lithium-base grease to lubricate components requiring grease. Some components require the extreme-pressure qualities of molybdenum disulfide grease, or the protective qualities of waterproof grease. When these greases are required, it is indicated in the procedures throughout the manual. Grease components frequently, as this will purge water and grit from the component and extend its life.

Chain Lubricant

Use a good-quality chain lubricant that is compatible with the type of chain installed on the machine. An O-ring chain was standard equipment for the years covered by this manual. If an O-ring chain is installed, use chain lubricant that is specifically for O-ring chains. Since the links of an O-ring chain are permanently lubricated and sealed, O-ring chain lubricant is formulated to prevent exterior corrosion of the chain and to condition the O-rings. It is not tacky and resists the adhesion of dirt. Avoid lubricants that are tacky and for conventional chains. These lubricants will attract dirt and subject the O-rings to unnecessary abrasion.

Control Cable Lubricant

Use lithium grease to lubricate the control cable pivots. Lubricate the cable with light oil or a commercial cable lubricant.

Air Filter Oil

Use a commercial air filter oil specifically for foam filters. This type of oil stays adhered to the foam and traps dust effectively.

PERIODIC LUBRICATION

Engine Oil Level Check

The oil level is checked and replenished at the dipstick (**Figure 3**) located in the oil tank. Check the oil after the engine has been warmed up, then allowed to stand for a few minutes.
1. Park the machine on level ground.
2. Remove the dipstick from the oil tank, then wipe the dipstick clean.
3. Insert the dipstick into the oil tank, but *do not* screw the dipstick into the tank.
4. Remove the dipstick and check the oil level.
   a. The oil level should be between the upper (F) and lower (E) level marks (**Figure 4**).
   b. Preferably, keep the oil level near the upper mark.
5. If the oil level is too low, add the appropriate grade of oil to bring the level to the upper mark. Add oil in small quantities and check the level often. Do not overfill the oil tank.

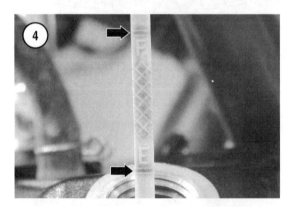

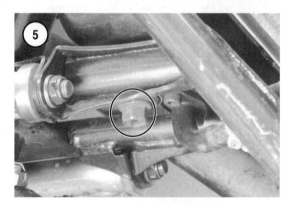

6. Screw the dipstick into place. If oil leakage is evident around the top of the oil tank, replace the O-ring on the dipstick.

Engine Oil and Filter Change

Change the oil and filter at the intervals recommended in **Table 1**. If the machine is used in extreme conditions (hot, cold, wet or dusty) change the oil more often and use the oil recommended in **Table 2**.

Always change the oil when the engine is warm. Contaminants will remain suspended in the oil and it will drain more completely and quickly. To decrease oil change time, have two drain pans available so the oil can be drained from both drain plugs simultaneously.

WARNING
Prolonged contact with used engine oil may cause skin cancer. Minimize contact with the engine oil.

1. Park the machine on level ground and set the parking brake.
2. Remove the engine skid plate (Chapter Fourteen).
3. Wipe the area around the dipstick, then loosen the dipstick (**Figure 3**).
4. Place a drain pan below the oil tank drain plug, then remove the drain plug (**Figure 5**). Allow the oil to drain from the engine. Although the frame is directly below the plug, the oil will drain through the holes and into the pan.
5. Place a drain pan below the crankcase drain plug (**Figure 6**), located by the shift lever. Remove the drain plug and allow the oil to drain from the engine.
6. Replace the oil filter as follows:
   a. Unscrew the oil filter (**Figure 7**) from the engine. If necessary, use a small, strap-type oil filter wrench. A wrench is available from Yamaha dealerships (part number YM-01469, 90890-01469).
   b. Wipe clean the mounting pin and filter contact area.
   c. Apply engine oil to the oil filter O-ring (**Figure 8**).
   d. Hand-tighten the new oil filter (Yamaha part No. 5DM-13440-00). Yamaha recommends torquing the filter to 17 N•m (13 ft.-lb.).
7. Install a new seal washer on both drain plugs. Replace the drain plugs if the threads are damaged or severely worn. If leakage is evident around the dipstick, replace the O-ring on the dipstick.
8. Wipe dirt and oil from around the drain plug holes, then install and torque the drain plugs.
   a. Torque the oil tank drain plug to 25 N•m (18 ft.-lb.).
   b. Torque the crankcase drain plug to 30 N•m (22 ft.-lb.).
9. Fill the oil tank with 1.75 L (1.85 qt.) of engine oil. Install and tighten the dipstick.
   a. Refer to **Table 2** for the required quantity and grade of engine oil.
   b. Note that oil capacity is greater when the filter is changed.
10. Start the engine, then raise and lower the engine speed to circulate oil out of the oil tank.
11. Stop the engine and add the remainder of the oil to the oil tank.
12. Start and warm the engine for a few minutes.
13. Stop the engine and check for leaks.

14. Check the engine oil level as described in *Engine Oil Level Check* in this section.

15. Install the skid plate.

16. Dispose the filter and used engine oil in an environmentally-safe manner.

NOTE
If engine oil pressure seems low, or if oil circulation is questionable, loosen (do not remove) the oil gallery bolt (Figure 9). Start the engine and allow it to idle. If oil does not seep from the bolt within one minute, stop the engine immediately. Check the engine oil filter, oil pump and oil passages for wear and clogs. Always perform this check after the engine has been submerged or subjected to contaminants in the crankcase.

Control Cable Lubrication

If binding or drag is detected in a cable, this can indicate a lack of cable lubrication or worn parts. Lubricate the control cable pivots with grease. Lubricate the cables with light oil or an aerosol cable lubricant and attachment (**Figure 10**). If the cable continues to operate poorly after lubrication, disconnect the cable(s) at both ends and check for binding or drag. Replace the cable if necessary.

If necessary, use these same techniques to lightly lubricate the parking brake cable and reverse cable. Preferably, these cables should remain dry, since excess lubricant can get on the brake pads, as well as accumulate dirt. If the cables are submerged, a light water-displacing lubricant can be used to prevent internal rusting of the cable.

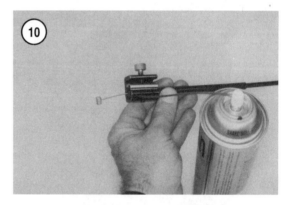

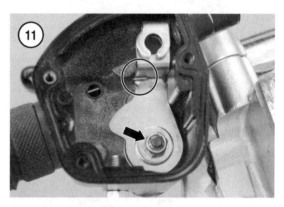

Clutch cable

1. Remove the clutch cable from the handlebar lever and release lever as described in *Clutch Cable Replacement* (Chapter Six).

2. Attach a cable lubricator, then lubricate the cable with aerosol cable lubricant. Keep the cable in a vertical position so the lubricant can pass to the opposite end. Move the cable in the housing to help distribute the oil. Stop lubrication when oil is seen at the opposite end of the cable.

3. Lubricate the lever pivot and cable ends with grease.

4. Install the cable as described in *Clutch Cable Replacement* (Chapter Six).

5. Adjust the clutch cable as described in this chapter.

Throttle cable and lever

1. Remove the throttle cable from the carburetor and handlebar as described in *Throttle Cable Replacement* (Chapter Eight).

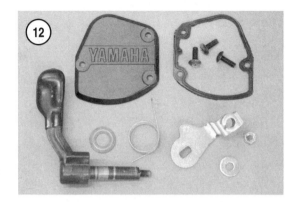

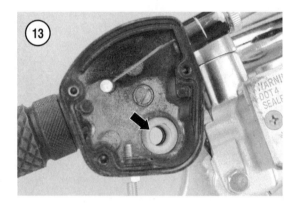

2. Attach a cable lubricator, then lubricate the cable with aerosol cable lubricant. Keep the cable in a vertical position so the lubricant can pass to the opposite end. Move the cable in the housing to help distribute the oil. Stop lubrication when oil is seen at the opposite end of the cable.

3. Disassemble and lubricate the throttle lever as follows:

    a. Remove the nut and washer from the throttle lever (**Figure 11**), then remove the cable lever, spring and lever.

    b. Inspect the parts for obvious wear (**Figure 12**).

    c. Inspect the bushings in the housing (**Figure 13**). Replace the bushings if worn.

    d. Apply grease to the lever shaft and washer, then insert the parts into the housing.

    e. Insert the spring with the hooked end pointing up (**Figure 14**).

    f. Pull back on the spring hook, then install the cable lever. Seat the hook on the lever (**Figure 11**).

    g. Install the cable as described in *Throttle Cable Replacement* (Chapter Eight).

Drive Chain Cleaning and Lubrication

The machine is equipped with an O-ring chain that requires routine cleaning and lubrication. If the chain has been replaced with a standard chain, it too requires regular cleaning, lubrication and adjustment for long life. Although O-ring chains are internally lubricated and sealed, the O-rings need to be kept clean and lubricated to prevent them from drying out and disintegrating.

Chains should never be cleaned with high-pressure water sprays or strong solvents. This is particularly true for O-ring chains. If water is forced past the O-rings, water will be trapped inside the links. Strong solvents can soften the O-rings so they tear or damage easily.

Although chains are often lubricated while they are installed on the machine, the chain should periodically be removed and thoroughly cleaned. The following procedure describes the preferred method for cleaning and lubricating the chain.

1. Refer to *Drive Chain* (Chapter Twelve) to remove the chain.

2. Immerse the chain in kerosene and work the links so dirt is loosened.

3. Lightly scrub the chain with a soft-bristle brush.

CAUTION
Brushes with coarse or wire bristles can damage O-rings.

4. Rinse the chain with clean kerosene and wipe dry.

NOTE
While the chain is removed, check that it is still within the wear limit as de-

*scribed in **Drive Chain and Sprockets Inspection** in this chapter.*

5. Lubricate the chain with chain lubricant. Lubricate an O-ring chain with lubricant specifically for O-ring chains.

CAUTION
Since the links of an O-ring chain are permanently lubricated and sealed, O-ring chain lubricant is formulated to prevent exterior corrosion of the chain and to condition the O-rings. It is not tacky and resists the adhesion of dirt. Avoid lubricants that are tacky and for conventional chains. These lubricants will attract dirt and subject the O-rings to unnecessary abrasion.

6. Install the chain (Chapter Twelve).
7. Adjust the chain as described in this chapter.

Air Filter Cleaning and Lubrication

The engine is equipped with a reusable foam air filter. Do not operate the engine without the air filter and cover, or with a damaged air filter. Performance will not be enhanced and rapid engine wear will occur.

1. Remove the seat (Chapter Fourteen).
2. Remove the crankcase breather hose from the front left corner of the air filter housing cover (**Figure 15**).
3. Remove the six clips securing the cover (**Figure 16**).
4. Lift out the air filter assembly (**Figure 17**).
5. Rotate and remove the end cap, then remove the air filter from the frame (**Figure 18**).
6. Wash all parts in solvent (kerosene), a commercial filter wash, or hot soapy water.
   a. *Squeeze* the cleaner from the filter. Do not wring the filter, as tearing may occur.
   b. Shake the filter of any particles that may remain on the filter.
   c. Allow the filter to completely dry.
7. Apply filter oil to the filter, squeezing the filter so the oil is distributed evenly. Squeeze out the excess oil. When performing this step, handle the filter with disposable gloves, or put the filter in a plastic bag to squeeze and distribute the oil. Follow the manufacturer's instructions when oiling the filter.

NOTE
Oil specifically formulated for foam filters should be used. This type of oil stays adhered to the foam and traps dust effectively.

8. Install the frame into the filter, seating the filter against the front of the frame. If desired, apply grease around the perimeter of the filter lip and the outside face of the frame. This will help seal the parts when installed.

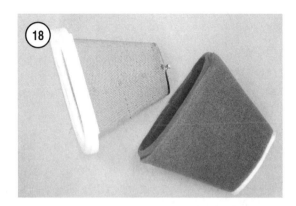

9. Install the end cap with the word OUTSIDE facing out.

10. Clean the air filter housing and cover.

11. Clean the inspection cup in the bottom of the air filter housing (**Figure 19**). This cup should be regularly inspected for water, dirt and other contaminants. When contaminants are evident, this indicates the air filter and housing should be inspected and cleaned, regardless of when it was last serviced.

12. View the front of the filter frame for the words UP SIDE. Orient the assembly, then seat it into the air filter housing. Check that the frame is tight against the front of the housing.

13. Install the cover and crankcase breather hose.

14. Install the seat.

MAINTENANCE AND INSPECTION

Speed Limiter Adjustment

The speed limiter screw restricts the travel of the throttle lever, thereby preventing maximum engine speed. This is helpful to enthusiasts that are learning to ride the machine. As rider skills increase, the limiter can be adjusted to increase power. It is recommended that the screw be fully turned in for beginning riders.

The limiter is also useful during the engine break-in period. By adjusting the limiter to accommodate the break-in intervals, possible engine damage can be avoided.

1. At the throttle housing, measure the distance from the housing to the screw head (**Figure 20**). Maximum distance should not exceed 12 mm (0.5 in.).

2. If necessary, loosen the locknut and screw the adjuster to the desired position. Tighten the locknut.

Fastener Inspection

Periodically inspect all fasteners on the machine for tightness and condition.

1. Retorque nuts, bolts and screws as specified in the tables at the end of each chapter. Refer to the *General Torque Specifications* table (Chapter One) when a torque value is not specified.

2. Check that all cotter pins are secure and undamaged.

3. Check that tie straps, used to secure cables and electrical wiring, are not broken or missing.

Muffler Cleaning

In order for the muffler to perform correctly and not affect engine performance, the internal baffle should be purged of carbon buildup. This is particularly important if the engine has been running too rich.

> *WARNING*
> *Do not spray solvents or other combustible liquids into the muffler to aid*

in removing buildup. If solvents are used to clean the spark arrester, use compressed air to completely dry the part before installing it in the muffler. An explosion and/or fire could occur if solvents are present in the muffler.

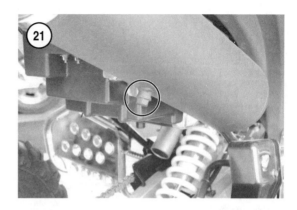

1. Park the machine in an open area, away from combustible materials.
2. Remove the plug on the bottom of the muffler (**Figure 21**).
3. Start the engine.
4. Wearing gloves, use a rubber mallet to tap on the surface of the muffler as the engine speed is raised and lowered. Also, momentarily place a folded shop cloth over the end of the muffler to force exhaust pressure out of the plug opening.
5. When no more carbon particles are purged, stop the engine and replace the plug. Allow the muffler to cool.
6. Remove the bolt securing the spark arrestor to the muffler (**Figure 22**).
7. Remove the spark arrestor and brush it clean.
8. Install and bolt the spark arrestor into place.

Carburetor Float Chamber Drain

The float chamber can be drained by *loosening* the drain screw (**Figure 23**). Removal of the screw is not necessary. When loosened, the fuel is drained out the hose attached to the float chamber.

> *WARNING*
> *Do not attempt to drain the float chamber while the engine is hot or running.*

> *NOTE*
> *If the screw is loose or damaged, the leaking fuel may be wrongly diagnosed as poor float adjustment.*

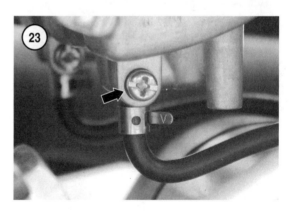

Coolant Level Inspection

> *WARNING*
> *Inspect the cooling system when the engine and coolant are cold. Severe injury could occur if the system is checked while it is hot. If the radiator cap must be removed while the coolant is still warm, cover the cap with a*

towel and open it slowly. Do not remove the cap until all pressure is relieved.

Refer to **Table 2** for the recommended coolant and mixing ratio.

1. Park the machine on level ground.

2. At the reserve tank, located under the left rear fender, visually check the coolant level. The level should be between the low and full marks embossed on the tank (**Figure 24**). If the level is too low, re-

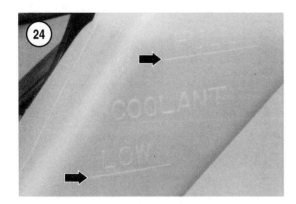

move the cap from the tank and add coolant. Do not allow the tank level to fall below the low mark.

3. Make the following checks, as necessary:

 a. Check the hoses for damage at the top and bottom of the tank.

 b. If the reserve tank is empty, check the level in the radiator. The coolant level should be to the bottom of the filler neck (**Figure 25**). If the coolant level is below the filler neck, add coolant mixture to raise the level.

 c. Install the radiator cap and start the engine. Inspect for leaks at all hoses and fittings. Check for leakage at the drain hole at the bottom of the water pump (**Figure 26**). If coolant is evident, this indicates that leakage is occurring at the mechanical seal in the water pump. If engine oil is evident, this indicates that leakage is occurring at the oil seal in the water pump. Refer to Chapter Ten for replacement of the seals.

> *CAUTION*
> *If the coolant level continues to drop, pressure test the cooling system. Severe engine damage can occur if the engine is allowed to overheat.*

Cooling System Inspection

Annually check the condition of the cooling system, or whenever it is suspected that overheating is occurring. The radiator cap and cooling system are checked individually, using a cooling system tester. This tester applies the required pressure to the cooling system and cap. A pressure gauge attached to the tester is observed and leakage can be detected. A Yamaha dealership can perform this inspection, or a tester can be purchased at an automotive parts supplier. Test the radiator cap and cooling system as follows:

> *WARNING*
> *Test the cooling system when the engine and coolant are cold. Severe injury could occur if the system is checked while it is hot.*

1. Park the machine on level ground.

2. Remove the radiator cap (**Figure 27**) and make the following checks. Replace the cap if any damage is detected.

a. Rubber seals. Check for cracks, compression and pliability.

b. Relief valve. Check for damage and seizure.

c. Radiator neck. Check for dents and distortion. The surfaces must be smooth and dent-free so the cap can seal and hold pressure. Repair or replace the radiator if the radiator neck is damaged.

3. Check the cap relief pressure. Wet the seal on the radiator cap, then attach the cap to a tester (**Figure 28**). Apply pressure to the cap. Relief pressure for the cap is 95-125 kPa (13.8-18.1 psi). Observe the pressure gauge and do the following:

a. If the gauge holds pressure up to the relief pressure range, the cap is in good condition.

b. If the gauge does not hold pressure, or the relief pressure is too high or low, replace the cap.

4. Check that the radiator is filled to the bottom of the filler neck (**Figure 25**). Attach the tester to the radiator (**Figure 29**), then pump the tester to 137 kPa (20 psi).

> *CAUTION*
> *Do not exceed 137 kPa (20 psi). Excessive pressure can damage the cooling system components.*

a. If the gauge holds the required pressure, the cooling system is in good condition.

b. If the gauge does not hold the required pressure, check for leakage at the radiator and all fittings. If the pressure lowers and then stabilizes, check for swollen radiator hoses. Replace or repair the cooling system components so it maintains the test pressure.

Coolant Draining and Replacement

> *WARNING*
> *Replace the coolant in the cooling system when the engine and coolant are cold. Severe injury can occur if the system is drained while it is hot.*

> *CAUTION*
> *Do not allow coolant to contact painted surfaces. If contact does occur, immediately wash the surface with water.*

1. Park the machine on level ground.

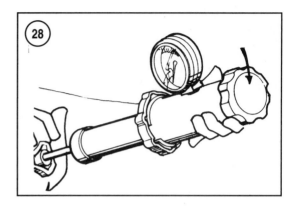

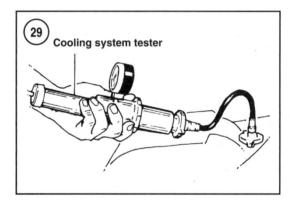

Cooling system tester

2. Remove the front panel (Chapter Fourteen).

3. Place a drain pan under the right side of the engine, below the water pump. Remove the drain plug from the bottom of the water pump (**Figure 30**).

4. As coolant begins to drain from the engine, stand to the side and slowly loosen the radiator cap so the flow from the engine increases. Be ready to reposition the drain pan.

5. Place a drain pan under the reserve tank, then remove the bottom hose from the tank (**Figure 31**). If

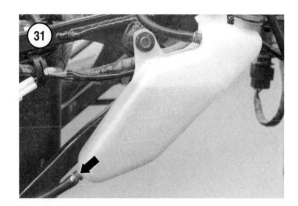

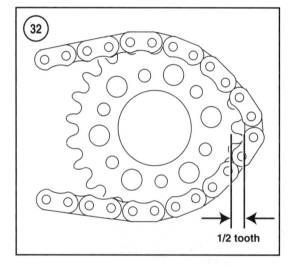

1/2 tooth

dirt or other buildup is in the tank, remove the mounting bolts and wash the tank.

6. Flush the cooling system and reserve tank with clean water. Check that all water drains from the system. Applying *light* air pressure to the radiator can aid in purging the water passages.

7. Inspect the condition of:

a. Radiator hoses. Check for leaks, cracks and loose clamps.

b. Radiator core. Check for leaks, debris and tightness of mounting bolts.

c. Radiator fan. Check for damaged wiring and tight connections.

8. Install a new seal washer on the coolant drain plug, then install and torque the plug to 10 N•m (88 in.-lb.).

9. Connect the hose to the reserve tank.

10. Refill the radiator with a coolant mixture as specified in **Table 2**.

a. Refill the radiator as the coolant level goes down.

b. When the coolant level no longer goes down, fill the radiator to the bottom of the filler neck (**Figure 25**). Install the radiator cap.

c. Fill the reserve tank to the full mark.

11. Start the engine and allow the coolant to circulate for about one minute. Shut off the engine and do the following:

WARNING
Cover the cap with shop cloths, then open the cap slowly. Do not remove the cap until all pressure is relieved.

a. Remove the radiator cap and check the coolant level. If necessary, add coolant to bring the level to the bottom of the filler neck.

b. Install the radiator cap.

12. Start the engine and allow it to reach operating temperature. Shut off the engine and do the following:

a. Check for leakage at the drain plug, hoses and reserve tank.

b. Check the level in the reserve tank. If necessary, remove the cap from the reserve tank and fill it to the full mark.

13. Rinse the frame and engine where coolant was splashed.

14. Install the front panel.

15. Dispose the used coolant in an environmentally-safe manner.

Drive Chain and Sprockets
Inspection

A worn drive chain and sprockets is both unreliable and potentially dangerous. Inspect the chain and sprockets for wear and replace if necessary. If wear is detected, replace both sprockets and the chain. Mixing old and new parts will prematurely wear the new parts.

A quick check will provide an indication of when to actually measure chain wear. At the rear sprocket, pull one of the links away from the sprocket. If the link pulls away more than 1/2 the height of a sprocket tooth, the chain is excessively worn (**Figure 32**). To measure chain wear, perform the following:

1A. If the chain is not removed from the sprockets, loosen the axle hub and turn the chain adjusters equally to take all slack out of the chain along its top run.

1B. If the chain is removed from the sprockets, lay the chain on a flat surface and pull the ends of the chain to remove the slack.

2. Measure the length of any 10-link (11 pin) span. Measure center-to-center from the pins.

    a. The service limit for the chain is 150.1 mm (5.91 in.). If the measured distance meets or exceeds the service limit, replace the chain.

    b. If the chain is within the service limit, inspect the inside surfaces of the link plates. The plates should be shiny at both ends of the chain roller. If one side of the chain is worn, the chain has been running out of alignment. This also causes premature wear of the rollers and pins. Replace the chain if abnormal wear is detected.

3. Inspect the teeth on the front and rear sprockets. Compare the sprockets to **Figure 33**.

    a. A new sprocket will have symmetrical and uniform teeth. A used sprocket will wear on the back side of each tooth.

    b. If the chain has been running out of alignment, the sprocket teeth will appear worn and shiny on one side of the sprocket (**Figure 34**).

Drive Chain Adjustment

The drive chain must have adequate play so it can adjust to the actions of the swing arm when the machine is in use. Too little play can cause the chain to become excessively tight and cause unnecessary wear to the driveline components. Too much play can cause excessive looseness and possibly cause the chain to derail.

1. Support the machine under the frame so the rear wheel is off the ground and the suspension is extended.

2. Rotate the rear wheel and determine when the chain is tightest along its top length (least amount of play).

3. Measure the free play in the top length of chain (**Figure 35**). The required amount of free play is 30-45 mm (1.2-1.8 in.).

4. If necessary, adjust the chain play as follows:

    a. Loosen the axle hub nuts (**Figure 36**).

    b. Loosen the chain adjuster locknuts (A, **Figure 37**).

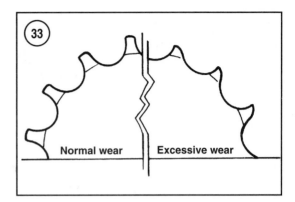

Normal wear   Excessive wear

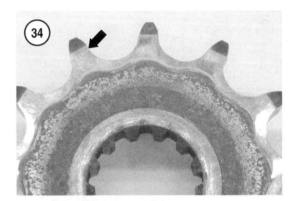

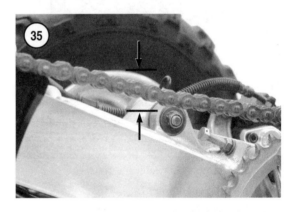

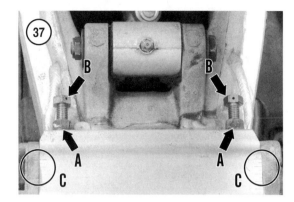

c. Equally turn the chain adjuster bolts (B, **Figure 37**) until the chain play is correct. Use the adjustment marks (C, **Figure 37**) on the swing arm to equally adjust the chain. If increasing chain play, push the axle forward to take the play out of the adjusters. This can also be achieved by slightly lowering the jack, allowing the wheels to force the axle against the adjusters.

NOTE
If free play cannot be adjusted within the limits of the adjusters, the chain is excessively worn and should be replaced.

d. When free play is correct, tighten the axle hub nuts and chain adjuster locknuts to lock the setting. Torque the axle hub nuts to 90 N•m (66 ft.-lb.). Torque the locknuts to 16 N•m (12 ft.-lb.).

e. Recheck the chain play. Adjust, if necessary.

Drive Chain Slider, Guard and Guide Inspection

Inspect the following parts for wear or damage. The parts support the chain and protect the frame and swing arm.

1. Chain slider (**Figure 38**).
    a. Inspect the upper and lower surface of the slider for wear or damage. The chain will contact the swing arm, possibly causing severe damage, if the slider is worn or missing.
    b. Check the mounting bolt for tightness.
2. Chain rollers (**Figure 39**).
    a. Clean and inspect the chain rollers, attached to the frame. Replace the rollers if worn or seized.
    b. Check the mounting bolts for tightness.

Throttle Cable Adjustment

To achieve accurate cable adjustment, the cable must not bind or drag. Engine idle speed should also be correct before adjusting the cable. If necessary, refer to Chapter Eight for throttle cable replacement procedures.

1. Measure the amount of free play at the throttle lever end (**Figure 40**). Free play should be 3-5 mm

(0.12-0.2 in.). If free play is incorrect, adjust the cable as described in the following step(s).

2. Loosen the locknut (A, **Figure 41**) and turn the cable adjuster (B) to increase/decrease play in the cable and lever. Note the following:

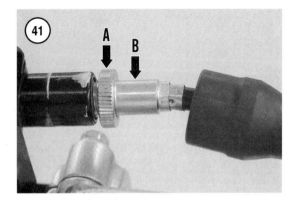

   a. If correct play can be achieved, and the adjuster is close to the middle of its range of travel, tighten the locknut. Adjustment is complete.

   b. If correct play cannot be achieved with the adjuster, or, if the adjuster is fully screwed in or out, set the adjuster to the middle of its travel. Proceed to Step 3 to make the adjustment at the carburetor.

3. Adjust the cable at the left carburetor as follows:

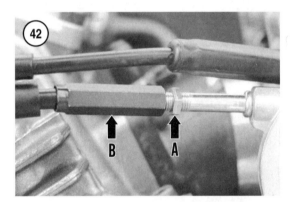

   a. Loosen the locknut (A, **Figure 42**) and turn the cable adjuster (B) to increase/decrease play in the cable and lever.

   b. Tighten the locknut.

   c. If necessary, make fine adjustments at the handlebar (Step 2).

4. At engine startup, turn the handlebar from side to side as the engine idles. If engine speed varies, check for proper cable adjustment and cable routing.

Clutch Cable Adjustment

The clutch cable must be properly adjusted to ensure smooth shifting, full clutch engagement and minimal wear on the clutch plates. The cable must not bind or drag. If necessary, refer to Chapter Six for clutch cable replacement procedures.

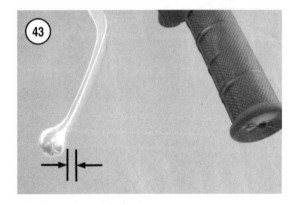

1. Measure the amount of free play at the lever end (**Figure 43**). Free play should be 5-10 mm (0.2-0.4 in.). If free play is incorrect, adjust the cable as described in the following step(s).

2. Loosen the locknut (A, **Figure 44**) and turn the cable adjuster (B) to increase/decrease play in the cable and lever. Note the following:

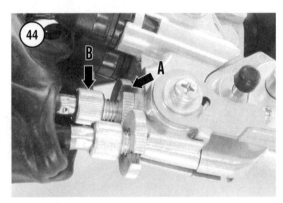

   a. If correct play can be achieved, and the adjuster is close to the middle of its range of travel, tighten the locknut. Adjustment is complete.

   b. If correct play cannot be achieved with the adjuster, or if the adjuster is fully screwed in or out, set the adjuster to the middle of its travel. Proceed to Step 3 to make the adjustment at the release lever.

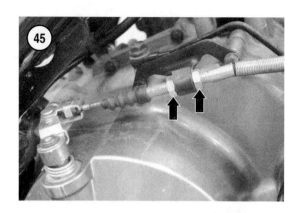

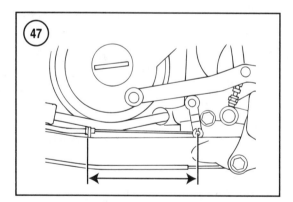

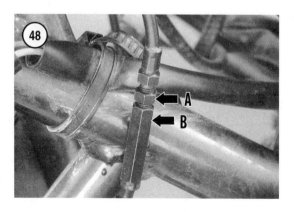

3. Adjust the cable at the release lever, located on the right crankcase cover, as follows:

   a. Loosen the locknuts (**Figure 45**) and reposition the cable so free play is correct at the lever.

   b. Tighten the locknuts.

   c. If necessary, make fine adjustments at the handlebar (Step 2).

4. At engine startup, check that the transmission properly engages and disengages from the clutch.

Reverse Cable Adjustment

The reverse cable must be adjusted properly so it will fully disengage the lockout mechanism in the transmission, allowing the transmission to be put into reverse. If adjusted properly, the cable will fully pull the reverse lever forward, as well as allow the cable to fully return to the seated lockout position.

1. Check that the lever is fully seated (toward the rear). If the lever will not seat, the cable is too tight and the lockout mechanism is partially disengaged. Proceed to Step 3 and adjust the cable.

2. Operate the reverse switch (**Figure 46**) and check that there is no free play in the cable.

   a. Check that the cable and switch actually move the reverse lever forward at the crankcase. While holding the cable taut with the reverse switch, try to push the lever forward, checking for any additional possible movement.

   b. If additional movement is available, the cable is not fully disengaging the lockout mechanism. Proceed to Step 3 and adjust the cable.

3. If necessary, adjust the cable as follows:

   a. Measure the cable length from the points shown in **Figure 47**. The cable should be 135 mm (5.3 in), or taut, when the reverse lever is fully seated.

   b. Under the right front fender, loosen the cable locknut (A, **Figure 48**) and turn the cable adjuster (B) until proper adjustment is achieved. Tighten the locknut.

   c. Operate the reverse switch and check the adjustment.

Parking Brake Cable Adjustment

The parking brake cable must be properly adjusted to ensure that it fully engages and disengages.

1. Measure the cable length between the cable holder and the center of the cable end. The length should be 64-68 mm (2.5-2.7 in.).

2. If necessary, adjust the cable as follows:

    a. At the handlebar, loosen the locknut (A, **Figure 49**) and turn the cable adjuster (B) until the proper length is achieved. Tighten the locknut.

    b. At the parking brake, loosen the locknut (A, **Figure 50**) and turn the adjuster bolt (B) counterclockwise until no resistance is felt. Turn the adjuster bolt clockwise until resistance is felt, then turn it back 1/8 turn counterclockwise. Hold the adjuster bolt in this position and tighten the locknut. There should be no play in the cable at the handlebar lever.

3. Check the parking brake for proper operation.

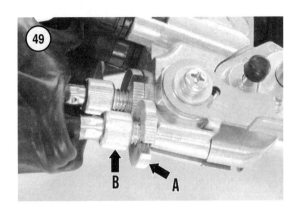

Choke Cable Adjustment

The choke cable must be properly adjusted to ensure that it fully opens and closes.

1. Remove the choke plunger from the left carburetor (**Figure 51**).

2. Lay the cable and plunger assembly on a flat surface so it can be measured.

3. At the handlebar, move the choke lever (**Figure 52**) to the left and right to ensure the cable moves freely. If the cable binds, inspect the the cable for damage and lack of lubrication. If necessary, replace the cable.

4. At the handlebar, move the choke lever *fully to the right*. In this position, the plunger should be extended. Measure the distance from the tip of the plunger to the edge of the housing (**Figure 53**). Record the measurement.

5. Move the choke lever *fully to the left*. In this position, the plunger should be retracted. Measure the distance from the tip of the plunger to the edge of the housing (**Figure 53**). Record the measurement.

6. The difference between the two measurements (plunger stroke) should be 15 mm (0.6 in.). If necessary, adjust the cable as follows:

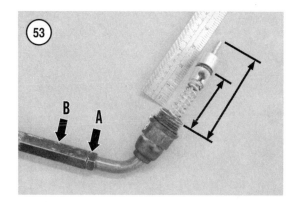

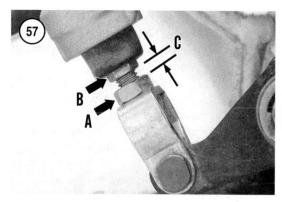

3

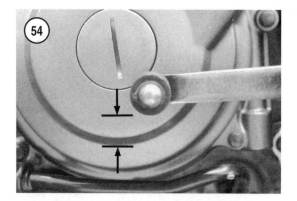

a. Loosen the locknut (A, **Figure 53**) and turn the cable adjuster (B) to increase/decrease the length of the plunger stroke.

b. When adjustment is correct, tighten the locknut.

7. Route the cable to the carburetor and install the plunger.

Shift Lever Adjustment

The shift lever should be positioned 22 mm (0.9 in.) above the point on the left crankcase cover, shown in **Figure 54**. Adjust the pedal and linkage as follows:

1. Loosen the locknuts (A, **Figure 55**) on the adjustment rod, then turn the adjuster (B) to increase/decrease the height of the lever.

2. Tighten the locknut.

Front Brake Lever Adjustment

There is no routine adjustment required for the front brake lever. If the master cylinder is in good condition and properly bled, the lever is automatically adjusted. If the brake drags, or brake lever play is unacceptable, inspect for worn or damaged parts in the master cylinder and brake caliper (Chapter Thirteen).

Rear Brake Pedal Adjustment

The brake pedal should be positioned 4 mm (0.16 in.) below the top of the footpeg (**Figure 56**). Adjust the pedal and linkage as follows:

1. Loosen the locknut at the master cylinder clevis (A, **Figure 57**), then turn the adjuster (B) to increase/decrease the height of the pedal.

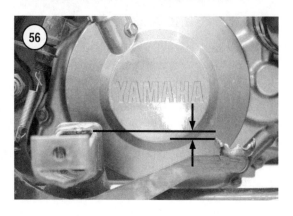

2. Tighten the locknut.

3. Check the distance between the nuts (C, **Figure 57**). The distance should be 2.2-3.2 mm (0.09-0.13 in.).

4. With the rear wheels off the ground, turn the wheels and operate the pedal to ensure the brake can be fully engaged and disengaged. If the brake drags, or if brake pedal height and free play cannot be achieved using the specified adjustments, inspect for worn or damaged parts in the master cylinder and caliper. Also check the pedal for damage.

5. Check brake light operation. If necessary, adjust the switch as described in this section.

Rear Brake Light Switch Adjustment

The rear brake light should turn on when the brake pedal is slightly depressed. The switch is located above the brake pedal and is attached by a spring. Adjust the brake light switch position by turning the nut (**Figure 58**) on the switch as follows:

1. If the light comes on too late (too much pedal travel), turn the switch adjustment nut and *raise* the switch position.

2. If the light comes on too early (too little pedal travel), turn the switch adjustment nut and *lower* the switch position.

> *NOTE*
> *If the light does not come on after adjustment, check the bulb condition. If necessary, disconnect the switch wires and use an ohmmeter to check for continuity. The switch is in the on position when the switch plunger is extended.*

Brake Fluid Level Inspection

1. Park the machine on a level surface and position the handlebar so the brake fluid reservoirs are level.

2. Inspect the front reservoir as follows:

  a. The fluid level should be between the lower level mark and the top of the sight glass (**Figure 59**).

  b. If the fluid level is below the low mark, remove the cap and diaphragm (**Figure 60**), then add DOT 4 brake fluid. Replace the diaphragm and cap.

  c. Check for master cylinder leaks and worn brake pads.

3. Inspect the rear reservoir (**Figure 61**) as follows:

  a. The fluid level should be between the upper and lower level marks embossed on the reservoir.

  b. If the fluid level is below the low mark, remove the guard assembly to access the reservoir.

  c. Remove the cap, diaphragm holder and diaphragm (**Figure 62**), then add DOT 4 brake fluid.

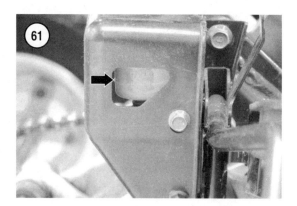

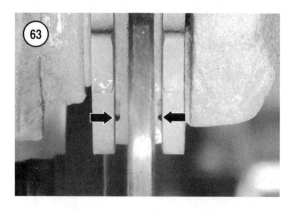

d. Replace the diaphragm, diaphragm holder and cap, then bolt the guard into place.

e. Check for master cylinder leaks and worn brake pads.

> *NOTE*
> *If the brake fluid is not clear to slightly yellow, the fluid is contaminated and should be replaced. Drain and bleed the brake system (Chapter Thirteen).*

Brake Pad and Disc Inspection

Regularly inspect the brake discs and pads to ensure they are in good condition. During severe riding conditions, the scoring of a disc can occur rapidly if the brake pads are damaged or have debris lodged in the pad material. If damage is evident for any of the following inspections, refer to Chapter Thirteen for brake pad replacement, disc specifications and service limits.

To inspect the front brake pads and discs, the front wheels and calipers must be removed. Refer to Chapter Thirteen for the caliper removal procedure. The rear brake pads and disc can be visually inspected for wear without removal of any parts. If disc scoring is evident, the caliper should be removed and the surface of the pads inspected.

1. Visually inspect the front and rear discs for the following:

   a. Scoring. The disc should be smooth in the friction area.

   b. Runout. Spin the wheel and visually check for lateral movement of the disc. Runout should not be evident. If runout is obvious, refer to Chapter Thirteen for measuring runout with a dial indicator.

   c. Disc thickness. If the disc shows wear in the friction area, refer to Chapter Thirteen for measuring wear with a micrometer.

2. Inspect the brake pads. The rear pads are visible by looking into the caliper on both sides of the disc. If the pads are worn to the wear indicator grooves (**Figure 63**), the pads are less than 1 mm (0.04 in.) thick and should be replaced. Refer to Chapter Thirteen for pad replacement procedures.

Front and Rear Suspension Adjustment

The front and rear shock absorbers are adjustable to meet the requirements of the riding conditions. Refer to *Shock Absorbers* (Chapter Eleven) to adjust the front shock absorbers. Refer to *Rear Suspension Adjustment* (Chapter Twelve) to adjust the rear shock absorber.

Tire Pressure

The tires must be inflated to meet the demands of the riding conditions. The standard air pressure recommendation is listed in **Table 4**. Slight over- or under-inflation is permissible if the riding conditions justify the change. However, do *not* exceed the inflation range embossed on the tire sidewall.

ENGINE TUNE-UP

Refer to *Carburetor Systems* (Chapter Eight) for information concerning the function of the carburetor jets and jet needle.

Valve Clearance

The engine is designed with three intake valves and two exhaust valves. The valves must be adjusted correctly so they will completely open and close during the combustion cycle. Valves that are out of adjustment can cause poor performance and engine damage. Check the valve clearance when the engine is cold. Read the entire procedure and understand the skill and equipment required to properly adjust the valves.

Commonly, when valve clearance is near the smallest acceptable clearance, the clearance is increased, even though the valve is technically within specification. Valves more often lose clearance than gain clearance between inspections, and therefore are adjusted toward the larger clearance specification. A small, marginally-acceptable clearance may be severely out of specification by the next inspection interval.

1. Park the machine on level ground and set the parking brake.
2. Remove the fuel tank and protectors (Chapter Fourteen).
3. Remove the spark plug cap (**Figure 64**) and spark plug.
4. Remove the two exhaust valve covers (**Figure 65**).
5. Remove the intake valve cover (**Figure 66**).
6. Remove the rotor nut and timing plugs (**Figure 67**).
7. Set the engine at TDC as follows:
   a. Fit a socket onto the rotor nut and turn the crankshaft *counterclockwise* until the **I** mark on the rotor is aligned with the index mark in the timing hole (**Figure 68**).
   b. Verify the engine is at TDC by watching the tops of the intake and exhaust valve adjusters. If properly set, all adjusters will be up when the rotor is set at the **I** mark. If the exhaust

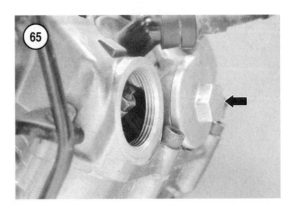

valve adjusters are down, rotate the crankshaft one full turn and realign the **I** mark.

8. For each valve, perform the following:

   a. Refer to **Table 3** for the correct valve clearance.

   b. Use a flat feeler gauge to determine the clearance between the top of the valve and adjuster (**Figure 69**). Clearance is correct if slight resistance is felt when the gauge is inserted and withdrawn.

9. If necessary, adjust the valve as follows:

   a. Loosen the locknut (A, **Figure 69**) and turn the adjuster (B) to achieve the correct clearance.

   b. Hold the adjuster and tighten the locknut.

   c. Check the clearance. Readjust if necessary.

10. Repeat the procedure for the remaining valves.

11. Reverse this procedure to install the removed components. Note the following:

   a. Install new, lubricated O-rings on the valve covers and case plugs.

   b. Torque the spark plug to 18 N•m (13 ft.-lb.).

   c. Torque the intake valve cover bolts to 12 N•m (106 in.-lb.).

   d. Torque the exhaust valve covers to 10 N•m (88 in.-lb.).

Carburetor Idle Speed and Mixture Adjustment

The carburetor must be adjusted so the idle speed keeps the engine running, but is also low enough to provide compression braking. Additionally, the pilot mixture screws must be adjusted so throttle response is good from an idle to about 1/4 throttle.

Use the following procedure to adjust the idle speed and pilot mixture screws for the *standard* jets:

1. Check the throttle cable for proper adjustment.

2. Check the air filter for cleanliness.

3. Set the pilot mixture screw for each carburetor (**Figure 70**) as follows:

NOTE
There is minimal clearance when accessing the pilot mixture screw. Unless special tools are available, a small, angled screwdriver with a straight blade will have to be fabricated. Yamaha does not offer a tool for making this adjustment.

   a. *Lightly* seat the screw. Turn the screw out the number of turns listed in **Table 3**. The settings are different for each carburetor. This is a starting point for adjustment.

   b. Start the engine and allow it to warm up.

   c. Set the engine idle speed to 1450-1550 rpm. Set the idle speed by turning the throttle stop screw (**Figure 71**). Raise and lower the engine speed a few times to ensure that it returns to the set idle speed.

d. Mark the position of the pilot air screw or tool. From its initial setting, turn the pilot air screw in and out in small increments to find the points where the engine speed begins to decrease. Set the pilot screw between the two points. Repeat this step for the remaining carburetor. The amount of adjustment to both carburetors should be similar.

e. Reset the idle speed to bring it within its required setting.

4. Test ride the machine and check throttle response. If throttle response is poor from an idle, adjust the pilot mixture screws out (richer) or in (leaner) by 1/8 turn increments until the engine accelerates smoothly.

5. If necessary, adjust the throttle cable for proper play.

Engine Timing Check

The ignition timing is electronically controlled by the CDI unit. No adjustment is possible to the timing. The timing is checked to verify the CDI unit is functioning properly. If ignition timing needs to be verified, perform the check as described in *Ignition Timing* (Chapter Nine).

Compression Check

A cylinder compression check can help verify the condition of the piston, rings and cylinder head assembly without disassembling the engine. By keeping a record of the compression reading at each tune-up, readings can be compared to determine if normal wear is occurring.

The standard, minimum and maximum pressures are listed in **Table 3**. It is recommended that the owner perform regular compression checks and record the readings. If a current reading is extremely different from a previous reading, troubleshooting can begin to pinpoint the problem. Operating the engine when compression readings are abnormal can lead to severe engine damage.

1. Warm the engine to operating temperature.

2. Remove the spark plug. Insert the spark plug into the cap, then ground the plug to the cylinder.

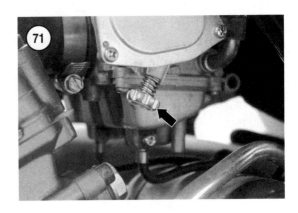

CAUTION
The spark plug must be grounded in order to prevent possible damage to the CDI unit.

3. Thread a compression gauge into the spark plug hole. The gauge must be fitted airtight in the hole for an accurate reading. If a gauge adapter is necessary, order part No. YU-33223-3, 90890-04082 from a Yamaha dealership.

4. Hold or secure the throttle fully open.

5. Operate the starter and turn the engine over until the highest gauge reading is achieved.

6. Record the reading. Compare the reading with previous readings, if available. Under normal operating conditions, compression will slowly lower from the original specification, due to wear of the piston rings and/or valve seats.

a. If the reading is higher than normal, this can be caused by a damaged compression release mechanism. Commonly, carbon buildup in the combustion chamber is another cause of high compression. This can cause high com-

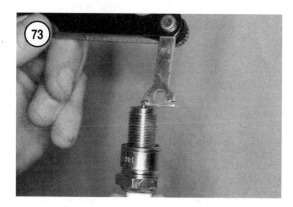

bustion chamber temperatures and potential engine damage.

b. If the reading is lower than normal, this can be caused by worn piston rings, worn valves, damaged piston, leaking head gasket, or a combination of these parts.

c. To help pinpoint the source of leakage, pour 15 cc (1/2 oz.) of four-stroke engine oil through the spark plug hole and into the cylinder. Turn the engine over to distribute the oil. Recheck compression. If compression increases, the piston rings are worn or damaged. If compression is the same, the piston, head gasket, valves or compression release are worn or damaged.

SPARK PLUG

Removal

Careful removal of the spark plug is important in preventing grit from entering the combustion chamber. It is also important to know how to remove a plug that is seized or is resistant to removal. Forcing a seized plug can destroy the threads in the cylinder head.

1. Remove the fuel tank and protectors (Chapter Fourteen).

2. Grasp the spark plug cap (**Figure 64**) and twist it loose from the spark plug. There may be slight suction and resistance as the cap is removed.

3. Clean dirt from the plug well, preferably with compressed air.

4. Fit a spark plug wrench onto the spark plug, then remove it by turning the wrench *counterclockwise*. If the plug is seized or drags excessively during removal, stop and try the following techniques:

a. Apply a penetrating lubricant such as Liquid Wrench or WD-40 and allow it to stand for 15 minutes.

b. If the plug is completely seized, apply moderate pressure in both directions with the wrench. Only attempt to break the seal so lubricant can penetrate under the spark plug and into the threads. If this does not work, and the machine is still operable, install the spark plug cap and fuel tank, then start the engine. Allow it to completely warm up. The heat of the engine may be enough to expand the parts and allow the plug to be removed.

c. When a spark plug has been loosened, but drags excessively during its removal, apply penetrating lubricant around the spark plug threads. Turn the plug *in* (clockwise) to help distribute the lubricant onto the threads. Slowly remove the plug, working it in and out of the cylinder head as lubricant is added.

d. Clean and true the threads with a spark plug thread-chaser. If severely damaged, remove the cylinder head from the engine and install a thread repair insert.

5. Inspect the removed plug to determine if the engine is operating properly.

6. A spark plug that is in good condition and will be reused after inspection should be cleaned with electrical contact cleaner and a shop cloth. Do not use abrasives or wire brushes to clean the plug.

Gap and Installation

Proper adjustment of the electrode gap is important for reliable and consistent spark. Also, the proper preparation of the spark plug threads will ensure that the plug can be removed easily in the future, without damage to the cylinder head threads.

1. Refer to **Table 3** for the required spark plug gap.

2. Insert a wire feeler gauge (the size of the required gap) between the center electrode and the ground electrode.

3. Pull the gauge through the gap. If there is slight drag, the setting is correct. If the gap is too large or small, adjust the gap by bending the ground electrode (**Figure 72**) to achieve the required gap. Use an adjusting tool (**Figure 73**) to bend the electrode. Do not pry the electrode with a screwdriver or other tool. Damage to the center electrode and insulator is possible.

4. Inspect the spark plug to ensure it is fitted with a crush washer.

5. Wipe a small amount of antiseize compound onto the spark plug threads. Do not allow the compound to get on the electrodes.

6. Finger-tighten the spark plug into the cylinder head. This will ensure the plug is not cross-threading.

7. Torque the spark plug to 18 N•m (13 ft.-lb.). If a torque wrench is not available, turn a new spark plug 1/4-1/2 turn from the seated position; a used spark plug 1/8-1/4 turn from the seated position.

8. Press and twist the cap onto the spark plug.

    a. To help prevent water from migrating under the cap, wipe a small amount of dielectric grease around the interior of the cap and at the upper boot before installing it on the plug.

    b. The spark plug cap should fit tight to the spark plug and be in good condition. A cap that does not seal and insulate the spark plug terminal can lead to flashover (shorting down the side of the plug), particularly when the machine is operated in wet conditions.

Spark Plug Selection

Refer to **Table 3** for the recommended spark plug type and gap.

> *NOTE*
> *The following paragraphs provide general information and operation fundamentals that apply to all spark plugs. However, before changing to a plug other than what is recommended by Yamaha, check with the spark plug manufacturer for specific part numbers and equivalents that apply to this machine. Poor performance or engine damage can occur by installing a spark plug that is not compatible with this engine.*

Heat range

Spark plugs are available in several heat ranges to accommodate the load and performance demands put on the engine. The standard spark plug recommended by manufacturers is usually a medium heat range plug that operates well over a wide range of

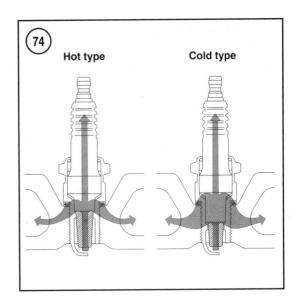

engine speeds. As long as engine speeds vary, these plugs will stay relatively clean and perform well.

If the engine is run in hot climates, at high speed or under heavy loads for prolonged periods, a spark plug with a colder heat range is recommended. A colder plug quickly transfers heat away from its firing tip and to the cylinder head (**Figure 74**). This is accomplished by a short path up the ceramic insulator and into the body of the spark plug. By transferring heat quickly, the plug remains cool enough to avoid overheating and preignition problems. If the engine is run slowly for prolonged periods, this type of plug will foul and result in poor performance.

If the engine is run in cold climates or at slow speed for prolonged periods, a spark plug with a hotter heat range is recommended. A hotter plug slowly transfers heat away from its firing tip and to the cylinder head. This is accomplished by a long path up the ceramic insulator and into the body of the spark plug (**Figure 74**). By transferring heat slowly, the plug remains hot enough to avoid fouling and buildup. If the engine is run in hot climates or fast for prolonged periods, this type of plug will overheat, cause preignition problems and possibly melt the electrode. Damage to the piston and cylinder assembly is possible.

If a spark plug will be changed to a different heat range, go one step hotter or colder from the recommended plug. Do not try to correct poor carburetor or ignition problems by using different spark plugs. This can only compound the existing problems and possibly lead to severe engine damage.

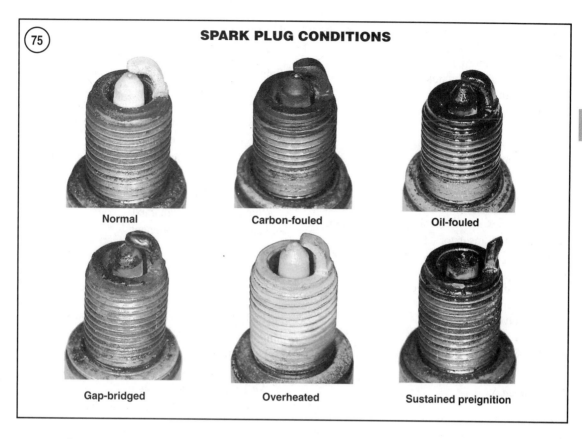

SPARK PLUG CONDITIONS

Normal   Carbon-fouled   Oil-fouled

Gap-bridged   Overheated   Sustained preignition

Reach

Reach is the length of the threaded portion of the plug. Always use a spark plug that is the correct reach. Too short of a reach can lead to deposits or burning of the exposed threads in the cylinder head. Misfiring can also occur since the tip of the plug is shrouded and not exposed to the fuel mixture. If the reach is too long, the exposed plug threads can burn, causing preignition. It is possible the piston may contact the plug on the upstroke, causing severe engine damage.

Inspection

The spark plug is an excellent indicator of how the engine is operating. By correctly evaluating (reading) the condition of the plug, potential problems can be diagnosed. Whenever the spark plug is removed, compare the firing tip with the ones shown in **Figure 75**. The following paragraphs provide a description, as well as common causes for each of the conditions.

> *CAUTION*
> *In all cases, when the spark plug does not read normal, find the cause of the problem before continuing engine operation. Severe engine damage is possible when abnormal plug readings are ignored.*

Normal

The plug has light tan or gray deposits on the tip. No erosion of the electrodes or abnormal gap is evident. This indicates an engine that has properly adjusted carburetion, ignition timing, and proper fuel. This heat range of plug is appropriate for the conditions in which the engine has been operated. The plug can be cleaned and reused.

Carbon-fouled

The plug is black with a dry, sooty deposit on the entire plug surface. This dry sooty deposit is conductive and can create electrical paths that bypass the electrode gap. This often results in misfiring of

the plug. One or more of the following conditions can cause carbon fouling:
1. Fuel mixture too rich.
2. Improperly adjusted choke.
3. Clogged air filter.
4. Spark plug heat range too cold.
5. Prolonged idling.
6. Faulty ignition component.
7. Poor compression.

Oil-fouled

The plug is wet with black, oily deposits on the electrodes and insulator. The electrodes do not show wear. Common causes for this condition are:
1. Incorrect carburetor jetting.
2. Prolonged idling or low idle speed.
3. Spark plug range too cold.
4. Worn valve guides.
5. Worn piston rings.
6. Ignition component failure.

Gap-bridged

The plug is clogged with deposits between the electrodes. The electrodes do not show wear. This condition can be caused by the following:
1. Incorrect oil being used.
2. Incorrect fuel or fuel contamination.
3. Carbon deposits in combustion chamber.
4. High-speed operation after excessive idling.

Overheated

The plug is dry and the insulator has a white or light gray cast. The insulator may also appear blistered. The electrodes may have a bluish-burnt appearance. If a hotter spark plug is not used and the plug is overheated, consider the following causes:
1. Fuel mixture too lean.
2. Spark plug heat range too hot.
3. Air leak into intake system.
4. No crush washer on plug.
5. Plug improperly tightened.
6. Faulty ignition component.

Preignition

The plug electrodes are severely eroded or melted. This condition can lead to severe engine damage. Common causes are:
1. Faulty ignition component.
2. Spark plug range too hot.
3. Air leak into intake system.
4. Carbon deposits in combustion chamber.

Worn out

The plug electrodes are rounded from normal combustion. There is no indication of abnormal combustion or engine conditions. Replace the plug.

Table 1 MAINTENANCE AND LUBRICATION SCHEDULE

	Initial first month	Every 6 months	Other
Adjust and lubricate drive chain			As required
Inspect/adjust speed limiter			As required
Inspect/charge battery			Monthly
Clean/replace air filter			Every 20-40 hours, or as required
Inspect brake fluid level	x		Monthly
Inspect/adjust brakes	x		Monthly
Inspect/adjust shift pedal	x		Monthly
Inspect fasteners	x		Monthly
Inspect valve clearance	x	x	
Change engine oil	x	x	
Replace engine oil filter	x		Every other oil change after break-in

(continued)

Table 1 MAINTENANCE AND LUBRICATION SCHEDULE (continued)

	Initial first month	Every 6 months	Other
Inspect/replace spark plug	x	x	Or as required
Inspect/adjust engine idle speed	x	x	Or as required
Inspect/adjust throttle cable	x	x	Or as required
Inspect/adjust clutch cable	x	x	Or as required
Inspect/adjust choke cable	x	x	Or as required
Inspect/adjust reverse cable	x	x	Or as required
Inspect/lubricate cables	x	x	Or as required
Inspect/replace brake pads	x	x	Or as required
Inspect drive chain and sprockets	x	x	Or as required
Inspect/replace coolant hoses	x	x	
Inspect/replace fuel hose	x	x	
Inspect/adjust steering toe-in	x	x	
Inspect wheels and bearings	x	x	
Inspect engine compression		x	
Inspect crankcase breather hose		x	
Lubricate rear shock linkage		x	
Lubricate swing arm pivots		x	
Lubricate front suspension arms		x	
Inspect exhaust system tightness		x	
Clean muffler		x	
Perform general lubrication		x	
Inspect/replace radiator cap		x	
Replace coolant			Every 2 years
Replace brake fluid			Every year
Replace brake hoses			Every 4 years

Table 2 FUEL, LUBRICANTS AND FLUIDS

Air filter	Foam air filter oil
Brake fluid type	DOT 4
Control cables	Cable lube
Cooling system	
Capacity	1.3 liters (1.4 U.S. qt.)
Radiator capacity	0.55 liter (0.58 U.S. qt.)
Reservoir capacity	0.29 liter (0.31 U.S. qt.)
Antifreeze type	Ethylene glycol containing anti-corrosion inhibitors for aluminum engines
Coolant mixture	50/50 (antifreeze/distilled water)
Drive chain	O-ring type chain lubricant
Engine oil	SG rated, four-stroke engine oil SAE 5W-30, 10W-30 or 20W-40
Engine oil	
Capacity	2.3 liters (2.43 U.S. qt.)
Without filter change	1.9 liters (2.01 U.S. qt.)
With filter change	1.95 liters (2.06 U.S. qt.)
Fuel type	Unleaded gasoline
Octane rating (minimum)	86 (R+M/2) or 91 RON
Fuel tank capacity	12 liters (3.17 U.S. gal.)
Reserve amount	2.6 liters (0.69 U.S. gal.)

Table 3 TUNE-UP SPECIFICATIONS

Battery	12 volt, 12 amp-hour
Battery type	YTX14-BS
Compression	
Standard	1250 kPa (181 psi)
Minimum	1050 kPa (152 psi)
Maximum	1350 kPa (196 psi)
Compression ratio	9.2:1
Idle speed	1450-1550 rpm
Ignition timing	12° BTDC at 1500 rpm
Pilot mixture screw (initial setting)	
Left carburetor	3 turns out
Right carburetor	2 turns out
Spark plug	
Type	NGK DPR8EA-9
Gap	0.8-0.9 mm (0.031-0.035 in.)
Valve clearance (cold)	
Intake	0.10-0.15 mm (0.004-0.006 in.)
Exhaust	0.15-0.20 mm (0.006-0.008 in.)

Table 4 ROUTINE ADJUSTMENT SPECIFICATIONS

Brake pad lining minimum thickness	1.0 mm (0.040 in.)
Brake pedal height	4.0 mm (0.16 in.)
Choke plunger stroke	15 mm (0.60 in.)
Clutch lever free play (at lever end)	5-10 mm (0.20-0.40 in.)
Drive chain	
Free play	30-45 mm (1.2-1.8 in.)
Length wear limit (10 pitch/11 pins)	150.1 mm (5.91 in.)
Parking brake	
Cable end length	64-68 mm (2.5-2.7 in.)
Lever free play	0 mm (0 in.)
Radiator cap relief pressure	95-125 kPa (13.8-18.1 psi)
Reverse cable length	135 mm (5.3 in.)
Reverse knob free play	0 mm (0 in.)
Rim runout (radial and lateral)	2.0 mm (0.08 in.)
Shift pedal height	22 mm (0.9 in.)
Speed limiter length (standard)	12 mm (0.47 in.)
Throttle lever free play	3-5 mm (0.12-0.20 in.)
Tire pressure (cold)	
Standard	27.5 kPa (4.0 psi) for maximum 100 kg (220 lb.) load
Mimimum	24.5 kPa (3.5 psi)
Maximum	30.5 kPa (4.4 psi)
Tire wear limit	3 mm (0.12 in.)
Tire toe-in	0-10 mm (0-0.40 in.)

Table 5 MAINTENANCE TORQUE SPECIFICATIONS

Item	N•m	in.-lb.	ft.-lb.
Axle hub nuts	90	–	66
Chain adjuster locknuts	16	–	12
Coolant drain plug	10	88	–
Crankcase drain plug	30	–	22
Oil filter	17	–	13
Oil tank drain plug	25	–	18
Spark plug	18	–	13
Valve cover bolts			
Intake	12	106	–
Exhaust	10	88	–
Wheel lug nuts	45	–	33

CHAPTER FOUR

ENGINE TOP END

This chapter provides information for the removal, inspection and replacement of the major assemblies that make up the engine top end. This includes the exhaust system, cylinder head cover, cylinder head, camshaft, valves, cylinder and piston. All the parts can be removed with the engine mounted in the frame. Refer to the tables at the end of this chapter for specifications.

Read this chapter before attempting any repair to the engine top end. Become familiar with the procedures, photos and illustrations to understand the skill and equipment required. Refer to Chapter One for tool usage and techniques. When special tools are required or recommended, the part number is provided. The special tools can be ordered from a Yamaha dealership.

SHOP CLEANLINESS

Always clean the engine before starting repairs. If the engine will remain in the frame, clean the surrounding framework, cables and harnesses. Avoid letting dirt enter the engine.

Keep the work environment as clean as possible. Store parts and assemblies in well-marked plastic bags and containers. Keep reconditioned parts wrapped until they will be installed.

EXHAUST SYSTEM

Removal and Installation

Do not attempt to remove the exhaust pipes or muffler when the engine is hot.

1. Remove the muffler as follows:
    a. Remove the bolt clamping the muffler to the exhaust pipe (**Figure 1**).
    b. Remove the two bolts securing the muffler to the frame (**Figure 2**).
    c. Pull the muffler from the exhaust pipe and out of the frame. Do not hammer on the muffler if it is stuck to the exhaust pipe. Twist the muffler off the pipe. If necessary, apply penetrating oil around the connection.
    d. Account for the mesh gasket sealing the muffler to the exhaust pipe.
2. Remove the heat shields (**Figure 3** and **Figure 4**) from the exhaust pipe.
3. Remove both exhaust pipes as follows:
    a. Remove the exhaust pipe clamp bolt and both nuts from each exhaust pipe flange (**Figure 5**). The flange nuts are often corroded. To prevent damaging the studs, apply penetrating oil as needed during removal.
    b. Pull the exhaust pipes off the cylinder head. Pivot the left pipe down and route the assembly out of the frame.
    c. Account for the mesh gasket sealing the left exhaust pipe to the right exhaust pipe.

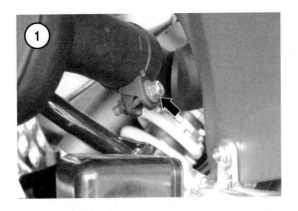

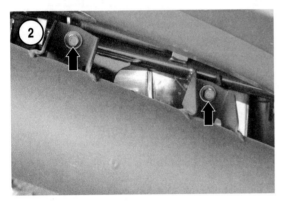

d. Remove the gaskets from the exhaust ports (**Figure 6**).

4. Reverse these steps to install the system. Note the following:

a. Clean the exhaust ports and install new exhaust pipe gaskets, seating them in the port before installing the exhaust pipe. The gasket can be held in place with a small amount of antiseize compound. Install the gasket with the round side facing out.

b. Install new mesh gaskets at the exhaust pipe joints.

c. Apply antiseize compound to all threads. Locking compound may be preferred on the heat shield threads.

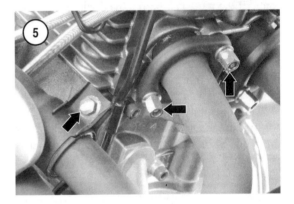

d. Install and align the entire exhaust system, with all fasteners finger-tight. Tighten the exhaust pipes squarely into the exhaust ports, then tighten the remaining fasteners.

5. Torque the exhaust system components to the following values:

a. Exhaust pipe flanges to cylinder head: 10 N•m (88 in.-lb.).

b. Exhaust pipe clamp: 16 N•m (12 ft.-lb.).

4

c. Heat shields: 10 N•m (88 in.-lb.).

d. Muffler to exhaust pipe: 20 N•m (15 ft.-lb.).

e. Muffler to frame: 26 N•m (19 ft.-lb.).

CYLINDER HEAD COVER

Removal and Installation

1. Park the machine on level ground and set the parking brake.

2. Remove the fuel tank and protectors (Chapter Fourteen).

3. Remove the spark plug (**Figure 7**).

4. Remove the bolts securing the upper engine mounting bracket to the engine and frame (**Figure 8**).

5. Remove the oil pressure check plate (**Figure 9**).

6. Remove the oil tank breather hose, front oil pipe and valve covers (**Figure 10**).

7. In the left crankcase cover, remove the plugs from the rotor nut and the timing holes (**Figure 11**). Turn the rotor nut until the **I** mark (**Figure 12**) is visible in the timing hole. The timing mark indicates the piston is at TDC (top dead center).

a. To check that the piston is at TDC on the compression stroke, there should be clearance between all valves and their rocker arms.

b. If there is no clearance, turn the crankshaft counterclockwise one revolution and recheck the clearances.

8. Loosen the cylinder head cover bolts. Work in a crossing pattern and loosen the bolts in several passes. Note the location of all guides that are secured by a bolt.

9. Loosen the cylinder head cover. The cover is sealed to the cylinder head with sealant. Pull up on the cover to break the seal between the parts. Do not pry on the sealing surfaces.

10. When the cylinder head cover is loosened, slowly pull up on the cover and account for the two dowels, located in the bores at the left side (A, **Figure 13**).

a. If the dowels are seated in the cylinder head, leave them in place until the cover is removed and the cam chain tunnel is stuffed with a shop cloth.

b. If the dowels are in the cylinder head cover, grip the dowels and remove the cylinder head cover from the engine (**Figure 14**). Stuff the cam chain tunnel with a shop cloth to prevent the entry of parts and debris.

NOTE
Verify the engine is at TDC by checking the position of the camshaft oil holes. If properly set, the oil holes will point up (B, Figure 13). If the holes point down, hold the camshaft in place and slowly rotate the crankshaft one full turn and realign the TDC I mark.

11. Inspect the cylinder head cover assembly as described in this chapter.

12. Reverse this procedure to install the cylinder head cover. Note the following:

a. Clean the mating surfaces on the cylinder head and cover. Apply Yamabond 1215 sealant (part No. 90890-85505) to all mating surfaces on the cylinder head. Do not apply too much sealant. Excess sealant can migrate into the engine components and oil passages.

b. Install the cylinder head, guides and bolts. Refer to **Figure 15** for bolt length locations. If the three bolts that are inline with the intake rocker shaft will not pass to the cylinder head,

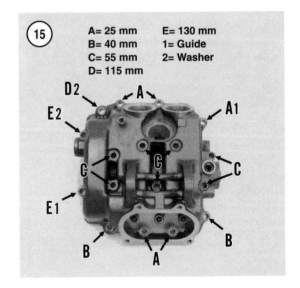

A= 25 mm E= 130 mm
B= 40 mm 1= Guide
C= 55 mm 2= Washer
D= 115 mm

check that the rocker shaft is vertically aligned. The shaft is notched to allow the bolts to lock the shaft into place.

c. Tighten the cylinder head cover bolts. Work in a crossing pattern and tighten the bolts in several passes to 10 N•m (88 in.-lb.).

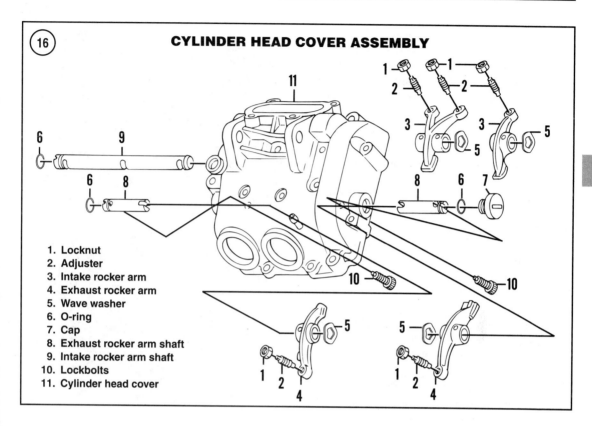

CYLINDER HEAD COVER ASSEMBLY

1. Locknut
2. Adjuster
3. Intake rocker arm
4. Exhaust rocker arm
5. Wave washer
6. O-ring
7. Cap
8. Exhaust rocker arm shaft
9. Intake rocker arm shaft
10. Lockbolts
11. Cylinder head cover

i. Torque the intake valve cover to 10 N•m (88 in.-lb.).

j. Torque the exhaust valve covers to 12 N•m (106 in.-lb.).

k. Torque the spark plug to 18 N•m (13 ft.-lb.).

l. Torque the front oil pipe banjo bolts to 20 N•m (15 ft.-lb.).

m. Torque the oil pressure check plate mounting bolt to 10 N•m (88 in.-lb.).

Inspection

Refer to **Figure 16**.

1. Clean the cylinder head cover in solvent and dry with compressed air. All sealant must be removed from the mating surfaces, threads and dowel bores. Sealant particles that remain on the cover can migrate through the engine, possibly causing damage.

2. Visually inspect the inner and outer surfaces of the cover. Check for cracks, scoring or other damage around bolt holes and all mating surfaces.

3. Inspect the valve covers and bolts (**Figure 17**) for obvious damage. Replace the O-ring on each cover.

d. If necessary, refer to Chapter Three for performing the valve clearance check and adjustment.

e. Install new seal washers on the front oil pipe banjo bolts.

f. Install new, lubricated O-rings on the valve covers, oil pressure check plate, and the rotor nut and timing hole plugs.

g. Torque the upper engine mounting bracket to frame bolts to 33 N•m (24 ft.-lb.).

h. Torque the upper engine mounting bracket to engine bolt to 40 N•m (30 ft.-lb.).

4. Inspect the rocker contact pads, valve adjusters and camshaft bearing surfaces (**Figure 18**).

    a. If the pads or bearing surfaces are pitted or scored, inspect the camshaft for damage. Also, clean and inspect the oil pockets below the camshaft lobes, for dirt and debris.

    b. The rockers should pivot freely on their shafts with no perceptible play.

    c. Replace adjusters and locknuts that are flared or worn.

    d. If the camshaft bearing surfaces are damaged, the cylinder head cover and cylinder head must be replaced as a set. The parts are only available as a single part number. The parts are machined as a set, so their dimensions and alignments are unique.

5. If necessary, remove the rocker arms and shafts as follows:

    a. For the intake assembly, thread a cylinder head cover bolt into the end of the shaft. Pull the shaft and O-ring from the cover (**Figure 19**).

    b. For the exhaust assemblies, remove the lockbolt from each shaft. The bolts are located by the rocker arms. Remove the shafts and O-rings with a cylinder head cover bolt.

6. Inspect the rocker arm and shaft assemblies.

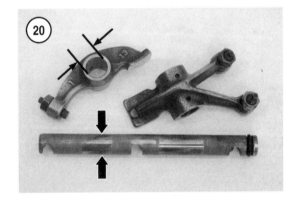

    a. Inspect the rocker bores and oil holes for scoring, cracks, debris or other damage.

    b. Measure the inside diameter of the rocker arm (**Figure 20**). Refer to **Table 2** for specifications.

    c. Measure the outside diameter of the rocker arm shaft where it contacts the rocker arm (**Figure 20**). Refer to **Table 2** for specifications.

    d. Inspect the wave washers and replace the O-ring on each shaft.

7. Install the rocker arm and shaft assemblies into the cylinder head cover. Note the following:

    a. Lubricate the O-rings before installing the shafts.

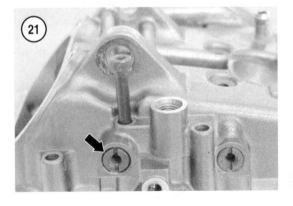

    b. Install all shafts so the O-ring is to the outside of the cover.

    c. Install the intake rocker shaft with the shaft notches aligned with the three cylinder head cover bolt holes. The shaft is notched to allow the cover bolts to lock the shaft into place. Turn the shaft so the slot in the shaft is vertical and the bolts will pass through the cover (**Figure 21**).

    d. Torque the exhaust shaft lockbolts to 10 N•m (88 in.-lb.).

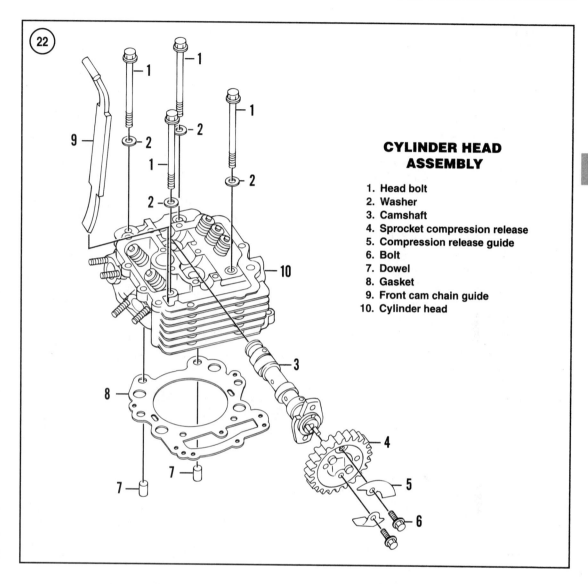

CYLINDER HEAD ASSEMBLY

1. Head bolt
2. Washer
3. Camshaft
4. Sprocket compression release
5. Compression release guide
6. Bolt
7. Dowel
8. Gasket
9. Front cam chain guide
10. Cylinder head

8. Install the cylinder head cover.

CAMSHAFT AND CAM CHAIN TENSIONER

Removal

The camshaft and cam chain tensioner can be removed with the engine mounted in the frame. Refer to **Figure 22.**

> *NOTE*
> *When working on the camshaft assembly, stuff the cam chain tunnel with a shop cloth to prevent the entry of parts and debris.*

1. Remove the cylinder head cover as described in this chapter.
2. Check that the engine is at TDC.
3. At the left side of the cylinder, remove the cam chain tensioner (**Figure 23**) from the cam chain tunnel as follows:
    a. Remove the center bolt (A, **Figure 23**), seal washer and internal spring.
    b. Remove the mounting bolts (B, **Figure 23**).
    c. Remove the tensioner and gasket.

> *CAUTION*
> *Anytime the tensioner mounting bolts are loosened, the tensioner must be completely removed and reset. Do not partially remove, then retighten, the*

bolts. The ratchet-type plunger will have extended and locked itself. Retightening the bolts will cause the cam chain and tensioner to be too tight, possibly causing engine damage if the engine is operated. Also, minimize any turning of the crankshaft when the tensioner is removed from the engine. Camshaft timing could be altered because of the excess slack in the cam chain. This also could result in engine damage if the engine is operated.

4. Remove the front cam chain guide.
5. Remove the camshaft sprocket as follows:
   a. Remove the bolt and compression release guide plate (A, **Figure 24**).
   b. Rotate the crankshaft and remove the remaining bolt and guide plate. Have a length of wire at the work area to secure the cam chain after the sprocket is removed.
6. Remove the camshaft.
7. Inspect the camshaft, compression release and cam chain tensioner as described in this section.
   a. Reset the cam chain tensioner as described in the inspection procedure. The tensioner must be reset before installation.
   b. If necessary, refer to Chapter Five for cam chain inspection. Although the chain cannot be removed from the engine, a partial inspection can be performed.

Installation

1. Prior to installing the camshaft and cam chain tensioner, refer to **Figure 22** and note the following:
   a. Check that the cam chain tensioner is disassembled and reset, as described in the inspection procedure.
   b. Lubricate parts with engine oil during assembly.
2. Inspect the cylinder head and ensure that all surfaces are clean. Remove any shop cloths from the cam chain tunnel.
3. Check that the engine is at TDC and is held in this position. The engine must remain at TDC when installing and timing the camshaft.
4. Install the camshaft with the oil holes pointing up (B, **Figure 13**). This is the TDC position for the camshaft.

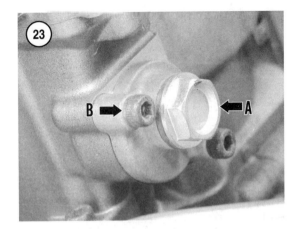

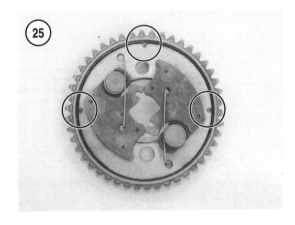

5. Identify the three alignment marks on the cam sprocket (**Figure 25**).

   a. When installed on the camshaft, the top mark must point up and be perpendicular to the cylinder head. This mark also aligns vertically with the mark on the end of the camshaft (**Figure 26**).

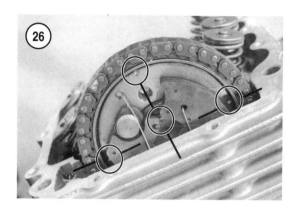

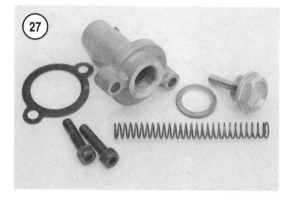

b. The marks to the front and rear of the sprocket must be parallel with the top of the cylinder head.

6. Align and install the cam sprocket and compression release guide plates. Note the following:

a. During installation, keep the front of the cam chain taut so there is no play in the chain when the sprocket is installed.

b. Check that the compression release levers are engaged with the pins on the camshaft (B, **Figure 24**).

c. When turning the crankshaft to install the second sprocket bolt, turn the crankshaft *counterclockwise* (forward) to keep the front side of the cam chain taut.

d. Torque the sprocket bolts to 20 N•m (15 ft.-lb.).

7. Install the cam chain tensioner as follows:

a. Install a new gasket, the tensioner and mounting bolts (B, **Figure 23**). Torque the bolts to 10 N•m (88 in.-lb.).

b. Insert the spring and a new seal washer, then install and tighten the center bolt (A, **Figure 23**). Torque the bolt to 22 N•m (16 ft.-lb.).

CAUTION
If for any reason the tensioner mounting bolts are loosened, the tensioner must be completely removed and reset. Do not partially remove, then retighten the bolts. The ratchet-type plunger will have extended and locked itself. Retightening the bolts will cause the cam chain and tensioner to be too tight, possibly causing engine damage if the engine is operated.

8. Install the front cam chain guide.

9. With the engine at TDC, inspect the installation.

a. The cam chain should be taut at the front and rear.

b. The alignment marks on the sprocket must be parallel to the top of the cylinder head.

c. Hold the camshaft in place and slowly rotate the crankshaft counterclockwise two full turns. Verify all alignments when the crankshaft is at the TDC **I** mark.

Cam Chain Tensioner and Front Guide Inspection

The tensioner assembly is a spring-loaded, ratcheting-type tensioner. As the cam chain wears and develops slack, the spring-loaded plunger extends and locks itself against the rear chain guide. The guide then pivots forward and retightens the chain.

Since the tensioner is self-adjusting, there is no routine maintenance required. However, anytime the tensioner is loosened or removed, the tensioner must be reset. Do not partially remove, then retighten, the bolts. The plunger will have extended and locked itself. Retightening the bolts will cause the cam chain and tensioner to be too tight, possibly causing engine damage if the engine is operated.

1. Inspect the parts (**Figure 27**) for obvious wear or damage. Install a new gasket and seal washer at installation.

2. Reset the plunger (**Figure 28**) as follows:

a. Press and hold the ratchet release.

b. Press and seat the plunger into the tensioner housing.

c. Do not install the spring, washer and bolt until the tensioner housing has been mounted and the camshaft and chain have been installed and timed.

3. Inspect the front cam chain guide for wear or deterioration. The guide must be in good condition to minimize chain oscillation.

Camshaft Sprocket and Compression Release Inspection

The compression release is located at the left end of the camshaft. The release slightly opens the left exhaust valve during engine cranking. The reduction in compression makes starting easier.

In operation, the notches in the spring-loaded release levers (A, **Figure 29**) are engaged with the drum and pins (B) in the camshaft. The pivoting action of the drum raises and lowers the lifter (C, **Figure 29**). When the engine is off, the release levers are contracted and the lifter is raised. During startup, the left exhaust rocker arm contacts the lifter and slightly opens the exhaust valve. When startup occurs, centrifugal force pivots the release levers outward and the drum lowers the lifter.

1. Clean the sprocket and release mechanism.

2. Inspect the parts.

   a. Pivot each lever outward and check for smooth operation. When the lever is pivoted and released, the spring should fully retract the lever. Replace the spring if it is fatigued.

   b. Inspect the springs and pivots for buildup, binding or other damage.

   c. Check the fit of the guide plates on the release assembly. The levers should not drag on the guide plates.

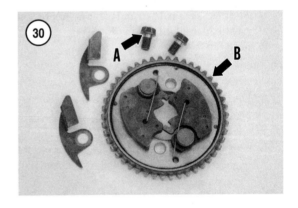

   d. Inspect the shoulders on the bolts (A, **Figure 30**). When installed, the bolts should fit in the sprocket with minimal play.

   e. Inspect the sprocket teeth (B, **Figure 30**) for wear or other damage. The profile of each tooth should be symmetrical. When mounted in the chain, maximum movement of the chain is 1/4 tooth. If the sprocket is worn, replace the cam sprocket and cam chain as a set. When this type of damage occurs, the crankshaft sprocket and chain guides should also be inspected for damage.

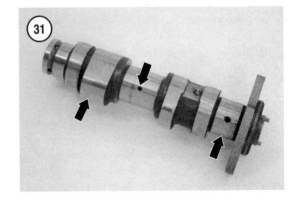

   f. Inspect the lifter (C, **Figure 29**), drum and pins (B) on the camshaft. The lifter should smoothly raise and lower as the drum is rotated.

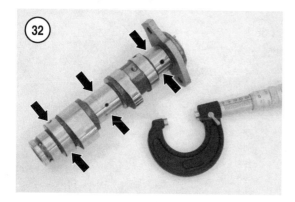

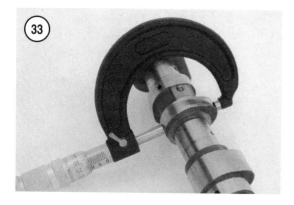

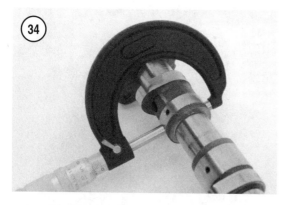

Camshaft Inspection

In the following procedure, replace the camshaft if it is obviously damaged, or not within specification.

1. Clean the camshaft in solvent and dry with compressed air.
2. Inspect the camshaft lobes, journals and oil holes (**Figure 31**).
   a. Check for pitting and scoring on the machined surfaces. If damage is evident, inspect the cylinder head, cylinder head cover and rocker arm assemblies for damage.
   b. Inspect the oil holes for dirt and debris.
3. Measure the camshaft with a micrometer.
   a. Measure the camshaft journals (**Figure 32**). Refer to **Table 2** for specifications.
   b. Measure the cam lobe heights (**Figure 33**). Refer to **Table 2** for specifications.
   c. Measure the cam lobe widths (**Figure 34**). Refer to **Table 2** for specifications.

CYLINDER HEAD

Removal

The cylinder head can be removed with the engine mounted in the frame. Refer to **Figure 22**.
1. Drain the engine coolant (Chapter Three).
2. Remove the carburetors (Chapter Eight).
3. Remove the exhaust system as described in this chapter.
4. Remove the water jacket outlet hose and fitting (**Figure 35**) from the cylinder.
5. Remove the cylinder head cover, camshaft and cam chain tensioner as described in this chapter.
6. Loosen the cylinder head bolts in the following order. Make several passes and loosen each bolt 1/4 turn until all bolts are loose.
   a. Left rear bolt (**Figure 36**).
   b. Right rear bolt (**Figure 37**).
   c. Front bolt (**Figure 38**).
   d. Head bolt (A, **Figure 39**).
   e. Head bolt (B, **Figure 39**)
   f. Head bolt (C, **Figure 39**).
   g. Head bolt (D, **Figure 39**).
7. Loosen the cylinder head by lightly tapping around its base with a soft mallet. Lift the head off the engine while routing the cam chain out of the head. Secure the chain so it will not fall into the engine.

8. Stuff shop cloths into the cam chain tunnel, then remove the head gasket. Account for the two dowels located at the right side of the cylinder (**Figure 40**).

9. At the workbench, remove the carburetor intake ducts (**Figure 41**).

10. If necessary, remove and inspect the valve assembly as described in this chapter.

11. Wash all parts in solvent and dry with compressed air. Note the following:

   a. Remove all gasket residue from the cylinder head and cylinder. Do not scratch or gouge the surfaces.

   b. Remove all carbon deposits from the combustion chamber. Use solvent and a soft brush or hardwood scraper. Do not use sharp-edged tools that could scratch the valves or combustion chamber. If the piston crown is cleaned, keep solvent and carbon deposits out of the gap between the piston and cylinder.

CAUTION
If the valves are removed from the head, the valve seats are exposed and can be damaged from careless cleaning. A scratched or gouged valve seat will not seal properly.

   c. If the cylinder head will be bead-blasted, wash the entire assembly in hot soapy water after it has been reconditioned. This will remove blasting grit lodged in crevices and threads. Clean and chase all threads to ensure no grit remains. Blasting grit that remains in the head will be picked up by the engine oil and circulated to other parts of the engine. This will damage the bearings, piston and rings.

   d. Check all oil passages for debris or blockage.

   e. Check all parts for obvious wear or damage.

12. Inspect the cylinder head as described in this chapter.

Inspection

Anytime the cylinder head is removed, the valves should be tested for leakage with a solvent test. This test is quick and easy to perform and will help identify problems in the valve train. Refer to *Valves* in this chapter for the solvent test.

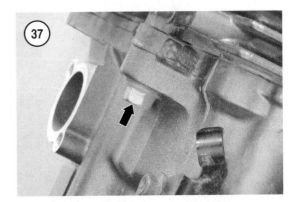

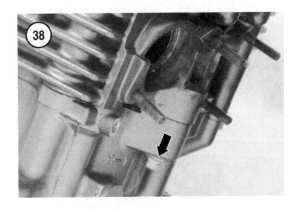

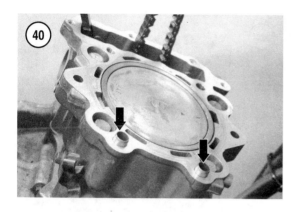

1. Inspect the spark plug hole threads. If the threads are dirty or mildly damaged, use a spark plug thread tap to clean and straighten the threads. Keep the tap lubricated while cleaning the threads.

NOTE
If the threads are galled, stripped or cross-threaded, the cylinder head should be fitted with a steel thread insert, such as a HeliCoil. Thread damage can be minimized by applying antiseize compound to the spark plug threads before installation. Do not overtighten the spark plug.

2. Clean the entire cylinder head assembly in fresh solvent.

3. Inspect the combustion chamber side of the cylinder head (**Figure 42**).
    a. Inspect for cracks or damage in the spark plug hole, combustion chamber, water jackets and exhaust port.
    b. Inspect the exhaust studs for damage or looseness.

4. Inspect the camshaft side of the cylinder head (**Figure 43**).
    a. Inspect for cracks or damage on the casting and mating surfaces.
    b. Inspect the camshaft bearing surfaces for obvious scoring or damage. If damaged, the cylinder head and cylinder head cover must be replaced as a set. The parts are only available as a single part number. The parts are machined as a set, so their dimensions and alignments are unique.
    c. If cracks are found anywhere in the cylinder head, take the head to a dealership or machine shop to see if the head can be repaired. If not, replace the head and cylinder head cover as a set.

5. Inspect the cylinder head for warp as follows:
    a. Lay a machinist's straightedge across the cylinder head (**Figure 44**).
    b. Try to insert a flat feeler gauge between the straightedge and the machined surface of the head. If clearance exists, record the maximum measurement.
    c. Repeat substeps a and b several times, laying the straightedge both across and diagonally on the head.
    d. Compare the measurements to the warp service limit listed in **Table 2**. If the clearance is

not within the service limit, take the cylinder head to a dealership or machine shop for further inspection and possible resurfacing.

6. Inspect the cylinder fasteners for damaged threads and heads. Replace fasteners that are rusted.

7. Inspect the carburetor intake ducts for cracks and damage.

8. Assemble and install the cylinder head as described in this section.

Installation

Check that all gasket residue is removed from all mating surfaces. All cylinder head surfaces must be clean and dry. Refer to **Figure 22**.

1. Install the carburetor intake ducts (**Figure 41**). Install new, lubricated O-rings, then torque the mounting bolts to 10 N•m (88 in.-lb.).

2. Install the dowels and a new cylinder head gasket onto the cylinder (**Figure 45**).

3. Lower the cylinder head onto the engine, routing the cam chain through the head.

   a. Keep adequate tension on the cam chain so it does not bind at the crankshaft sprocket. Secure the cam chain when the cylinder head is seated.

   b. Avoid dislodging the dowels as the head is positioned.

   c. Cover engine openings as needed.

4. Install and torque the seven cylinder head bolts. Note the following:

   a. Refer to the torque sequence in **Figure 46**.

   b. Torque the bolts in two passes. Torque the 9 mm bolts equally in the first pass.

   c. Final torque the 9 mm bolts (bolts 1-6) to 38 N•m (28 ft.-lb.).

   d. Torque the 6 mm bolt (bolt 7) to 10 N•m (88 in.-lb.).

5. Install the camshaft, cam chain tensioner and cylinder head cover as described in this chapter.

6. Install the water jacket outlet hose and fitting (**Figure 35**). Install a new O-ring on the fitting and torque the bolt to 10 N•m (88 in.-lb.).

7. Install the exhaust system as described in this chapter.

8. Install the carburetors (Chapter Eight).

9. Fill the engine with coolant (Chapter Three).

10. Install a new spark plug (Chapter Three).

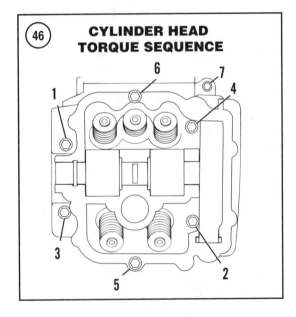

CYLINDER HEAD TORQUE SEQUENCE

VALVES

Solvent Test

A solvent test is performed with the valve assembly in the cylinder head. The test can reveal if valves

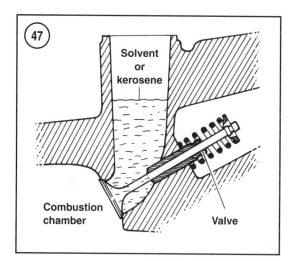

47

Solvent
or
kerosene

Combustion
chamber

Valve

48

49

are fully seating, as well as expose undetected cracks in the cylinder head.

1. Remove the cylinder head as described in this chapter.

2. Check that the combustion chamber is dry and the valves are seated.

3. Support the cylinder head so the port faces up (**Figure 47**).

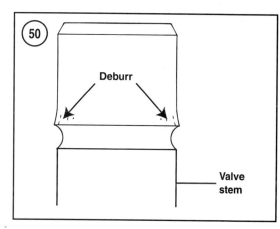

50

Deburr

Valve
stem

4

4. Pour solvent or kerosene into the port.

5. Inspect the combustion chamber for leakage around the valve.

6. Repeat Steps 3-5 for the other valves.

7. If leakage is detected, this can be caused by:
   a. A worn or damaged valve face.
   b. A worn or damaged valve seat (in the cylinder head).
   c. A bent valve stem.
   d. A crack in the combustion chamber.

Valve Removal

1. Perform the solvent test on the intake and exhaust valves as described in this chapter.

2. Install a valve spring compressor squarely over the valve head and the spring retainer (**Figure 48**).

3. Tighten the compressor until the spring retainer no longer holds the valve keepers in position. Lift the keepers from the valve stem (**Figure 49**).

> *CAUTION*
> *Do not overtighten and compress the valve spring. This can result in loss of valve spring tension.*

4. Slowly relieve the pressure on the valve spring and remove the compressor from the head.

5. Remove the upper spring seat, valve spring, oil seal and lower spring seat.

6. Inspect the valve stem for sharp and flared metal (**Figure 50**) around the groove for the keepers. If necessary, deburr the valve stem before removing the valve from the head. Burrs on the valve stem can damage the valve guide.

7. Remove the valve from the cylinder head.

8. Store all components of each valve assembly together (**Figure 51**). Prevent parts from being intermixed.

> *CAUTION*
> *Valve components that are within specification should be installed in their original positions. The oil seal should be replaced.*

9. Repeat this procedure for the remaining valves.

10. Inspect the components as described in this section.

Valve Component Inspection

During the cleaning and inspection of the valve assemblies, do not intermix the sets of parts. Work with one set of parts at a time, repeating the procedure until all parts are inspected. After each set of parts is inspected, return them to their storage container.

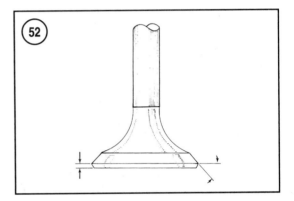

> *NOTE*
> *In the following procedure, whenever the valves, valve guides and valve seats must be replaced or reconditioned, it is recommended that the work be done by a dealership. These parts should be replaced or reconditioned as a set. Replacement and servicing of these parts requires special equipment, as well as experience in replacing and fitting the parts.*

1. Clean the valve assembly in solvent.

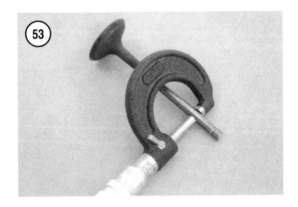

> *CAUTION*
> *The valve seating surface is a critical surface and must not be damaged. Do not scrape the seating surface or place the valve where it could roll off the work surface.*

2. Inspect the valve head as follows:
   a. Inspect the top and perimeter of each valve. Check for burning or other damage on the top and seating surface. Replace the valve if damage is evident. If the valve head appears uniform, with only minor wear, the valve can be lapped (described in this section) and reused, if the other valve measurements are acceptable.

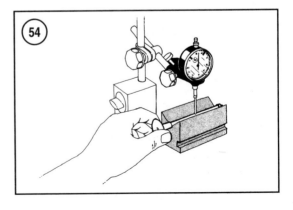

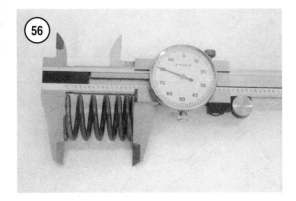

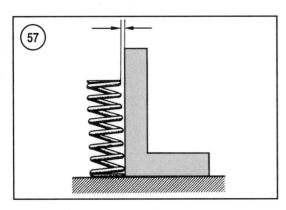

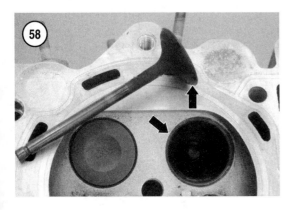

b. Measure the margin (thickness) (**Figure 52**). Record the measurement. Refer to **Table 2** for specifications.

3. Inspect the valve stem as follows:

   a. Inspect the stem for obvious wear and scoring. Also check the end of the valve stem for flare.

   b. Measure the valve stem diameter (**Figure 53**). Record the measurement. Refer to **Table 2** for specifications.

   c. Check the valve stem for runout. Place the valve in a V-block and measure runout with a dial indicator (**Figure 54**). Record the measurement. Refer to **Table 2** for the specification.

4A. If a small bore gauge and micrometer are available, inspect the valve guides as follows:

   a. Clean the valve guides so they are free of all carbon and varnish. Use solvent and a stiff, narrow brush.

   b. Measure each valve guide hole (**Figure 55**) at the top, center and bottom. Record the measurements. Refer to **Table 2** for specifications.

4B. If a small bore gauge and micrometer are not available, inspect the valve guides as follows:

   a. Insert the appropriate valve into the guide.

   b. With the valve head off the seat, move the valve stem side to side in the valve guide. Move the valve in several directions, checking for obvious play. If movement is easily detected, the valve guide and/or valve is worn. Take the valves and cylinder head to a dealership and have the parts accurately measured to determine the extent of wear.

5. Check the valve springs as follows:

   a. Visually check the springs for damage.

   b. Measure the length of each valve spring (**Figure 56**). Refer to **Table 2** for specifications.

   c. Measure the valve spring tilt (**Figure 57**). Refer to **Table 2** for specifications.

6. Inspect the valve spring seats and keepers for wear or damage.

7. Inspect the valve seats (**Figure 58**) to determine if they must be reconditioned.

   a. Clean and dry the valve seats with contact cleaner.

   b. Coat the seat on the valve with machinist's marking fluid.

c. Install the valve into the appropriate guide, then *lightly* tap the valve against the seat to make a clear pattern on the cylinder head. Do not rotate the valve.

d. Remove the valve from the guide and measure the imprinted valve seat width (**Figure 59**) at several locations. Refer to **Table 2** for specifications.

e. Clean all marking fluid from the valves and seats.

Valve Installation

Perform the following procedure for each set of valve components (**Figure 51**). All components should be clean and dry.

1. Coat the valve stem and interior of the oil seal with molybdenum disulfide grease.

2. Install the lower spring seat into the head. Install the seat so the perimeter rests on the head.

3. Install and seat a new oil seal on the valve guide.

4. Insert the appropriate valve into the cylinder head. Rotate the valve stem as it enters and passes through the seal. Check that the seal remains seated, then hold the valve in place.

5. Install the valve springs with the *small* coil pitch facing down.

6. Install the upper spring seat, fitting the center of the seat into the spring.

7. Install a valve spring compressor over the valve assembly. Fit the tool squarely onto the upper spring seat.

8. Tighten the compressor until the spring retainer is compressed enough to install the valve keepers.

> *CAUTION*
> *Do not overtighten and compress the valve springs. This can result in loss of valve spring tension.*

9. Insert the keepers around the groove in the valve stem (**Figure 49**).

10. Slowly relieve the pressure on the spring retainer, then remove the compressor from the head.

11. Tap the end of the valve stem with a soft mallet to ensure that the keepers are seated in the valve stem groove (**Figure 60**).

12. After all valves are installed, perform the solvent test as described in this chapter.

13. Install the cylinder head as described in this chapter.

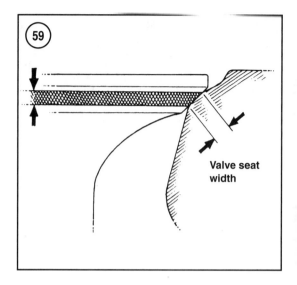

Valve seat width

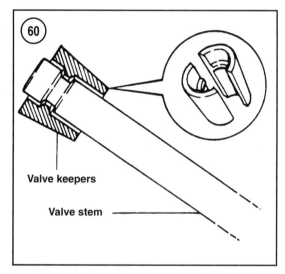

Valve keepers

Valve stem

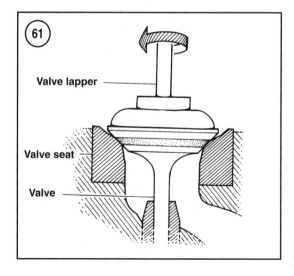

Valve lapper

Valve seat

Valve

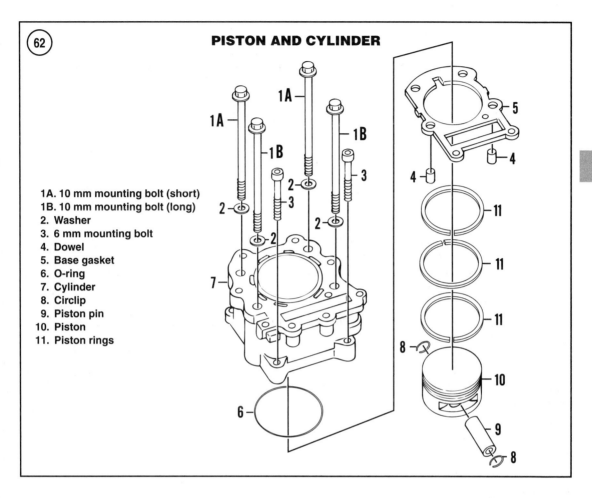

PISTON AND CYLINDER

1A. 10 mm mounting bolt (short)
1B. 10 mm mounting bolt (long)
2. Washer
3. 6 mm mounting bolt
4. Dowel
5. Base gasket
6. O-ring
7. Cylinder
8. Circlip
9. Piston pin
10. Piston
11. Piston rings

Valve Lapping

Valve lapping restores sealing between the valve seat and valve contact area, without machining. Lapping should be performed on valves and valve seats that have been inspected and are within specifications. Lapping should also be performed on valves and valve seats that have been reconditioned.

1. Lightly coat the valve face with fine-grade lapping compound.

2. Lubricate the valve stem, then insert the valve into the head.

3. Wet the suction cup on the lapping tool and press it onto the head of the valve (**Figure 61**).

4. Spin the tool back and forth between the hands to lap the valve to the seat . Every five to ten seconds, rotate the valve 180° and continue to lap the valve into the seat.

5. Frequently inspect the valve seat. Stop lapping the valve when the valve seat is smooth, even and polished. Keep each lapped valve identified so it can be installed in the correct seat during assembly.

6. Clean the valves and cylinder head in solvent and remove all lapping compound. Any abrasive allowed to remain in the head will cause premature wear and damage to other engine parts.

7. After the valves are installed in the head, perform a *Solvent Test* as described in this section. If leakage is detected, remove that valve and repeat the lapping process.

CYLINDER

Removal

The cylinder and piston can be removed with the engine mounted in the frame. Read all procedures completely before attempting a repair. Refer to **Figure 62**.

1. Remove the cylinder head as described in this chapter.
2. Remove the cable guide from the right rear of the cylinder.
3. Remove the water jacket inlet housing from the front of the cylinder.
4. Remove the two cylinder mounting bolts (6 mm) at the left side of the cylinder.
5. Remove the four cylinder mounting bolts (10 mm) at the top of the cylinder (**Figure 63**). Note that the left bolts are longer than the right bolts.
6. Loosen the cylinder by tapping around the base. If necessary, apply penetrating oil to the joint.
7. *Slowly* lift the cylinder from the crankcase.
   a. Account for the two dowels under the cylinder (**Figure 64**). If loose, remove the dowels to prevent them from possibly falling into the engine.
   b. Route and secure the cam chain out of the cylinder.
8. Remove the base gasket.
9. Stuff shop cloths into the cam chain tunnel and around the piston. Support the piston and rod so it does not contact the crankcase (**Figure 65**).
10. Remove the O-ring from the bottom of the cylinder (**Figure 66**).
11. Inspect the cylinder as described in this chapter.

Inspection

1. Remove all gasket residue from the top and bottom cylinder block surfaces.
2. Wash the cylinder in solvent and dry with compressed air.
3. Inspect the overall condition of the cylinder (**Figure 67**) for obvious wear or damage.
   a. Inspect the cylinder bore for scoring or gouges. If damaged, overbore the cylinder.
   b. Inspect the water jackets for deposits.
   c. Inspect all threads for condition and cleanliness.
4. Measure and check the cylinder for wear. Measure the inside diameter of the cylinder with a bore gauge or inside micrometer as follows:
   a. Measure the overall cylinder wear at three points along the bore axis (**Figure 68**). At each point, measure the cylinder front to back (measurement X) and side to side (measurement Y). Make the middle measurement 50 mm down from the top of the cylinder. Record the measurements for each location.

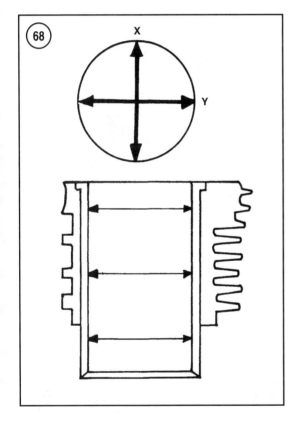

b. To determine if the cylinder is within specifications, Yamaha recommends finding the average of the X and Y measurements recorded at the *middle* position only. Compare this averaged measurement to the specifications and service limit listed in **Table 2**. If the cylinder bore is not within the service limit, rebore and hone the cylinder.

5. If cylinder boring is necessary, take the cylinder to a dealership or machine shop to have any machine work performed. If the cylinder is to be overbored and fitted with the next size piston and rings, take the new piston to the shop so the cylinder can be accurately bored and honed to accommodate the actual piston size.

6. If the cylinder is within all service limits, and the current piston and rings are reusable, deglaze the cylinder, preferably with a ball hone (**Figure 69**). Cylinder glaze appears as a hard, shiny surface. After deglazing, the crosshatching in the cylinder provides a uniform surface, capable of retaining oil and mating with the rings.

7. Thoroughly wash and scrub the cylinder in hot soapy water after inspection and service, to remove all fine grit and material/residue left from machine operations. Check cleanliness by rubbing a clean, white cloth over the bore. No residue should be evident. When the cylinder is thoroughly clean and dry, immediately coat the cylinder bore with oil to prevent corrosion. Wrap the cylinder until engine reassembly.

CAUTION
Wash the cylinder in hot soapy water. Solvents will not remove the fine grit left in the cylinder. This grit will cause premature wear of the rings and cylinder.

8. Perform any service to the piston assembly before installing the cylinder.

Installation

Refer to **Figure 62**.
1. Check that all gasket residue is removed from all mating surfaces.
2. Install the dowels and a new base gasket onto the crankcase (**Figure 64**).
3. Install a new, lubricated O-ring on the bottom of the cylinder (**Figure 66**).

4. Lubricate the following components with engine oil:
  a. Piston and rings.
  b. Piston pin and connecting rod.
  c. Cylinder bore.

5. Support the piston so the cylinder can be lowered into place.

6. Stagger the piston ring gaps on the piston. Yamaha recommends the positions shown in **Figure 70**. Note that the top and second ring gaps are opposite one another, as well as the gaps in the oil ring rails.

7. Lower the cylinder onto the crankcase.
  a. Route the cam chain and guide through the chain tunnel. Secure the cam chain so it cannot fall into the engine.
  b. As the piston enters the cylinder, compress each ring so it can enter the cylinder. A ring compressor can also be used. When the bottom ring is in the cylinder, remove any holding fixture and shop cloths from the crankcase.

8. Install the four 10 mm cylinder mounting bolts into the top of the cylinder.

CAUTION
The two long bolts must be installed on the left side of the cylinder.

  a. Working in a crossing pattern, torque the bolts equally in several passes.
  b. Torque the bolts to 42 N•m (31 ft.-lb.).

9. Install the two 6 mm cylinder mounting bolts at the left side of the cylinder. Torque the bolts to 10 N•m (88 in.-lb.).

10. Install the water jacket inlet housing at the front of the cylinder.
  a. Install a new, lubricated O-ring.
  b. Torque the bolts to 10 N•m (88 in.-lb.).

11. Install the cable guide at the right rear of the cylinder.

12. Install the cylinder head as described in this chapter.

PISTON AND PISTON RINGS

The piston is made of aluminum alloy and fitted with three rings. The piston is held on the small end of the connecting rod by a chrome-plated, steel piston pin. The pin is a precision fit in the piston and rod, and is held in place by circlips.

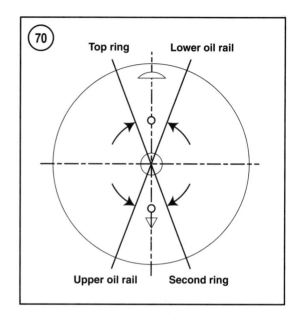

Top ring   Lower oil rail

Upper oil rail   Second ring

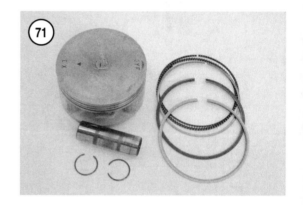

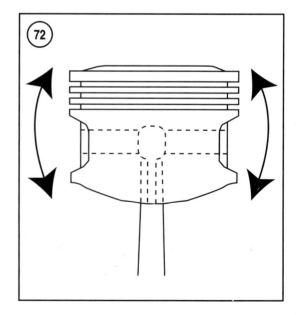

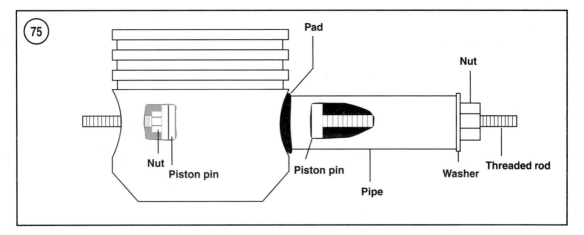

Pad

Nut

Nut
Piston pin

Piston pin

Pipe

Washer

Threaded rod

4

As each component of the piston assembly (**Figure 71**) is cleaned and measured, record and identify all measurements. The measurements will be referred to when checking dimensions and wear limits.

Piston Removal

1. Remove the cylinder as described in this chapter.

2. Before removing the piston, check the piston and piston pin for obvious play. Hold the rod and try to tilt the piston side to side (**Figure 72**). If tilting (not sliding) motion is detected, this indicates wear on either the piston pin, pin bore or connecting rod. Wear could be on any combination of the three parts. Careful inspection will be required to determine which parts should be replaced.

3. Stuff shop cloths around the connecting rod and in the cam chain tunnel to prevent parts from entering the crankcase.

4. Rotate the ends of the circlips to the removal gaps, then remove the circlips from the piston pin bore (**Figure 73**). Discard the circlips.

CAUTION
New circlips must be installed during assembly.

5. Press the piston pin out of the piston by hand (**Figure 74**). If the pin is tight, a simple removal tool can be made as shown in **Figure 75**. The end of the padded pipe rests against the piston, not the piston pin. The hole in the pipe must be larger than the diameter of the piston pin. As the nut on the end of the rod is tightened, the nut and washer at the opposite end drive the piston pin into the pipe.

CAUTION
Do not attempt to drive the pin out with a hammer and drift. The piston and connecting rod assembly will likely be damaged.

6. Lift the piston off the connecting rod.

7. Inspect the piston and piston pin as described in this section.

Piston Inspection

1. Remove the piston rings as described in this section.

2. Clean the piston.

    a. Clean the carbon from the piston crown. Use a soft scraper, brushes and solvent. Do not use tools that can gouge or scratch the surface. This type of damage can cause hot spots on the piston during engine operation.

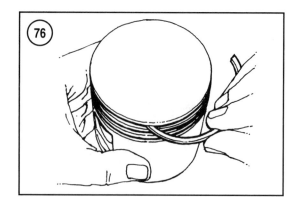

    b. Clean the piston pin bore, ring grooves and piston skirt. Clean the ring grooves with a soft brush, or use a broken piston ring to remove carbon and oil residue (**Figure 76**). Mild galling or discoloration can be polished off the piston skirt with fine emery cloth and oil.

3. Inspect the piston (**Figure 77**). Replace the piston if damage is detected.

    a. Inspect the piston crown for damage. If the piston is pitted, overheating is likely occurring. This can be caused by a lean fuel mixture and/or preignition.

    b. Inspect the ring grooves for dents, nicks, cracks or other damage. The grooves should be square and uniform for the circumference of the piston. Particularly inspect the top compression ring groove. It is lubricated the least and is nearest the combustion temperatures. If the oil ring appears worn, or if the oil ring was difficult to remove, the piston has likely overheated and distorted.

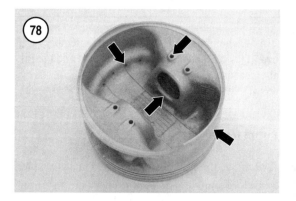

    c. Inspect the piston skirt. If the skirt shows signs of severe galling or partial seizure (bits of metal imbedded in the skirt), replace the piston.

    d. Inspect the interior of the piston (**Figure 78**). Check the crown, skirt and bosses for cracks or other damage. Check the oil holes and circlip grooves for cleanliness and damage.

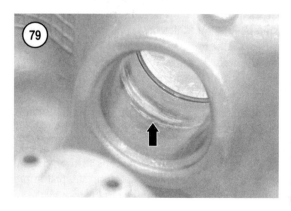

    e. Inspect the pin bores for scoring (**Figure 79**), wear or discoloration from overheating.

    f. Measure the inside diameter of the pin bores. Refer to **Table 2** for specifications.

4. Inspect the piston ring to ring groove clearance as described in *Piston Ring Inspection and Removal* in this section.

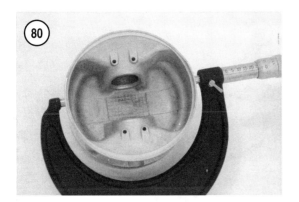

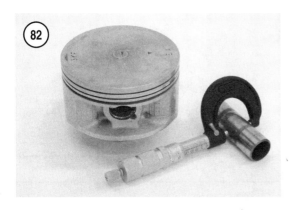

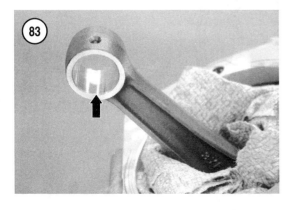

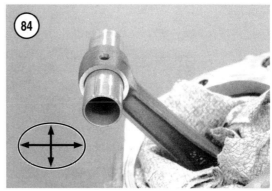

Piston to Cylinder Clearance Check

Calculate the clearance between the piston and cylinder to determine if the parts can be reused. If parts do not fall within specification, the cylinder should be bored oversize to match an oversize piston assembly. Clean and dry the piston and cylinder before measuring.

1. Measure the outside diameter of the piston. Measure 5 mm (0.2 in.) from the bottom edge of the piston skirt and 90° to the direction of the piston pin (**Figure 80**). Record the measurement.

2. Determine clearance by subtracting the piston measurement from the averaged cylinder measurement. If cylinder measurements are not yet known, the procedure is described under *Cylinder Inspection* in this chapter. If the clearance exceeds the specifications in **Table 2**, the cylinder must be overbored and fitted with an oversize piston assembly.

Piston Pin Inspection

1. Clean the piston pin.

2. Inspect the pin for chrome flaking, scoring (**Figure 81**), wear or discoloration from overheating.

3. Measure the outside diameter of the pin (**Figure 82**). Refer to **Table 2** for specifications.

4. Determine the pin to pin bore clearance. Subtract the pin outside diameter from the pin bore inside diameter. Refer to **Table 2** for specifications.

5. Inspect the bore in the small end of the connecting rod (**Figure 83**). Check for scoring, uneven wear, and discoloration from overheating.

6. Lubricate the piston pin and slide it into the connecting rod. Slowly rotate the pin and check for radial play (**Figure 84**). If play is detectable, one or

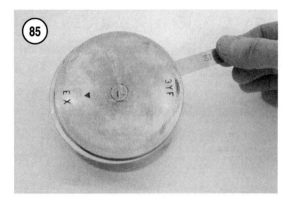

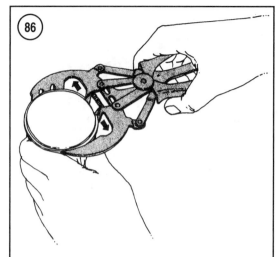

both of the parts are worn. Yamaha does not provide specifications for the connecting rod bore. Therefore, if the pin diameter is marginally within specification, check the fit of a new pin. If play still exists, replace the connecting rod.

Piston Ring Inspection and Removal

The piston is fitted with two compression rings and an oil control ring assembly. The oil ring assembly consists of two side rails and an expander ring.

1. Check the piston ring to ring groove clearance as follows:

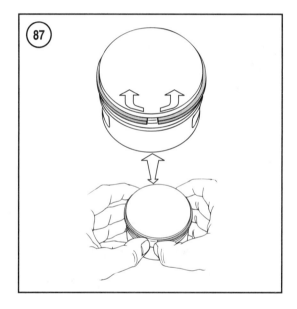

   a. Clean the rings and grooves so accurate measurements can be made with a flat feeler gauge.

   b. Press the top ring into the piston groove.

   c. Insert a flat feeler gauge between the ring and groove (**Figure 85**). Record the measurement. Repeat this step at other points around the piston. Replace the rings if any measurement exceeds the service limit in **Table 2**. If excessive clearance remains after new rings are installed, replace the piston.

   d. Repeat substeps b and c for the remaining rings.

2. Remove the top and second rings with a ring expander (**Figure 86**) or by hand (**Figure 87**).

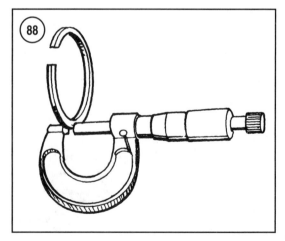

   a. Spread the rings only enough to clear the piston.

   b. The top ring and oil ring rails on Yamaha ring sets are not marked with a *top* mark. If the rings may possibly be reused, mark the top surface of the rings so they can be installed in their original direction. The second ring is marked with an *R* on its top surface. Since this

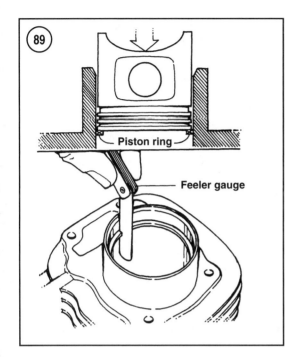

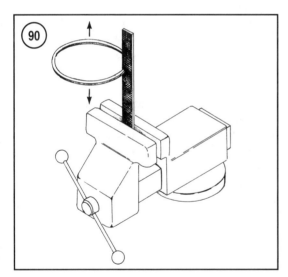

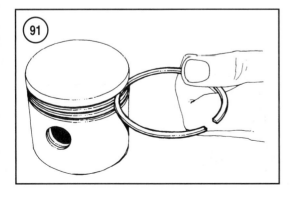

ring is tapered, it must be installed with the mark facing up.

3. Remove the oil ring assembly by first removing the top rail, followed by the bottom rail. Remove (by hand) the expander ring last.

4. Clean and inspect the piston as described in this section.

5. Measure the height and width of the rings (**Figure 88**). Replace all the rings if any measurement exceeds the specifications listed in **Table 2**.

6. Inspect the end gap of the rings as follows:

    a. Insert a ring into the bottom of the cylinder. Use the piston to square the ring to the cylinder wall. Push the ring 50 mm (2 in.) into the cylinder (**Figure 89**).

    b. Measure the end gap with a feeler gauge. For the oil control ring, measure only the rails.

    c. Replace all the rings if any measurement exceeds the service limit listed in **Table 2**. Always replace rings as a set. If new rings are to be installed, gap the new rings after the cylinder has been serviced. If the new ring gap is too narrow, carefully widen the gap using a fine-cut file as shown in **Figure 90**. Work slow and measure often.

7. Roll each ring around its piston groove and check for binding or snags (**Figure 91**). Repair minor groove damage with a fine-cut file.

Piston Ring Installation

If new piston rings will be installed, the cylinder must be honed. This is necessary to deglaze and crosshatch the cylinder surface. The newly honed surface is important in providing lubrication pockets for the new rings, helping them seat and seal against the cylinder. A dealership or machine shop can hone the cylinder for a minimal cost. Refer to *Cylinder Inspection* in this chapter to determine if the cylinder should be honed and reused. If the cylinder needs to be overbored, a larger piston and rings will have to be installed.

1. Check that the piston and rings are clean and dry. When installing, spread the rings only enough to clear the piston.

2. Install the rings as follows:

    a. Install the oil ring expander in the bottom groove, followed by the bottom rail and top rail. The ends of the expander must *not* overlap. The rails can be installed in either posi-

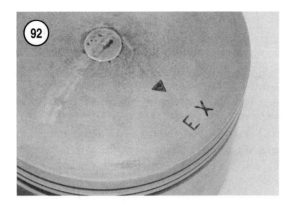

tion or direction for new rings. Used rings should be installed in their original position.

b. Install the second ring. Check that the *R* mark faces up.

c. Install the top ring. The ring can be installed in either direction for new rings. A used ring should be installed in its original direction.

3. Check that all rings rotate freely in their grooves.

Piston Installation

1. Install the piston rings onto the piston as described in this section.

2. Check that all parts are clean and ready to be installed. Use new circlips when installing the piston.

CAUTION
Never install used circlips. Severe engine damage could occur. Circlips fatigue and distort when they are removed, even though they appear reusable.

3. Install a new circlip into one of the piston pin bosses. Rotate the ends of the circlip away from the gap.

4. Lubricate the following components with engine oil:

a. Piston pin.

b. Piston pin bores.

c. Connecting rod bore.

5. Start the piston pin into the open pin bore, then place the piston over the connecting rod. The arrow and letters EX, stamped on the piston crown (**Figure 92**), must point forward.

CAUTION
The piston must be installed correctly. Failure to install the piston correctly can lead to severe engine damage.

6. Align the piston with the rod, then slide the pin through the rod (**Figure 74**) and into the other piston bore.

7. Support the piston so it is stable. Stuff shop clothes into crankcase openings to prevent the accidental entry of the remaining circlip.

8. Install a new circlip into the remaining piston pin boss (**Figure 73**). Rotate the ends of the circlip away from the gap.

9. Stagger the piston ring gaps on the piston. Yamaha recommends the positions shown in **Figure 70**. Note that the top and second ring gaps are opposite one another, as well as the gaps in the oil ring rails.

10. Install the cylinder as described in this chapter.

11. Refer to Chapter Three for break-in procedures.

Table 1 GENERAL ENGINE SPECIFICATIONS

Engine type	Four-stroke single cylinder
Lubrication system	Forced pressure, dry sump
Valve system	5 valve, chain-driven SOHC
Cooling system	Liquid cooled
Engine displacement	660 cc (40.26 cu. in.)
Bore × stroke	100.0 × 84.0 mm (3.94 × 3.31 in.)
Compression ratio	9.2:1

Table 2 ENGINE TOP END SPECIFICATIONS

	New mm (in.)	Service limit mm (in.)
Camshaft		
Journal diameter	22.967-22.980 (0.9042-0.9047)	–
Lobe height		
Intake	35.69-35.79 (1.4051-1.4091)	35.59 (1.4012)
Exhaust	36.50-36.60 (1.437-1.441)	36.40 (1.4331)
Lobe width (intake and exhaust)	30.15-30.25 (1.1870-1.1909)	30.05 (1.1831)
Runout	–	0.03 (0.0012)
Camshaft cap inside diameter	23.0-23.021 (0.9055-0.9063)	–
Camshaft cap to journal clearance	0.020-0.054 (0.0008-0.0021)	–
Cylinder head warp limit		
2001	–	0.05 (0.002)
2002-on	–	0.03 (0.001)
Cylinder		
Inside diameter	100.005-100.045 (3.9372-3.9388)	100.10 (3.94)
Measurement point from top of cylinder	50 (2.0)	
Piston		
Mark direction	Arrow pointing forward	
Outside diameter measurement point	2.5 (0.10) from bottom	–
Outside diameter	99.945-99.995 (3.9348-3.9368)	–
Pin bore diameter	22.004-22.015 (0.8663-0.8667)	22.045 (0.8679)
Pin bore offset (toward intake side)	1.0 (0.04)	–
Piston to cylinder clearance	0.05-0.07 (0.0020-0.0028)	0.15 (0.006)
Piston pin diameter	21.991-22.0 (0.8658-0.8661)	21.971 (0.8650)
Piston pin to pin bore clearance	0.004-0.024 (0.00016-0.00094)	0.07 (0.0028)
Piston rings		
Top ring profile	Barrel	
Top ring height and width	1.2 × 3.8 (0.0472 × 0.1496)	–
Top ring end gap	0.30-0.45 (0.0118-0.0177)	0.70 (0.0276)
Top ring to piston groove clearance	0.04-0.08 (0.0016-0.0031)	0.13 (0.0051)
Second ring profile	Taper	
Second ring height and width	1.2 × 4.0 (0.0472 × 0.1575)	–
Second ring end gap	0.30-0.45 (0.0118-0.0177)	0.80 (0.0315)
Second ring to piston groove clearance	0.03-0.07 (0.0012-0.0028)	0.13 (0.0051)
Oil ring height and width	2.5 × 3.4 (0.0984 × 0.1339)	–
Oil ring end gap	0.2-0.7 (0.0079-0.0276)	–
Oil ring to piston groove clearance	0.06-0.15 (0.0024-0.0059)	0.13 (0.0051)
Piston ring top mark identification	R (second ring only)	
Rocker arm inside diameter		
Intake and exhaust	12.0-12.018 (0.4724-0.4731)	–
Rocker arm shaft diameter		
Intake and exhaust	11.976-11.991 (0.4715-0.4721)	–
Rocker arm to rocker arm shaft clearance	0.009-0.042 (0.0004-0.0017)	–
Valve clearance (cold)		
Intake	0.10-0.15 (0.004-0.006)	–
Exhaust	0.15-0.20 (0.006-0.008)	–
Valve dimensions		
Head diameter		
Intake	29.9-30.1 (1.1772-1.1850)	–
Exhaust	31.9-32.1 (1.2559-1.2638)	–
Face width		
Intake	2.25 (0.0886)	–
Exhaust	2.26 (0.0890)	–
Seat angle	45°	

(continued)

4

Table 2 ENGINE TOP END SPECIFICATIONS (continued)

	New mm (in.)	Service limit mm (in.)
Seat width		
Intake		
2001	0.9-1.1 (0.0354-0.0433)	1.6 (0.0630)
2002-on	1.1-1.3 (0.0433-0.0512)	1.6 (0.0630)
Exhaust	0.9-1.1 (0.0354-0.0433)	1.6 (0.0630)
Margin thickness		
Intake and exhaust	0.85-1.15 (0.0335-0.0453)	–
Stem diameter		
Intake	5.975-5.990 (0.2352-0.2358)	5.945 (0.2341)
Exhaust	5.960-5.975 (0.2346-0.2352)	5.930 (0.2335)
Stem runout	–	0.01 (0.0004)
Valve guide inside diameter		
Intake and exhaust	6.0-6.012 (0.2362-0.2367)	6.040 (0.2378)
Valve stem to guide clearance		
Intake	0.010-0.037 (0.0004-0.0015)	0.08 (0.0031)
Exhaust	0.025-0.052 (0.0010-0.0020)	0.10 (0.0039)
Valve spring		
Free length		
Intake	35.95 (1.42)	34.15 (1.34)
Exhaust	37.75 (1.49)	35.86 (1.41)
Set length (valve closed)		
Intake	27.2 (1.07)	–
Exhaust	30.7 (1.21)	–
Compressed pressure		
Intake	149-173 N (33.5-38.89 lbs.)	
Exhaust	165-191 N (37.09-42.94 lbs.)	
Tilt limit	–	1.6 (0.06)

Table 3 ENGINE TOP END TORQUE SPECIFICATIONS

	N•m	in.-lb.	ft.-lb.
Cam chain tensioner center bolt	22	–	16
Cam chain tensioner mounting bolts	10	88	–
Cam sprocket bolts	20	–	15
Carburetor intake duct bolts	10	88	–
Cylinder head bolts (6 mm)	10	88	–
Cylinder head bolts (9 mm)	38	–	28
Cylinder head cover bolts	10	88	–
Cylinder mounting bolts (6 mm)	10	88	–
Cylinder mounting bolts (10 mm)	42		31
Exhaust heat shield bolts	10	88	–
Exhaust pipe clamp bolt	16	–	12
Exhaust pipe flange to cylinder head nuts	10	88	–
Exhaust rocker shaft lockbolt	10	88	–
Exhaust valve covers	12	106	–
Intake valve cover bolts	10	88	–
Muffler to exhaust pipe bolt	20	–	15
Muffler to frame bolts	26	–	19
Oil pipe banjo bolts	20	–	15
Oil pressure check plate bolt	10	88	–
Spark plug	18	–	13
Upper engine mounting bracket to engine bolt	40	–	30
Upper engine mounting bracket to frame bolts	33	–	24
Water jacket hose fitting bolt	10	88	–

CHAPTER FIVE

ENGINE LOWER END

This chapter provides procedures for servicing or removing the following major lower end components:

1. Cam chain and rear guide.
2. Crankcase, bearings and seals.
3. Crankshaft and connecting rod.
4. Balancer.
5. Transmission.

To access and service the components that are in the crankcase, the engine must be removed from the frame, then dismantled of all assemblies attached to the crankcase.

Read this chapter before attempting repairs to the engine lower end. Become familiar with the procedures, photos and illustrations to understand the skill and equipment required. Refer to Chapter One for tool usage and techniques.

SHOP CLEANLINESS

Prior to removing and disassembling the engine, clean the engine and frame with degreaser. The disassembly job will go easier and there will be less chance of dirt entering the assemblies. Keep the work environment as clean as possible. Store parts and assemblies in well-marked plastic bags and containers. Keep reconditioned parts wrapped and lubricated until they will be installed.

ENGINE

The following removal and installation procedure outlines the basic steps necessary to remove the engine from the frame. Depending on the planned level of disassembly, consider removing top end components, and those located in the crankcase covers, while the engine remains in the frame. Since the frame keeps the engine stabilized, tight nuts and bolts are easier to remove if the engine is held steady. Also, if the actual engine problem is unknown, it may be discovered in another assembly, other than the crankcase.

During engine removal, make note of mounting bolt directions and how cables and wire harnesses are routed. Refer to the appropriate chapters for removal, inspection and installation procedures for the components in the engine top end and crankcase covers.

Removal and Installation

1. Park the machine on level ground and set the parking brake.

2. If possible, perform a compression test (Chapter Three) and leakdown test (Chapter Two) before dismantling the engine.

3. Remove the skid plate, seat, bodywork, fuel tank, protectors, footguard assemblies and footpegs (Chapter Fourteen).

4. Remove the exhaust pipes (Chapter Four).

5. Drain the engine oil (Chapter Three).

6. Drain the engine coolant (Chapter Three).

7. Disconnect the coolant hoses at the engine.

8. Remove the carburetors (Chapter Eight).

9. Remove the spark plug lead and oil tank breather hose from the cylinder head.

10. Disconnect the starter motor lead (Chapter Nine).

11. Disconnect the clutch cable at the engine (Chapter Six).

12. Disconnect the parking brake cable.

13. Disconnect the battery ground lead at the engine.

14. Remove the sprocket guard and remove the drive chain from the drive sprocket.

15. Disconnect the stator and pickup coil wiring harness connectors, located at the back of the engine.

16. Remove the speed sensor from the right crankcase.

17. Remove the crankcase breather hose.

18. Disconnect the reverse switch, neutral switch, reverse cable and lower oil pipe from the left side of the engine (**Figure 1**).

> *NOTE*
> *Remove the upper oil pipe (**Figure 2**) after the engine has been moved forward in the frame. Access to the rear bolt is limited.*

19. Inspect the engine and verify that it is ready for removal. If desired, remove any additional components that will make engine removal and handling easier.

20. Remove the engine mounting bolts and brackets as follows:

> *WARNING*
> *When removing the bolts, be aware that the engine may shift in the frame. Keep*

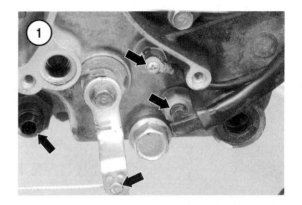

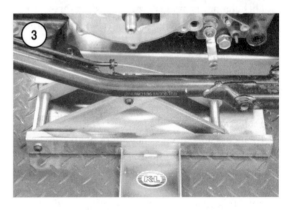

*hands protected and check the stability of the engine after each set of bolts is removed. Get assistance when removing the engine from the frame. Use a jack to support the engine as it is being prepared for removal (**Figure 3**).*

a. Remove the bolts and upper mounting bracket (**Figure 4**).

b. Remove the bolts from the middle and lower mounting brackets (**Figure 5**). Mark the mid-

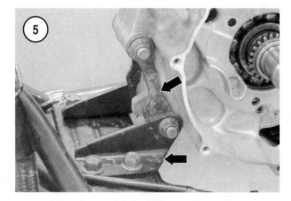

dle brackets so they can be installed in their original positions.

c. Remove the swing arm pivot nut. Do not remove the pivot bolt at this time.

WARNING
*In the following step, do not completely remove the swing arm pivot bolt from the frame (**Figure 6**). Pull the bolt out only far enough to slide the engine forward. Complete removal will allow the swing arm to fall. As the*

pivot bolt is withdrawn from the swing arm, insert a large drift or bolt into the swing arm from the right side. This will help keep the right side of the swing arm in place.

d. Pull the swing arm pivot bolt out so it clears the engine, then slide the engine forward. If not already removed, remove the upper oil pipe from the left side of the engine.

e. Remove the engine from the frame.

f. Push the swing arm pivot bolt back into the frame.

g. Clean and inspect the frame in the engine bay. Check for cracks and damage, particularly at welded joints.

21. Refer to the procedures in this chapter for servicing the crankcase assembly.

22. Reverse this procedure to install the engine. Note the following:

a. If the chain is endless (no master link) and has been removed from the swing arm, check that it is routed over the swing arm pivot before installing the pivot bolt.

b. Install new O-rings, where used.

c. Install the engine mounting brackets, bolts and nuts. Finger-tighten all nuts before torquing. Note the original direction of the bolts during installation.

NOTE
If the engine top end is not installed when the engine is mounted in the frame, do not tighten any mounting bolts until the upper mounting bracket has been installed and aligned.

d. Torque the upper engine mounting bracket to frame bolts to 33 N•m (24 ft.-lb.).

e. Torque the upper engine mounting bracket to engine bolt to 40 N•m (30 ft.-lb.).

f. Torque the middle and lower engine mounting bracket bolts to 56 N•m (41 ft.-lb.).

g. Torque the swing arm pivot nut to 95 N•m (70 ft.-lb.).

h. Torque the lower oil pipe nut to 35 N•m (26 ft.-lb.).

i. Torque the upper oil pipe bolts to 10 N•m (88 in.-lb.).

j. Carefully route electrical wires so they are not pinched or in contact with surfaces that get hot.

k. Apply dielectric grease to electrical connections before reconnecting.

l. If assemblies have been removed from the top end or crankcase covers, install those components. Refer to the appropriate chapters for inspection and installation procedures.

m. Fill the engine with engine oil (Chapter Three).

n. Fill the cooling system with coolant (Chapter Three).

o. Adjust the clutch (Chapter Three).

p. Adjust the throttle cable (Chapter Three).

q. Adjust the rear brake pedal (Chapter Three).

r. Adjust the parking brake cable (Chapter Three).

s. Adjust the chain (Chapter Three).

t. Start the engine and check for leaks.

u. Check throttle and clutch operation.

v. If the engine top-end has been rebuilt, perform a compression check. Record the result and compare it to future checks.

w. Read the *Engine Break-In* procedure in Chapter Three.

CAM CHAIN AND REAR GUIDE

The cam chain and rear guide are located behind the rotor and starter clutch, at the left side of the crankcase (**Figure 7**). The front guide can be removed when the cylinder head cover is removed.

Removal, Inspection and Installation

1. Remove the camshaft, then remove the cam chain from the camshaft sprocket (Chapter Four).

2. Remove the left crankcase cover, rotor and starter clutch (Chapter Nine).

3. Remove the rear guide and cam chain.

4. Inspect the cam chain and guide (**Figure 8**).

a. Pull the chain tight and check for play between the links. If play is evident, inspect the condition of the chain sprockets.

b. Inspect the guide for wear and deterioration.

5. Reverse this procedure to install the cam chain and guide. Note the following:

a. Apply threadlocking compound to the bolt threads.

b. Torque the rear guide bolts to 8 N•m (71 in.-lb.).

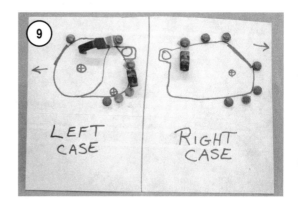

CRANKCASE

The following procedures detail the disassembly and reassembly of the crankcase. When the two halves of the crankcase are disassembled or split the crankshaft, balancer and transmission assemblies can be removed for inspection and repair. Before performing this procedure, remove the engine from the frame as described in this chapter. All assemblies located in the crankcase covers must be removed. It may be easier to remove these assem-

Disassembly

Any reference to the *left* or *right* side of the engine, refers to the side of the engine as it is mounted in the frame not on the workbench. As components are removed, keep the parts organized and clean. Leave the left case facing up until the balancer and transmission assembly have been removed from the case.

1. Place the engine on wooden blocks and loosen the crankcase bolts on both sides of the engine. Loosen each bolt 1/4 turn, working in a crossing pattern. Loosen the bolts until they can be removed by hand.

NOTE
*Since the bolt lengths vary, make a drawing of the crankcase shape on a piece of cardboard. Punch holes in the cardboard at the bolt locations. As the bolts and clamps are removed from the crankcase, put each bolt in its respective hole in the template (**Figure 9**). If desired, mark each bolt hole with a reference number, indicating which of the five bolt sizes is used at that location. After the template is marked, the bolts can be removed and cleaned. After cleaning, return the bolts to the template.*

2. Separate the crankcase halves as follows:
   a. With the right side of the engine facing up, lightly and evenly pry the cases at the reinforced areas around the perimeter of the engine. Do not pry on gasket surfaces. Pry the case slowly and only enough to break the seal between the cases. If necessary, a heat gun can be used to soften the joint sealant, making separation easier.
   b. When the case seal breaks, raise and lower the right case until it is fully released. Evenly lift the right case from the left case.
   c. Account for the three dowels between the cases when the cases are separated (**Figure 10**). The middle dowel is fitted with an O-ring.

3. Remove and inspect the balancer (**Figure 11**) as described in this chapter.

4. Remove the transmission assembly from the case as follows:
   a. Remove the two shift fork shafts (A, **Figure 12**) and three shift forks (B).

blies with the engine in the frame. The engine will remain steady during the disassembly process.

The crankcase halves are made of cast aluminum alloy. Do not hammer or excessively pry on the cases. The cases will fracture or break. The cases are aligned at the joint by dowels, and joined with liquid sealant.

The crankshaft is press-fitted to the crankpin. The assembly is supported at each end by a ball bearing. The connecting rod has a needle bearing fitted at the large end.

b. Remove the shift drum (A, **Figure 13**), disengaging the reverse lockout lever (B) from the drum.

c. Remove the washer and first gear from the output shaft (A, **Figure 14**), then remove the input shaft assembly (B).

d. Remove the output shaft and reverse shaft assemblies (**Figure 15**). Keep the output shaft upright to prevent parts from falling from the shaft.

e. Disassemble and inspect the transmission components (Chapter Seven).

> *CAUTION*
> *Take extreme care when removing, handling and storing the transmission. Wrap and store the assembly until it will be inspected. Do not expose the assembly to dirt or place it in an area where it could roll and fall to the floor.*

5. On the outside of the case, remove the neutral switch, reverse switch, lower oil pipe fitting and reverse lockout lever assembly (**Figure 16**). Inspect the reverse lockout assembly (Chapter Seven).

6. Remove the crankshaft and left main bearing (**Figure 17**) from the case as follows:

a. Attach a crankcase separating tool (part No. YU-01135-A, 90890-01135) or similar two-point puller as shown in **Figure 18**. Check that the tool is fully threaded through the case. Lubricate the tool threads and contact point on the crankshaft.

b. If available, use a heat gun to warm the case around the bearing. This will slightly expand the bore and aid in bearing removal. Avoid directly heating the bearing.

c. Working on a stable surface, turn the centerbolt and pull the case from the crankshaft and bearing.

> *CAUTION*
> *Take extreme care when removing, handling and storing the crankshaft. Do not expose the assembly to dirt or place it in an area where it could roll and fall to the floor. If the crankshaft is dropped, the crankpin will likely be knocked out of alignment. The connecting rod may also be damaged.*

d. Inspect the crankshaft assembly and cases as described in this chapter.

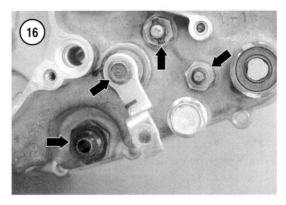

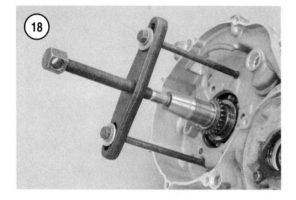

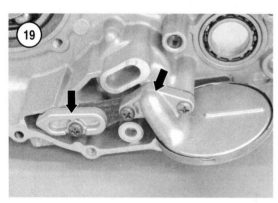

7. In the right crankcase, remove the oil strainer, cover and gasket (**Figure 19**). Inspect the oil strainer as described in this chapter.

Assembly

Read the entire procedure to ensure that all tools, parts and supplies are on hand, as well as proper preparation of the case halves.

To install the crankshaft, a special Yamaha crankshaft installation set (**Figure 20**) is required. The parts include: crankshaft installation kit (part No. YU90050) (pot, bolt, nut and spacer), 14 mm × 1.5 mm RH female adapter (part No. YM90069) and pot spacer (No. YM91044). A similar set is available from dealerships that carry K&L Supply Co. tools (1-800-727-6767).

1. Note the following prior to beginning assembly:
   a. Check that all mating surfaces are smooth, clean and dry. Minor irregularities can be repaired with an oil stone. After thorough removal of the old sealant, clean all mating surfaces with a highly-evaporative solvent, such as brake cleaner or electrical contact cleaner. The new sealant will not adhere to oily surfaces.
   b. Lubricate the crankshaft, bearings and transmission assembly with engine oil.
   c. Lubricate seal lips with grease.
   d. If possible, have assistance when installing the crankshaft into the crankcase. Assemble the crankshaft installation tool and understand how it operates before actually starting the installation.
   e. To seal the crankcase halves, a *liquid gasket* sealant is used. Use Yamabond 1215 or Yamabond 4, available at dealerships. These sealants are durable and can be submerged in oil.

> *CAUTION*
> *Do not attempt to seal the cases with RTV silicone sealant, commonly found at auto parts stores. The sealant is inadequate for this application. Oil leakage and engine damage is possible.*

2. Install the crankshaft and bearing into the left crankcase as follows:
   a. Place the left crankcase on wooden blocks, with the open side of the case facing down.

b. If available, use a heat gun to warm the case around the bearing bore. This will slightly expand the bore and aid in bearing installation.

c. Thread the adapter onto the crankshaft (**Figure 21**). Note that the adapter has a different thread pitch at each end. Check that the correct end of the adapter is being threaded onto the crankshaft. Lubricate the exterior of the adapter after it is seated.

d. Lubricate the interior of the installer pot (**Figure 22**).

e. Align the pot spacer over the crankcase bore, then install the large spacer, pot, bolt and nut (**Figure 23**). The pot spacer must be level on the case and the bolt must fully thread into the adapter.

f. Hold the assembly stable and turn the nut to draw the crankshaft bearing toward the bore. As the adapter nears the pot, check that the pin on the adapter enters the groove in the pot.

g. Turn the nut and fully seat the bearing into the crankcase.

h. Remove the tool and place the left crankcase so the open side is facing up (**Figure 24**).

3. On the outside of the case, install the neutral switch, reverse switch and lower oil pipe fitting (**Figure 16**). Note the following:

a. Install new seal washers, where required.

b. Torque the lower oil pipe fitting to 50 N•m (37 ft.-lb.).

c. Torque the neutral switch and reverse switch to 20 N•m (15 ft.-lb.).

4. Install the reverse lockout assembly as follows:

a. Install the reverse lockout shaft through the case, checking that the lever is positioned as shown in A, **Figure 25**.

b. On the outside of the case install the washer, E-clip (sharp edge out), spring, lever and bolt. Check that the spring is seated against the case and lever (**Figure 16**).

c. Torque the bolt to 13 N•m (10 ft.-lb.). When torquing the bolt, support the lever inside the case to prevent jamming the lever against the case.

d. Check that the lever is spring-loaded and pivots forward. When released, the lever should return toward the rear of the case.

5. Install the transmission as follows:

a. Install the reverse shaft assembly, fully seating it in the bore (B, **Figure 25**).

5

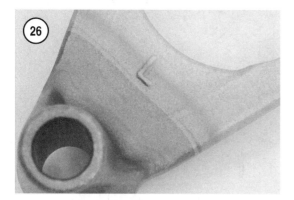

b. Install the output shaft, meshing it with the reverse shaft assembly (**Figure 15**). Keep the output shaft upright to prevent parts from falling from the shaft.

c. Temporarily remove the washer and first gear from the output shaft (A, **Figure 14**), then install the input shaft (B), fully seating it with the gears.

d. Install the shift drum (A, **Figure 13**), engaging the reverse lockout lever (B) with the groove in the drum.

e. Identify the shift forks by the letter cast on the fork (**Figure 26**). The left (L, **Figure 27**) and right (R) forks engage with the output shaft, while the center (C) fork engages with the input shaft. When installed, the letter on each shift fork must face up.

f. Install the shift forks, engaging them with the appropriate gears. Check that the guide pin on each fork engages with the appropriate groove in the shift drum.

g. Install the fork shafts (A, **Figure 12**). Install the short shaft in the center fork.

h. Check that all parts are engaged and seated.

5. Install the balancer (**Figure 11**). The left case should appear as shown in **Figure 28**.

6. In the right crankcase, install a new gasket, the cover and oil strainer (**Figure 19**). Apply threadlocking compound to the screws, then torque the screws to 7 N•m (62 in.-lb.).

7. Install the right crankcase onto the left crankcase as follows:

a. Check that all mating surfaces are clean and dry.

b. On the left crankcase, insert the three dowels (**Figure 29**). Install a new O-ring on the middle dowel.

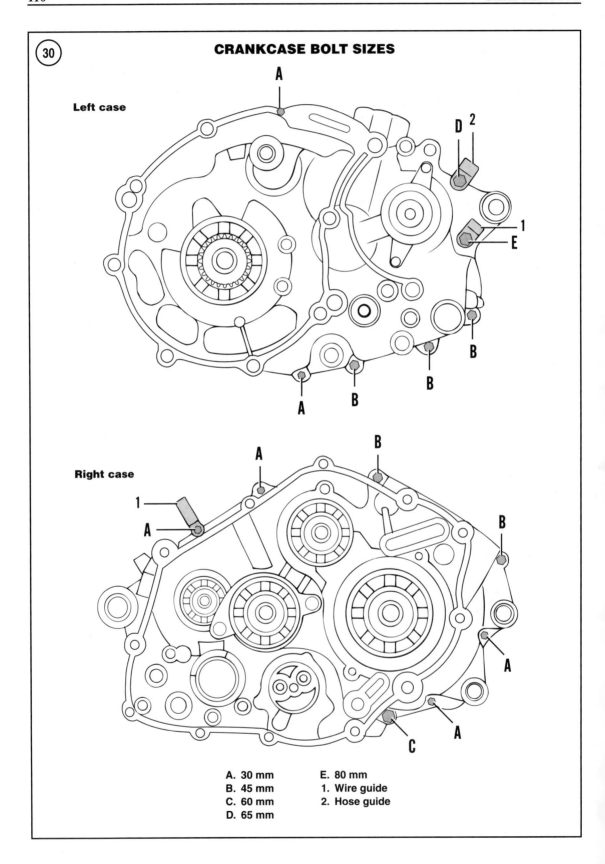

30

CRANKCASE BOLT SIZES

Left case

Right case

A. 30 mm
B. 45 mm
C. 60 mm
D. 65 mm
E. 80 mm
1. Wire guide
2. Hose guide

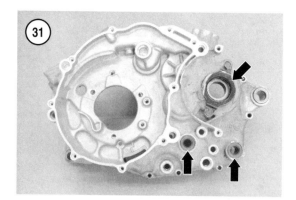

c. Apply liquid gasket sealant, such as Yamabond 1215 or Yamabond 4, to all mating surfaces. This includes applying the sealant around all bolt holes and the passage above the middle dowel (**Figure 29**). Use enough sealant to fill voids and provide a continuous seal on the entire joint. Excessive amounts of sealant should be avoided.

d. Check that all shafts are aligned vertically, then fit the left case squarely onto the right case.

e. If necessary, *tap* the left case with a mallet to evenly seat the cases. Do not force the cases. If the cases are not seating, a shaft is probably misaligned with its bore. Lift the case and slightly move it side to side until the shaft(s) are properly guided.

8. Remove each crankcase bolt from the template and insert the bolts and guides into the appropriate holes. Finger-tighten the bolts. If necessary, refer to **Figure 30** for bolt and guide locations.

9. Tighten the bolts equally in several passes and in a crossing pattern. Torque the bolts to 10 N•m (88 in.-lb.).

10. Rotate the crankshaft and check for smooth operation. If binding is evident, separate the cases and correct the problem.

11. Rotate the transmission shafts and check for smooth operation. If binding or poor operation is evident, separate the cases and correct the problem.

a. Thread a bolt and locknut into the end of the shift drum and check for proper shifting through the gears. Rotate the shafts to aid in shifting.

b. To check reverse gear operation, rotate the shift drum *clockwise* and place the transmission in first gear. Pull the reverse lever for-

ward and rotate the shift drum clockwise to engage reverse gear. Release the reverse lever, then rotate the shift drum counterclockwise to go back to first gear. From first gear, with the reverse lever released, attempt to put the transmission into reverse gear. The transmission must not be able to go into reverse gear without pulling on the reverse lever.

12. Allow the sealant to set for at least an hour before handling the crankcase.

13. The crankcase assembly is ready for installation into the frame. If desired, top end components and those located in the side covers can be installed at this time. Refer to the appropriate chapters for inspection and installation procedures for the components in the engine top end and crankcase covers.

Inspection

1. In the left crankcase, remove the oil seals from the output shaft bearing, reverse shaft bore and shift shaft bore (**Figure 31**). Remove the seals as described in this chapter.

2. Remove all sealant from the gasket surfaces. Avoid gouging or scratching the surfaces.

3. Clean the crankcase halves with solvent. Flush all bearings last, using clean solvent.

4. Dry the cases and passages with compressed air.

WARNING
When drying the bearings with compressed air, minimize spinning the bearings. Do not spin them at high speed. Since the bearing are not lubricated, damage could occur.

5. Inspect the bearings as follows:

a. Oil the engine bearings before inspecting their condition.

b. Check each bearing for roughness, pitting, galling and play. If rust is evident on the bearing, the engine oil has likely been contaminated with water. Replace any bearing that is not in good condition, or is a loose fit in the crankcase bore. Always replace the opposing bearing at the same time.

6. Inspect the cases for fractures around all mounting and bearing bosses, stiffening ribs and threaded holes. If repair is required, the case should be taken to a dealership or machine shop that repairs precision aluminum castings.

7. Check all threaded holes for damage or sealant buildup. Clean threads with the correct size metric tap. Lubricate the tap with oil or aluminum tap fluid.

SEAL REPLACEMENT

Output Shaft

1. Remove the seal retainer (**Figure 32**), then pry out the seal. If necessary, place a block of wood on the case to improve leverage and protect the case from damage.

> *CAUTION*
> *When prying, do not allow the end of the tool to touch the seal bore or snag the oil hole in the bore (**Figure 33**). Scratches in the bore will cause leakage and heavy-handed prying can break the casting.*

2. If a new bearing will be installed, replace the bearing before installing the new seal.
3. Clean the oil seal bore.
4. Apply grease to the lip and sides of the new seal.
5. Place the seal over the bore, with the closed side of the seal facing out. The seal must be square to the bore.
6. Press the seal by hand until it is flush with the outside edge of the bore.
   a. If a driver is used, use a driver that fits at the perimeter of the seal.
   b. Another method for driving the seal is to install the seal retainer over the seal, then equally tightening the retainer bolts in several passes, driving the seal flush with the case. Whichever method is used to drive the seal, always check that the oil hole in the bore (**Figure 33**) is not blocked.
   c. Torque the retainer bolts to 10 N•m (88 in.-lb.).

Shift Shaft and Reverse Shaft

Both seals are removed and replaced identically.
1. Pry out the old seal (**Figure 34**). If necessary, place a block of wood on the case to improve leverage and protect the case from damage.

> *CAUTION*
> *When prying, do not allow the end of the tool to touch the seal bore.*

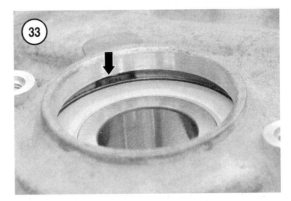

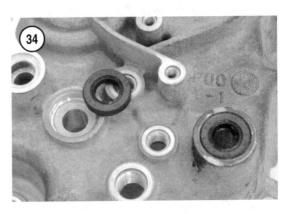

Scratches in the bore will cause leakage.

2. Clean the oil seal bore.

3. Apply grease to the lip and sides of the new seal.

4. Place the seal over the bore, with the closed side of the seal facing out. The seal must be square to the bore.

5. Press the seal into place by hand.

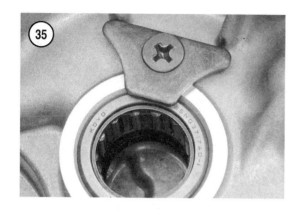

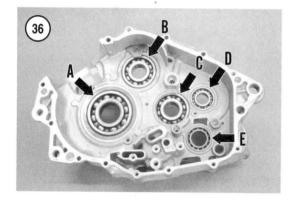

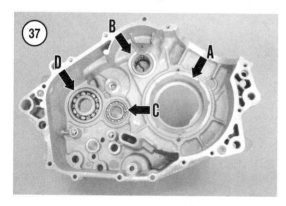

**CRANKCASE BEARING
REPLACEMENT**

Refer to Chapter One for additional removal and installation techniques for bearings. Also refer to *Interference Fit* if it is desired to use heat for the removal and installation of the bearings in the housings.

Crankcase Bearing Identification

1. When replacing crankcase bearings, note the following:

a. Where used, remove bearing retainers (**Figure 35**) before attempting bearing removal. When installing retainers, clean the screw threads and install the screws using threadlocking compound. Torque bearing retainer screws to 7 N•m (62 in.-lb.).

b. Identify and record the size code of each bearing before it is removed from the case. This will eliminate confusion when installing the bearings in their correct bores.

c. Record the orientation of each bearing in its bore. Note if the size code faces toward the inside or outside of the case. Commonly, the markings should *face up* when installing the bearing.

d. Use a hydraulic press or a set of bearing drivers to remove and install bearings. Removal and installation of the bearings is eased by using heat, as described in *Interference Fit* in Chapter One.

e. Bearings that are only accessible from one side of the case can be removed with a blind bearing puller. The puller is fitted through the bearing, then expanded to grip the back side of the bearing. A sliding weight on the tool is quickly pulled back to impact and dislodge the bearing.

2. Refer to the following substeps to identify the *right* crankcase bearings (**Figure 36**). The direction of the manufacturer's marks on each bearing is also indicated. When the marks are facing *in*, this indicates they face the *inside* of the case. When the marks are facing *out*, this indicates they face the *outside* of the case.

a. Crankshaft bearing (A). Manufacturer's marks facing out.

b. Balancer bearing (B). Manufacturer's marks facing out.

c. Input shaft bearing (C). Manufacturer's marks facing out.

d. Output shaft bearing (D). Manufacturer's marks facing in.

e. Shift drum bearing (E). Manufacturer's marks facing in.

3. The following list identifies the *left* crankcase bearings (**Figure 37**). The direction of the manufacturer's marks on each bearing is also indicated. When the marks are facing *in*, this indicates they face the *inside* of the case. When the marks are

facing *out*, this indicates they face the *outside* of
the case.

   a. Crankshaft bearing (A) (mounted on crank-
     shaft). Manufacturer's marks facing out.

   b. Balancer bearing (B). Manufacturer's marks
     facing in. Use a blind bearing puller to re-
     move this bearing.

   c. Input shaft bearing (C). Manufacturer's
     marks facing out. This bearing is shielded on
     the outside. Use a blind bearing puller to re-
     move this bearing.

   d. Output shaft bearing (D). Manufacturer's
     marks facing in. This bearing is shielded on
     the outside.

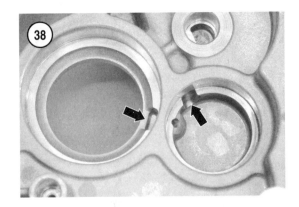

Crankcase Bearing Replacement

All crankcase bearings can be removed and installed using the following steps. Read the entire
procedure before replacing any bearing.

> *NOTE*
> *Before performing this procedure, re-*
> *fer to the **Crankcase Bearing***
> ***Identification** section to determine if*
> *there is specific information related to*
> *the bearing being replaced.*

1. Remove the seal from the bearing, if applicable.
2. Make note of which side of the bearing is facing
up.
3. Heat the crankcase as described in *Interference
Fit* in Chapter One. Observe all safety and handling
procedures when the case is heated.

> *CAUTION*
> *Do not heat the housing or bearing*
> *with a propane or acetylene torch.*
> *The direct heat will destroy the case*
> *hardening of the bearing and will*
> *likely warp the housing.*

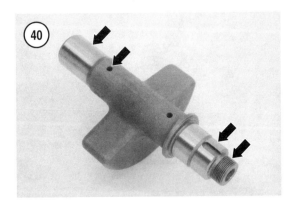

4. Support the heated crankcase on wooden blocks,
allowing space for the bearing to fall from the bore.
5. Remove the damaged bearing from the bore, using a press, hand-driver set or bearing puller.
6. Clean and inspect the bore. Check that all oil
holes (where applicable) are clean (**Figure 38**).
7. Place the new bearing in a freezer and chill for at
least one hour.
8. When the bearing is chilled, reheat the crankcase.

9. Support the heated crankcase on wooden blocks,
checking that the case is supported directly below
the bearing.

10. Lubricate the mating surface of the bore and
bearing (**Figure 39**). Place the bearing squarely
over the bore and check that it is properly oriented.

   a. If the correct orientation of a bearing is not
     known, *generally*, bearings that are not sealed
     on either side should be installed with the
     manufacturer's marks (stamped on the side of
     the bearing) facing up.

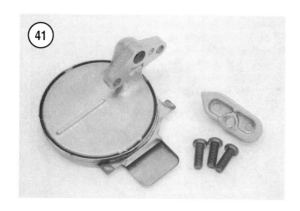

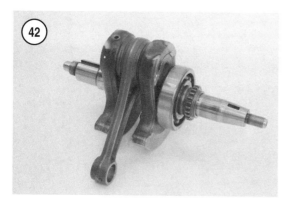

b. Bearings with one side shielded should have the sealed side facing down.

11. Press the bearing into place using a driver that fits on the outer bearing race.

> *CAUTION*
> *If a press is not available, the bearing can be seated by hand, using a driver and hammer. Place the driver squarely over the bearing, then drive the bearing into the case. Avoid using excessive force when driving the bearing. Bearing and case damage could occur.*

12. Install the seal (if applicable) as described in this chapter.

ENGINE BALANCER

Inspection

The engine utilizes a rotating balancer to dampen vibration that is inherent to a single-cylinder engine. The balancer weight is synchronized with the crankshaft, and is gear-driven by the primary drive gear, located on the right end of the crankshaft. Inspect the balancer (**Figure 40**).

1. Install the balancer into its crankcase bearings and check for play between the parts.
2. Inspect the bearing surfaces, oil holes, keyway and threads for damage and cleanliness.
3. Inspect the fit of the drive gear, key and nut on the balancer shaft.
4. Replace parts that are worn or damaged.

OIL STRAINER

Inspection

1. The oil strainer (**Figure 41**) is not designed to be disassembled. It is normal for the bottom of the strainer to feel slightly loose from the top of the strainer.
2. Flush the strainer with solvent and compressed air. If significant accumulations of dirt or metal particles continue to be flushed from the strainer, replace the strainer.
3. After cleaning and drying, pour engine oil into the strainer and allow it to drain.
4. Install a new gasket when installing the strainer.

CRANKSHAFT

Inspection

Carefully handle the crankshaft assembly during inspection. Do not place the crankshaft where it could accidentally roll off the workbench. The crankshaft (**Figure 42**) is an assembly-type, with its two halves joined by a crankpin. The crankpin is hydraulically pressed into the flywheels and aligned, both vertically and horizontally, with calibrated equipment. If any part of the crankshaft assembly is worn or damaged, have a dealership evaluate all the parts to determine the practicality of repair. The connecting rod is available as a separate part number, however, the crankshaft, left main bearing and cam chain sprocket are only available as a complete assembly.

1. Clean the crankshaft with *clean* solvent and dry with compressed air. Lubricate the rod bearing and shaft bearing with engine oil.
2. Inspect the right end of the crankshaft (**Figure 43**).
   a. Inspect the oil passage in the end of the shaft for cleanliness.

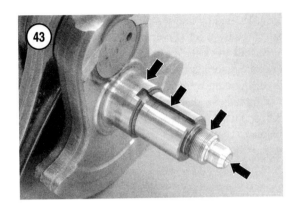

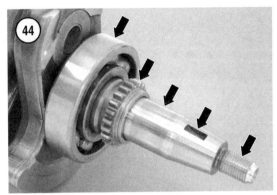

b. Inspect the shaft threads. The primary drive-gear nut is torqued to these threads. Light damage can be corrected with a thread file.

c. Inspect the keyway and seating surfaces for the primary drive gear.

d. Inspect the bearing surface for scoring, heat discoloration or other damage. Burnishing can be removed with 320-grit carborundum cloth.

3. Inspect the left end of the crankshaft (**Figure 44**).

a. Inspect the shaft threads. Light damage can be corrected with a thread file.

b. Inspect the keyway and seating surface for the rotor and starter clutch bearing. Burnishing can be removed with 320-grit carborundum cloth.

c. Inspect the cam chain sprocket for wear and broken teeth.

d. Inspect the bearing for heat discoloration, roughness, pitting, galling and play. If rust is evident on the bearing, the engine oil has likely been contaminated with water.

4. Inspect the connecting rod.

a. Inspect the rod small end (**Figure 45**) for scoring, galling or heat damage. Refer to Chapter Four for additional inspections of the rod bore, piston pin and piston.

b. Inspect the rod small end for play (tilt) (**Figure 46**). Mount the crankshaft in a set of V-blocks and accurately measure play. Refer to **Table 1** for the specification.

c. Inspect the rod big end and bearing for obvious scoring, galling or heat damage.

d. Inspect the rod for radial clearance (**Figure 47**). Mount the crankshaft in a set of V-blocks and accurately measure play. Refer to **Table 1**

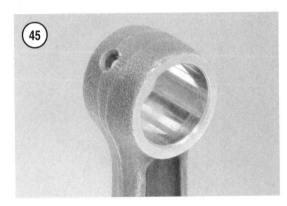

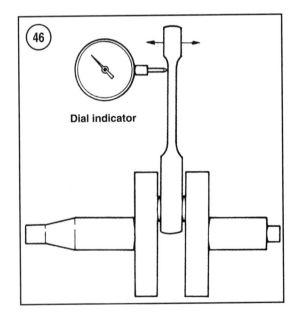

Dial indicator

for specifications. An acceptable method is to grasp the rod and feel for radial play in all directions. There should be no perceptible play.

e. Measure the connecting rod side clearance (**Figure 48**). Fully seat the feeler gauge

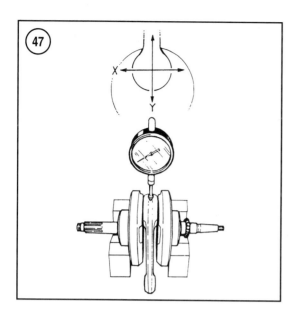

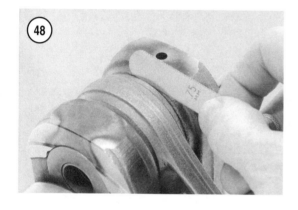

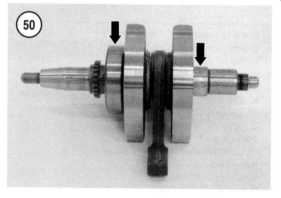

against the crankpin to make the measurement. Refer to **Table 1** for specifications.

NOTE
If the connecting rod must be replaced, the crankshaft and crankpin oil passages must be realigned with a maximum tolerance of 1 mm (0.040 in.) or less.

5. Measure the flywheel width (**Figure 49**). If the width exceeds the specification listed in **Table 1**,

have a dealership evaluate and possibly true the crankshaft.

6. Place the crankshaft in a flywheel alignment jig and measure crankshaft runout with a dial indicator. The jig centers should be inserted into the ends of the crankshaft. Measure at the two points shown in **Figure 50**. If the runout exceeds the specification listed in **Table 1**, have a dealership evaluate and possibly true the crankshaft.

NOTE
If it is known that the crankshaft was dropped or damaged, or if the engine exhibited abnormal vibration, have the crankshaft alignment checked before assembling the engine.

Tables 1 and 2 are on the following page.

Table 1 ENGINE LOWER END SPECIFICATIONS

	New mm (in.)	Service limit mm (in.)
Connecting rod		
Big end side clearance	0.32-0.64 (0.0126-0.0252)	1.0 (0.0394)
Big end radial clearance	0.010-0.025 (0.0004-0.0010)	–
Small end free play (tilt movement)	0.8 (0.0315)	–
Crankshaft		
Flywheel width	74.95-75.0 (2.9508-2.9528)	
Runout	–	0.03 (0.012)

Table 2 ENGINE LOWER END TORQUE SPECIFICATIONS

	N•m	in.-lb.	ft.-lb.
Bearing retainer screws	7	62	–
Crankcase bolts	10	88	–
Lower engine mounting bracket bolts	56	–	41
Lower oil pipe fitting	50	–	37
Lower oil pipe nut	35	–	26
Middle engine mounting bracket bolts	56	–	41
Neutral switch	20	–	15
Oil strainer and cover screws	7	62	–
Rear cam chain guide bolts	8	71	–
Reverse lever bolt	13	–	10
Reverse switch	20	–	15
Seal retainer bolts	10	88	–
Swing arm pivot nut	95	–	70
Upper engine mounting bracket to engine bolt	40	–	30
Upper engine mounting bracket to frame bolts	33	–	24
Upper oil pipe bolts	10	88	–

CHAPTER SIX

CLUTCH, GEARSHIFT LINKAGE AND LUBRICATION SYSTEM

This chapter provides service procedures for the following components on the right side of the engine:

1. Right crankcase cover.
2. Clutch.
3. Oil pump.
4. Balancer shaft driven gear.
5. Primary drive gears.
6. Speed sensor.
7. Shift lever.
8. External gearshift linkage.
9. Clutch cable replacement.

Read this chapter before attempting repairs to the components in the right crankcase cover. Become familiar with the procedures, photos and illustrations to understand the skill and equipment required. Refer to Chapter One for tool usage and techniques.

RIGHT CRANKCASE COVER

Removal and Installation

1. Remove the right footguard and peg (Chapter Fourteen).
2. Strap the brake pedal in the down position.
3. Drain the engine oil and remove the oil filter (Chapter Three).
4. Drain the cooling system (Chapter Three).
5. Remove the water pump (Chapter Ten).
6. Remove the front and rear oil pipes (A, **Figure 1**) from the case. Loosen the remaining connection points of the pipes to prevent bending during cover removal and installation.
7. Remove the clutch cable from the holder and release lever (B, **Figure 1**). Bend the small tab at the release lever to remove the cable.
8. Remove the 12 bolts from the perimeter of the crankcase cover.

    a. Since the cover bolts are different lengths, keep the bolts organized by making a drawing of the case on a piece of cardboard. As each bolt is removed, punch the bolt through the drawing at the appropriate location.

    b. One of the bolts is located inside the water pump cavity (A, **Figure 2**).

    c. The lower left bolt (B, **Figure 2**) cannot be removed from the cover until the cover is removed.

9. Pull the cover straight out. If necessary, lightly tap the cover to loosen it from the engine. It is normal for the clutch release lever to move since it is

disengaging from the clutch pull rod, located behind the cover.

10. Account for the two dowels that fit between the crankcase and cover (**Figure 3**).

11. Remove the cover gasket.

12. Inspect the cover assembly as described in this section.

13. Reverse these steps to install the right crankcase cover assembly. Note the following:

    a. Clean all residue and oil from the engine and cover gasket surfaces.

    b. Apply grease to the crankshaft oil seal, located in the cover.

    c. Install the dowels and a new cover gasket on the crankcase. To keep the gasket in place while installing the cover, apply small spots of sealant to the crankcase gasket surface. It is not necessary to apply sealant to the entire surface.

    d. Turn the clutch pull rod so the teeth point toward the rear (**Figure 4**).

    e. Apply molybdenum disulfide grease to the mating teeth on the clutch pull rod and release lever shaft.

    f. Rotate the clutch release lever *clockwise* until it is engaged with the spring, then turn the lever so it points to the back. Install the cover. As the cover is seated, the release lever should rotate *clockwise*, indicating that it is engaged. The spring pressure on the lever will be felt as the cover is seated.

    g. After the cover is seated, install a bolt at each side of the cover to hold it in place. Check the alignment marks on the release lever and cover (A, **Figure 5**). The marks should be closely, if not exactly, aligned. If the marks are severely misaligned, either remove the cover and reposition the release lever, or remove the snap ring from the top of the release lever shaft and reposition the lever and spring so they are aligned. Install the snap ring with the sharp edge facing out.

    h. Torque the crankcase cover bolts to 10 N•m (88 in.-lb.).

    i. Torque the rear oil pipe banjo bolts to 18 N•m (13 ft.-lb.).

    j. Torque the front oil pipe banjo bolts to 20 N•m (15 ft.-lb.).

    k. Adjust the clutch (Chapter Three).

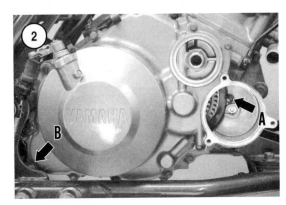

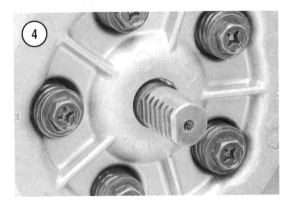

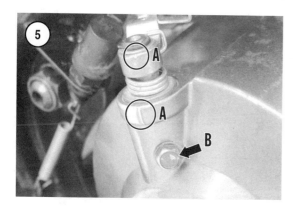

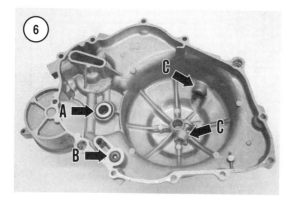

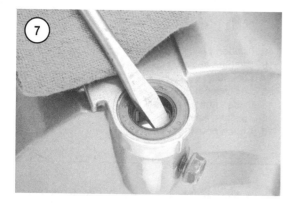

Inspection and Disassembly

1. Wipe the cover clean. Do not submerge the cover in solvent unless all bearing and seal assemblies are removed.

2. Inspect the crankshaft oil seal in the crankcase cover (A, **Figure 6**). This seal fits over the end of the crankshaft and must be in good condition. Oil under pressure passes into the end of the crankshaft, where it then goes to the crankpin and connecting rod. If this seal leaks, oil pressure will be reduced to these parts. Replace the seal as follows:

   a. Pry the seal from its bore.

   b. Lubricate the new seal with grease.

   c. Support the cover under the seal bore with a block of wood.

   d. Place the seal over the bore.

   e. Place a driver or socket over the seal. The driver should fit toward the perimeter of the seal.

   f. Drive the seal into place.

3. Inspect the oil check valve (B, **Figure 6**).

   a. The valve assembly and cavity should be clean.

   b. Apply light pressure on the ball and check that it opens and seats freely.

4. Inspect the clutch release lever seal and bearings (C, **Figure 6**).

   a. Remove the release lever shaft from the case by removing the retaining bolt (B, **Figure 5**). Inspect the release lever assembly as described in *Clutch Inspection* in this chapter.

   b. Inspect the seal. If oil leakage is evident, replace the seal. Pry the seal from its bore (**Figure 7**), then apply grease to the new seal. Seat the seal using a driver that fits on the perimeter of the seal.

   c. Inspect the bearings. If the upper bearing is damaged or worn, remove the seal and drive the bearing out of the bore. Lubricate the new bearing, then drive and seat it into the bore. Use a driver that fits on the perimeter of the bearing. Install the bearing with the manufacturer's marks facing up. If necessary, replace the lower bearing in a similar manner.

CLUTCH

The clutch assembly (**Figure 8**) consists of a clutch housing and a clutch hub. A set of clutch

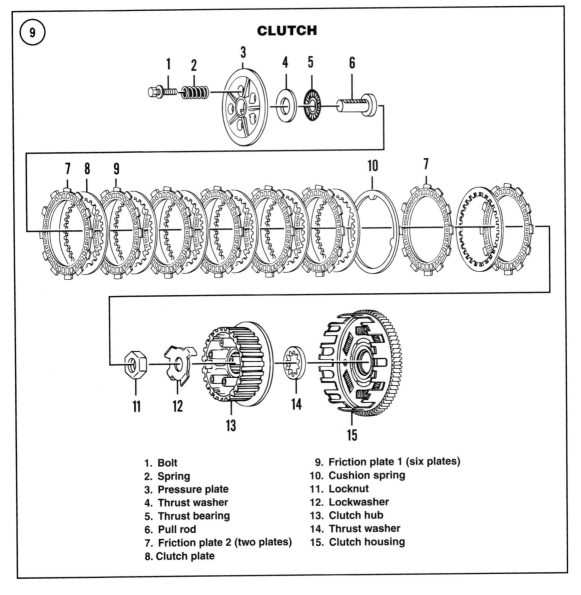

CLUTCH

1. Bolt
2. Spring
3. Pressure plate
4. Thrust washer
5. Thrust bearing
6. Pull rod
7. Friction plate 2 (two plates)
8. Clutch plate
9. Friction plate 1 (six plates)
10. Cushion spring
11. Locknut
12. Lockwasher
13. Clutch hub
14. Thrust washer
15. Clutch housing

plates and friction plates are alternately locked to the two parts. The gear-driven clutch housing is mounted on the transmission input shaft and can rotate freely. The housing receives power from the primary drive gear mounted on the crankshaft. As the clutch is engaged, the housing and friction plates transfer the power to the clutch plates, locked to the clutch hub. The clutch hub is splined to the input shaft and powers the transmission. The plate assembly is engaged by springs and disengaged by a cable-actuated release lever and pull rod assembly.

The clutch operates immersed in the engine oil supply. Oil additives should not be added to the oil supply, since these can cause poor clutch operation. The friction plates can also become contaminated.

Removal

Refer to **Figure 9**.

1. Remove the right crankcase cover as described in this chapter.

2. Remove the five bolts compressing the clutch springs (**Figure 10**). Make several passes to relieve the pressure equally on the bolts. Remove the bolts and springs from the clutch.

3. Hold the end of the pull rod and remove the pressure plate assembly. Remove the pull rod, thrust bearing and thrust washer from the pressure plate.

4. Remove the plates and cushion spring (between the plates) from the clutch housing and clutch hub (**Figure 11**).

5. Remove the clutch locknut as follows:

    a. Bend the lockwasher tab (**Figure 12**) away from the locknut.

    b. Attach a clutch holder tool to the clutch hub (**Figure 13**). If long enough, the tool can be braced against the frame.

CAUTION
Do not jam the gears with screwdrivers or other tools. This can cause gear breakage. A clutch holder tool (part No. YM-91042, 90890-04086) can be ordered from a Yamaha dealership.

    c. Using a 30 mm socket, loosen the locknut.

    d. Remove the clutch locknut and lockwasher.

6. Remove the clutch hub.

7. Remove the thrust washer (**Figure 14**) and clutch housing.

8. Inspect the clutch assembly as described in this section.

Inspection

Always replace clutch plates, friction plates or springs as a set if they do not meet specifications. If any part shows signs of wear or damage, replace it, regardless of its specification. Refer to the specifications listed in **Table 1** for component service limits, when applicable. Refer to **Figure 9**.

1. Clean the parts in solvent and dry with compressed air. Also clean the transmission shaft.

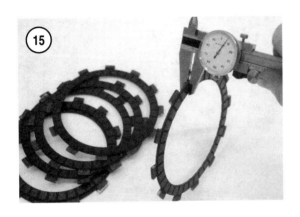

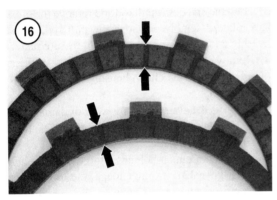

2. Measure the thickness of each friction plate (**Figure 15**). Measure at several locations around the perimeter.

    a. Note that there are two friction plates that are narrower than the other six friction plates (**Figure 16**). These plates have a different specification, as noted in **Table 1**. The plates also have specific positions in the clutch assembly.

3. Inspect the tabs on the friction plates (A, **Figure 17**). The tabs must not be damaged. Check that each plate slides smoothly in the clutch housing.

4. Measure each clutch plate for warping. Lay each plate on a surface plate, or thick piece of glass, and measure any gap around the perimeter of the plate (**Figure 18**).

5. Measure the thickness of each clutch plate (**Figure 19**). Measure at several locations around the perimeter.

6. Inspect the inner teeth on the clutch plates (A, **Figure 20**). The teeth must not be damaged. Check that each plate slides smoothly on the clutch hub.

7. Inspect both sides of the clutch housing (**Figure 21** and **Figure 22**).

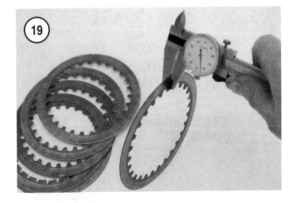

a. Inspect the surface of the housing bore for wear and damage. Check the fit of the housing on the transmission shaft. The housing should move freely, but have no obvious play.

b. Inspect the oil pockets in the housing bore for cleanliness.

c. Inspect the gear teeth for wear or damage.

d. Inspect the damper springs and rivets on both sides of the housing for looseness or damage.

e. Inspect the slots for nicks, wear and damage (B, **Figure 17**). The slots must be smooth and free of defects so the friction plates will smoothly engage and disengage. If chatter marks are evident, light damage can be smoothed using a fine-cut file or oilstone.

8. Inspect the clutch hub (**Figure 23**).

a. Inspect the shaft splines. The hub should fit on the transmission shaft with no obvious play.

b. Inspect the perimeter of the hub for wear and damage on the contact area.

c. Inspect the bosses for damage.

d. Inspect the outer splines for nicks, wear and damage (B, **Figure 20**). The splines must be smooth and free of defects so the clutch plates will smoothly engage and disengage. If chatter marks are evident, light damage can be smoothed using a fine-cut file or oilstone.

9. Measure the free length of each clutch spring (**Figure 24**).

10. Inspect the pressure plate (**Figure 25**).

a. Inspect the pressure plate for cracks, particularly around the bosses and bearing seat.

b. Inspect the perimeter of the pressure plate for wear and damage on the contact area.

11. Inspect the pull rod and release lever assembly (**Figure 26**).

a. Inspect the thrust bearing and washer for obvious wear or damage. Also inspect the pull rod surface that contacts the bearing.

b. Inspect the pull rod fit with the release lever teeth. Replace both parts if either part is damaged.

c. Inspect the release lever shaft for wear and fit in the cover bearing.

12. Inspect the bolts, thrust washer, cushion spring and nut for obvious damage. The cushion spring should be wavy.

13. Inspect the oil hole, splines, threads and polished surfaces on the transmission shaft for damage (**Figure 27**).

14. Install the clutch assembly as described in this section.

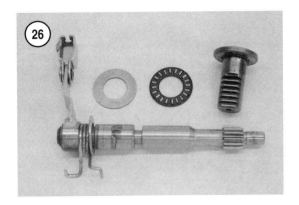

Installation

During assembly, lubricate the parts and transmission shaft with engine oil, unless specified otherwise. Refer to **Figure 9**.

1. Install the clutch housing.

2. Install the thrust washer.

3. Install the clutch hub. Align the index mark (**Figure 28**) on the hub so the mark points up.

4. Install a new lockwasher, engaging the tab with the slot in the hub (**Figure 29**).

5. Install and finger-tighten the locknut.

6. Torque and secure the clutch locknut as follows:

a. Attach a clutch holder tool to the clutch hub.

> *CAUTION*
> *Do not jam the gears with screwdrivers or other tools. This can cause gear breakage. A clutch holder tool (part No. YM-91042, 90890-04086) can be ordered from a Yamaha dealership.*

b. Using a 30 mm socket, torque the locknut to 90 N•m (66 ft.-lb.).

c. Flatten one side of the lockwasher against the nut (**Figure 12**).

7. Install the plates into the clutch housing and clutch hub as follows:

> *NOTE*
> *Refer to **Figure 9** and identify the locations for friction plate 2 (narrow plates) and the cushion spring. The two plates and spring must be installed in the positions indicated.*

a. Lubricate the plates with engine oil. To prevent possible seizure, particularly with new friction plates, it is important that the face of the friction plates be completely coated with oil. If possible, allow the plates to soak in engine oil prior to installation.

b. Beginning with a friction plate, alternately install friction plates and clutch plates into the clutch housing and clutch hub.

8. Apply molybdenum disulfide grease to the thrust bearing and thrust washer, then install the parts onto the clutch pull rod.

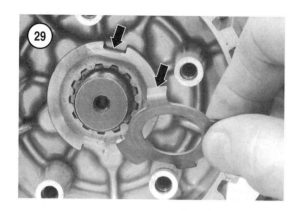

9. Insert the pull rod into the pressure plate.

10. Install the pressure plate, aligning the arrow (**Figure 30**) on the plate with the index mark on the clutch hub. Seat the pressure plate in this position.

11. Lock the pressure plate to the clutch hub as follows:

    a. Install the clutch springs on the hub bosses.

    b. Finger-tighten the five bolts.

    c. Tighten the bolts, working in a crossing pattern. Make several passes so all bolts are

tightened in equal steps. Torque the bolts to 8 N•m (71 in.-lb.).

12. If removed, install the clutch release lever into the right crankcase cover, then install the cover as described in this chapter.

OIL PUMP

The oil pump (**Figure 31**) is driven by a gear on the back of the clutch housing. The clutch assembly must be removed to service the oil pump.

Removal and Installation

Refer to **Figure 32**.

1. Remove the right crankcase cover and clutch assembly as described in this chapter.

2. Remove the snap ring and driven gear from the shaft (**Figure 33**).

3. Remove the three mounting bolts and the oil pump (**Figure 34**).

4. Remove the gasket and two O-rings (**Figure 35**).

5. Disassemble, inspect and assemble the oil pump as described in this section.

6. Reverse these steps to install the oil pump. Note the following:

    a. Fill the pump with engine oil prior to mounting.

    b. Install a new oil pump gasket and O-rings.

    c. Apply threadlocking compound to the threads of the mounting bolts before installing.

    d. Torque the mounting bolts to 10 N•m (88 in.-lb.).

    e. Install the driven gear with the dished side facing out.

    f. Install a new snap ring with the sharp edge facing out.

7. Install the clutch and right crankcase cover as described in this chapter.

Disassembly and Assembly

Refer to **Figure 32**.

1. Remove the retaining screw from the back of the pump, then disassemble the pump (**Figure 36**).

2. Inspect the parts as described in this section.

3. Assemble the pump as follows:

    a. Lubricate the parts with engine oil.

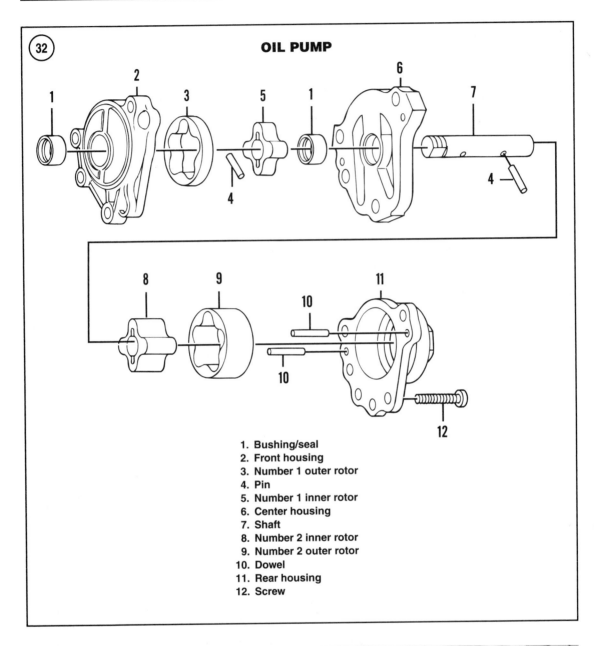

OIL PUMP

1. Bushing/seal
2. Front housing
3. Number 1 outer rotor
4. Pin
5. Number 1 inner rotor
6. Center housing
7. Shaft
8. Number 2 inner rotor
9. Number 2 outer rotor
10. Dowel
11. Rear housing
12. Screw

b. Install the number 2 rotor set into the rear housing, with the rotor marks aligned (**Figure 37**).

c. Install the shaft and pin, engaging the pin with the inner rotor. The grooves on the shaft should face out.

d. Install the dowels and center housing, with the bushing seal facing out.

e. Install the number 1 inner rotor with the pin groove facing out, then install the pin (**Figure 38**).

f. Install the number 1 outer rotor. There is no alignment required for this rotor set.

g. Install the front housing, with the bushing seal facing out.

h. With the assembly held tight, check that the three grooves on the shaft are visible (**Figure 39**). If not, check assembly. Usually, the number 1 inner rotor is installed backwards.

i. Apply threadlocking compound to the threads of the retaining screw, then install and tighten the screw.

j. Check that the pump shaft turns freely and smoothly.

k. Install the oil pump and driven gear as described in this section.

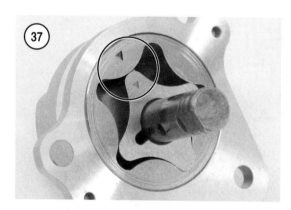

Inspection

1. Clean the parts in solvent.

2. Visually inspect all parts for obvious wear or damage.

3. Inspect the pump shaft, gear and pins (**Figure 40**) for wear or scoring.

   a. The pins should firmly fit in the shaft.

   b. The pump shaft should fit in the pump housings with minimal perceptible play.

  c. If the gear is worn or damaged, also inspect the gear on the clutch housing.

4. Inspect the rotor sets.

  a. Inspect each rotor set for wear or scoring (**Figure 41**). When assembled, the inner rotor and pin should firmly fit on the shaft.

  b. Check the clearance at the inner rotor tip and at the outer rotor-to-housing (**Figure 42**). Refer to **Table 2** for specifications.

5. Assemble the oil pump as described in this section.

BALANCER SHAFT DRIVEN GEAR

The balancer shaft driven gear (A, **Figure 43**) is meshed with the primary drive gear assembly (B). The clutch assembly must be removed to service the balancer shaft driven gear.

Removal and Installation

1. Remove the right crankcase cover and clutch assembly as described in this chapter.

2. Remove the driven gear locknut as follows:

  a. If the primary drive gear assembly will not be removed, turn the crankshaft so the synchronization marks on the driven gear and primary drive gear are aligned (**Figure 44**).

  b. Bend the lockwasher tab (**Figure 45**) away from the locknut.

  c. Hold the crankshaft steady at the rotor nut (**Figure 46**).

  d. Using a 30 mm socket, loosen the locknut.

  e. Remove the locknut, lockwasher, gear and Woodruff key.

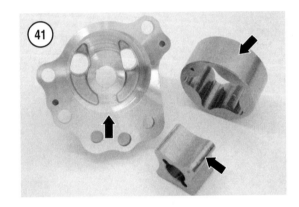

CAUTION
After the gear is removed, the balancer shaft weight will hang freely. With the weight in the down position, use caution if it is necessary to turn the crankshaft. The weight will jam against the crankshaft unless the weight is first pivoted rearward.

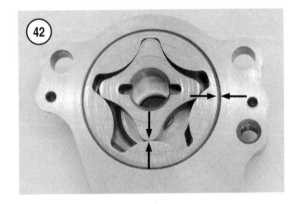

3. Inspect the parts.

  a. Clean the parts and shaft with solvent.

  b. Inspect the gear for worn or broken teeth.

  c. Check the fit of the key in the gear and balancer shaft (**Figure 47**). The key must fit in all parts with no play.

d. Inspect the shaft threads.

4. Install the parts as follows:

   a. Install the Woodruff key onto the shaft.

   b. If not already positioned, turn the crankshaft so the synchronization marks on the driven gear and primary drive gear can be aligned (**Figure 44**). Turn the shafts and seat the driven gear when alignment is verified.

   c. Install a new lockwasher, engaging the tab with the slot in the shaft (**Figure 48**).

   d. Lubricate the shaft threads with molybdenum disulfide grease.

   e. Install and finger-tighten the locknut.

5. Torque and secure the locknut as follows:

   a. Hold the crankshaft steady at the primary drive gear nut (B, **Figure 43**). If the primary drive gear assembly is not installed, the locknuts for both the primary drive gear assembly and balancer shaft driven gear can be tightened at the same time. Each locknut can be held while the other locknut is torqued.

   b. Using a 30 mm socket and torque wrench, torque the locknut to 140 N•m (103 ft.-lb.).

   c. Flatten one tab of the lockwasher against the nut (**Figure 45**).

6. Install the clutch and right crankcase cover as described in this chapter.

PRIMARY DRIVE GEARS

The primary drive gear assembly (B, **Figure 43**) is meshed with the balancer shaft driven gear and the clutch housing. The clutch assembly must be removed to service the primary drive gears.

Removal and Installation

1. Remove the right crankcase cover and clutch assembly as described in this chapter.
2. Remove the drive gear locknut as follows:
   a. Bend the lockwasher tab (**Figure 49**) away from the locknut.
   b. Hold the crankshaft steady at the rotor nut (**Figure 46**).
   c. Using a 30 mm socket, loosen the locknut.
   d. Remove the locknut, lockwasher, gear assembly, plate, Woodruff key and washer (**Figure 50**).

> *CAUTION*
> *After the gear assembly is removed, the balancer shaft weight will hang freely. With the weight in the down position, use caution if it is necessary to turn the crankshaft. The weight will jam against the crankshaft unless the weight is first pivoted rearward.*

3. Inspect and repair the parts as described in this section.
4. Install the parts (**Figure 51**) as follows:
   a. Install the washer and Woodruff key onto the shaft.
   b. Install the plate.
   c. If not already positioned, turn the crankshaft so the synchronization marks on the gear assembly and balancer shaft driven gear can be aligned (**Figure 44**). Turn the shafts and seat the gear assembly when alignment is verified. If the balancer shaft driven gear is not installed, synchronization can be performed during installation of that part.
   d. Install the lockwasher, engaging the tab with the slot in the shaft (**Figure 52**).
   e. Lubricate the shaft threads with molybdenum disulfide grease.
   f. Install and finger-tighten the locknut.
5. Torque and secure the locknut as follows:
   a. Hold the crankshaft steady at the balancer shaft locknut (A, **Figure 43**). If the balancer shaft driven gear is not installed, the locknuts for both the primary drive gear assembly and balancer shaft driven gear can be tightened at the same time. Each locknut can be held while the other locknut is torqued.
   b. Using a 30 mm socket, torque the locknut to 150 N•m (111 ft.-lb.).

c. Flatten one tab of the lockwasher against the nut (**Figure 49**).

6. Install the clutch and right crankcase cover as described in this chapter.

Inspection

1. Clean the parts and shaft with solvent.

2. Inspect the gears for worn or broken teeth.

3. Inspect the springs and pins located between the two gears (**Figure 53**). The springs should be lightly compressed and the pins should be loose. If damaged or missing, the pins and springs are replaced as follows:

    a. Lightly tap the gears to begin separation (**Figure 54**). To prevent the loss of small parts, disassemble the gears in a large bag.

    b. Separate the gears and replace the dowels and springs, as required.

    c. Locate the alignment marks on both gears (**Figure 55**).

    d. Align and assemble the gears.

4. Inspect the key, plate, washer and nut for obvious damage.

5. Inspect the shaft (**Figure 56**).

    a. Check the fit of the key in the shaft and gear. The key must fit in all parts with no play.

    b. Inspect the oil hole in the end of the shaft for cleanliness.

    c. Inspect the shaft threads.

6. Install the primary drive gears as described in this chapter.

SPEED SENSOR

The speed sensor limits engine speed when the transmission is in reverse. Continuous, high engine speed will cause the sensor to temporarily shut off the CDI unit. When engine speed drops to a safe level, the CDI unit continues operation. The sensor is located at the rear of the engine case and the rotor is mounted on the transmission output shaft (**Figure 57**). The clutch assembly must be removed to service the speed sensor rotor.

Removal and Installation

1. Remove the right crankcase cover and clutch assembly as described in this chapter.

2. To remove the rotor, remove the outer snap ring, washer, wave washer and rotor. If the crankcase will be split, also remove the inner snap ring.

3. Clean the parts in solvent.

4. If necessary, remove the bolt and sensor from the engine case.

5. Inspect the parts (**Figure 58**) for obvious wear and damage. The wave washer should not be flat. The washer is distorted so it will apply light pressure to the rotor when the parts are installed

6. Reverse this procedure to install the parts. Note the following:

    a. Install new snap rings.

    b. Install the inner snap ring with the sharp edge facing in.

    c. Install the outer snap ring with the sharp edge facing out.

SHIFT LEVER

The shift lever pivots on the left footpeg and is clamped to the transmission shift shaft. The following procedure provides steps for partial and complete removal of the linkage and pedal from the machine.

Removal and Installation

1. If only the shift lever linkage must be removed from the shift shaft, do the following:

    a. Completely remove the linkage bolt (**Figure 59**), then remove the linkage from the shaft.

    b. To install the linkage onto the shift shaft, install the linkage so the gap is aligned level with the center of the shift shaft (**Figure 60**).

    c. Torque the bolt to 10 N•m (88 in.-lb.).

2. If complete removal of the shift lever assembly is necessary, do the following:

    a. Remove the bolts securing the left footpeg to the footguard.

    b. Remove the bolts securing the footpeg to the frame.

    c. Remove the shift lever linkage as described in Step 1.

    d. Disassemble, clean and lubricate the pivot as described in this section.

    e. Reverse these steps to install the shift lever assembly.

    f. Check pedal height adjustment (Chapter Three).

Inspection

1. Remove the E-clip from the lever shaft, then remove the lever and washers.

2. Carefully pry the seals out of each side of the bore, then clean the shaft and parts (**Figure 61**).

3. Inspect the parts for obvious wear and damage. If water or grit has been in the bore, replace the seals.

4. Lubricate the parts.

   a. Lubricate the shaft and seals with waterproof grease.

   b. Lubricate the pivot joints with waterproof grease or engine oil.

5. Press the seals into the bore by hand.

6. Assemble the parts, installing a new E-clip with the sharp edge facing out.

EXTERNAL GEARSHIFT LINKAGE

The external shift mechanism includes all that are not within the crankcase halves (**Figure 62**).

Removal

1. Remove the right crankcase cover and clutch assembly as described in this chapter.

2. Put the transmission in neutral, then remove the shift lever from the shift shaft as described in this chapter.

3. Slowly pull the shift shaft, torsion spring, spacer and washer from the engine (**Figure 63**).

4. Remove the roller from the lever (**Figure 64**).

5. Remove the spring and stopper lever (**Figure 65**). Account for the bushing in the stopper lever.

6. Remove the bolts securing the shift guide and lever assembly (**Figure 66**). To prevent the loss of internal parts, note the following:

a. As the bolts are removed, hold the shift guide in place to prevent the lever assembly from falling.

b. When the bolts are removed, slowly pull the guide and lever assembly from the shift drum stopper.

c. When the spring-loaded pawls are visible at the rear of the lever, grasp the pawls to prevent the pawl pins and springs from ejecting.

7. Remove the center bolt and shift drum stopper (**Figure 67**).

8. Inspect the parts as described in this section.

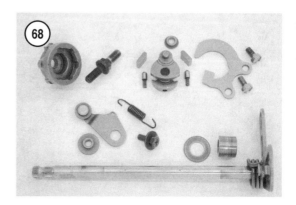

Inspection

During inspection, replace all parts that are obviously worn or damaged.

1. Clean all parts in solvent, then group the assemblies (**Figure 68**).

2. Inspect the shift shaft assembly (**Figure 69**).

a. Inspect the shaft for straightness.

b. Inspect the shaft splines for damage.

c. Inspect the roller engagement hole for wear. The hole should be symmetrical and not excessively worn.

d. Inspect the torsion spring for wear and fatigue cracks. If the spring is worn, inspect the condition of the spring post (**Figure 70**).

e. Inspect the spacer and washer for obvious wear and damage.

3. Inspect the stopper lever assembly (**Figure 71**).

a. Inspect the roller on the lever. It must be symmetrical and turn freely, but be firmly attached to the lever.

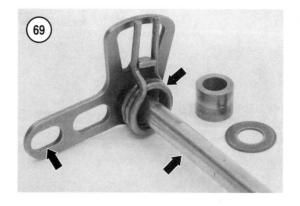

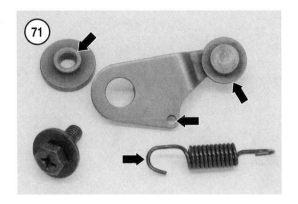

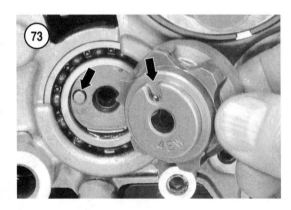

b. Inspect the fit of the shouldered bushing in the lever pivot. The bushing must fit in the pivot firmly, with minimal play.

c. Inspect the spring for wear or fatigue.

d. Inspect the bolt and washer for obvious wear and damage.

4. Inspect the shift drum stopper and center bolt (**Figure 72**).

   a. Inspect the shift detents and ramps on the outside of the shift drum stopper. The detents and ramps must not be worn, or shifting will be imprecise.

   b. Inspect the detents inside the shift drum stopper. If the depressions are rounded at their shoulders, the pawls in the shift lever assembly can slip.

   c. Inspect the fit of the shift drum stopper on the shift drum pin (**Figure 73**). The pin must be in good condition in order to properly engage with the notch in the back of the shift drum stopper.

   d. Inspect the center bolt. The smooth part of the bolt must be smooth to allow the lever to pivot.

5. Inspect the lever, roller and shift guide (**Figure 74**).

   a. The roller should be symmetrical, with no perceptible wear. The roller and lever must fit together firmly, with minimal play.

   b. Inspect the shift guide for obvious wear.

6. Inspect the lever and pawl assembly (**Figure 75**).

   a. Inspect the springs and pawl pins for wear and fatigue.

   b. Inspect the pawls for wear at their square end. The ends must be square in order to stay engaged in the shift drum stopper.

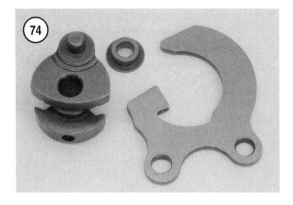

c. Assemble the lever and pawl assembly (**Figure 76**), then insert it into the shift drum stopper. Check that the springs fully extend the pawls against the sides of the shift drum stopper.

Installation

1. Install the shift drum stopper and center bolt (**Figure 67**). Note the following:
   a. Engage the shift drum pin with the notch in the shift drum stopper (**Figure 73**).
   b. Torque the center bolt to 30 N•m (22 ft.-lb.).
   c. Check that the transmission is in neutral. The neutral detent on the shift drum stopper should be near vertical. If necessary, turn the transmissions shafts and shift to the neutral position.
2. Install the shift guide and lever assembly (**Figure 66**). Note the following:
   a. Apply threadlocking compound to the bolt threads, then place the bolts within reach of the installation point.
   b. Insert the springs, pawl pins and pawls into the lever. Check that the rounded ends of the pawls are seated in the lever (**Figure 76**). The pawls must compress and retract smoothly in the lever.
   c. Compress the pawls and install the shift guide onto the assembly (**Figure 77**).
   d. Install the assembly into the shift drum stopper. The lever should be positioned as shown in **Figure 66**. Hold the assembly in place and install the bolts.
   e. Torque the bolts to 10 N•m (88 in.-lb.).
3. Install the stopper lever assembly (**Figure 65**). Note the following:
   a. Insert the bushing from the back of the stopper lever.
   b. Torque the bolt to 10 N•m (88 in.-lb.).
   c. Install the spring.
   d. Check that the roller on the stopper lever is engaged with the neutral detent on the shift drum stopper. If necessary, place the transmission in the neutral position.
4. Install the roller onto the lever (**Figure 64**).
5. Install the shift shaft assembly (**Figure 63**). Note the following:
   a. Slide the spacer completely under the torsion spring, then install the washer.

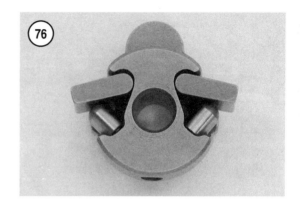

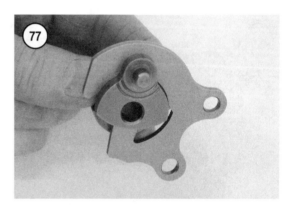

   b. Lubricate the shaft and slowly slide it through the engine cases. As the lever and spring approach the engine, engage the torsion spring with the post and the lever with the roller (**Figure 78**).

6. Temporarily install the shift lever and check for proper shifting.

   a. When installing the shift lever, the shift shaft will want to push out of the crankcase. If possible, have an assistant hold the shaft in place while the lever is installed.

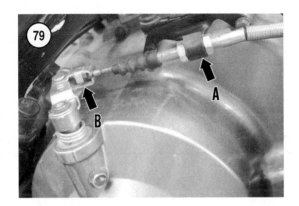

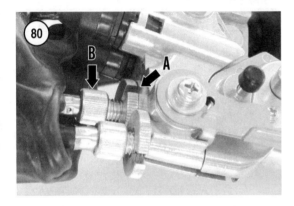

a. Loosen the locknuts and remove the clutch cable from the holder (A, **Figure 79**).

b. Bend the small tab (B, **Figure 79**) at the release lever and remove the cable.

2. Remove the cable at the handlebar as follows:

a. Pull back the dust cover from the clutch lever.

b. Loosen the clutch cable locknut (A, **Figure 80**), then turn the adjuster (B) in until the cable can be removed from the lever and the slots in the adjuster assembly.

3. Remove the cable from the machine, noting the routing of the cable.

4. Clean the levers and clutch lever housing.

5. Lubricate the new cable with an aerosol cable lubricant. Lubricate the cable ends with lithium grease.

6. Route the cable from the engine to the handlebar lever.

7. At the engine, place the cable in the cable holder, then attach the cable end to the release lever. Do not center the cable at this time.

8. At the handlebar, attach the cable to the lever and thread the adjuster to the center of its travel.

9. At the engine, center the adjuster and locknuts in the cable holder.

10. Bend the small tab down, trapping the cable in the release lever.

11. Adjust the clutch cable (Chapter Three).

b. If working alone, bolt a simple brace across the right end of the shaft. Use one of the crankcase bolt holes to secure the brace.

7. Install the clutch and right crankcase cover as described in this chapter.

CLUTCH CABLE REPLACEMENT

1. Remove the cable at the engine as follows:

Table 1 CLUTCH SPECIFICATIONS

	New mm (in.)	Service limit mm (in.)
Friction plate 1 thickness (six plates)	2.74-3.86 (0.108-0.113)	2.6 (0.102)
Friction plate 2 thickness (two plates)	2.94-3.06 (0.116-0.120)	2.8 (0.110)
Steel plate thickness (seven plates)	1.1-1.3 (0.043-0.051)	–
Steel plate warpage	–	0.2 (0.008)
Spring free length	42.8 (1.69)	40.7 (1.60)

Table 2 OIL PUMP SPECIFICATIONS

	New mm (in.)	Service limit mm (in.)
Lubrication system	Troichoid pump, forced pressure, dry sump	
Oil pump		
Inner rotor tip clearance	0.12 (0.005)	0.20 (0.008)
Outer rotor-to-housing (side) clearance	0.03-0.08 (0.001-0.003)	–
Oil pressure at 1500 rpm	65 kPa (9.4 psi)	
Bypass valve set pressure	80-120 kPa (11.6-17.4 psi)	

Table 3 CLUTCH TORQUE SPECIFICATIONS

	N•m	in.-lb.	ft.-lb.
Balancer shaft driven gear locknut	140	–	103
Banjo bolts			
Front oil pipe	20	–	15
Rear oil pipe	18	–	13
Clutch locknut	90	–	66
Clutch springs	8	71	–
Crankcase cover bolts	10	88	–
Oil pump mounting bolts	10	88	–
Primary drive gear locknut	150	–	111
Shift drum stopper center bolt	30	–	22
Shift guide bolts	10	88	–
Shift lever bolt	10	88	–
Stopper lever bolt	10	88	–

CHAPTER SEVEN

TRANSMISSION AND INTERNAL SHIFT MECHANISM

This chapter provides service procedures for the transmission and internal shift mechanism. Read this chapter and become familiar with the procedures, photos and illustrations to understand the skill and equipment required. Refer to Chapter Five for transmission removal and installation. Refer to Chapter One for tool usage and techniques.

TRANSMISSION OPERATION

The machine is equipped with a five-speed constant-mesh transmission, plus a reverse gear. The gears on the input shaft (A, **Figure 1**) are meshed with the gears on the output shaft (B). Each pair of meshed gears represents one gear ratio. For each pair of gears, one of the gears is splined to its shaft, while the other gear freewheels on its shaft.

Next to each freewheeling gear is a gear that is splined to the shaft. This locked gear can slide on the shaft and lock into the freewheeling gear, making that gear ratio active. Anytime the transmission is in gear, one pair of meshed gears are locked to their shafts, and that gear ratio is selected. All other meshed gears have one freewheeling gear, making those ratios inoperative.

To engage and disengage the various gear ratios, the splined gears are moved by shift forks. The shift forks are guided by the shift drum, which is operated by the shift lever. As the machine is upshifted and downshifted, the shift drum rotates and guides the forks to engage and disengage pairs of gears on the transmission shafts.

SERVICE NOTES

The engine crankcase must be split to remove the transmission and shift assemblies (**Figure 2**). Remove and install the transmission assemblies as described in *Crankcase* in Chapter Five.

After the transmission is removed from the crankcase, disassembly, inspection and assembly can be performed. Careful inspection of the parts is required, as well as keeping the parts oriented so they can be reinstalled in the correct direction on the shafts. If necessary, slide the parts onto a long dowel or screwdriver as the parts are removed, or make an identification mark on each part to indicate position and orientation.

Always install new snap rings. The snap rings will fatigue and distort when they are removed. Do not reuse them, although they appear to be in good condition. To install a new snap ring without distorting it, hold the closed side of the snap ring with a pair of pliers while the open side is spread with snap ring pliers (**Figure 3**). While holding the spread ring with both tools, slide it over the shaft and into position. This technique is particularly useful when removing the notched-type snap ring shown in **Figure 3**. During removal or installation, this type of snap ring tends to bind and grip the shaft. Avoid excessive spreading of the snap ring during installation. Spread the snap ring only enough to slide it down the shaft. If necessary, practice the technique prior to final assembly with a discarded snap ring.

Usually, snap rings have one rounded edge, while the other side has a sharp edge (**Figure 4**). The inner sharp edge prevents the snap ring from lifting out of the shaft groove when lateral pressure is applied to the snap ring. Always look at the inner and outer edges of the snap ring. Some snap rings are manufactured with the inner and outer sharp edge on opposite sides. If a snap ring has no identifiable sharp edge, the snap ring can be installed in either direction. When a snap ring is installed on a splined shaft, the snap ring gap should be positioned over a groove in the shaft (**Figure 5**).

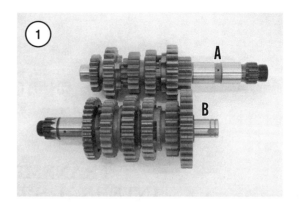

NOTE
*For all the snap rings used on the input and output shafts in this transmission, Yamaha recommends positioning the sharp edge of the snap ring away from the adjacent spline washer, regardless of the direction of thrust. Although both inner edges appear identical on the notched snap rings, identify the sharpest barb (**Figure 6**) on the snap ring. Position this side of the snap ring away from the spline washer.*

EARLY AND LATE
TRANSMISSION DIFFERENCES

For 2002-on models, the gear ratios were changed for first, second, third and reverse gears. Refer to **Table 1** for the ratio changes. In addition to these changes, the actual design of second and fourth gears was changed. On the input shaft, fourth gear was changed from six recesses to four recesses, and second gear was changed from three dogs to four dogs (**Figure 7**). On the output shaft, second gear was changed from six recesses to four recesses,

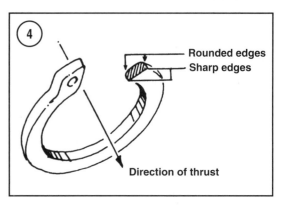

Rounded edges
Sharp edges

Direction of thrust

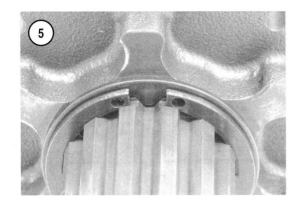

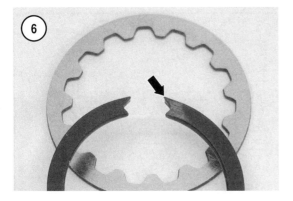

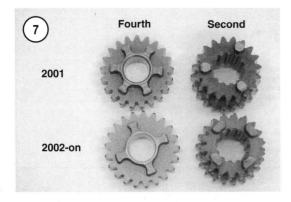

Fourth   Second

2001

2002-on

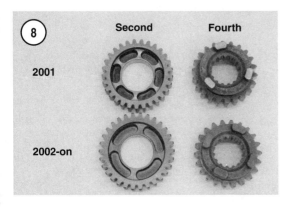

Second   Fourth

2001

2002-on

and fourth gear was changed from three dogs to four dogs (**Figure 8**).

If the later gear ratios are desired for a 2001 model, the conversion can be made by replacing all gears, input shaft and center shift fork. Although fifth gear on the input shaft is not a revised part number, use of the original gear with a new gear set is not recommended.

The shift drum, left shift fork, right shift fork, fork shafts, reverse gear shaft, output shaft and washers can be reused if they are in good condition. Replace all snap rings and bushings.

INPUT SHAFT

Use the following procedures to disassemble and assemble the input shaft. Refer to **Figure 9** for part identifications and locations on the shaft.

Disassembly

> *NOTE*
> *The input shaft is a press-fitted assem-*
> *bly. To disassemble the shaft, a hy-*
> *draulic press is required to remove*
> *reverse gear from the end of the shaft*
> *(**Figure 10**). The press is also re-*
> *quired to accurately press the gear*
> *onto the shaft after assembly. If the*
> *equipment and skill are not available*
> *to perform these procedures, have the*
> *gear removed and installed by a deal-*
> *ership or machine shop.*

Remove the parts from the input shaft in the order below. Keep parts oriented and note their direction and original location on the shaft. Preferably, mark the outer face of each part as it is removed from the shaft.

1. Measure and record the clearance between fourth gear and where it contacts the splined edge of the shaft (**Figure 11**). This clearance will aid assembly.

2. Using a hydraulic press, drive the shaft out of reverse gear.

3. Disassemble the input shaft in the following order:

  a. Reverse gear.

  b. Fourth gear.

  c. Second and third gear.

  d. Snap ring.

  e. Spline washer.

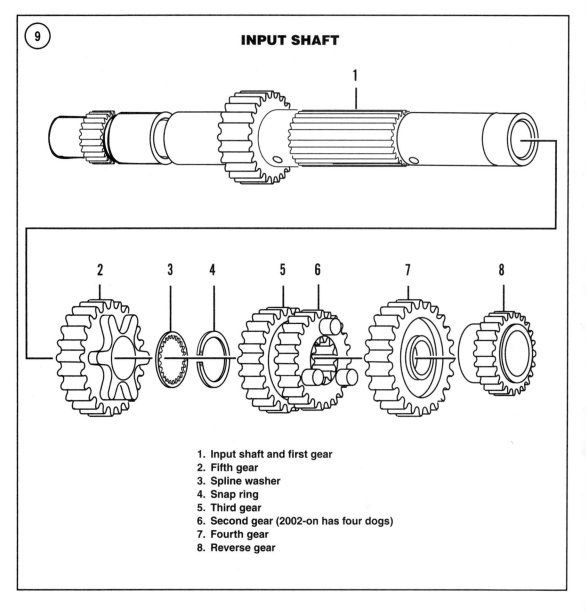

⑨   **INPUT SHAFT**

1. Input shaft and first gear
2. Fifth gear
3. Spline washer
4. Snap ring
5. Third gear
6. Second gear (2002-on has four dogs)
7. Fourth gear
8. Reverse gear

f. Fifth gear.

4. Inspect each part as described in this chapter, then return it to its place until assembly.

Assembly

Before beginning assembly, have a new snap ring on hand. Throughout the procedure, the orientation of many parts is made in relation to first gear, on the input shaft. If desired, lock the lower portion of the shaft (below first gear) in a *padded* vise. With the shaft held stable and vertical, installation of the snap ring will be easier. Do not allow the vise to damage the shaft.

NOTE
*Refer to **Service Notes** in this chapter for the recommended snap ring installation technique.*

1. Clean and dry all parts before assembly. Lubricate all parts with engine oil.

2. Install fifth gear. The gear recesses must face *out* (away from first gear).

3. Install the spline washer.

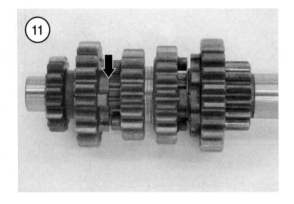

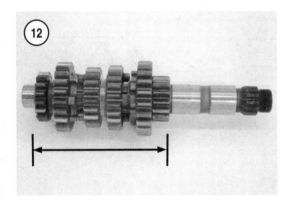

6. Install fourth gear. The flat side must face *out* (away from first gear).

7. If available, use a heat gun to warm reverse gear prior to installing it on the shaft. The heat will slightly expand the gear and aid in driving it into position.

8. Install reverse gear. The flat side must face *out* (away from first gear). Note the following:

    a. Refer to the clearance measured during Step 1 of disassembly (**Figure 11**). While pressing the gear into place, hold a feeler gauge that is this clearance, or slightly larger, in the gap between the gear and the shaft to prevent reverse gear from jamming against fourth gear.

    b. Remove the feeler gauge and measure the total installed length of the gear set. The measurement must be between 115.65-115.85 mm (4.553-4.561 in.). Measure close to the shaft and against the widest part of the gears (**Figure 12**).

9. Check that all parts are secure and that the gears spin, slide and engage freely on the shaft. Wrap and store the assembly until it is ready for installation into the crankcase. Install the complete transmission assembly as described in Chapter Five.

OUTPUT SHAFT

Use the following procedures to disassemble and assemble the output shaft. Refer to **Figure 13** for part identifications and locations on the shaft.

Disassembly

Keep parts oriented and note their direction and original location on the shaft. Preferably, mark the outer face of each part as it is removed from the shaft.

1. Disassemble the output shaft in the following order:

    a. Washer.
    b. First gear.
    c. Fifth gear.
    d. Snap ring.
    e. Spline washer.
    f. Third gear.
    g. Third gear bushing.
    h. Splined lockwasher.
    i. Splined lockwasher retainer.
    j. Second gear.
    k. Second gear bushing.

4. Install the snap ring. The sharp edge of the snap ring must face *out* (away from first gear) The snap ring must seat in the shaft groove. Position the snap ring gap over a groove in the shaft (**Figure 5**).

5. Install second and third gear. Second gear must face *out* (away from first gear). Second gear has fewer teeth and is smaller in diameter than third gear.

    a. For the 2001 model, second gear has three dogs, as shown in **Figure 9**.

    b. For 2002-on models, second gear has four dogs.

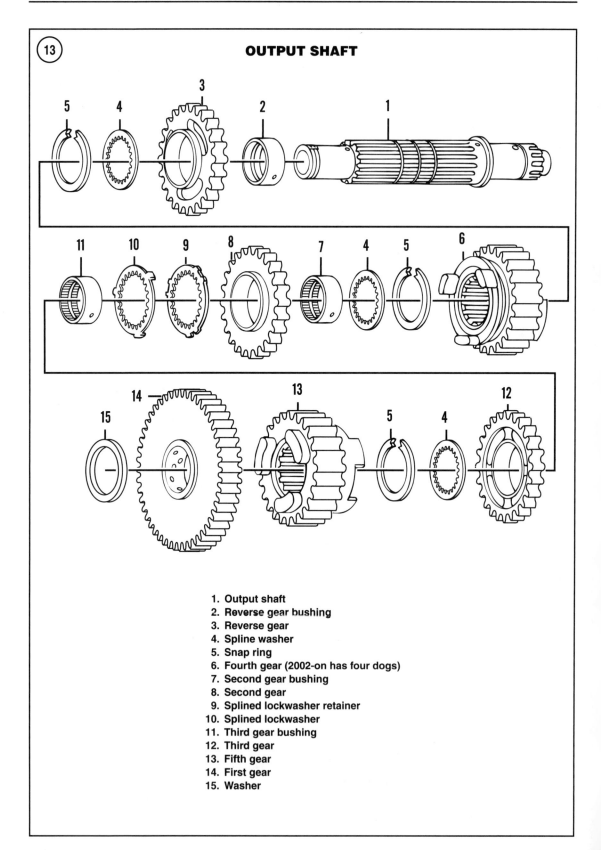

OUTPUT SHAFT

1. Output shaft
2. Reverse gear bushing
3. Reverse gear
4. Spline washer
5. Snap ring
6. Fourth gear (2002-on has four dogs)
7. Second gear bushing
8. Second gear
9. Splined lockwasher retainer
10. Splined lockwasher
11. Third gear bushing
12. Third gear
13. Fifth gear
14. First gear
15. Washer

l. Spline washer.

m. Snap ring.

n. Fourth gear.

o. Snap ring.

p. Spline washer.

q. Reverse gear.

r. Reverse gear bushing.

2. Inspect each part as described in this chapter, then return it to its place until assembly.

Assembly

Before beginning assembly, have new snap rings on hand. Throughout the procedure, the orientation of the parts is made in relation to the splined end of the shaft, where the drive sprocket is mounted. If desired, lock the splined end of the shaft in a *padded* vise. With the shaft held stable and vertical, installation of the snap rings will be easier. Do not allow the vise to damage the shaft.

NOTE
*Refer to **Service Notes** in this chapter for the recommended snap ring installation technique.*

1. Clean and dry all parts before assembly. Lubricate all parts with engine oil.

2. Install the reverse gear bushing.

3. Install reverse gear. The gear recesses must face *out* (away from splined end).

4. Install the spline washer.

5. Install the snap ring. The sharp edge of the snap ring must face *out* (away from splined end) The snap ring must seat in the shaft groove. Position the snap ring gap over a groove in the shaft (**Figure 5**).

6. Install fourth gear. The side of the gear with the shift fork groove must face *out* (away from splined end).

    a. For the 2001 model, fourth gear has three dogs facing out, as shown in **Figure 13**.

    b. For 2002-on models, second gear has four dogs facing out.

7. Install the snap ring. The sharp edge of the snap ring must face *in* (toward splined end) The snap ring must seat in the shaft groove. Position the snap ring gap over a groove in the shaft (**Figure 5**).

8. Install the spline washer.

9. Install the second gear bushing. Align the oil hole in the bushing with the oil hole in the shaft (**Figure 14**).

10. Install second gear. The flat side must face *out* (away from splined end).

11. Install the splined lockwasher retainer.

12. Install the splined lockwasher, engaging the tabs with the retainer.

13. Install the third gear bushing. Align the oil hole in the bushing with the oil hole in the shaft (**Figure 14**).

14. Install third gear. The gear recesses must face *out* (away from splined end).

15. Install the spline washer.

16. Install the snap ring. The sharp edge of the snap ring must face *out* (away from splined end) The snap ring must seat in the shaft groove. Position the snap ring gap over a groove in the shaft (**Figure 5**).

17. Install fifth gear. The side of the gear with the shift fork groove must face *in* (toward splined end).

18. Install first gear. The flat side must face *out* (away from splined end).

19. Install the washer.

20. With the parts in their correct positions, wrap a strong rubber band around the end of the shaft. Check that all parts are secure and that the gears spin, slide and engage freely on the shaft. Wrap and store the assembly until it is ready for installation into the crankcase. Install the complete transmission assembly as described in Chapter Five

TRANSMISSION INSPECTION

Use the following procedures to inspect the shaft assemblies for all models. If the shafts are not disassembled, many of the checks can be performed by spreading the gears and visually inspecting the condition of the parts. Before inspection, clean all parts

7

in solvent and dry with compressed air. Keep parts organized with their respective shaft.

Shaft Inspection

1. Inspect each shaft for the following:
   a. Damaged keyway (A, **Figure 15**).
   b. Clean oil holes (B, **Figure 15**).
   c. Worn or damaged splines (C, **Figure 15**).
   d. Rounded or damaged snap ring grooves (D, **Figure 15**).
   e. Damaged threads (A, **Figure 16**). Mildly damaged threads can be trued with a thread die.
   f. Damaged O-ring groove (B, **Figure 16**).
   g. Wear, galling or other damage on the bearing/bushing surfaces (C, **Figure 16**). A blue discoloration on any surface (**Figure 17**) indicates excessive heat.
   h. Broken or damaged gear teeth on the input shaft.
   i. Shaft runout. With the shaft mounted in a centering jig, use a dial indicator to measure runout. Measure on a smooth surface near the center of the shaft. Refer to **Table 1** for the specification.
2. Assemble the shafts as described in this chapter.

Gear, Bushing and Washer Inspection

1. Inspect the gears for the following:
   a. Broken or damaged teeth (A, **Figure 18**).
   b. Worn, damaged or rounded gear recesses (B, **Figure 18**).
   c. Scored, galled or fractured bore (C, **Figure 18**). The oil pockets should not be worn away A blue discoloration indicates excessive heat. In **Figure 19**, excessive heat caused this gear to crack in all the gear recesses. Additionally, the bushing is torn from the bore and seized to the shaft (**Figure 17**). The outer washer is fused to the gear. This type of damage can be caused by diluted oil or oil starvation.
   d. Worn or damaged shift fork groove (A, **Figure 20**).
   e. Worn or damaged splines (B, **Figure 20**).
   f. Worn, damaged or rounded gear dogs (C, **Figure 20**). Any wear on the dogs and mating recesses should be uniform. If the dogs are not worn evenly, the remaining dogs will be over-

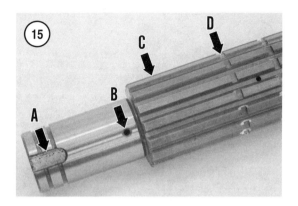

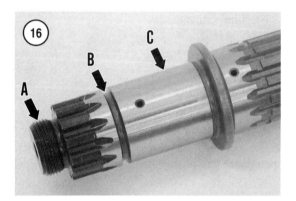

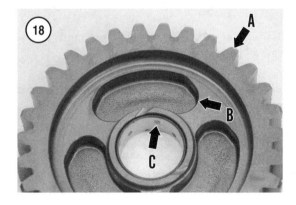

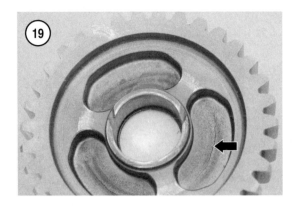

stressed and possibly fail. Check the engagement of the dogs by placing the gears at their appropriate positions on the countershaft, then twisting the gears together. Check for positive engagement in both directions. If damage is evident, also check the condition of the shift forks as described in this chapter.

NOTE
The side of the gear dogs that carries the engine load will wear and eventually become rounded. The unloaded side of the dogs will remain unworn. Rounded dogs will cause the transmission to jump out of gear.

g. Smooth gear operation on the shafts. Bored gears should fit firmly on the shaft, yet spin smoothly and freely. Splined gears should fit snugly at their position on the shaft, yet slide smoothly and freely from side to side. If a gear is worn or damaged, also replace the gear it mates to on the other shaft.

2. Inspect the bushings and washers (**Figure 21**). All parts should show no signs of wear or damage.
3. Install the parts onto their shafts as described in this chapter.

REVERSE SHAFT AND LOCKOUT ASSEMBLIES

Disassembly, Inspection and Assembly

1. Disassemble the reverse shaft as follows:
   a. Remove the snap rings from the shaft, then remove the gear and washers (**Figure 22**).
   b. Clean the parts.
   c. Inspect the gear for broken teeth and wear. Inspect the gear bushing for wear, galling, fractures or heat damage.
   d. Inspect the shaft for wear and clean oil holes.
   e. Inspect the washers for obvious wear. Replace the snap rings.
2. Assemble the reverse shaft as follows:
   a. Install a snap ring on the shaft. The sharp edge of the snap ring must face away from the gear location.
   b. Install a washer, the gear and the remaining washer onto the shaft.

c. Install the remaining snap ring onto the shaft. The sharp edge of the snap ring must face away from the gear.

d. Lubricate the assembly with engine oil.

3. Inspect the reverse lockout assembly (**Figure 23**) as follows:

a. Inspect all parts for obvious wear or damage.

b. Inspect the guide pin that engages with the shift drum. The pin should be symmetrical and not flat on the side.

4. Install the parts as described in Chapter Five.

SHIFT DRUM AND FORKS

As the machine is upshifted and downshifted, the shift drum and fork assembly engages and disengages pairs of gears on the transmission shafts. Gear shifting is done by the shift forks, that are guided by cam grooves in the shift drum.

It is important that the shift drum grooves, shift forks and mating gear grooves be in good condition. Excessive wear between the parts will cause unreliable and poor engagement of the gears. This can lead to premature wear of the gear dogs and other parts.

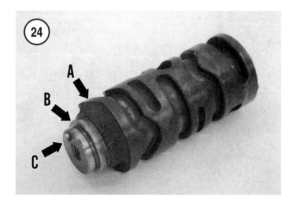

Inspection

When inspecting the shift fork and drum assembly, replace parts that are worn or obviously damaged.

1. Clean all parts in solvent and dry with compressed air.

2. Inspect the shift drum (**Figure 24**) for the following:

a. Worn shift drum grooves and cam points (A, **Figure 24**). The grooves should be a uniform width. Worn grooves can prevent complete gear engagement, which can cause rough shifting and allow the transmission to disengage.

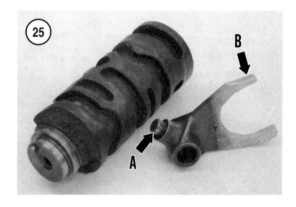

b. Worn or damaged bearing surfaces (B, **Figure 24**). Besides wear, look for signs of overheating discoloration and lack of lubrication. Fit the shift drum into each crankcase half and check for play. If necessary, replace the shift drum bearing (Chapter Five).

c. Damaged or loose shift drum pin (C, **Figure 24**).

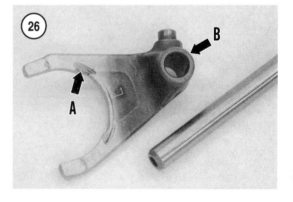

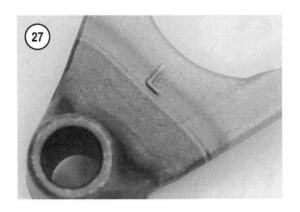

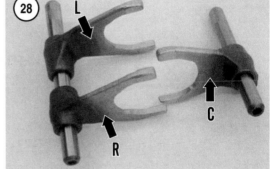

3. Inspect each shift fork (**Figure 25**) for wear and damage. Inspect the following:

    a. Guide pin (A, **Figure 25**). The pin should be symmetrical and not flat on the side. The pin should pass through its mating groove on the shift drum without binding or excessive looseness.

    b. Shift fork claw (B, **Figure 25**). The claw should not be worn. A polished appearance at the contact points is acceptable.

    c. Shift fork radius (A, **Figure 26**). The radius and sides should not be worn. If wear is evident, the fork is binding in the gear groove. This could be caused by a worn or damaged fork bore, fork shaft, shift drum or gear.

4. Inspect the shift fork bore (B, **Figure 26**) and shaft. The bore should be smooth and the fork should slide and pivot smoothly on the shaft. There should be no excessive play or tightness. The shaft should roll freely on a flat surface.

5. After inspection, match the forks to the shafts. Each fork is identified by a location letter cast on the side of the fork (**Figure 27**). The left (L) and right (R) forks go on the long shaft, while the center fork goes on the short shaft (**Figure 28**). All forks should be oriented with their location letter facing in the same direction. When the forks and shafts are installed, all letters must face the right crankcase.

6. Install the parts as described in Chapter Five.

Table 1 TRANSMISSION SPECIFICATIONS

Transmission	Five-speed constant mesh with reverse
Primary reduction ratio	2.088 (71/34)
Final reduction	3.076 (40/13)
Gear ratios	
First gear	
2001	2.428 (34/14)
2002-on	2.583 (31/12)
Second gear	
2001	1.526 (29/19)
2002-on	1.6673 (30/18)
Third gear	
2001	1.238 (26/21)
2002-on	1.286 (27/21)
Fourth gear	1.0471 (22/21)
Fifth gear	0.904 (19/21)
Reverse	
2001	1.750 (28/23 × 23/16)
2002-on	1.833 (33/25 × 25/18)
Input and output shaft runout	0.08 mm (0.0031 in.)
Gear set installed length	115.65-115.85 mm (4.553-4.561 in.)

CHAPTER EIGHT

FUEL SYSTEM

This chapter provides service procedures for removing, disassembling, inspecting and repairing the carburetor. Also included is information on how the different carburetor systems operate within the carburetor. **Table 1** at the end of the chapter lists the standard carburetor specifications.

Refer to this chapter for fuel valve servicing and throttle cable replacement. Refer to Chapter Three for air filter service, throttle cable adjustment and cable lubrication.

When working on the fuel system, observe the shop and safety practices outlined in Chapter One.

CARBURETORS

Fundamental Operation

The machine is equipped with two carburetors. Although the carburetors are essentially identical, the left carburetor feeds one intake valve and is fitted with an air cutoff valve, starter (choke) jet, choke plunger, and throttle cable lever. The right carburetor feeds two intake valves and is fitted with a larger main jet and pilot air jet. When installed, the carburetors are joined by screws and controlled by a single throttle cable.

The Mikuni BSR33 is a vacuum-controlled, or constant velocity, carburetor. It uses both a throttle valve and diaphragm-operated slide to regulate fuel to the engine. The throttle valve (**Figure 1**) is located on the output side of the carburetor and is connected to the throttle cable. It is not connected to any fuel-regulating device. The slide and diaphragm assembly, located at the center of the carburetor (**Figure 2**), regulate fuel by a jet needle at the bottom of the slide (**Figure 3**). The diaphragm is sealed at the top of the carburetor by the vacuum chamber cover. The diaphragm divides and seals the large chamber into a lower and upper chamber.

During operation, when the throttle valve is opened, air demand and speed through the carburetor is increased. As air passes under the slide, air pressure drops in that area. This low air pressure is vented to the upper diaphragm chamber. The lower

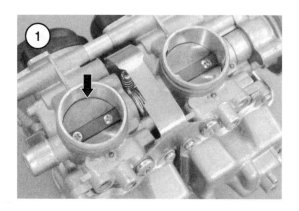

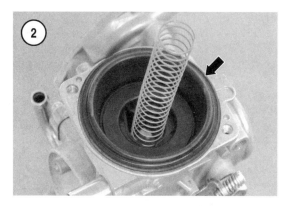

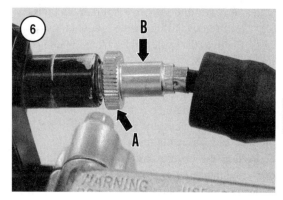

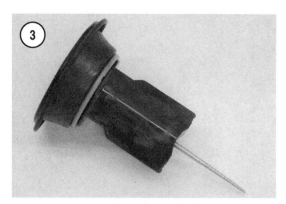

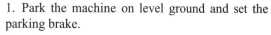

diaphragm chamber is vented to atmospheric pressure. This difference in pressure causes the slide and jet needle to rise, allowing fuel to pass into the carburetor throat. When the throttle valve is closed, the pressure differential lowers, allowing the slide and jet needle to lower.

Refer to *Carburetor Systems* in this chapter for operational details of specific fuel circuits within the carburetor.

Removal and Installation

1. Park the machine on level ground and set the parking brake.

2. Remove the fuel tank and rear protector (Chapter Fourteen).

3. Remove the carburetor air vent hoses and float chamber vent hose (**Figure 4**).

4. At the left carburetor, remove the throttle cable as follows:

    a. Remove the throttle valve cover (**Figure 5**).

    b. At the handlebar, loosen the cable locknut (A, **Figure 6**) and turn the adjuster (B) in to create slack in the cable.

c. Turn the throttle valve counterclockwise to ease removal of the cable holder (**Figure 7**).

d. Remove the cable holder from the cable end (**Figure 8**).

e. Loosen the locknut (A, **Figure 9**) and remove the cable adjuster (B) from the carburetor.

5. At the left carburetor, remove the choke plunger (**Figure 10**). If necessary, remove and inspect the plunger as described in this chapter.

6. Loosen the clamps from the air filter housing ducts and intake ducts (**Figure 11**).

7. Remove the carburetors.

8. Reverse this procedure to install the carburetors. Note the following:

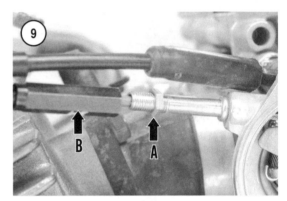

a. Before installing, check that the carburetors are synchronized as described in this chapter.

b. If necessary, set the pilot mixture screws to their initial settings.

c. Clean and lightly lubricate the inside edges of the ducts so the carburetors will easily seat.

d. Check the fuel, vent and drain hose routing.

e. Inspect and adjust the throttle cable (Chapter Three).

f. Check the carburetors for leaks.

g. If necessary, adjust the idle speed and pilot mixture screw settings (Chapter Three).

Disassembly and Assembly

The following procedure shows disassembly of the left carburetor, which includes the throttle valve housing, air cutoff valve assembly, starter (choke) jet and choke plunger. Except for these differences, the right carburetor can be disassembled using this procedure. During disassembly, keep all parts identified and organized. Refer to **Figure 12**.

1. Remove the float chamber drain hoses.

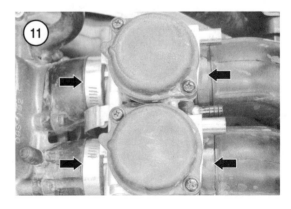

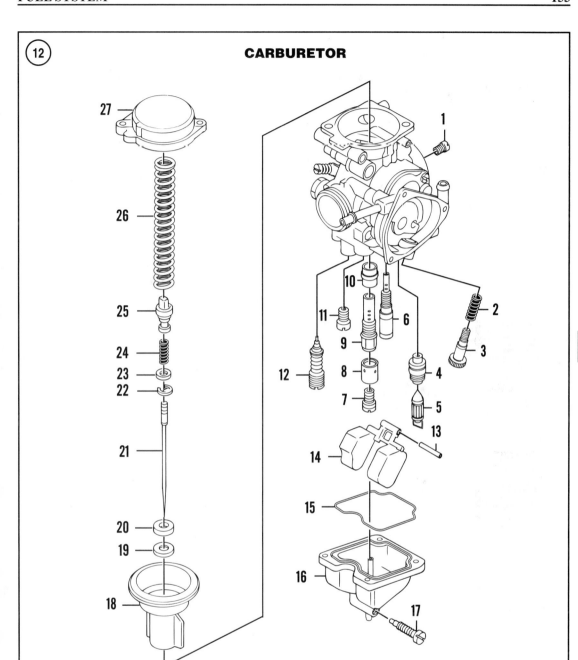

⑫ **CARBURETOR**

1. Pilot air jet
2. Spring
3. Throttle stop screw
4. Float valve seat
5. Float valve
6. Pilot jet
7. Main jet
8. Main jet sleeve
9. Needle jet holder
10. Needle jet
11. Starter (choke) jet
12. Pilot mixture screw
13. Pin
14. Float
15. O-ring
16. Float chamber
17. Drain screw
18. Diaphragm and slide
19. Washer (thin)
20. Spacer
21. Jet needle
22. Clip
23. Washer (thick)
24. Spring
25. Jet needle holder
26. Spring
27. Vacuum chamber cover

8

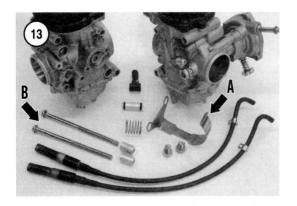

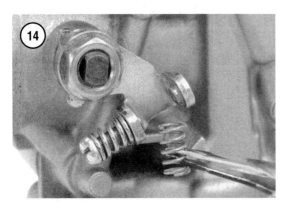

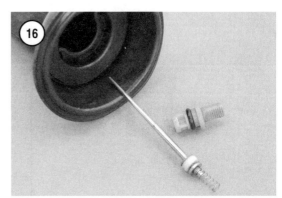

2. Separate the carburetors (**Figure 13**) as follows:

   a. Remove the synchronizer guard (A, **Figure 13**).

   b. Remove the two screws joining the carburetors (B, **Figure 13**).

   c. Separate the carburetors and account for the spacers, spring, fuel crossover tube and vent hose fitting.

3. Remove the spring from the synchronizer lever (**Figure 14**).

4. Remove the vacuum chamber cover and slide assembly as follows:

   a. Remove the cover (**Figure 15**). The cover is under slight spring pressure. Hold the cover in place as the two screws are removed, then lift off the cover.

   b. Remove the spring (**Figure 2**).

   c. From the intake side, push up on the slide so it can be lifted from the carburetor (**Figure 3**).

CAUTION
Do not lift or hold the slide by the diaphragm. Prevent damaging the jet needle as it is raised and handled.

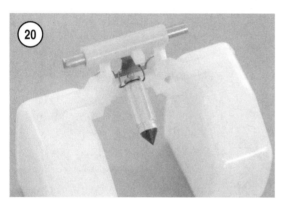

d. Pull the jet needle holder from the slide, then remove the jet needle assembly (**Figure 16**).

5. Remove the pilot air jet (**Figure 17**).

6. Remove the float chamber screws (**Figure 18**). Remove the drain screw and O-ring from the chamber.

7. Remove and disassemble the float assembly as follows:

    a. Remove the pin retaining screw (**Figure 19**).

    b. Carefully lift out the float, pin and float valve (**Figure 20**).

    c. Remove the clip and float valve from the float tab.

8. Remove the float valve seat as follows:

    a. Remove the retaining screw (**Figure 21**).

    b. Twist and remove the float seat (**Figure 22**). Do not grip the seat inside the bore. Scratches in the seat will cause leakage past the float valve.

9. Remove the main jet assembly as follows:

    a. Remove the main jet (**Figure 23**).

    b. Remove the main jet sleeve (**Figure 24**).

    c. Remove the needle jet holder (**Figure 25**).

d. Remove the needle jet (**Figure 26**). The jet is a friction fit, passing into the venturi. Unseat the jet from the carburetor venturi by hand. If necessary, use a wood or plastic dowel to help free the jet. Do not use tools that could scratch the inner surface of the jet.

10. Remove the pilot jet (**Figure 27**).

11. Remove the starter (choke) jet (**Figure 28**).

12. Remove the pilot mixture screw (**Figure 29**) as follows:

a. Make a scratch on the edge of the bore in line with the slot in the screw. This will be used as a reference point when installing the screw.

b. Turn the screw clockwise and accurately count the number of turns it takes to *lightly* seat the screw into the carburetor.

c. Record the number of turns.

d. Remove the pilot mixture screw, spring, washer and O-ring.

13. Remove the throttle stop screw and spring.

14. If the carburetors are severely clogged and must be completely disassembled and cleaned, it is necessary to remove the air cutoff valve diaphragm from the left carburetor. The carburetor should not be flooded with solvent if the diaphragm remains in the carburetor. If the carburetor had no prior problems and is only being inspected and lightly cleaned, removal of the assembly is not necessary. Since the location of the inside screw on the air cut-off valve cover is not easily accessible (**Figure 30**), the removal of the screw can be achieved by one of the following methods. If specialty tools are on hand, a simpler method of removal may be devised.

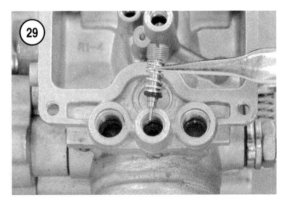

a. Partial removal of the throttle valve housing. This method requires a 4 mm ball-end Allen wrench to remove the housing screws (**Figure 31**). This wrench is required since one of

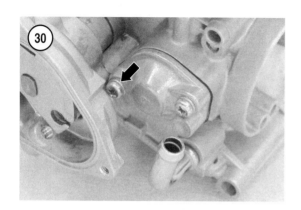

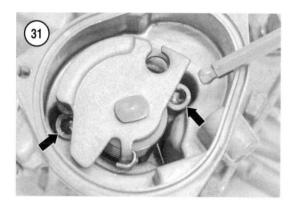

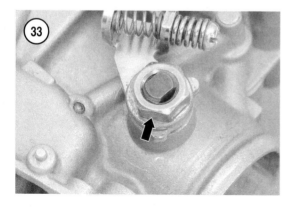

the screws is partially blocked by the throttle valve assembly. This method is preferred since it does not disturb the throttle shaft assembly. Proceed to Step 15 for removal of the air cutoff valve assembly using this method.

b. Complete removal of the throttle shaft assembly from the carburetor. If this method is used, remove the throttle valve screws (**Figure 32**) and throttle shaft nut (**Figure 33**). Pull the assembly out of the throttle valve housing. In most cases, this method is *not* preferred, since the parts are assembled with threadlocking compound and part damage during removal is possible. Use this method only if throttle shaft repair is required.

15. If necessary, partially remove the throttle valve housing as follows. Read the entire procedure before starting disassembly to understand the required technique.

a. Turn the throttle valve and remove the lower housing screw. A standard 4 mm Allen wrench will work for removing this screw.

b. Turn the throttle valve until maximum access to the upper housing screw is achieved, then remove the upper screw using the 4 mm ball-end Allen wrench. As the screw is removed, pull the housing away from the carburetor to maintain clearance. The screw cannot be removed from the housing, but it can be completely unthreaded.

c. When the upper housing screw is completely unthreaded, turn the housing so the notch in the housing is aligned with the screw in the air cutoff valve cover. Align a screwdriver in the notch and remove the cover screw (**Figure 34**).

d. Remove the remaining cover screw, then remove the cover, spring and diaphragm (**Figure **35**). The cover is under spring pressure. Keep pressure on the cover as the screw is removed.

16. Reverse Step 15 to install the parts.

   a. Install the diaphragm with the spring seat facing out (**Figure 36**).

   b. When installing the air cutoff valve cover, check that the throttle valve housing is on the correct side of the cover. If incorrect, the cover will prevent the housing from being aligned with its screw holes.

   c. Start the upper housing screw into its threads first, then start the lower housing screw. Tighten both screws equally in several passes.

   d. Check that the throttle shaft O-ring (**Figure 37**) is seated before tightening the housing screws.

17. Clean and inspect the parts as described in this chapter.

18. Refer to *Carburetor Systems* in this chapter for the function of the jets and their affect on performance.

19. Reverse this procedure to assemble the carburetor. Note the following:

   a. Install new, lubricated O-rings.

   b. When installing the needle jet, check that the leading edge of the jet aligns squarely with the carburetor bore. Do not allow the leading edge to jam against the step in the bore.

   c. Attach the float valve and clip to the float before installing the parts.

   d. Check and adjust the float height. Refer to *Float Adjustment* in this chapter.

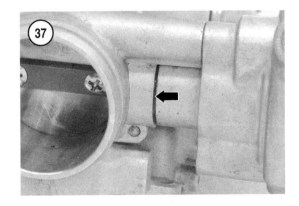

   e. When installing the pilot mixture screw, *lightly* seat the screw, then turn it out the number of turns recorded during disassembly. Refer to the reference mark on the carburetor for the original setting. If the number of turns is not known, refer to **Table 1** for the initial setting.

   f. When installing the slide and diaphragm, the diaphragm must be seated at its edge (**Figure 38**) before installing the cover.

   g. To join the carburetors, invert the carburetors and assemble the screws, spacers, fuel crossover tube and vent hose fitting to the right carburetor (**Figure 39**). Seat the spring on the left carburetor (**Figure 39**). Join the parts and check that the right carburetor throttle lever

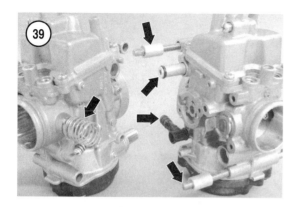

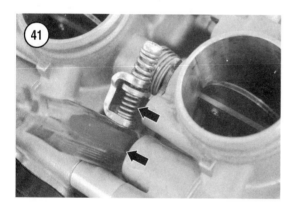

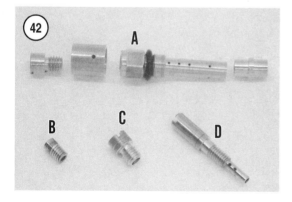

fits into the synchronizer lever located on the left carburetor. Tighten the screws.

h. Check that the spring ends are seated on the stops (**Figure 40**).

i. To install the spring between the synchronizer lever and throttle lever, jam the synchronizer lever in the fully open position with the handle of a small screwdriver. This will allow two-hand installation of the spring (**Figure 41**).

j. Synchronize the carburetors before installing. Refer to *Carburetor Synchronization* in this chapter.

k. Install the carburetors as described in this chapter.

CARBURETOR CLEANING AND INSPECTION

Use the following procedure to clean and inspect the carburetors. Refer to *Carburetor Systems* in this chapter to gain an understanding of how the carburetor passages for each system are interconnected. When cleaning, this will help in verifying whether the entire length of a passage is clean. Always replace worn or damaged parts.

It is recommended to use a commercial cleaner specifically for carburetors, since the cleaner contains agents for removing fuel residues and buildup. Use a cleaner that is harmless to rubber and plastic parts. Follow the manufacturer's instructions when using the cleaner.

CAUTION
Do not attempt to clean the jet orifices or seats with wire or drill bits. These items can scratch the surfaces and alter flow rates or cause leaking.

NOTE
Because of heat and age, O-rings eventually lose their flexibility and do not seal properly. It is standard practice to replace all O-rings and gaskets when rebuilding a carburetor.

1. Clean all parts in carburetor cleaner. Use compressed air to clean all passages, orifices and vents in the carburetor body.

2. Inspect the main jet and needle jet assembly (A, **Figure 42**), pilot air jet (B), starter (choke) jet (C)

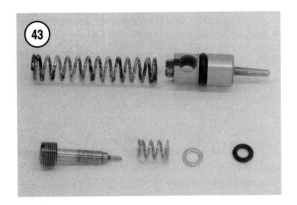

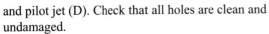

and pilot jet (D). Check that all holes are clean and undamaged.

3. Inspect the pilot mixture screw assembly and choke plunger (**Figure 43**).

   a. Inspect the screw and plunger tips for dents or wear.

   b. The spring coils should be resilient and not crushed.

   c. The plunger should move freely in its bore in the carburetor.

4. Inspect the throttle stop screw, spring, cable holder and throttle valve cover (**Figure 44**). Inspect the throttle stop screw for straightness and thread damage. The spring coils should be resilient and not crushed.

5. Inspect the diaphragm, slide, vacuum chamber cover and spring (**Figure 45**).

   a. Inspect the slide for wear and scratches. Fit the slide into the carburetor body and check for smooth vertical operation (**Figure 46**). The slide should have minimal front-to-back play.

   b. Inspect the diaphragm for dryness, tears and holes. The diaphragm *must* be undamaged in order to isolate the pressure differences that are above and below the diaphragm. A leaking diaphragm will prevent the slide from reaching/maintaining its normal level, for any throttle position off idle. Engine performance will be noticeably diminished.

   c. The vacuum chamber cover *must* be undamaged in order to maintain low pressure in the upper chamber of the carburetor. A cracked or loose cover will affect engine performance similarly to a damaged diaphragm.

6. Inspect the jet needle assembly (**Figure 47**). The jet needle must be smooth, straight and evenly ta-

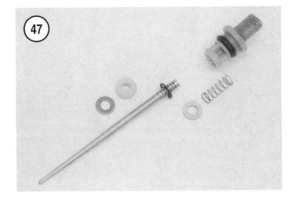

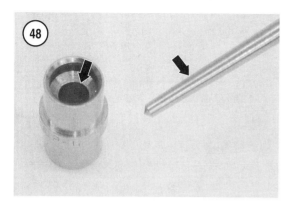

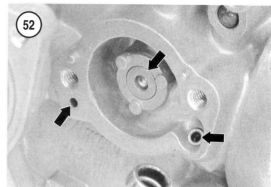

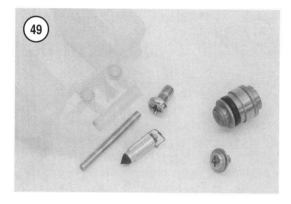

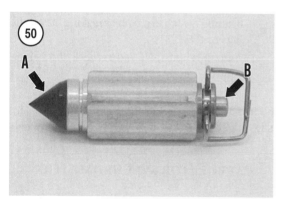

pered. If the needle or needle jet (**Figure 48**) is stepped, dented, worn or bent, replace the parts.

7. Inspect the float and float valve assembly (**Figure 49**).

    a. Inspect the tip of the float valve (A, **Figure 50**). If it is stepped or dented, replace the float valve.

    b. Lightly press on the spring-loaded pin (B, **Figure 50**) in the float valve. The pin should easily move in and out of the valve. If it is varnished with fuel residue, replace the float valve.

    c. Inspect the float valve seat. The seat should be clean and scratch-free. If it is not, the float valve will not seat properly and the carburetor will overflow.

    d. Inspect the float and pin. Submerge the float in water and check for leakage. Replace the float if water or fuel is detected inside the float. Check that the float pin is straight and smooth. It must be a slip-fit in the float.

8. Inspect the float chamber assembly (**Figure 51**).

    a. Check that all residue is removed from the interior of the bowl.

    b. Inspect threaded parts for damage.

    c. Inspect the tip of the drain screw. If damaged, the drain screw will allow fuel to pass into the drain hose.

    d. Inspect the overflow tube for cleanliness.

9. If removed, inspect the air cutoff valve assembly (**Figure 35**).

    a. The diaphragm must be free of damage in order to operate properly.

    b. The pin on the back of the diaphragm should not be worn.

10. If removed, inspect the air cutoff valve chamber on the left carburetor (**Figure 52**).

a. Inspect the vent holes and ball valve for cleanliness.

b. Check the ball valve for free movement. Apply light pressure to unseat the ball, then release pressure. The spring-loaded ball should seat itself.

11. Inspect the assembly hardware and fittings for damage.

FLOAT ADJUSTMENT

The float and float valve maintain a constant and measured fuel level in the float chamber. As fuel is used, the float lowers and allows more fuel past the valve. As the fuel level rises, the float closes the valve when the required fuel level is reached. If the float is out of adjustment, the fuel level will be too high or low. A low fuel level will cause the engine to run as if the jetting is too lean. A high fuel level will cause the engine to run as if the jetting is too rich. It may also cause fuel overflow.

> *NOTE*
> *If fuel is overflowing from the float chamber drain hose, check that the drain screw is in good condition and tight. The float chamber overflow tube and drain screw share the hose. If the screw is loose or damaged, the leaking fuel may be wrongly diagnosed as poor float adjustment.*

1. Remove the carburetors as described in this chapter.

2. Remove the float chamber.

3. Lightly touch the float to ensure the float valve is seated.

4. With the float valve seated, position the carburetor on its side and allow the float to lightly pivot inwards until it rests against the spring-loaded pin in the valve (B, **Figure 50**). The tab should only touch the pin so the pressure against the pin is minimized.

5. Measure the distance from the carburetor gasket surface to the highest point on the float (**Figure 53**). Refer to **Table 1** for the required float height.

6. If necessary, reset float height as follows:

   a. Remove the float assembly from the carburetor.

   b. Remove the float valve and clip.

   c. Bend the float tab in the appropriate direction to raise or lower the float. Use care when

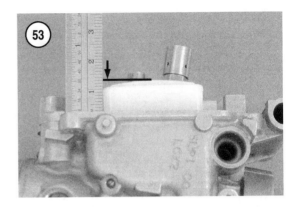

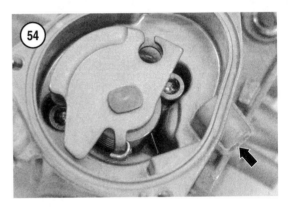

bending the tab to prevent breaking the plastic lugs or float.

   d. Assemble the float and recheck the height. Adjust, if necessary.

7. Install the float chamber.

8. Install the carburetors as described in this chapter.

CARBURETOR SYNCHRONIZATION

Synchronization of the carburetors is necessary to achieve efficient combustion and maximum engine performance. Always synchronize the carburetors whenever they have been disassembled, or whenever the carburetors are diagnosed as the cause of poor performance. When synchronizing, the right carburetor throttle valve is adjusted to match the left carburetor throttle valve.

1. Remove the carburetors as described in this chapter.

2. Remove the throttle stop screw from the throttle valve housing (**Figure 54**).

3. Remove the synchronizer guard (**Figure 55**).

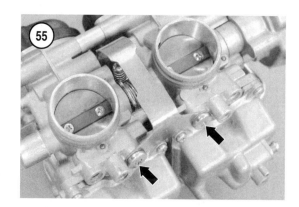

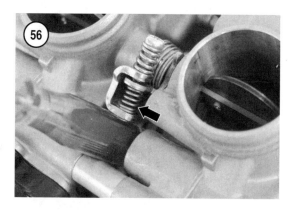

RIGHT   LEFT

4. Check that the spring ends are seated on the stops (**Figure 40**).

5. Check that the spring between the synchronizer lever and throttle lever is installed, and that the synchronizer screw is fully backed out (**Figure 56**).

6. Synchronize the right carburetor with the left carburetor (**Figure 57**) as follows:

    a. Place the carburetors with the throttle valves facing up.

    b. Check that the throttle valve is fully closed in the left carburetor. If it is not, make repairs to

the throttle shaft assembly as necessary. Do not try to synchronize damaged parts.

    c. Turn the synchronizer screw while lightly touching the edge of the throttle valve on the right carburetor. By touching the throttle valve, movement is accurately detected. Turn the screw until the throttle valve just becomes fully seated, and no more. Fine adjustment is achieved by turning the screw in small increments in both directions to determine when the throttle valve initially seats.

7. Operate the lever in the throttle valve housing and verify the synchronized movement of both throttle valves.

8. Install the synchronizer guard.

9. Install the throttle stop screw. Do not turn the screw in excessively or idle speed will be high at startup.

10. Install the carburetors as described in this chapter.

11. Set the idle speed at the next engine startup (Chapter Three).

8

CARBURETOR SYSTEMS

Common factors that affect carburetor performance are altitude, temperature and engine load. If the engine is not running or performing up to expectations, check the following before adjusting or replacing the components in the carburetor:

1. Throttle cable. Check that the cable is not dragging and is correctly adjusted.

2. Choke. Check that the choke fully opens and closes.

3. Fuel flow. Check that fuel is adequately flowing from the fuel tank to the carburetors.

4. Carburetor synchronization. Check that both carburetors open and close equally.

5. Air filter. Check that the filter is clean.

6. Ignition timing. Check that timing is correct.

7. Muffler. Check that the muffler is not restricting flow.

8. Brakes. Check that the brake pads are not dragging on the discs.

Before disassembling the carburetors, understand the function of the pilot, needle and main jet systems. When evaluating or troubleshooting these systems, keep in mind that their operating ranges overlap one another during the transition from closed to fully open throttle.

Pilot Jet System

The pilot system controls the air/fuel ratio from closed throttle to about 1/4 throttle. The pilot system is in operation across the entire throttle range, but its effectiveness diminishes after 1/4 throttle. Air enters the pilot air jet (A, **Figure 58**), where it passes to the pilot jet (A, **Figure 59**). The pilot jet draws fuel from the float chamber and mixes it with the air from the pilot air jet. The atomized air/fuel mixture passes to the pilot mixture screw (B, **Figure 59**), where it is regulated into the throat of the carburetor. The mixture is discharged from the pilot hole (A, **Figure 60**). Turning the pilot mixture screw in will *lean* the air/fuel mixture entering the engine, while turning the screw out will *richen* the mixture.

The pilot hole and mixture screw affects idle and low engine speeds. As the throttle valve is opened, it uncovers the bypass pilot holes (B, **Figure 60**), which then become effective. These holes are connected to the passage between the pilot jet and pilot mixture screw. They are not affected by the mixture screw. As engine speed increases, fuel is drawn from these passages directly from the pilot jet.

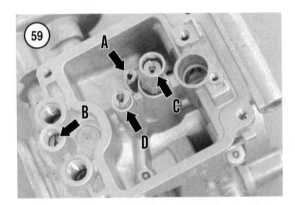

Jet Needle System

The jet needle is connected to the slide and controls the mixture from approximately 1/4 to 3/4 throttle. Air enters the main air jet (B, **Figure 58**), where it passes to the needle jet holder and needle jet. These parts are located above the main jet (C, **Figure 59**). The needle jet holder mixes fuel from the float chamber with the air from the main air jet. The atomized air/fuel mixture passes to the needle jet, where it is regulated by the jet needle into the throat of the carburetor. As the throttle is opened, the needle rises and fuel is regulated by the needle taper. The vertical position of the needle in the slide is adjustable to increase (richen) or decrease (lean) fuel flow from the needle jet.

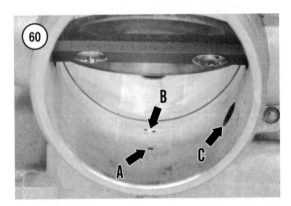

Main Jet System

The main jet (C, **Figure 59**) is screwed to the bottom of the needle jet holder and controls the mixture from approximately 3/4 to full throttle. The main jet is numbered and is interchangeable with jets that will provide a leaner or richer air/fuel mixture.

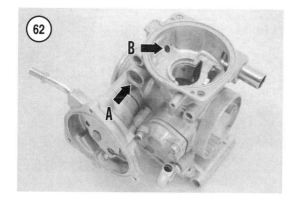

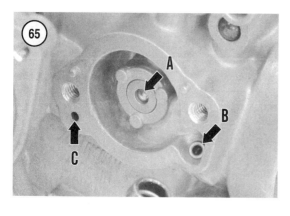

Starter (Choke) System

The starter (choke) system consists of a plunger assembly (**Figure 61**) and starter jet (D, **Figure 59**). The jet passes fuel to an orifice in the plunger bore. The plunger bore (A, **Figure 62**) also intersects an air passage (B). The air passage goes from the bottom of the slide diaphragm chamber and into the throat of the carburetor (**Figure 63**).

When the choke knob is operated, the plunger needle is withdrawn from the fuel orifice and opens the air passage. As the engine is cranked, a rich air/fuel mixture is drawn into the carburetor throat. When closed, the choke plunger blocks the air and fuel passages.

This type of choke is most effective if the throttle remains closed during startup, in order to maintain high vacuum at the air and fuel passages.

Air Cutoff Valve System

The function of the air cutoff valve is to richen the pilot jet system air/fuel mixture during compression braking, such as descending steep grades, when the engine speed is high, but the throttle is closed. Without this valve, the engine will develop a lean air/fuel mixture in the pilot system, which will cause backfiring and possibly engine damage. The air cutoff valve consists of a diaphragm, spring and cover (**Figure 64**). The function of the assembly is to open and close a spring-loaded ball valve (A, **Figure 65**) in the diaphragm chamber. The ball valve controls air flow through the passage and into the pilot system.

During acceleration and steady running speeds, the diaphragm is in the down position, holding the ball valve open. This allows air to pass from the pilot air jet and into the chamber (B, **Figure 65**). The air passes under the diaphragm and into the pilot system. During deceleration, when the throttle valve is closed, engine vacuum vents through a passage (C, **Figure 60**) leading to the air cutoff valve cover (C, **Figure 65**). The vacuum pulls the diaphragm out, allowing the ball to block the air passage in the bore. This reduces the amount of air going to the pilot jet system, and a rich fuel mixture is discharged from the pilot hole (A, **Figure 60**).

When acceleration resumes, the vacuum holding the diaphragm out is reduced and the spring pushes the diaphragm and pin down, again creating a normal fuel mixture in the pilot jet system.

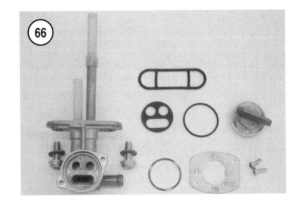

FUEL VALVE

Removal, Inspection and Installation

1. Remove the fuel tank (Chapter Fourteen).
2. Drain the fuel from the tank.

> *WARNING*
> *Drain the fuel into an approved container. Perform the draining procedure a safe distance away from the work area.*

3. Remove the two screws securing the fuel valve to the tank, then pull the valve straight out of the tank.

4. Remove the two screws from the lever plate, then pull the complete lever and plate assembly out of the fuel valve.

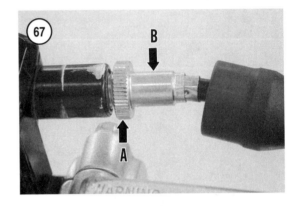

5. Disassemble, clean and inspect the parts (**Figure 66**).

    a. Inspect for buildup in the screen filters. If buildup is evident, lightly scrub the screens with a nylon brush and solvent. Carefully blow compressed air through the screen, from the inside to the outside.

    b. Inspect and clean buildup from the valve passages.

    c. Replace all O-rings.

    d. The wave washer must be capable of applying pressure to the outside of the lever. If resistance is not felt when tightening the lever plate screws, the washer is fatigued.

    e. Inspect the remaining parts for obvious damage.

6. Assemble the valve. Note the following:

    a. Lightly lubricate the O-rings.

    b. Assemble the O-ring, lever, wave washer and plate, then install the parts into the valve.

7. Install the fuel valve into the fuel tank and equally tighten the screws.

8. Install the fuel tank (Chapter Fourteen).

9. When filling the tank, start with a small amount of fuel and check for leaks. Operate the lever and check that all positions are leak-free.

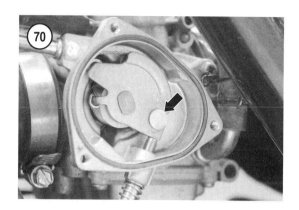

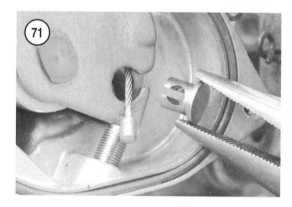

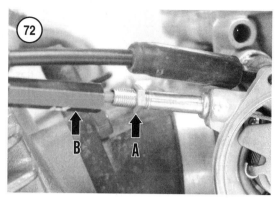

THROTTLE CABLE REPLACEMENT

The throttle uses a single cable to operate both carburetors. Use the following procedure to replace the throttle cable.

1. Park the machine on level ground and set the parking brake.

2. Remove the fuel tank and rear protector (Chapter Fourteen).

3. At the handlebar, remove the cable as follows:

    a. Loosen the cable locknut (A, **Figure 67**) and turn the adjuster (B) in to create slack in the cable.

    b. Remove the throttle housing cover, then remove the cable from the throttle lever (**Figure 68**).

    c. Turn the cable adjuster out and remove the cable from the handlebar.

4. At the left carburetor, remove the throttle cable as follows:

    a. Remove the throttle valve cover (**Figure 69**).

    b. Turn the throttle valve counterclockwise to ease removal of the cable holder (**Figure 70**).

    c. Remove the cable holder from the cable end (**Figure 71**).

    d. Loosen the locknut (A, **Figure 72**) and remove the cable adjuster (B).

    e. Remove the cable from the carburetor.

5. Note how the cable is routed, then pull the cable from the frame.

6. Reverse this procedure to install the new cable. Note the following:

    a. Clean the housings and levers before assembly.

    b. Lubricate the cable with aerosol cable lubricant. Lubricate the cable ends, lever, holder and cable guide with grease.

    c. Adjust the cable (Chapter Three).

    d. Install the fuel tank when proper adjustment and operation is verified.

8

Table 1 is on the following page.

Table 1 CARBURETOR SPECIFICATIONS

Carburetor type	Mikuni BSR constant velocity
Carburetor bore diameter	33 mm
Fuel level	3-4 mm (0.12-0.16 in.) below float chamber gasket surface
Float height	13 mm (0.51 in.)
Identification number	
2001	5LP1 00
2002-on	5LP5 20
Idle speed	1450-1550 rpm
Intake vacuum	32.0-33.3 kPa (9.45-9.83 in. Hg)
Jet needle	
Clip groove position	3
Number	5ND16-56-3
Main air jet number	130
Main jet number	
Carburetor (left)	140
Carburetor (right)	145
Needle jet number	P-6M (#826)
Pilot air jet number	
Carburetor (left)	80
Carburetor (right)	150
Pilot jet number	22.5
Pilot mixture screw turns out	
Carburetor (left)	3
Carburetor (right)	2
Starter jet number	95
Throttle valve number	80

CHAPTER NINE

ELECTRICAL SYSTEM

This chapter provides access and service procedures for the following components and electrical systems:

1. Upper idle gear cover.
2. Left crankcase cover.
3. Lower idle gear.
4. Stator and pickup coil.
5. Rotor and starter clutch.
6. Starter.
7. Starting system switches.
8. Ignition system.
9. Charging system.
10. Fan system.
11. Water temperature warning circuit.
12. Indicator circuits.
13. Headlight.
14. Taillight.
15. Left handlebar switches.

Also provided in this chapter is the basic operation of the ignition and charging systems. An understanding of the system operation is often helpful to logically troubleshoot and test the components.

RESISTANCE TESTING GUIDELINES

1. When testing component resistance, use the provided specifications as a *guide* in judging the condition of a component. Electrical test results vary, depending on ambient temperature and the quality and condition of the meter being used. Other factors include the cleanliness and overall condition of the wiring harness, terminals and connectors.

2. Use caution when considering the replacement of a component, particularly when it is marginally out of specification. Test the parts that interact with the component to ensure the problem is isolated. Perform a continuity test on appropriate wiring harnesses before assuming the part is faulty. Knowledge of how the system operates is also helpful in correctly determining faulty components.

3. Whenever in doubt of the test results, take the component to a dealership for evaluation. Comparison to a new part will often reveal the condition of the component.

4. Refer to the wiring diagram at the end of the manual to identify wires, plugs and components.

CONTINUITY TESTING GUIDELINES

Circuits, switches, light bulbs and fuses can be checked for continuity (a completed circuit) using an ohmmeter connected to the appropriate color-coded wires in the circuit. Tests can be made at the connector plug or at the part itself. Use the following procedure as a guide in performing general continuity tests.

> *CAUTION*
> *When performing continuity checks, do not turn on the ignition switch.*

Damage to parts and test equipment could occur. Also, verify that power from the battery is not routed directly into the test circuit, regardless of ignition switch position.

1. Refer to the wiring diagram at the back of the manual and find the part to be checked.

2. Identify the wire colors leading to the part and determine which pairs of wires should be checked. For any check, the circuit should begin at the plug, pass through the part, then return to the plug.

3. Determine when continuity should exist.

    a. Typically, whenever a switch or button is turned on, it *closes* the circuit, and the meter should indicate continuity.

    b. When the switch or button is turned off, it *opens* the circuit, and the meter should not indicate continuity.

4. Trace the wires from the part to the nearest connector plug. Separate the connector plug.

5. Connect an ohmmeter to the plug half that leads to the part being checked. If the test is being made at the terminals on the part, remove all other wires connected to the terminals so they do not influence the meter reading.

6. Operate the switch/button and check for continuity.

BASIC IGNITION AND CHARGING SYSTEM OPERATION

A permanent magnet alternator is located on the left end of the crankshaft, and is the source of energy for charging the battery. The capacitor discharge ignition (CDI) system is charged by the battery. When the engine is cranking or running, the current from the battery goes to the CDI unit and is stored in a capacitor. When the alternator rotor is in the correct position for ignition, the ignition pickup coil signals the CDI unit to release the stored charge to the coil. The charge of current into the coil primary windings induces a much higher voltage in the secondary windings, which fire the spark plug. This system is essentially maintenance free, with the spark plug being the only part requiring routine replacement.

When the engine is running, the current produced by the alternator is sent to the regulator/rectifier. The power is converted to direct current and regulated to the battery. If the battery is fully charged,

the excess current is shunted and dissipated as heat by the regulator/rectifier.

UPPER IDLE GEAR COVER

The starter drives the starter clutch assembly by two idle gears, located between the starter and starter clutch. The upper idle gear is accessed at the upper idle gear cover, while the lower idle gear is accessed by removing the left crankcase cover.

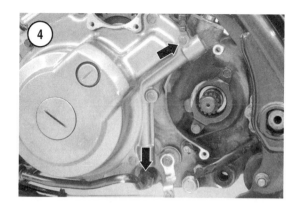

Removal, Inspection and Installation

1. Remove the four bolts at the perimeter of the upper idle gear cover (**Figure 1**).

2. Remove the cover, gasket, gear, bearing and shaft (**Figure 2**). Account for the dowel in the cover.

3. Inspect the parts (**Figure 3**).

   a. Inspect the bearing in the cover. The bearing should operate smoothly with no play.

   b. Assemble the needle bearing, shaft and gear. The parts should operate smoothly with no play.

   c. Insert the shaft into the crankcase and cover bores. The shaft should fit firmly with no play.

   d. Inspect the gear teeth and bore. If the gear is obviously worn, check the condition of the starter motor gear, lower idle gear and starter clutch gear.

4. Reverse this procedure to install the parts. Note the following:

   a. Lubricate the parts with engine oil.

   b. Install a new cover gasket.

   c. Torque the cover bolts to 10 N•m (88 in.-lb.).

LEFT CRANKCASE COVER

Removal and Installation

The left crankcase cover must be removed to access the lower idle gear for the starter, rotor, stator and pickup coil. The stator and pickup coil are mounted on the inside of the cover.

1. Drain the engine oil (Chapter Three).

2. Remove the shift lever (Chapter Six).

3. Remove the oil pipe and ground cable (**Figure 4**).

4. Disconnect the stator and pickup coil leads.

5. Remove the upper idle gear cover and gear assembly as described in this chapter.

6. Remove the bolts from the perimeter of the cover (**Figure 5**).

7. Pull the cover away from the engine (**Figure 6**). Magnetic resistance will be felt as the cover is unseated.

8. Remove the cover gasket and account for the three cover dowels and two O-rings on the rear dowels (**Figure 7**).

9. Remove and/or test the stator and pickup coil as described in this chapter.

10. Reverse this procedure to install the stator and left crankcase cover. Note the following:

a. Lubricate the gears, shafts and bearings with engine oil.

b. Install new O-rings on the dowels.

c. Install a new cover gasket.

d. Apply sealant to the electrical lead grommet, then seat the lead into the cover.

e. Check that all wires are routed and secured.

f. Clean electrical connections, then apply dielectric grease when assembling.

g. Torque the cover bolts to 10 N•m (88 in.-lb.). Work in a crossing pattern when torquing the bolts.

h. Torque the oil pipe nut to 35 N•m (26 ft.-lb.).

LOWER IDLE GEAR

The lower idle gear for the starter is accessed by removing the left crankcase cover.

Removal, Inspection and Installation

1. Remove the left crankcase cover as described in this chapter.

2. Remove the lower idle gear, shaft and bearing (**Figure 8**). On 2002-on models, a bearing is not used.

3. Inspect the parts (**Figure 9**).

a. Assemble the needle bearing (2001 model only), shaft and gear. The parts should operate smoothly with no play.

b. Insert the shaft into the crankcase and cover bores. The shaft should fit firmly with no play.

c. Inspect the gear teeth and bore. If the gear is obviously worn, check the condition of the starter gear, upper idle gear and starter clutch gear.

4. Reverse this procedure to install the parts. Lubricate the parts with engine oil.

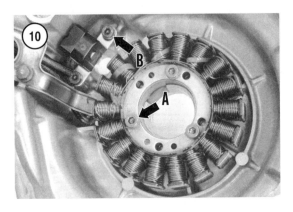

STATOR AND PICKUP COIL

Removal and Installation

The stator and pickup coil are mounted on the inside of the left crankcase cover. The stator and pickup coil can be tested without removing them from the cover. Disconnect the stator and pickup coil connectors, then test the parts at the connectors. Refer to *Charging System* to test the stator charging

coil resistance and *Ignition System* to test the pickup coil.

1. Remove the left crankcase cover as described in this chapter.

2. Remove the three bolts from the stator (A, **Figure 10**).

3. Remove the two screws from the pickup coil (B, **Figure 10**).

4. Remove the wiring harness clamp from the cover.

5. Remove the wire grommet from the cover, then remove the parts.

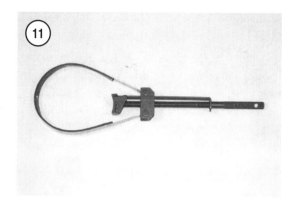

wise. The clutch gear should turn freely and smoothly in that direction. Attempt to turn the gear counterclockwise. The gear should not turn. If the gear turns in both directions or is always locked up, disassemble and inspect the clutch assembly.

Removal and Installation

1. Remove the left crankcase cover and lower idle gear as described in this chapter.
2. Remove the rotor bolt as follows:
    a. Hold the rotor stationary with the rotor holder tool (**Figure 11**). When installing the tool, do not allow it to grip the metal strip located on the perimeter of the rotor.
    b. Remove the rotor nut and washer.
3. Loosen the rotor and starter clutch as follows:
    a. To aid in removal, spray penetrating lubricant into the rotor bore and Woodruff key area. Apply grease to the end and threads of the rotor puller.
    b. Thread the rotor nut onto the shaft (**Figure 12**), keeping it spaced away from the rotor. The nut will protect the shaft threads and prevent the rotor assembly from accidentally falling when it is loosened.
    c. Install the puller onto the crankshaft and rotor. Use 8 mm, grade 8 bolts to secure the puller to the rotor. The bolts must be fully seated and the puller must be square to the end of the shaft.
    d. Hold the rotor stationary with the rotor holder tool or at the primary drive gear nut.
    e. Tighten the rotor puller. The rotor is tightly seated and will require a wrench that provides high leverage.
    f. With the rotor puller tightened, the application of heat to the rotor is recommended to ease removal. Use a heat gun or propane torch to evenly heat the rotor around the shaft only. Do not heat the rotor magnet. Apply additional pressure to the puller until the rotor breaks free from the crankshaft taper.
    g. Remove the rotor puller and nut from the crankshaft.
4. Remove the rotor, starter clutch, Woodruff key, sprocket bearing and spacer from the crankshaft (**Figure 13**).

6. Reverse this procedure to install the stator and pickup coil. Note the following:
    a. Apply threadlocking compound to the bolt threads.
    b. Torque the stator and pickup coil bolts to 7 N•m (62 in.-lb.).
    c. Torque the wiring harness clamp bolts to 10 N•m (88 in.-lb.).

ROTOR AND STARTER CLUTCH

The starter clutch is mounted on the back of the rotor. The starter gears and rotor must be removed to access the clutch. In order to remove the rotor, it must be held with a rotor holder tool (**Figure 11**) to remove the nut. The rotor is then removed with a three-point rotor puller. If the right crankcase cover is removed, the primary drive gear nut can be held while the rotor nut is loosened.

NOTE
If troubleshooting the starter clutch, the clutch can be checked for freewheel and lockup without removing the rotor. Turn the clutch gear clock-

9

5. Inspect and lubricate the parts as described in this section.

6. Reverse this procedure to install the rotor and starter clutch assembly. Note the following:

a. Install the large washer onto the crankshaft before installing the starter clutch and rotor.

b. Lubricate the sprocket bearing with engine oil.

c. Torque the rotor nut to 150 N•m (111 ft.-lb.).

d. Install the lower idle gear and left crankcase cover as described in this chapter.

Inspection

1. Inspect the clutch for proper operation as follows:

a. With the clutch gear facing up, turn the gear counterclockwise. The gear should freely and smoothly turn in that direction (**Figure 14**).

b. Attempt to turn the gear clockwise. The gear should not turn.

c. If the gear turns in both directions or is always locked up, disassemble and inspect the clutch assembly.

2. Remove the clutch gear from the rotor. Turn the gear counterclockwise and twist it squarely away from the rotor.

3. Clean and inspect the clutch assembly (**Figure 15**).

a. Inspect the clutch gear teeth for wear or damage.

b. Inspect the clutch rollers. The rollers should be undamaged and operate smoothly.

CAUTION
The starter clutch rollers can potentially be damaged if the engine kicks back, particularly at engine startup. The reversal of the crankshaft direction puts a high load on the rollers. To minimize potential damage to the rollers, keep the starter button engaged until the engine is definitely started.

c. Inspect the gear bearing and washer for damage. Fit the bearing and gear onto the crankshaft. The parts should operate smoothly with no play.

4. If the clutch is damaged, remove the clutch from the rotor as follows:

a. Remove the bolts, then remove the clutch assembly from the rotor. Use a heat gun to help loosen the threadlocking compound on the bolts.

b. Install a new clutch assembly.

c. Apply threadlocking compound to the bolts, then torque the bolts equally in several passes to 16 N•m (12 ft.-lb.).

5. Lubricate the clutch rollers with engine oil.

6. Install the clutch gear into the rotor. Turn the gear counterclockwise and twist it squarely into the rotor. When the gear is fully seated, check that it turns only in the counterclockwise direction.

7. Clean and inspect the rotor components.

a. Inspect the rotor for cracks and damage.

WARNING
The rotor must be replaced if it is damaged. The rotor can fly apart at high crankshaft speeds, causing severe personal injury and damage to the engine.

b. Inspect the taper in the bore of the rotor and on the crankshaft (**Figure 16**) for damage.

c. Inspect the Woodruff key, crankshaft keyway, rotor nut and washer for damage.

NOTE
If the Woodruff key is bent or sheared, the rotor will not be properly aligned on the crankshaft, causing the engine to be out of time.

8. Install the parts as described in this section.

STARTER

Removal and Installation

Refer to **Figure 17**.
1. Remove the exhaust pipe (Chapter Four).
2. Disconnect the parking brake cable. If desired, the cable can be removed when the starter mounting bolts are removed.
3. Remove the rear oil pipe.
4. Disconnect the ground (negative) cable from the battery.
5. Disconnect the positive cable from the starter (A, **Figure 18**).

6. Remove the mounting bolts and bracket (B, **Figure 18**), then pull and twist the starter out of the left crankcase cover. The starter is sealed to the cover by an O-ring, which will cause resistance during removal.
7. Disassemble, inspect and test the starter as described in this section.
8. Reverse this procedure to install the starter. Note the following:
   a. Lubricate the O-ring on the starter end cover before inserting it into the crankcase cover.
   b. Check that the fiber washers on the cable post are in good condition. The washers must insulate the cable from the starter housing.
   c. Clean all cable connections, then apply dielectric grease to fittings and connectors before tightening.
   d. Torque the starter mounting bolts to 10 N•m (88 in.-lb.).
   e. Install new seal washers on the oil pipe banjo bolts, then torque the bolts to 18 N•m (13 ft.-lb.).

Disassembly and Assembly

Refer to **Figure 17**.
1. Remove the snap ring and drive gear from the shaft (A, **Figure 19**).
2. Note the alignment marks on the housing and end covers (B, **Figure 19**), then remove the two housing bolts, rear end cover (C) and O-ring (D). Account for the shims on the armature shaft.

NOTE
If the starter is disassembled only to check brush condition, remove only the rear end cover. The brushes can be inspected and the cover reinstalled if further disassembly is not required. The remainder of this procedure details the complete disassembly and inspection of the starter.

3. Remove the front end cover and O-ring. Account for the spacer and washers on the armature shaft.
4. Remove the armature, brush plate assembly and insulator from the starter housing.
5. Note the small projection on the positive brush assembly and make a reference mark on the brush plate (**Figure 20**). If the positive brushes are removed from the brush plate, the terminal should be

9

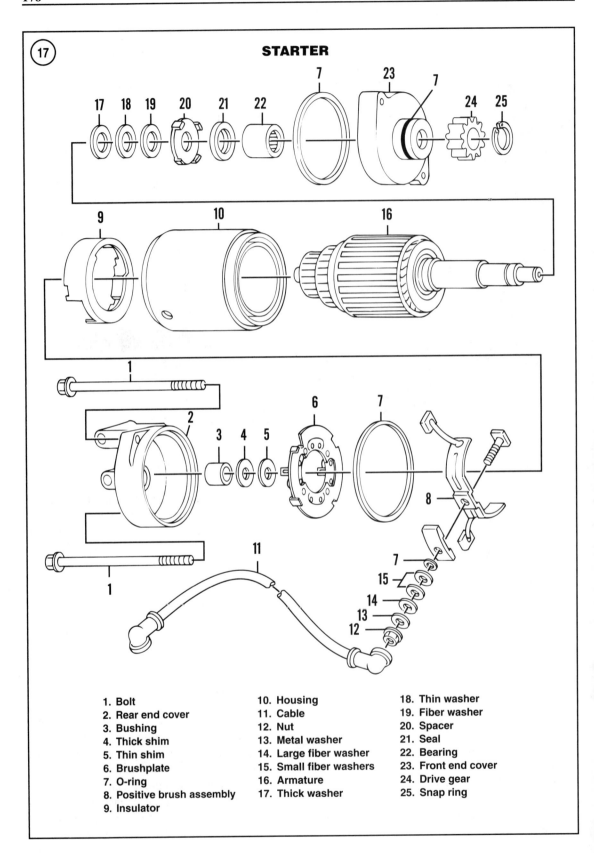

STARTER

1. Bolt
2. Rear end cover
3. Bushing
4. Thick shim
5. Thin shim
6. Brushplate
7. O-ring
8. Positive brush assembly
9. Insulator
10. Housing
11. Cable
12. Nut
13. Metal washer
14. Large fiber washer
15. Small fiber washers
16. Armature
17. Thick washer
18. Thin washer
19. Fiber washer
20. Spacer
21. Seal
22. Bearing
23. Front end cover
24. Drive gear
25. Snap ring

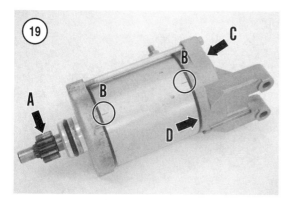

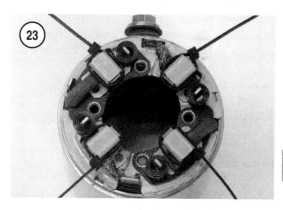

reinstalled on this side of the plate. The projection should point toward the mark. Installation of the brush plate will not be possible if these marks are not correctly oriented.

6. Inspect and test the starter components as described in this section.

7. Assemble the starter as follows:

    a. Align and install the insulator (**Figure 21**).

    b. Check the orientation of the small projection on the insulator, and the brush plate reference mark (**Figure 20**), then install the parts. The brush plate must seat in the housing and the insulation on the positive brushes must pass through the plate and into the insulator (**Figure 22**).

    c. Install the O-ring, washers and nut onto the terminal. The O-ring must fit between the terminal and housing to prevent shorting.

    d. To allow the armature to be installed, the brushes must be held back so the commutator can pass between the brushes. Use small plastic ties, positioned near the upper edge of each brush holder, to retain the brushes and springs (**Figure 23**).

e. Hold the brush plate in position and install the armature. Remove the plastic ties as the commutator passes between the brushes. The assembly should appear as shown in **Figure 24**.

f. Install the spacer, washers and shims at their appropriate end of the armature shaft.

g. Install the O-rings onto the housing, then install the end covers.

h Align the marks on the end covers and housing (B, **Figure 19**), then install and tighten the bolts.

i. Install a new, lubricated O-ring on the front end cap.

j. Install the drive gear and a new snap ring onto the shaft (A, **Figure 19**). Install the snap ring with the sharp edge facing out.

k. Perform an operational test as described in this chapter.

l. Install the motor as described in this chapter.

Inspection and Testing

Use an ohmmeter for all electrical tests in this procedure. If the result for any test is incorrect, the part is either shorted, or there is an open circuit between the test points. Replace or recondition parts that are worn, damaged or marginally acceptable. Refer to **Figure 17**.

1. Clean the parts (**Figure 25**) as required. Use a solvent specifically for electric motors to remove buildup and contamination, particularly between the commutator bars.

2. Inspect the condition of the housing and end covers (**Figure 26**).

a. The armature should fit in the covers with little or no play.

b. Inspect the condition of the bushing, bearing and seal. Lubricate the parts with waterproof grease. Remove excess grease that could migrate to the armature, commutator or brush assembly.

3. Inspect and test the commutator.

a. Measure the outside diameter (**Figure 27**). Refer to **Table 2** for specifications.

b. Inspect the bar height. The commutator bars should be taller than the insulation between the bars (**Figure 28**). Refer to **Table 2** for the undercut specification.

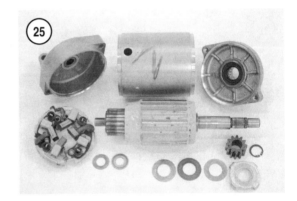

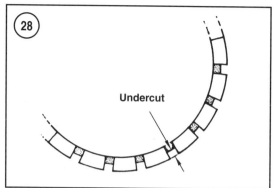

Undercut

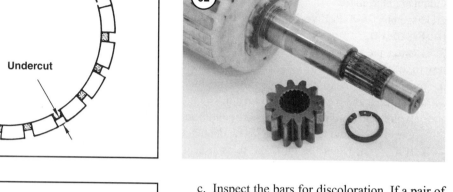

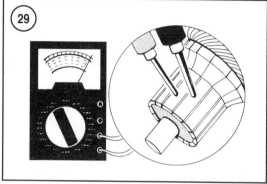

c. Inspect the bars for discoloration. If a pair of bars is discolored, this indicates grounded armature coils.

d. Inspect the bars for scoring. Mild scoring can be repaired with fine emery cloth.

e. Check for continuity across all adjacent pairs of commutator bars (**Figure 29**). There should be continuity across all pairs of bars.

f. Check for continuity between each commutator bar and the armature shaft (**Figure 30**). There should be no continuity.

4. Inspect the brush plate assembly.

a. Inspect the condition of the brush springs. If rusted or broken, replace the brush plate.

b. Measure the length of each brush (**Figure 31**). Refer to **Table 2** for specifications.

5. Inspect the drive gear, splines and armature shaft (**Figure 32**). If the gear is obviously worn, check the condition of the idle gears, located in the upper idle gear cover and left crankcase cover.

6. Inspect the spacer, shims, washers and insulator for obvious damage.

7. Assemble as described in this section.

Operational Test

The starter can be tested either mounted or removed from the engine.

> *WARNING*
> *When connecting a battery to the starter, use jumper cables to make the connections. Light gauge wire will burn. Since sparks will likely occur when the test connection is made, make the check away from all flammable sources.*

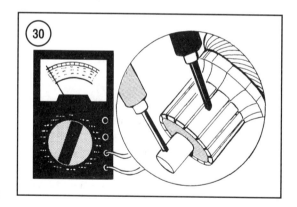

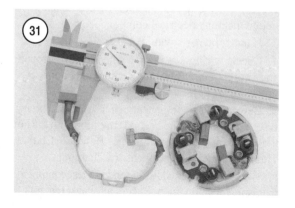

9

1. Place the transmission in neutral if the starter is mounted in the engine.

2. Disconnect the positive cable from the starter (A, **Figure 18**).

3. Connect the negative cable from a 12-volt battery to the starter mount.

4. Touch the positive battery cable to the positive starter terminal and then quickly remove it.

    a. If the starter turns, it is in good condition. Check the starter relay and cables for damage.

    b. If the starter does not turn, and the starter is not mounted in the engine, the starter is faulty.

    c. If the starter does not turn, and it is mounted in the engine, remove the starter and repeat the test. If the starter works after it is removed, check for possible jamming of the starter idle gears or starter clutch.

STARTING SYSTEM SWITCHES

The starting system switches include the switches necessary to safely start and stop the engine. This includes the starter relay, ignition switch, engine stop switch, starter button, neutral switch and clutch switch. All of these switches, except the starter relay, can be tested by following the *Continuity Testing Guidelines* in this chapter.

Starter Relay Testing

The starter relay (A, **Figure 33**) is located under the seat. The starter relay connects the battery to the starter. The relay is designed to temporarily carry the high electrical load between the parts during startup. The relay is activated when the starter button is pressed.

1. Disconnect the battery ground cable, then the positive cable.

2. Remove the starter relay from the machine.

3. Connect an ohmmeter to the cable terminals on the relay. Set the meter to the R × 1 scale.

4. Connect a 12-volt battery to the relay. Connect the positive lead to the terminal for the yellow/black wire.

5. Observe the meter, then touch the negative battery lead to the terminal for the blue/black wire.

    a. If the meter reads 0 (no resistance in relay), the relay is in good condition. Check the starter and cables for damage.

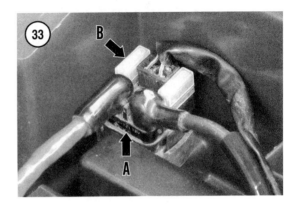

    b. If the meter does not read 0 (resistance in relay), the relay is faulty.

IGNITION SYSTEM

This section includes many of the components required for the engine to run. Since some components have a function in the starting and/or charging system, refer to those sections if the component is not found in this section.

Before checking components in the ignition system, verify the condition of the battery, fuse, ignition switch and engine stop switch. Switches can be tested by following *Continuity Testing Guidelines* in this chapter.

Precautions and Inspections

The CDI unit and other components of the ignition system can be damaged if precautions are not taken during testing and troubleshooting. Note the following:

1. Never disconnect electrical connections while the engine is running or cranking.

2. Turn off the ignition switch before disconnecting/connecting electrical components.

3. Handle the parts with care.

4. Check wiring for poor connections, corrosion and shorts before replacing components connected to the wiring.

5. Before testing components, check that the battery, fuse and spark plug are in good condition, and are not the cause of poor performance. Refer to Chapter Three for battery replacement and charging.

6. Work slowly, methodically, and use test equipment that is in good condition. Record all measurements.

CDI Unit

No specifications are provided by Yamaha for testing the CDI unit. If the components in the following tests pass inspection, Yamaha recommends replacing the CDI unit. The CDI unit is located under the seat (**Figure 34**).

Ignition Coil and Spark Plug Cap Testing

The ignition coil is located under the left fender (**Figure 35**). Check the coil for resistance in the primary and secondary coils.

1. Disconnect the orange wire at the coil.
2. Remove the spark plug cap from the plug.
3. Check primary coil resistance as follows:
   a. Set the meter to the R × 1 scale.
   b. Connect one meter probe to the orange wire terminal on the coil and the other meter probe to the coil base.
   c. Measure the resistance. Refer to **Table 2** for the specification.
4. Check secondary coil resistance as follows:
   a. Set the meter to the R × 100 scale.

b. Remove the spark plug cap from the spark plug lead.
c. Connect one meter probe to the spark plug lead and the other meter probe to the orange wire terminal on the coil.
d. Measure the resistance. Refer to **Table 2** for the specification.

5. Check spark plug cap resistance as follows:
   a. Set the meter to the R × 100 scale.
   b. Remove the spark plug cap from the spark plug lead.
   c. Connect the meter probes to each side of the cap.
   d. Measure the resistance. Refer to **Table 2** for the specification.

Pickup Coil Testing

The pickup coil is located in the left crankcase cover. The pickup coil can be checked at the wire connector, located above the starter, at the left side of the frame. Check the pickup coil for resistance.

1. Separate the connector.
2. Identify the half of the connector that leads to the pickup coil.
3. Measure the coil resistance as follows:
   a. Set the ohmmeter to R × 10 ohms.
   b. Insert the meter probes into the terminals of the white/red wire and the white/green wire. Refer to **Table 2** specifications.
   c. If the pickup coil is not within specification, check the wiring harness for obvious damage and shorting.
   d. If necessary, remove the left crankcase cover and recheck the wiring harness and coil (A, **Figure 36**). Flex the harness as the check is being made to detect erratic continuity. If the coil fails the check, replace the pickup coil/stator assembly.
4. Measure the resistance between the coil and ground as follows:
   a. Set the ohmmeter to R × 1 ohm.
   b. Ground one of the meter probes to the engine (or the left crankcase cover, if removed). Touch the other probe to the white/red wire, then the white/green wire.
   c. The resistance should be infinity. Any other reading indicates a short to ground, and the pickup coil/stator assembly should be replaced. Check for a pinched wire under the

pickup coil, or damage that would allow it to short out.

Rotor Rotation Direction Detection Coil Testing

The rotor rotation direction detection coil is located in the left crankcase cover. The coil is checked at the same connector as for the pickup coil. The connector is located above the starter, at the left side of the frame. Check the rotor rotation coil for resistance.

1. Separate the connector.
2. Identify the half of the connector that leads to the coil.
3. Measure the coil resistance as follows:
   a. Set the ohmmeter to R × 1 ohms.
   b. Insert the meter probes into the terminals of the white/blue wire and the red wire. Refer to **Table 2** for specifications.
   c. If the coil is not within specification, check the wiring harness for obvious damage and shorting.
   d. If necessary, remove the left crankcase cover and recheck the wiring harness and coil. Flex the harness as the check is being made to detect erratic continuity. If the coil fails the check, replace the pickup coil/stator assembly.
4. Measure the resistance between the coil and ground as follows:
   a. Set the ohmmeter to R × 1 ohm.
   b. Ground one of the meter probes to the engine (or the left crankcase cover, if removed). Touch the other probe to the white/blue wire, then the red wire.
   c. The resistance should be infinity. Any other reading indicates a short to ground, and the pickup coil/stator assembly should be replaced.

Ignition Timing

The ignition timing is electronically controlled by the CDI unit. No adjustment is possible to the ignition timing. The timing is checked to verify the CDI unit and pickup coil are functioning properly.

1. Warm up the engine to operating temperature.
2. Remove the cap from the timing hole (**Figure 37**).

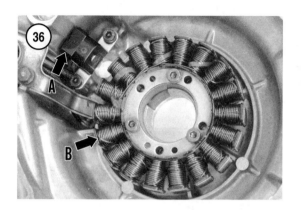

3. Connect a timing light, following the manufacturer's instructions.

4. Start the engine and allow it to idle at 1450-1550 rpm.

5. Direct the timing light into the timing hole and observe the timing mark. The index mark should be aligned between the vertical marks (**Figure 38**).

6. If the timing check is incorrect:

   a. Test the pickup coil. If the pickup coil is in good condition, the CDI unit should be checked against an identical CDI unit that is known to be in good condition. Specifications for testing the CDI unit are not available.

   b. If the CDI unit passes all checks, inspect the Woodruff key securing the rotor to the crankshaft. If the key is bent or sheared, the rotor will not be properly aligned on the crankshaft, causing the engine to be out of time.

7. Turn off the engine and disconnect the test equipment.

8. Lubricate the O-ring on the cap, then screw the cap into the timing hole.

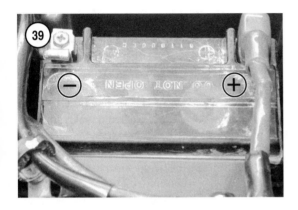

CHARGING SYSTEM

This section includes the components that charge and regulate power to the battery.

Precautions and Inspections

The components of the charging system can be damaged if precautions are not taken during testing and troubleshooting. Note the following:

1. Never disconnect electrical connections while the engine is running or cranking.
2. Turn off the ignition switch before disconnecting/connecting electrical components.
3. Handle the parts with care.
4. Check wiring for poor connections, corrosion and shorts before replacing components connected to the wiring.
5. Before testing components, check that the battery is in good condition, and is not the cause of poor performance.
6. Work slowly, methodically and use test equipment that is in good condition. Record all measurements.

Fuse Holder

The fuse holder is located under the seat, on top of the starter relay (B, **Figure 33**). Use an ohmmeter to check the fuse for continuity. Even though a fuse may appear to be in good condition, a fine break in the fuse element is not always visually detected. A fine break in the element can also indicate continuity when tested cold, then break continuity when it is under load and heated in the circuit.

Battery Replacement and Charging

Refer to Chapter Three for battery replacement and charging.

Battery Voltage Test (Unloaded)

For a maintenance-free battery (original equipment), check the unloaded voltage using a voltmeter. An unloaded test will indicate the basic state of charge.

1. Disconnect the battery cables and allow the battery to remain undisturbed for at least 4 hours.
2. Connect a voltmeter to the negative and positive terminals (**Figure 39**).
3. Measure the voltage.
   a. A fully charged battery will have a minimum of 12.8 volts.
   b. A battery that is approximately 75 percent charged will have a minimum of 12.5 volts.
   c. A battery that is approximately 50 percent charged will have a minimum of 12.0 volts.
4. If battery charging or replacement is required, refer to the procedures in Chapter Three.

Battery Voltage Test (Loaded)

For a maintenance-free battery (original equipment), check the loaded voltage using a voltmeter. A load test requires the battery to discharge current. A load test will indicate whether the battery is adequate to operate the machine.

1. Connect a voltmeter to the negative and positive terminals (**Figure 39**).
2. Turn on the headlights to the high beam.
3. Measure the voltage.
   a. A battery in good condition will have a minimum of 11.5 volts.

b. If battery charging or replacement is required, refer to the procedures in Chapter Three.

Regulator/Rectifier Output Voltage Test

For the 2001 model, the regulator/rectifier is located in front of the taillight (**Figure 40**). For 2002-on models, the unit is mounted under the seat, at the left side of the frame. The regulator/rectifier converts the alternating current produced by the alternator into direct current to charge the battery and power the electrical system. The unit also regulates the charging voltage to the battery. Excess voltage is dissipated as heat and radiated from the finned regulator.

The following test checks for output voltage of the regulator/rectifier to charge the battery. The battery must be in good condition and charged before performing the test.

1. Start the engine and allow it to reach operating temperature, then turn off the engine.

2. Check the regulator/rectifier output voltage as follows:

    a. Set a voltmeter to DC volts. Use a scale in the 25-50 volt range.

    b. Connect a voltmeter to the negative and positive battery terminals (**Figure 39**).

    c. Start the engine and momentarily raise the engine speed to 5000 rpm.

    d. The meter should indicate 14.1-14.9 volts (unloaded) as the engine speed is raised.

    e. If the output voltage is significantly higher than 15 volts, the regulator/rectifier may not be adequately grounded, or is faulty. If the output voltage does not rise with engine speed, the regulator/rectifier or stator coils are faulty. Before replacing parts, check the condition of the stator charging coils, wiring harness and battery.

Stator Charging Coils Testing

The stator coils are located in the left crankcase cover. The stator coils can be checked at the wire connector, located above the starter, at the left side of the frame. Check the charging coils for resistance and continuity.

1. Separate the connector.

2. Identify the half of the connector that leads to the stator.

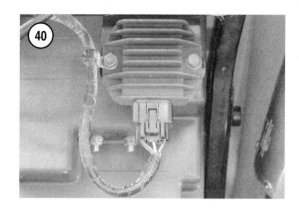

3. Measure the resistance as follows:

    a. Set the ohmmeter to R × 1 ohm.

    b. Refer to **Table 2** for specifications.

    c. Insert the meter probes into the terminals of the white wires. Check all three combinations of the white wires. The resistance between all pairs of white wires should be within the specification.

    d. If the charging coils are not within specification, check the wiring harness for obvious damage and shorting.

    e. If necessary, remove the left crankcase cover and recheck the wiring harness and coils (B, **Figure 36**). Individually check the full length of the harness wires for continuity. There should be near zero resistance in all wires. Flex the harness as the check is being made to detect erratic continuity.

    f. If the harness is not shorted, check the coils at the white wire connections on the stator. If the coils fail the check, replace the pickup coil/stator assembly.

5. Measure the resistance between the coils and ground as follows:

    a. Set the ohmmeter to R × 1 ohm.

    b. Ground one of the meter probes to the engine (or the crankcase cover, if removed). Touch the other probe to the white wires. The resistance should be infinity. Any other reading indicates a short to ground, and the pickup coil/stator assembly should be replaced.

FAN SYSTEM

When coolant temperature cannot be maintained by air passing through the radiator, an electric fan, located behind the radiator (**Figure 41**) turns on to

increase airflow through the radiator fins. Besides the fan, the fan circuit consists of the sending unit and fan circuit breaker. The fan is turned on and off by the sending unit, located at the bottom of the radiator (**Figure 42**). The sending unit is thermally sensitive and controls power to the fan. When the engine coolant is cold, the sending unit has an open circuit and the fan is inoperative. As coolant temperature rises and begins to exceed normal operating temperature, resistance in the sending unit lowers and the circuit closes. The fan turns on and runs until the coolant temperature falls, causing resistance in the sending unit and opening the circuit.

When testing or troubleshooting the fan system it is important that all connections are clean and tight. During assembly, apply dielectric grease to connections to prevent corrosion and the entry of moisture.

Fan Testing

1. Separate the fan connector.

2. Identify the half of the connector that leads to the fan.

3. Connect a 12-volt battery to the motor leads. Connect the positive lead to the blue wire and the negative lead to the black wire.

    a. If the fan does not turn on, replace the fan.

    b. If the fan turns on, test the fan circuit breaker.

Fan Circuit Breaker Testing

The fan circuit breaker is located near the front of the engine, under the fuel tank. The circuit breaker is encased in a small vinyl pack.

1. Disconnect the circuit breaker leads.

2. Measure the resistance in the circuit breaker as follows:

    a. Set the ohmmeter to R × 1 ohm.

    b. Connect the meter probes to the circuit breaker leads.

    c. If the resistance is anything other than 0, replace the circuit breaker.

Fan Sending Unit Testing

The following test requires that the sending unit be placed in heated water, to simulate actual operating conditions. Read and understand the procedure so the proper equipment is on hand to safely perform the test.

1. Drain the cooling system (Chapter Three).

2. Remove the connector from the sending unit (**Figure 42**), then remove the part from the radiator.

3. Clean and inspect the sending unit for obvious damage.

4. Test the sending unit at ambient temperature as follows:

    a. Connect an ohmmeter to the sending unit terminals. Note the meter reading.

    b. If the reading indicates continuity, the sending unit is faulty. Low resistance in the part could cause the fan to come on too soon and/or not turn off.

5. Test the sending unit at operating temperature as follows:

    a. Connect an ohmmeter to the sending unit terminals.

    b. Suspend the part (A, **Figure 43**) and an accurate thermometer (B) in a container of water. The temperature sensor and threads must be submerged. Do not allow the parts to touch the bottom or side of the container.

9

c. Slowly heat the water and observe the thermometer and ohmmeter readings. Do not excessively overheat the switch.

d. As the sending unit is heated, there should be continuity at approximately 95° C (203° F).

e. As the sending unit is cooled, there should be no continuity at approximately 89° C (192° F).

f. Replace the sending unit if it does not operate within the specifications.

6. Apply sealant to the sending unit threads, then install the part into the radiator. Torque the sending unit to 20 N•m (15 ft.-lb.).

7. Fill and bleed the cooling system (Chapter Three).

WATER TEMPERATURE WARNING CIRCUIT

The water temperature warning light (**Figure 44**) is turned on and off by the sending unit, located on the thermostat housing (**Figure 45**).

Water Temperature Warning Light Testing

The water temperature warning light (**Figure 44**) should turn on in the following situations:

1. When the engine start button is pressed. When the start button is pressed, the warning light circuit momentarily becomes grounded and the light should turn on.

a. If the light does not turn on, check the bulb for continuity.

b. Check the bulb socket for voltage and cleanliness.

2. When the water temperature sending unit detects high water temperature. The sending unit grounds the warning light circuit, and remains grounded until the water temperature is reduced to its normal operating range.

a. If the light does not turn on when overheating has occurred, check the bulb and socket condition. If the parts are in good condition, test the sending unit.

b. If the light is on at all times, or turns on soon after start up, test the sending unit. If the sending unit is in good condition, check for a short in the wire between the light and sending unit.

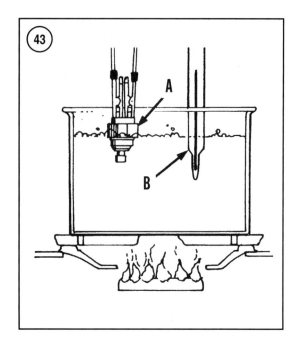

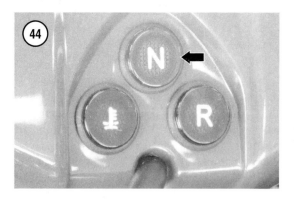

Water Temperature Sending Unit Testing

If the warning light is on all the time, or comes on soon after the engine startup, perform the following sending unit test. The test checks for continuity when the switch is at ambient to normal operating temperature. Normally, the switch should *not* have continuity in this temperature range.

If the warning light does not turn on, and all other causes of failure checked, replace the sending unit. Since the sending unit normally closes (creates continuity) at 112° C (234° F) to 117° C (234° F) to turn on the warning light, it is not practical or safe to attempt to heat and test the switch.

1. Remove the necessary bodywork to access the sending unit.

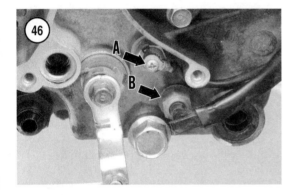

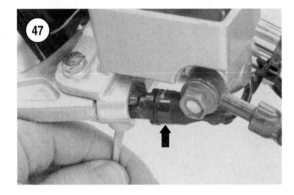

2. Remove the connector from the sending unit (**Figure 45**).

3. Clean and inspect the terminals for obvious corrosion or damage.

4. Test the sending unit at ambient temperature as follows:

   a. Connect an ohmeter to the sending unit terminals. Note the meter reading.

   b. If the reading indicates continuity, the sending unit is faulty. Low resistance in the part can cause the light to some on too soon and/or not turn off.

   c. Replace the sending unit (Chapter Ten).

5. Test the sending unit at operating temperatures as follows:

   a. Connect an ohmeter to the sending unit terminals.

   b. Start the engine and observe the meter as the engine coolant is brought to operating temperature.

   c. If the meter indicates continuity at any time during the warmup, the sending unit is faulty.

   d. Replace the sending unit (Chapter Ten).

Circuit Diode Testing

The circuit diode is located near the front of the engine, at the left side of the frame. The diode allows current to flow in one direction. Use an ohmmeter to test the diode for directional continuity.

1. Disconnect the diode.

2. Test the diode as follows:

   a. Set the ohmmeter to R × 1 ohm.

   b. Connect the negative meter probe to the white/blue wire terminal and the positive meter probe to the blue/black wire terminal. There should be continuity.

   c. Reverse the meter probe connections. There should be no continuity.

3. Replace the diode if it fails either of these tests.

INDICATOR CIRCUITS

The indicator circuits for reverse, neutral and the brakes can be checked for continuity using an ohmmeter. The bulbs and switches are tested by connecting the meter to the appropriate color-coded wires in the connector plug, or to the part itself. Simulate the conditions when the part should activate and make the check. Refer to the *Continuity Testing Guidelines* in this chapter for the test procedure.

The neutral switch (A, **Figure 46**) and reverse switch (B) are located on the left side of the engine, near the oil drain plug. The brake switches are located at the front brake lever (**Figure 47**) and above the rear brake pedal (**Figure 48**).

HEADLIGHT

Bulb Replacement

1. Remove the headlight assembly from the frame (Chapter Fourteen).

2. Remove the screws and disassemble the case and lens pieces.

3. Remove the bulb.

> *NOTE*
> *When handling the new bulb, do not touch the glass with bare hands. Handle the bulb with a clean cloth. Bulbs are sensitive to oil or other contaminants on their surface. Contaminants prevent heat dissipation from the bulb, which can result in shortened bulb life.*

4. Seat the new bulb in the socket.

5. Assemble and install the headlight.

Headlight Adjustment

1. Loosen the screw at the bottom of the headlight assembly.

2. Slide the reflector forward to raise the beam, or slide the reflector back to lower the beam.

3. Tighten the screw.

TAILLIGHT

Bulb Replacement

1. Remove the rubber cover from the back of the taillight assembly.

2. Turn the bulb holder counterclockwise and remove the holder.

3. Remove the bulb.

4. Seat the new bulb in the socket.

5. Install the bulb holder and rubber cover.

LEFT HANDLEBAR SWITCHES

The left handlebar switch unit houses the headlight switch, starter button and engine stop switch. The switches can be checked for continuity using an ohmmeter connected to the appropriate color-coded wires in the connector plug. Refer to *Continuity Testing Guidelines* in this chapter for the test procedure.

Table 1 ELECTRICAL SYSTEM GENERAL SPECIFICATIONS

Alternator	
Type	Three-phase AC
Output	14 volts/16 amps at 5000 rpm
Battery	
Type	YTX14-BS
Capacity	12 volt, 12 amp hour
Fuse	20 amp
Ignition timing	12° BTDC at 1500 rpm
Light bulbs	
Headlights (krypton bulb)	12 volt, 30W/30W each bulb
Taillight/brake light	12 volt, 5W/21W
Indicators	12 volt, 1.7W
Spark plug	
Type	NGK DPR8EA-9
Gap	0.8-0.9 mm (0.031-0.035 in.)

Table 2 ELECTRICAL SYSTEM SPECIFICATIONS

Ignition coil resistance	
Primary coil	0.18-0.28 ohm
Secondary coil (spark plug lead cap removed)	6.32-9.48K ohms
Ignition spark gap (minimum gap with spark plug cap installed)	6 mm (0.24 in.)
Pickup coil resistance (white/red-to-white/green wires)	445-545 ohms
Rectifier no-load output voltage	14.1-14.9 volts
Rotor rotation direction coil resistance (red-to-white/blue wires)	0.069-0.085 ohm
Spark plug cap resistance	10K ohms
Stator coil resistance (white-to-white wires)	0.43-0.65 ohm
Starter	
Armature coil resistance	0.025-0.035 ohm
Brush length	12.5 mm (0.49 in.)
Service limit	5 mm (0.20 in.)
Commutator outside diameter	28 mm (1.10 in.)
Service limit	27 mm (1.06 in.)
Mica undercut	0.7 mm (0.03 in.)
Starter relay coil resistance	4.18-4.62 ohms

Table 3 ELECTRICAL SYSTEM TORQUE SPECIFICATIONS

	N•m	in.-lb.	ft.-lb.
Fan sending unit	20	–	15
Left crankcase cover bolts	10	88	–
Lower oil pipe nut	35	–	26
Pickup coil bolts	7	62	–
Rear oil pipe banjo bolts	18	–	13
Rotor nut	150	–	111
Starter clutch bolts	16	–	12
Starter mounting bolts	10	88	–
Stator bolts	7	62	–
Upper idle gear cover bolts	10	88	–
Water temperature sending unit	20	–	15
Wire harness (stator) clamp bolts	10	88	–

9

CHAPTER TEN

COOLING SYSTEM

This chapter provides service procedures for the thermostat, water temperature sending unit, radiator, fan, fan sending unit and water pump. Read this chapter before attempting repairs to the cooling system. Become familiar with the procedures and photos to understand the skill and equipment required. Refer to Chapter One for tool usage and techniques.

SAFETY PRECAUTIONS

WARNING
Do not remove the radiator cap immediately after or during engine operation. When the engine has been operated, the liquid in the cooling system is scalding hot and under pressure. Attempting to remove the cap while the engine is hot can cause the coolant to spray from the radiator opening, possibly causing personal injury.

Wait for the engine to cool, then place a shop cloth over the cap. *Slowly* turn the cap to relieve any pressure. Turn the cap to the safety stop and check that all pressure is relieved. To remove the cap from the radiator, press down on the cap and twist it free.

To prevent potential damage to the engine, change the coolant regularly, as described in Chapter Three. Always use an antifreeze solution. Antifreeze contains lubricants and rust inhibitors that protect the components of the cooling system. Always dispose of coolant in an environmentally-safe manner.

THERMOSTAT

The engine thermostat (**Figure 1**) is located in a housing on the right side of the steering shaft and below the front fender. The thermostat is a temperature-sensitive valve that opens and closes, depending on the coolant temperature in the cylinder head. At startup, the thermostat is closed to retain coolant in the water jackets. When the cylinder head coolant temperature begins to exceed the ideal operating temperature, the thermostat opens and allows the coolant to pass to the radiator, where it is cooled. Since the temperature of the incoming coolant is low, the thermostat closes and reduces the flow to the radiator. As the temperature of the coolant rises, the cycle is repeated.

For the engine to run properly, the thermostat is necessary to maintain a specific amount of heat around the cylinder and cylinder head. Do not remove the thermostat, assuming that cooling or engine performance will be enhanced.

Removal, Inspection and Installation

1. Remove the front fender (Chapter Fourteen).
2. Drain the cooling system (Chapter Three).
3. Disconnect the top radiator hose (A, **Figure 2**).
4. Remove the mounting bolt and collar from both sides of the radiator (B, **Figure 2**). Raise and position of the radiator to the left side of the frame.
5. Remove the two bolts securing the thermostat cover to the housing (**Figure 3**), then remove the cover, O-ring and thermostat (**Figure 4**).

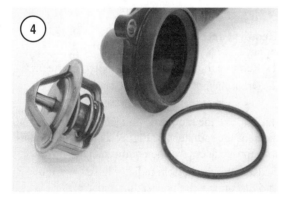

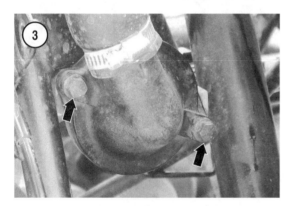

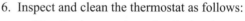

10

6. Inspect and clean the thermostat as follows:

   a. Visually inspect the valve in the thermostat. The valve should be closed when the thermostat is cold. If the valve is cold and open, replace the thermostat.

   b. Wash the thermostat in cool water. If necessary, use a soft brush to scrub accumulation off the thermostat. If accumulation of rubber particles is evident, inspect the radiator hoses for internal deterioration.

   c. Inspect the condition of the O-ring. Install a new O-ring if installing a new thermostat, or if leakage is evident.

   d. If desired, open the drain bolt at the water pump and flush the cylinder head, cylinder and water pump with clean water.

   e. Clean the bolts, thermostat housing and threaded bores (**Figure 5**).

7. Test the thermostat as follows:

   a. Suspend the thermostat and an accurate thermometer in a container of water (**Figure 6**). Do not allow the parts to touch the bottom or side of the container.

b. Slowly heat the water and observe the thermostat valve.

c. When the thermostat begins to open, observe the temperature on the thermometer. The thermostat should open between 69-73° C (156-163° F). Continue to raise the temperature to 85° C (185° F). At this temperature, the thermostat valve should be fully open, which is about 8 mm (0.31 in.).

d. Replace the thermostat if it does meet the conditions of the tests.

8. Install the thermostat with the air bleed hole at the top of the opening (**Figure 1**). The thermostat will only seat correctly in this position.

9. Lubricate the O-ring with coolant, then install it onto the housing cover. Bolt the cover into place. Torque the bolts to 10 N•m (88 in.-lb.).

10. Install the radiator and hose. Torque the radiator mounting bolts to 7 N•m (62 in.-lb.).

11. Fill and bleed the cooling system (Chapter Three). Check for leaks.

12. Install the front fender (Chapter Fourteen).

WATER TEMPERATURE SENDING UNIT

The water temperature sending unit is mounted on the thermostat housing (**Figure 7**), which is located on the right side of the steering shaft and below the front fender. Refer to Chapter Nine for testing.

NOTE
It is normal for the water temperature light to momentarily turn on when the engine start button is pressed. If the light does not turn on, check the condition of the bulb, wiring and water temperature sending unit.

Removal and Installation

1. Remove the fuel tank and front protector (Chapter Fourteen).

2. Drain the cooling system (Chapter Three).

3. Disconnect the wire connector from the sending unit.

4. Remove the sending unit from the thermostat housing.

5. Clean the sending unit and the threads in the housing.

6. Test the sending unit as described in Chapter Nine.

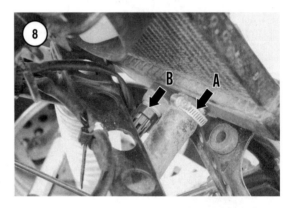

7. Reverse these steps to install the sending unit. Note the following:

a. Apply waterproof sealant to the sending unit threads.

b. Torque the sending unit to 28 N•m (21 ft.-lb.).

RADIATOR AND FAN

The machine is equipped with one radiator and a thermostatically-controlled fan. Refer to Chapter Nine for testing.

Radiator and Fan
Removal and Installation

1. Remove the front fender (Chapter Fourteen).

2. Drain the cooling system (Chapter Three).

3. Disconnect the top radiator hose (A, **Figure 2**).

4. Remove the mounting bolt and collar from both sides of the radiator (B, **Figure 2**). Tilt the radiator to improve access to the bottom radiator hose.

5. Remove the bottom radiator hose (A, **Figure 8**) and disconnect the fan sending unit (B).

6. Disconnect the overflow hose, fan breather hose and fan connector.

7. Remove the radiator and fan assembly. If fan removal is necessary, remove the bolts securing the fan to the radiator (**Figure 9**).

8. Inspect the radiator as described in this section.

9. If necessary, refer to Chapter Nine to test the fan.

10. Reverse this procedure to install the radiator and fan. Note the following:

   a. Replace hoses that are hard, cracked or show signs of deterioration, both internally and externally. Hold each hose and flex it in several directions to check for damage. For a hose that is difficult to install on a fitting, dip the hose end in hot water until the rubber has softened, then install the hose.

   b. Install clamps in their original positions.

   c. Fill and bleed the cooling system (Chapter Three). Check for leaks.

Radiator Inspection

1. Clean the exterior of the radiator with a low-pressure water spray. Allow the radiator to dry.

2. Check for damaged cooling fins. Straighten bent fins with a screwdriver. If more than 20% of the cooling area is damaged, replace the radiator.

3. Check the seams and other soldered connections for corrosion (green residue). If corrosion is evident, there could be a leak in that spot. Perform a cooling system pressure check as described in *Cooling System Inspection* in Chapter Three. If the equipment is not available, take the radiator to a radiator repair shop to have it flushed and pressure checked.

4. Fill the radiator with water and check the flow rate out of the radiator. If the flow rate is slow, or if corrosion or other buildup is seen, take the radiator to a radiator repair shop to have it flushed and pressure checked.

FAN SENDING UNIT

The fan sending unit is mounted at the bottom of the radiator (B, **Figure 8**). When coolant temperature is too high, the switch has low internal resistance and turns on the fan. At normal coolant temperature, the sending unit has high resistance and the fan remains off.

Removal and Installation

1. Remove the front fender (Chapter Fourteen).

2. Drain the cooling system (Chapter Three).

3. Disconnect the wire connector from the sending unit.

4. Remove the sending unit from the thermostat housing.

5. Clean the sending unit and the threads in the radiator.

6. Test the sending unit as described in Chapter Nine.

7. Reverse these steps to install the sending unit. Note the following:

   a. Apply waterproof sealant to the sending unit threads.

   b. Torque the sending unit to 28 N•m (21 ft.-lb.).

WATER PUMP

An inspection hole for the water pump (**Figure 10**) is located at the bottom of the housing. If coolant leakage is detected at this hole, the pump mechanical seal is leaking. If oil leakage is detected, the oil seal is leaking.

10

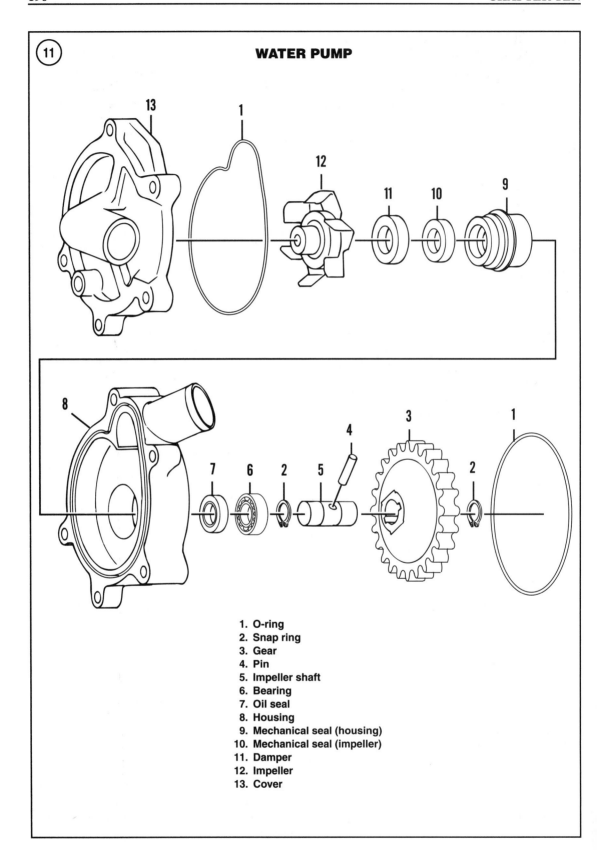

WATER PUMP

1. O-ring
2. Snap ring
3. Gear
4. Pin
5. Impeller shaft
6. Bearing
7. Oil seal
8. Housing
9. Mechanical seal (housing)
10. Mechanical seal (impeller)
11. Damper
12. Impeller
13. Cover

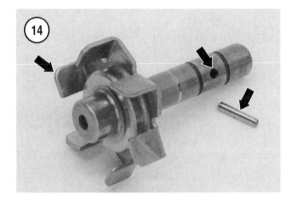

Removal, Inspection and Installation

Refer to **Figure 11**.
1. Drain the cooling system (Chapter Three).
2. Remove the hoses from the water pump (**Figure 12**).
3. Remove the three bolts securing the water pump to the engine (**Figure 13**).
   a. If desired, loosen the two cover bolts while the pump is stable in the engine.
   b. If necessary, lightly tap the pump to loosen it from the crankcase.
   c. Pull the pump straight out.
4. Remove the two cover bolts, O-ring and cover.
5. At the back of the pump, remove the O-ring, outer snap ring, gear, pin and inner snap ring.
6. Pull the impeller and shaft out of the housing.
7. Inspect the parts as follows:
   a. Inspect the impeller, shaft and pin for obvious damage (**Figure 14**).
   b. Inspect the gear and the fit of the gear on the pin and shaft (**Figure 15**). It is normal for the gear to be loose on the pin. However, if the pin and gear seat are worn or damaged, replace the parts.
   c. Inspect the face of the mechanical seal on the impeller and in the housing (**Figure 16**). In order to seal properly, both faces must be smooth and free of damage. When installed, the impeller seal should fit firmly against the seal in the housing. Since the seal in the housing is spring loaded, it maintains pressure on the seals and compensates for wear. If necessary, replace the mechanical seal and oil seal as described in this section.
   d. Inspect the bearing in the housing (**Figure 17**). The bearing should rotate turn smoothly with no play. If necessary, replace the bearing as described in this section.

10

e. Inspect the cover for damage and cleanliness. Install a new, lubricated O-ring on the cover (**Figure 18**).

f. Inspect and clean the bolt holes and impeller shaft boss in the engine (**Figure 19**).

8. Reverse these steps to assemble and install the water pump. Note the following:

a. Install the gear with the cupped side facing out (A, **Figure 20**).

b Install new snap rings with the sharp edge facing out (B, **Figure 20**).

c. Install a new, lubricated O-ring on the back of the pump (C, **Figure 20**).

d. Lubricate the bearing with engine oil.

e. Lubricate both faces of the mechanical seal with coolant.

f. Torque all bolts to 10 N•m (88 in.-lb.).

g. Fill the cooling system (Chapter Three).

Bearing and Seal Replacement

The water pump has a two-piece mechanical seal (9 and 10, **Figure 11**) and an oil seal (7). The mechanical seal prevents coolant in the pump chamber from passing into the crankcase, while the oil seal prevents oil in the crankcase from passing into the pump chamber. A drain hole (**Figure 10**) is located between the seals to allow any coolant or oil leakage to drain to the outside of the engine. Whenever leakage is detected at the drain hole, the seals should be replaced.

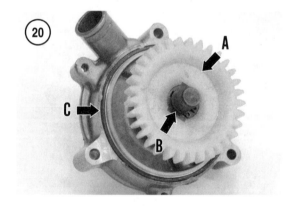

1. Replace the mechanical seal in the impeller as follows:

a. Support the impeller close to the shaft, then drive the shaft out of the impeller (**Figure 21**). Preferably, press the shaft out of the impeller.

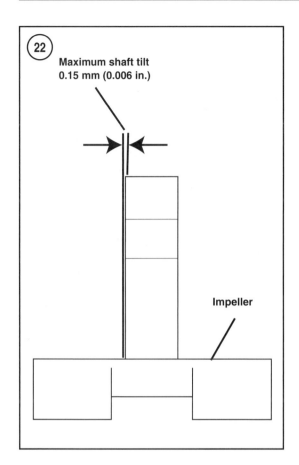

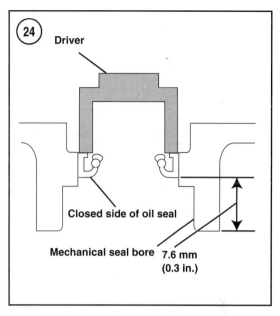

f. Check the shaft for tilt in the impeller (**Figure 22**). Maximum allowable tilt is 0.15 mm (0.006 in.). If tilt is excessive, the two halves of the mechanical seal will not make full contact and leakage is possible. If necessary, remove and reseat the shaft in the impeller and seal.

2. In the water pump housing, replace the remaining half of the mechanical seal and the oil seal. This procedure also includes the removal of the bearing.

a. Place a narrow drift against the back of the mechanical seal (**Figure 23**). Work around the seal and drive it from the bore. Avoid any contact with the surface of the bore. Do not attempt to pry the seal from the front side of the housing.

b. Support the housing with the bearing side down. Provide clearance for the bearing and seal to fall from the bore. Place a driver on the outside edge of the oil seal and drive it and the bearing from the bore.

c. Clean and inspect the housing.

d. Lubricate the oil seal with coolant.

e. Working from the bearing side of the housing, place the seal over the bore, with the closed side of the seal facing down (**Figure 24**). Note the required clearance that must exist after the seal is driven (**Figure 24**). This clearance must exist for the drain hole to be effective. Press the seal into the bore using a

b. Lift the seal and damper from the impeller. Clean the seal bore.

c. Lubricate the new damper with coolant.

d. Seat the new parts into impeller by hand.

e. Apply threadlocking compound to the end of the impeller shaft, then press the impeller onto the shaft. The impeller must be fully seated.

10

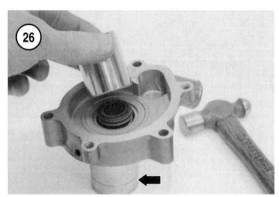

driver or socket that fits on the outer edge of the seal. Check the clearance.

f. Apply engine oil to the outer surface of the bearing, then place the bearing over the housing bore with the manufacturer's marks facing down. Drive the bearing until it is fully seated. Use a driver that fits on the outer race of the bearing (**Figure 25**).

g. Support the housing with the bearing side down. A socket that fits on the bearing boss works well (**Figure 26**). Apply coolant to the outer surface of the mechanical seal, then place the seal over the housing bore. Drive the seal until it is fully seated. Use a driver that fits on the outer edge of the seal housing (**Figure 25**).

Table 1 COOLING SYSTEM SPECIFICATIONS

Antifreeze type	Ethylene glycol containing anti-corrosion inhibitors for aluminum engines
Coolant mixture	50/50 (antifreeze/distilled water)
Cooling system	
Capacity	1.3 liters (1.4 U.S. qt.)
Radiator capacity	0.55 liter (0.58 U.S. qt.)
Reservoir capacity	0.29 liter (0.31 U.S. qt.)
Radiator cap relief pressure	95-125 kPa (13.8-18.1 psi)
Thermostat valve opening temperature	69-73° C (156-163° F)
Water pump impeller shaft	0.15 mm (0.006 in.) maximum tilt

Table 2 COOLING SYSTEM TORQUE SPECIFICATIONS

	N•m	in.-lb.	ft.-lb.
Fan sending unit	28	–	21
Radiator mounting bolts	7	62	–
Thermostat housing bolts	10	88	–
Water pump bolts	10	88	–
Water pump drain plug	10	88	–
Water temperature sending unit	28	–	21

FRONT SUSPENSION AND STEERING

This chapter provides service procedures for the front wheel, hub, suspension and steering components. Refer to the tables at the end of this chapter for specifications.

FRONT WHEEL

Removal and Installation

1. Park the machine on level ground and set the parking brake.
2. Loosen the lug nuts (**Figure 1**).
3. Raise and support the machine. The front wheels must be off the ground.
4. Remove the lug nuts and washers from the studs, then remove the wheel from the hub. If more than one wheel will be removed, mark each wheel so it can be installed in its original location.
5. If damaged or dirty, remove the outer brake disc guard (**Figure 2**).
6. If tire repair is required, make the repair as described in this chapter.
7. Clean the lug nuts, washers and studs. If studs are broken or damaged, replace them.
8. If removed, install the outer brake disc guard onto the hub. Install the burred side against the hub.
9. Install the wheel onto the studs, with the valve stem facing out.

WARNING
If more than one wheel has been removed from the machine, check that the tire direction arrow (on the tire sidewall, if applicable) is pointing forward, when the wheel is mounted. The arrow must point forward to prevent the possibility of tire ply failure during operation.

10. Install the washers and finger-tighten the lug nuts.
11. Lower the machine to the ground, then equally tighten the lug nuts in a crossing pattern. Make several passes when tightening and torque the nuts to 45 N•m (33 ft.-lb.).
12. Raise the machine and spin the wheel, checking that the wheel runs true.
13. Lower the machine to the ground.

FRONT HUB

Removal and Installation

1. Remove the front wheel and outer brake disc guard as described in this chapter.
2. Remove the cotter pin, hub nut and washer (**Figure 3**).

11

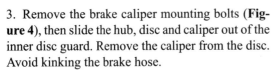

3. Remove the brake caliper mounting bolts (**Figure 4**), then slide the hub, disc and caliper out of the inner disc guard. Remove the caliper from the disc. Avoid kinking the brake hose.

> *NOTE*
> *If the hub is corroded to the axle, place a drift against the back of the hub and tap it free. Do not strike the outer edge of the brake disc.*

  a. Suspend the caliper with a length of wire. Do not let the caliper hang by the brake hose.
  b. Insert a small wood block between the brake pads. This will prevent the caliper piston from extending out of the caliper, if the brake lever is operated.

4. Remove the inner washer from the axle.

5. Inspect and repair the front hub assembly (**Figure 5**) as described in this section.

6. If additional suspension or steering components will be serviced, remove the inner brake disc guard (**Figure 6**).

7. If necessary, remove the brake disc from the hub as described in Chapter Thirteen.

8. Reverse this procedure to install the front hub. Note the following:

  a. Inspect the steering knuckle condition before installing the hub. Check for cracks and damage on bearing surfaces and threads (**Figure 7**).
  b. Torque the hub nut to 70 N•m (52 ft.-lb.).
  c. Install a new cotter pin.
  d. Install and torque the caliper mounting bolts to 28 N•m (21 ft.-lb.).
  e. Operate the brake lever several times to seat the pads.
  f. With the hub raised, check that it spins freely and the brake operates properly.

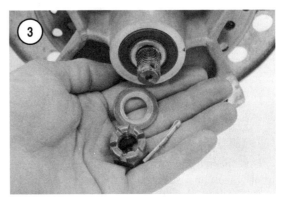

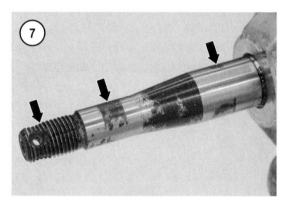

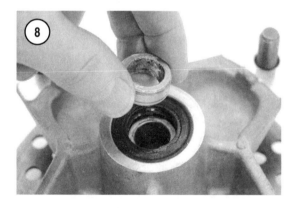

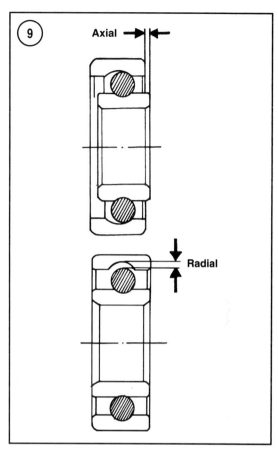

5. Check the tightness of the bearings in the hub. Replace the bearings if they are loose.

6. Install the spacers if the bearings and seals are in good condition. Leave the spacers out if the bearings and/or seals will be replaced.

Bearing and Seal Replacement

Two methods for removing bearings from the wheel hub are provided in the following procedure. The first method (Step 3A) uses a wheel bearing removal set and the second method (Step 3B) uses common shop tools.

CAUTION
In the following procedure, do not allow the wheel to rest on the brake disc. Support the wheel to prevent pressure being applied to the disc.

1. Pry the seals from both sides of the hub (**Figure 10**). Protect the hub as shown.
2. Examine the bearings. Note the following:

Inspection

1. Remove the spacers (**Figure 8**) from both sides of the hub.
2. Inspect the seals for damage.
3. Turn each bearing inner race by hand. The bearing should operate smoothly and quietly. If binding or roughness is detected, replace both bearings.
4. Check each bearing for axial and radial play (**Figure 9**). If obvious play is detected, the bearing should be replaced. Replace both bearings if either bearing is worn or damaged.

a. The bearings are open on the outer face and shielded on the inner face. The new bearings must be installed with the open side facing out.

b. If bearing damage is severe, determine which bearing is damaged the least. This bearing will be removed first.

3A. Remove the bearings using the wheel bearing removal set as follows:

> *NOTE*
> *The tools used in this procedure are part of the Kowa Seiki Wheel Bearing Remover set (**Figure 11**). The set is distributed by K & L Supply Co., (1-800-727-6767). The set is designed so a proper-size remover head can be wedged against the inner bearing race. The bearing can then be driven from the hub (**Figure 12**).*

a. Select the appropriate-size remover head. The small, split end of the remover must fit inside the bearing race.

b. Insert the split end of the remover head into the bearing. Seat the remover head against the bearing.

c. Insert the tapered end of the driver through the back side of the hub. Fit the tapered end into the slot of the remover head.

d. Position the hub so the remover head is against a solid surface, such as a concrete floor.

e. Strike the end of the driver so it wedges firmly in the remover head. The remover head should now be jammed tight against the inner bearing race.

f. Reposition and support the assembly so the remover head is free to move and the driver can be struck again. Support the hub so there is no pressure applied to the outside of the brake disc.

g. Strike the driver, forcing the bearing and hub spacer from the hub.

h. Remove the driver from the remover head.

i. Repeat the procedure to remove the remaining bearing.

3B. Remove the bearings using a hammer, drift and heat gun, or propane torch. The purpose for using heat is to slightly expand the hub bores so the bearings can removed with minimal resistance. Remove the bearings as follows:

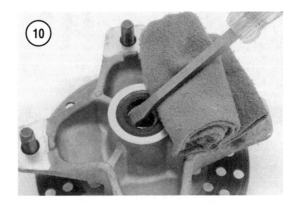

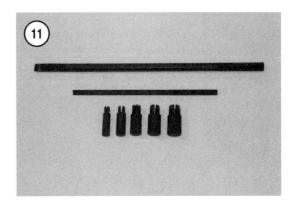

> *WARNING*
> *When using a heat gun or propane torch to heat the hub, care must be taken to prevent burning finished or combustible surfaces. Work in a well-ventilated area and away from combustible materials. Wear protective clothing, including eye protection and insulated gloves.*

a. Clean all lubricants from the wheel.

b. Insert a long drift into the hub and tilt the hub spacer away from the bearing to be removed (**Figure 13**).

c. Heat the hub around the bearing to be removed. Keep the heat source moving at an steady rate and avoid heating the bearing. A large washer placed over the bearing will help insulate the bearing from the heat.

d. Turn the wheel over and use the drift to tap around the inner bearing race (**Figure 14**). Make several passes until the bearing is removed from the hub.

e. Remove the hub spacer.

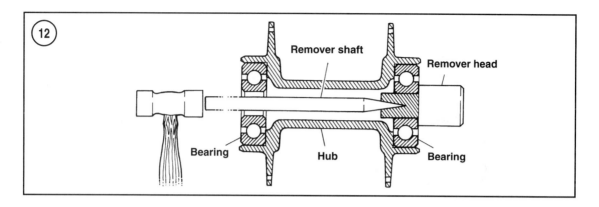

Remover shaft
Remover head
Bearing
Hub
Bearing

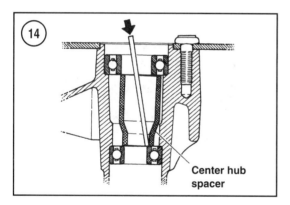

Center hub spacer

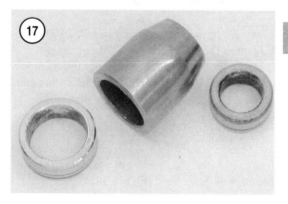

11

f. Heat the hub around the remaining bearing. Drive out the remaining bearing using a large socket or bearing driver that fits on the outer bearing race.

4. Clean and inspect all parts (**Figure 15**).

5. Inspect the hub bore (**Figure 16**) for:

   a. Cracks, corrosion or other damage.

   b. Fit of the new bearings. If a bearing easily enters the hub bore, the hub should be replaced. The bearings must be a driven-fit.

6. Inspect the hub spacers (**Figure 17**) for:

a. Cracks, corrosion or other damage.

b. Fit. Check the fit of the spacer against the back side of the bearings. It should fit flat against the bearings. Repair minor nicks and flaring with a file. Do not grind or shorten the spacer. The spacer must remain its full length, in order to prevent binding of the bearings when the axle is tightened.

7. Before installing the new bearings, note the following:

a. Apply waterproof grease to bearings that are not lubricated by the manufacturer. Work the grease into the cavities between the balls and races.

b. Always support the bottom side of the hub, near the bore, when installing bearings.

c. To aid in driving the bearings, chill them in a freezer, to temporarily reduce their diameter.

8. Heat the hub around the bearing bore.

9. Place a bearing *squarely* over the bearing bore. The open side of the bearing must face out.

10. Place a suitable-size driver or socket over the bearing. The driver should seat against the outside diameter of the bearing (**Figure 18**).

11. Hold the driver, then squarely drive the bearing, seating it in the hub (**Figure 19**).

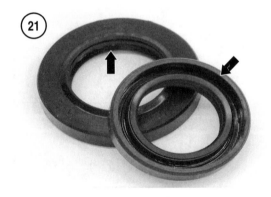

> *CAUTION*
> *Do not press or strike the bearing directly. Bearing damage will occur.*

12. Turn the hub over and install the hub spacer (**Figure 20**). Check that the spacer is oriented correctly.

13. Drive in the remaining bearing, seating it in the hub.

14. Install the seals as follows:

a. Pack grease into the lips and back sides of the new seals (**Figure 21**).

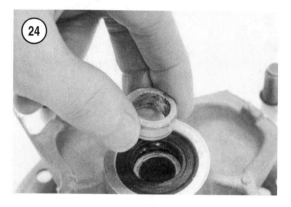

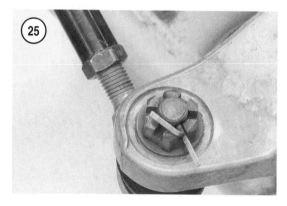

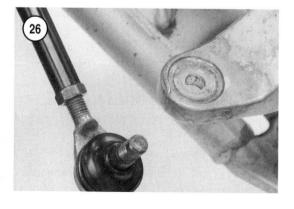

b. Lubricate the seal bores.

c. Place a seal *squarely* over the bore, with the manufacturer's marks facing out (**Figure 22**).

d. Place a suitable-size driver or socket over the seal. The driver should seat against the outside diameter of the seal. Hold the driver, then squarely drive the seal, seating it in the hub (**Figure 23**).

15. Install the spacers on both sides of the hub (**Figure 24**).

TIE RODS

Removal and Installation

1. Before removing the tie rods, make the following check for obvious play and wear.

   a. Park the machine on level ground with the wheels pointing straight ahead.

   b. Lightly turn the handlebar toward the left, then right while observing the tie rod ends. It is not necessary to actually turn the wheels. If the tie rod ends move vertically (removing play) as pressure is applied, they are worn or damaged.

   c. Repeat the check with the wheels fully locked to the left, then the right. If vertical play is observed in this position, this also indicates worn tie rod ends.

2. Remove the front wheel as described in this chapter. Access to the tie rod ends will be easier.

3. Remove the cotter pin and nut from the tie rod end at the steering knuckle (**Figure 25**). Use a small drift and tap the center of the tie rod to free it from the steering knuckle (**Figure 26**). If the tie rod end is seized in the bore do the following:

   a. If a ball joint remover is available (**Figure 27**), it can be used to separate the parts. If the tie rod end will be reused, there is a risk of tearing the rubber boot when using this tool.

   b. If a ball joint remover is not available, use a heat gun or propane torch to heat the area around the joint. Place a drift on the center of the tie rod and drive it out of the steering knuckle. If the tie rod end will be reused, avoid damaging the threads.

4. Repeat Step 3 to remove the tie rod from the steering shaft (**Figure 28**). If the tie rod end is seized in the bore, and must be driven out, it may be necessary to remove the brush guard and upper control arm to gain the necessary clearance.

5. Reverse these steps to install the tie rods. Note the following:

   a. Install the tie rods so the tie rod wrench flats (**Figure 29**) are nearest the wheel.

   b. Torque both tie rod nuts to 25 N•m (18 ft.-lb.).

   c. Install new cotter pins.

6. Check wheel toe-in as described in this chapter.

Inspection

> *NOTE*
> *The tie rod ends are packed with grease and sealed. Do not immerse the tie rod ends in solvent or any other liquid that could penetrate the boots. Wipe the ends with a shop cloth prior to inspection.*

1. Inspect the tie rod for straightness. Replace the rod if it is bent.

2. Inspect the ball joint boot for tears and the entry of moisture or dirt into the joint.

3. Grasp the ball joint (**Figure 30**) and swivel it in all directions, as well as vertically. Check for roughness, dryness and play. Replace the tie rod end if wear is detected.

Tie Rod Ends
Disassembly and Assembly

> *NOTE*
> *The outer tie rod end and locknut is a left-hand thread. The inner tie rod end and locknut is a right-hand thread. Note which direction each set of parts must be turned when loosening and tightening the parts.*

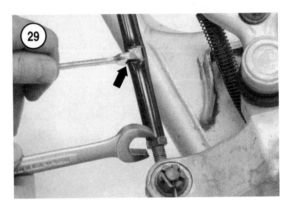

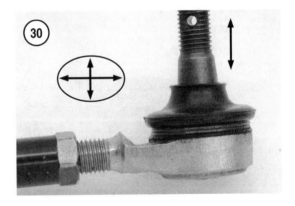

1. Hold the tie rod with a wrench placed on the tie rod flats (A, **Figure 31**).

2. Loosen the locknut (B, **Figure 31**) and remove the tie rod end.

3. Clean the tie rod threads.

4. Thread the correct tie rod end onto the tie rod.

5. Repeat the procedure for the remaining tie rod end.

6. Adjust the tie rod ends as follows:

   a. Equally adjust the tie rod ends so the number of exposed threads (C, **Figure 31**) is identical.

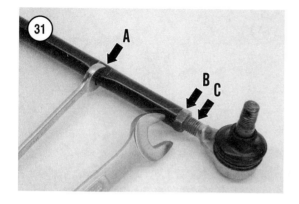

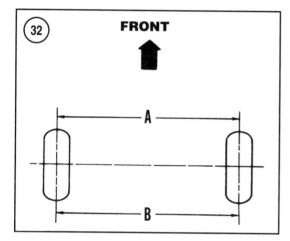

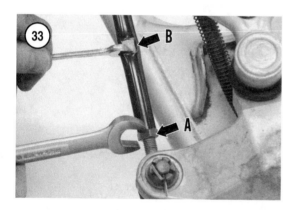

Both tie rod assemblies must be identically adjusted.

b. When the adjustments are achieved, finger-tighten the locknuts to hold the positions. Tighten the locknuts after the tie rods have been installed and the toe-in adjustment has been made.

c. Check toe-in adjustment as described in this section.

Toe-In Adjustment

In order to maintain stable steering and minimize tire wear, the front wheels must be set for toe-in. When correctly set, the front of the tires will be pointed *in* slightly, while the rear of the tires will be pointed *out*. Toe-in is checked by accurately measuring the distance between the tires at the front and rear (**Figure 32**). If toe-in is incorrect, the tie rods are adjusted to bring the measurement to within specifications.

Proper toe-in adjustment cannot be achieved if the tie rods, wheel bearings or ball joints are worn. Replace worn parts before adjusting toe-in.

1. Inflate all tires to the recommended pressure, **Table 2**.
2. Park the machine on level ground and set the parking brake.
3. Raise and support the machine. The front wheels must be off the ground.
4. Point the handlebar straight ahead.
5. On both front tires, make a chalk mark at the center of the tread. The mark should be level with the centerline of the axle.
6. Measure distance A between the tires as shown in **Figure 32**. Record the measurement.
7. Rotate both wheels until the marks are at the back, and level with the axle.
8. Measure distance B between the tires as shown in **Figure 32**. Record the measurement.
9. Subtract measurement A from measurement B.
   a. If the difference is 0-10 mm (0-0.4 in.), toe-in is correct.
   b If toe-in is not correct, perform Step 10.
10. Adjust *both* tie rods equally as follows:

NOTE
The outer tie rod end and locknut is a left-hand thread. The inner tie rod end and locknut is a right-hand thread. Note which direction each set of parts must be turned when loosening and tightening the parts.

a. Loosen both tie rod end locknuts (A, **Figure 33**) on both tie rods.
b. Equally turn each tie rod with a wrench fitted to the flats on the rod (B, **Figure 33**).

NOTE
If the tie rods are not adjusted identically, handlebar alignment will not be centered with the wheels.

11

c. Recheck the measurements.

d. Tighten the locknuts when toe-in is correct.

e. Turn the handlebar from side to side and check that all ball joints pivot properly.

f. Test ride the machine slowly to ensure that all adjustments are correct.

STEERING KNUCKLE

Removal and Installation

1. Remove the front hub as described in this chapter.

2. Remove the brake hose guide (**Figure 34**).

3. Remove the outer tie rod end (**Figure 26**) as described in this chapter.

4. Remove the cotter pins and nuts from the studs (**Figure 35**).

5. Remove the ball joints from the steering knuckle. Two methods of removal are as follows:

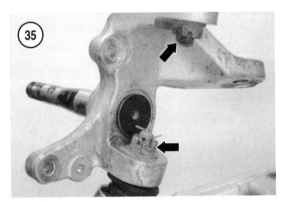

a. If a ball joint remover is available (**Figure 27**), or similar tool, it can be used to separate the parts (**Figure 36**). If the ball joint will be reused, there is a risk of tearing the rubber boot when using this tool.

b. If a ball joint remover is not available, support the steering knuckle and thread the nut onto the stud. Use a heat gun or propane torch to heat the area around the joint, then use a drift to drive the ball joint from the steering knuckle (**Figure 37**). Keep the drift centered on the stud. If the tie rod end will be reused, avoid damaging the threads.

6. Inspect the steering knuckle as described in this section.

7. Reverse these steps to install the steering knuckle. Note the following:

a. Torque both ball joint nuts to 25 N•m (18 ft.-lb.).

b. Install new cotter pins.

Inspection

1. Clean and dry the steering knuckle.

2. Inspect the following areas for cracks and other damage (**Figure 38**). If damage is detected, replace the steering knuckle.

a. Cotter pin hole.

b. Axle threads.

c. Bearing surfaces.

d. Bores.

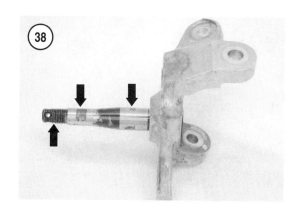

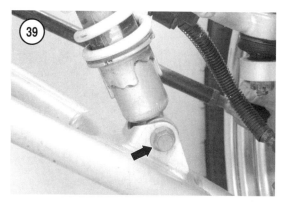

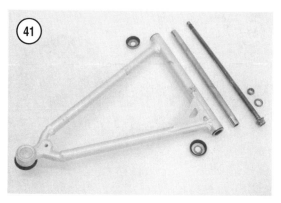

CONTROL ARMS

Removal and Installation

The following procedure describes the complete removal of the control arms for reconditioning or replacement.

1. Remove the front hub as described in this chapter.

2. Remove the lower mounting bolt from the shock absorber (**Figure 39**). If increased work space is desired, remove the entire shock absorber as described in this chapter.

3. Remove the brake hose guide and disconnect the control arm ball joints as described in *Steering Knuckle* in this chapter.

4. Remove the brush guard.

5. Before removing the control arms, grasp each arm and leverage it side to side. If play is noticeable, check the bushings for wear.

6. Remove the bolt from the upper control arm (**Figure 40**), then remove the control arm assembly (**Figure 41**). Note that the bolt head is at the front of the control arm. If both upper control arms are removed, identify the arms so they can be installed in their original positions.

7. Remove the bolts from the lower control arm (**Figure 42**), then remove the control arm assembly (**Figure 43**). Note that the bolt heads are at the outside of the control arm. If both lower control arms are removed, identify the arms so they can be installed in their original positions.

8. Inspect the control arms as described in this section.

9. Reverse these steps to install the control arms. Note the following:

    a. If both pairs of control arms have been removed, verify that they are being installed on the correct side of the machine.

11

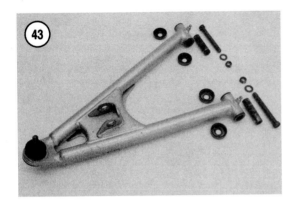

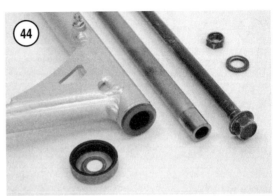

b. Install the control arm bolts so the heads face in the correct direction.

c. Torque the lower control arm nuts to 32 N•m (24 ft.-lb.).

d. Torque the upper control arm nut to 38 N•m (28 ft.-lb.).

e. Torque the ball joint nuts to 25 N•m (18 ft.-lb.).

f. Torque the shock absorber nuts to 45 N•m (33 ft.-lb.).

g. Torque the brush guard bolts to 31 N•m (23 ft.-lb.).

Inspection

1. Remove the caps and pivot spacer(s) from the upper control arm (**Figure 44**) and lower control arm (**Figure 45**). Keep all parts with their respective control arm.

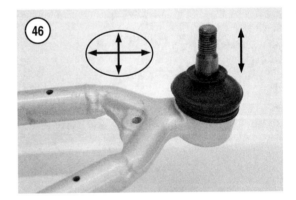

> *NOTE*
> *Unless the bushings are obviously damaged, do not remove them from the control arms. The bushings are made of synthetic material that is easily damage during removal.*

2. Clean the control arm parts. Keep all bolts identified so they can be reinstalled in their original positions.

> *NOTE*
> *The ball joints are packed with grease and sealed. Do not immerse the ball joints in solvent or any other liquid that could penetrate the boots. Wipe the ball joints clean with a shop cloth prior to inspection.*

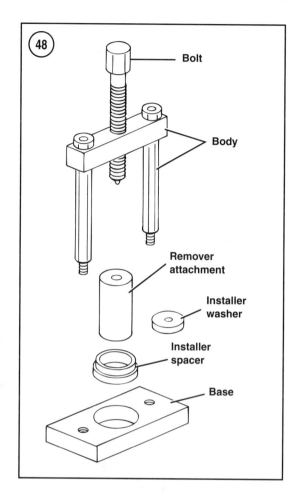

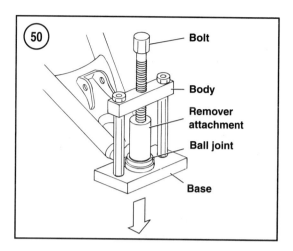

5. Grasp each ball joint (**Figure 46**) and swivel it in all directions, as well as vertically. Check for roughness, dryness and play.

   a. For the upper control arm, the ball joint is integral to the control arm and the complete assembly must be replaced if the ball joint is damaged.

   b. For the lower control arm, the ball joint is a replaceable part. Replace the ball joint as described in this section if wear is detected.

6. Inspect the control arm pivot assemblies.

   a. Insert each pivot spacer into its bushing and check for play (**Figure 47**). If necessary, remove a damaged bushing by carefully prying at the edge of the bushing. When the bushing is unseated, twist it from the bore. Install a new bushing by lightly tapping it into place with a soft mallet.

   b. Check the fit of the bolt in the spacer. If play is evident, replace the worn parts.

   c. Check the fit of each dust cover on the control arm. The cover should fit snugly to prevent the entry of moisture and dirt.

Lower Control Arm Ball Joint Replacement

Removal of the ball joint requires the Yamaha removal/installation set (part No. YM-01474, 90890-01474 and part No. YM-01480, 90890-01480) (**Figure 48**), or an equivalent.

1. Remove the clip, boot and snap ring from the ball joint (**Figure 49**).

2. The ball joint is driven out of the control arm by installing the tool as shown in (**Figure 50**).

3. Inspect all welded joints on the control arm. Check for fractures, bending or other damage. If damage is detected, replace the control arm, or, have a dealership or machine shop weld and test the strength of the control arm.

4. Inspect the ball joint boots for tears and the entry of moisture or dirt into the joint.

11

a. Center the bolt on the ball joint stud.

b. Center the base so the ball joint can pass through the hole in the base.

c. Turn the bolt and apply pressure to the ball joint, driving it from the control arm.

3. The new ball joint is driven into the control arm by installing the tool as shown in (**Figure 51**).

a. Check that all parts are aligned and the ball joint can pass into the control arm.

b. Turn the bolt and apply pressure to the ball joint, driving it into the control arm.

c. Lubricate the ball joint and boot interior with waterproof grease, then install the snap ring, boot and clip.

SHOCK ABSORBERS

The front shock absorbers are equipped with five spring preload positions. Set both shock absorbers to the same setting. Preload is set by using a shock absorber spanner to rotate the cam at the bottom of the spring (A, **Figure 52**). The least amount of spring preload is in the first position (B), while the most preload is in the fifth position (C). The standard setting is the third position.

The shock absorber body is a sealed unit that must be replaced if it becomes damaged. Parts are not available separately. If a shock absorber is damaged, replace the shock absorbers as a pair.

Removal and Installation

1. Raise and support the machine. The front wheels must be slightly off the ground.

2. Remove the lower mounting bolt (**Figure 39**).

3. Remove the upper mounting bolt (**Figure 53**).

4. Remove the shock absorber and inspect it as described in this section.

5. Reverse these steps to install the shock absorbers. Note the following:

a. Apply molydisulfide grease to the bushings and mounting bolts.

b. Install the bolts so the heads face to the front of the machine.

c. Torque the shock absorber nuts to 45 N•m (33 ft.-lb.).

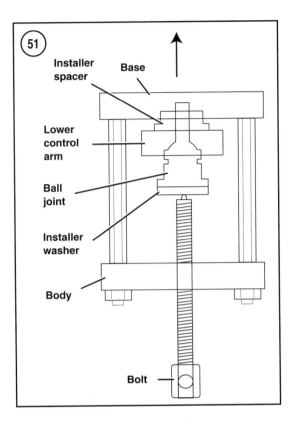

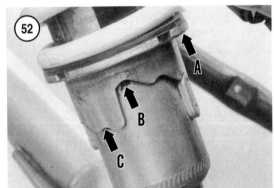

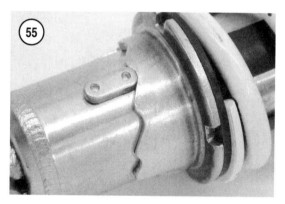

Inspection

1. Inspect and clean the lower bushing, pivot and mounting bolt (**Figure 54**). Fit each part into its mating part and check for wear and play.
2. Inspect the preload adjuster and notches for damage (**Figure 55**).
3. Inspect the body for major dents that can affect shock operation.
4. Inspect the rod seal for oil leakage (**Figure 56**).
5. Inspect the spring for damage or looseness. If the spring is loose, it is fatigued.
6. Inspect and clean the upper bushing and mounting bolt (**Figure 57**). Fit the bolt into the bushing and check for wear and play.
7. When inspection is complete, apply molybdenum disulfide grease to the lower and upper bushings and mounting bolts.

STEERING SHAFT

Removal and Installation

Refer to **Figure 58**.

1. Remove the front fender and fuel tank (Chapter Fourteen).
2. Remove the handlebar as described in this chapter. Reposition and secure the handlebar out of the way. Avoid kinking the cables and brake hose. Keep the brake fluid reservoir upright.
3. Remove the pin, nut and washer from the end of the steering shaft (**Figure 59**). If the pitman arm must also be removed, remove the tie rod ends as described in this chapter.
4. Bend the lockwasher tabs away from the bolt heads, then remove the two bolts from the steering shaft holders (**Figure 60**).
5. Lift and remove the steering shaft from the lower bearing (**Figure 61**).
6. Inspect the steering shaft assembly as described in this section.
7. Reverse these steps to install the steering shaft. Note the following:
   a. Apply waterproof grease to the shaft splines, seals, bearing and steering shaft holder.
   b. When installing the steering shaft splines into the pitman arm splines, check that the wheels and handlebar mounts are centered with one another. Finger-tighten all bolts and verify correct alignment of the parts before torquing any bolts.

11

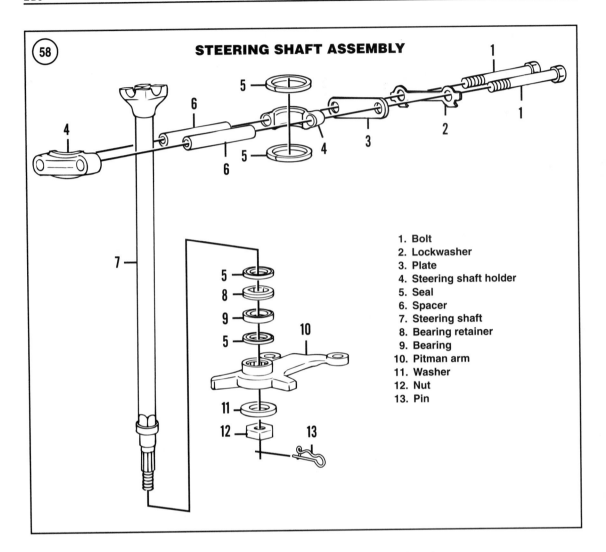

STEERING SHAFT ASSEMBLY

1. Bolt
2. Lockwasher
3. Plate
4. Steering shaft holder
5. Seal
6. Spacer
7. Steering shaft
8. Bearing retainer
9. Bearing
10. Pitman arm
11. Washer
12. Nut
13. Pin

c. Torque the steering shaft nut to 110 N•m (81 ft.-lb.).

d. Install a new lockwasher on the steering shaft holder, then torque the steering shaft holder nuts to 23 N•m (17 ft.-lb.). Bend the lockwasher tabs against the bolt heads.

e. Check toe-in as described in this chapter.

Inspection

Refer to **Figure 58**.

1. Wipe the steering shaft clean.
2. Inspect the steering shaft for the following:
   a. Distortion or damage.
   b. Enlarged tie rod holes in the pitman arm, if removed.
   c. Cracked cotter pin hole.
   d. Damaged threads.
3. Inspect the steering shaft holders and seals for wear or damage.
4. Inspect the steering shaft seals and bearing.
   a. Inspect the seals for wear and deterioration.
   b. Inspect the bearing by turning its inner race. The bearing should turn smoothly and have minimal, if any play.
   c. If necessary, replace the bearing and seals as described in this section.

Steering Shaft Bearing and Seals Replacement

Refer to **Figure 58**.

1. Pry the upper and lower seals out of the bearing holder.

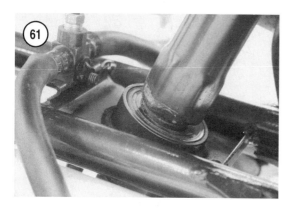

2. Remove the bearing retainer from the top of the bearing holder. Removal of the retainer requires the Yamaha damper rod holder (part No. YM-01327, 90890-01327), or an equivalent.

3. Drive the bearing out the top of the holder.

4. Clean the retainer and the bearing holder bore.

5. Apply waterproof grease to the new bearing and seals.

6. Insert the bearing into the bearing holder. Install the bearing so the manufacturer's marks face up.

7. Install and torque the bearing retainer to 40 N•m (30 ft.-lb.).

8. Place the seals squarely over the bores in the bearing holder, then seat the seals into the bore. When driving the seals, use a driver or socket that fits on the outer edge of the seals.

HANDLEBAR

Adjustment

The handlebar and controls must be tight and not move or pivot when pressure is applied. If the handlebar needs to be repositioned, adjustment can be made by loosening the *rear* bolts securing the upper holders. Tilt the handlebar to the desired position, then torque the front holder bolts, followed by the rear holder bolts. Torque the bolts to 23 N•m (17 ft.-lb.).

Removal and Installation

Refer to **Figure 62**.

1. If replacing the handlebar, remove the following components:

   a. Fuel tank breather hose and handlebar cover.

   b. Security bands.

   c. Front brake master cylinder and brake light switch. If the switch must be removed from the master cylinder, first disengage the barbed fitting on the switch, accessible from below the master cylinder.

   d. Throttle assembly.

   e. Clutch lever, park switch and brake switch assembly. If the switches must be removed from the clutch lever assembly, first disengage the barbed fitting on each switch, accessible from below the lever assembly.

   f. Handlebar switch assembly.

   g. If removal of the grips is necessary, use solvent or a spray lubricant to flood under the grip to soften the adhesive. Compressed air can also be used to lift and free the grips. Remove the collar from the handlebar and install it on the new handlebar.

   h. Handlebar holder bolts, cover brackets and holders.

2. Inspect the handlebar as described in this section.

11

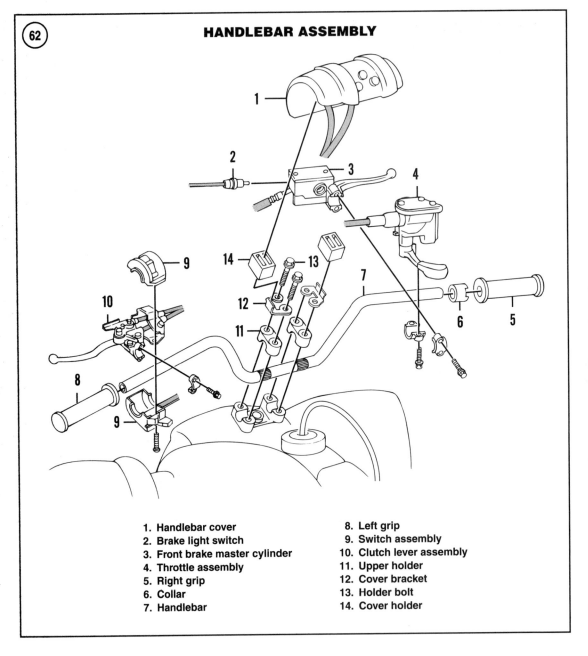

HANDLEBAR ASSEMBLY

1. Handlebar cover
2. Brake light switch
3. Front brake master cylinder
4. Throttle assembly
5. Right grip
6. Collar
7. Handlebar
8. Left grip
9. Switch assembly
10. Clutch lever assembly
11. Upper holder
12. Cover bracket
13. Holder bolt
14. Cover holder

3. Reverse these steps to install the handlebar. Note the following:

a. The punch marks on the upper holders must face forward (**Figure 63**). Torque the front holder bolts, followed by the rear holder bolts. Torque all bolts to 23 N•m (17 ft.-lb.).

b. Check that the indentions on the collar are engaged with the throttle assembly and front brake master cylinder.

c. Torque the front brake master cylinder mounting bolts to 7 N•m (62 in.-lb.).

d. If new grips will be installed, clean the handlebar grip surface with solvent, such as electrical contact cleaner. Apply a hand grip cement following the manufacturer's instructions.

e. Check the riding position and adjust the handlebar, if necessary. Turn the handlebar side to side and check for cable binding.

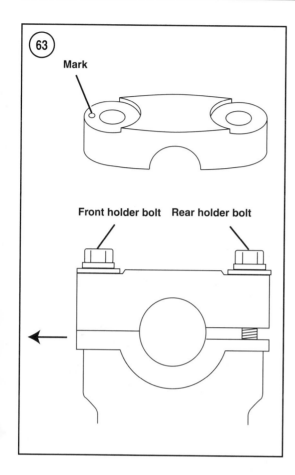

63

Mark

Front holder bolt   Rear holder bolt

64

Inspection

1. Inspect the handlebar for cracks, bends or other damage. If the handlebar is made of aluminum, check closely where the handlebar is clamped to the holders, and at the clutch lever. If cracks, scores or other damage is found, replace the handlebar. Damage in these areas can cause the handlebar to break.

WARNING
Never attempt to straighten, weld or heat a damaged handlebar. The metal can weaken and possibly break when subjected to the shocks and stresses that occur when riding the machine.

2. Inspect the threads on the mounting bolts and in the holders. Clean all residue from the threads. Replace damaged or stressed bolts.

3. Clean the handlebar holders and handlebar with solvent or electrical contact cleaner.

TIRES AND WHEELS

The machine is equipped with tubeless, low-pressure tires. The tires are designed for off-road use. Rapid wear will occur if the machine is ridden on paved surfaces. If a puncture occurs, a tire plug may be used temporarily. A tire plug is not suitable as a permanent repair. Repair the tire as soon as possible. The procedures in this section detail how to remove a tire from the rim and how to make a permanent cold patch tire repair.

Tire Changing

The severe operating conditions in which an ATV may operate and the design of ATV tires can create a seal that makes tire bead and wheel separation extremely difficult. A bead breaker tool, tire irons and rim protectors are required to remove and install the tire. K&L Supply Co., (1-800-727-6767) offers a heavy-duty tire breakdown tool (**Figure 64**) that is available through motorcycle dealerships.

1. Remove the valve stem core and deflate the tire.

2. Lubricate the tire bead and rim flanges with a rubber lubricant. Press the sidewalls down to allow the lubricant to penetrate the bead. Also lubricate the sidewall where the bead breaker will make contact.

3. Position the wheel under the bead breaker tool (**Figure 65**).

4. With the tool seated against the rim, press down on the lever to break the tire bead from the rim. Work around the rim, using the bead breaker and hand pressure to break the tire free (**Figure 66**).

5. Turn the rim over and repeat Steps 2-4.

6. Relubricate the tire beads and rim flanges to prepare for using the tire irons.

11

7. Place rim protectors or other padding (split rubber hose works well) on the rim edge. Position the protectors where the tire irons will be inserted.

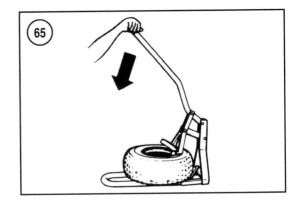

> *CAUTION*
> *Failure to use rim protectors could allow the tire irons to damage the wheel finish, as well as damage the bead seating area. This could result in air leakage at the bead.*

8. Insert the tire irons between the rim and tire (**Figure 67**). Pry the tire bead over the rim. If removal is difficult, move the tire irons closer together and remove smaller sections at a time.

9. When the upper sidewall is free, lift the lower sidewall up so it can be removed as described in Steps 6-8.

10. Clean and inspect the rim sealing surfaces (**Figure 68**). The sealing surface must be straight, clean and smooth in order to seal properly.

11. Replace the valve stem as follows:

  a. Remove the valve stem by pulling it out from inside the rim.

  b. Lubricate the new valve stem with tire lubricant.

  c. Insert the new valve stem through the rim hole, then pull it out until it seats into place (**Figure 69**).

12. Inspect the tire bead and rim for cleanliness.

13. Check the tire sidewall for the *direction arrow* or the *This Side Out* marking.

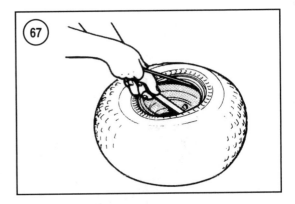

14. Place the tire with the sidewall markings facing up, then wet the tire bead with water.

> *NOTE*
> *Tire lubricants applied to the bead during installation may cause the tire to slip on the rim, resulting in a loss of air pressure. Preferably, use water as a lubricant during tire installation.*

15. Insert the rim (valve stem facing up) into the tire (**Figure 70**). Hand-fit as much of the rim into the tire as possible.

16. Use the rim protectors and tire irons to finish installing the bead. Push the rim to the opposite side of the tire so the second bead can be installed.

17. Turn the assembly over and hand-fit as much of the rim into the tire as possible **Figure 71**.

18. Use the rim protectors and tire irons to finish installing the bead.

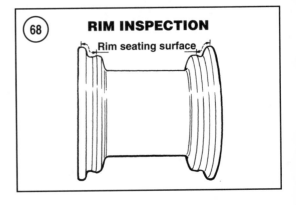

RIM INSPECTION

Rim seating surface

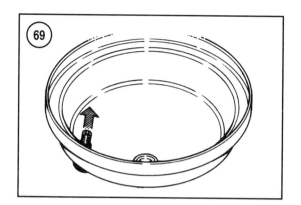

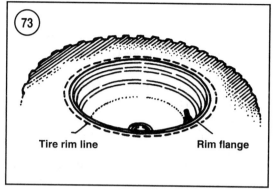

Tire rim line   Rim flange

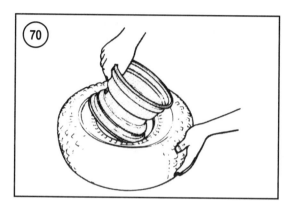

19. Install the valve stem core.

20. Apply water to the rim beads, then inflate the tire to the bead seating pressure, indicated on the sidewall.

> *WARNING*
> *Do not inflate the tire past the recommended bead seating pressure. Tire explosion and severe personal injury is possible. The pressure shown in **Table 2** is for original equipment tires. Check the sidewall if replacing with aftermarket tires.*

> *NOTE*
> *If the tire beads will not seat because of air leakage, a tight strap around the perimeter of the tread will aid in driving the beads into place. If correctly sized, a discarded motorcycle tire will also work (**Figure 72**).*

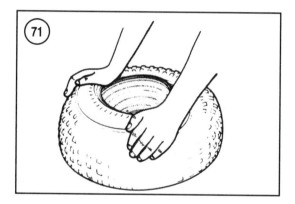

21. After inflation, check the rim lines on both sides of the tire to ensure the beads are seated. If the beads are seated correctly, the rim lines will be parallel with the rim flanges as shown in **Figure 73**. If the beads are not seated correctly, deflate the tire and break the bead so additional water can be applied to the tire bead. Reinflate the tire and check the beads.

22. When the tire is properly seated, do the following:

    a. Remove the valve core to deflate the tire.

    b. Wait one hour to allow adjustment of the tire on the rim.

    c. Install the valve core and inflate the tire to the operating pressure listed in **Table 2**.

    d. Apply water to the beads and valve stem and check for leaks.

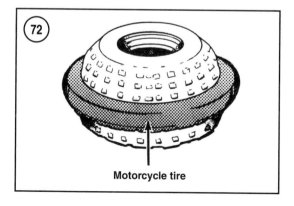

Motorcycle tire

11

Cold Patch Repair

Follow the manufacturer's instructions when using a repair kit. If instructions are not available, use the following procedure:

1. Remove the tire as described in this section.
2. Mark the puncture location, then remove the object puncturing the tire.
3. Working from inside the tire, roughen the area around the puncture. The roughened area should be larger than the patch to be applied. If the repair kit does not provide a tool to roughen the area, use coarse sandpaper or any object that will lightly scrape and roughen the surface.
4. Clean the roughened area with a non-oily solvent.
5. Apply a small amount of the repair adhesive to the roughened area. Allow the adhesive to dry for about 30 seconds to become tacky.

6. Remove the backing from the patch.

CAUTION
To ensure good adhesion of the patch, do not touch the newly exposed surface of the patch.

7. Center the patch over the puncture, then press the patch into place. Do not attempt to raise or slide the patch once it contacts the adhesive.

8. If a roller is available, burnish the patch, checking that the edges are tightly sealed. If a roller is not available, use a smooth hard object, to burnish the patch.

9. Install the tire on the rim as described in this section.

Table 1 STEERING AND FRONT SUSPENSION SPECIFICATIONS

Front suspension	Double wishbone
Front shock absorber	
Type	Coil spring/oil damper
Travel	110 mm (4.33 in.)
Spring installed length	293.5 mm (11.56 in.)
Spring rate	19.6-29.4 N/mm (111.92-167.87 lb./in.)
Front wheel travel	230 mm (9.06 in.)
Steering	
Camber angle	-1°
Caster angle	8°
Kingpin angle	14.5°
Kingpin offset	5 mm (0.20 in.)
Toe-in	0-10 mm (0-0.4 in.)
Trail	47 mm (1.85 in.)

Table 2 TIRE AND WHEEL SPECIFICATIONS

Tires	
Type	Tubeless radial
Sizes	
Front	AT21 × 7-10 Dunlop KT331
Rear	AT20 × 10-9 Dunlop KT335
Recommended cold pressure	
Standard	27.5 kPa (4.0 psi) for maximum 100 kg (220 lb.) load
Mimimum	24.5 kPa (3.5 psi)
Bead seating pressure	250 kPa (36 psi) maximum
Wheels	
Rim sizes	
Front	10 × 5.5 AT
Rear	9 × 8.5 AT
Runout (radial and lateral)	2 mm (0.08 in.)

Table 3 FRONT SHOCK ABSORBER SETTING

	Standard	Minimum	Maximum
Spring preload	3	1	5

Table 4 FRONT SUSPENSION TORQUE SPECIFICATIONS

	N•m	in.-lb.	ft.-lb.
Ball joint nuts	25	–	18
Brush guard bolts	30	–	23
Front brake caliper mounting bolts	28	–	21
Front brake master cylinder mounting bolts	7	62	–
Front wheel hub nut	70	–	52
Front wheel lug nuts	45	–	33
Handlebar holder bolts	23	–	17
Lower control arm nuts	32	–	24
Shock absorber mounting nuts	45	–	33
Steering shaft bearing retainer	40	–	30
Steering shaft nut	110	–	81
Steering shaft holder nuts	23	–	17
Tie rod nuts	25	–	18
Upper control arm nut	38	–	28

11

CHAPTER TWELVE

REAR SUSPENSION

This chapter provides service procedures for the rear wheel, rear wheel hub, rear axle, rear axle hub, sprockets, drive chain, shock absorber, shock linkage and swing arm. Refer to the tables at the end of this chapter for specifications.

For tire changing and repair refer to Chapter Eleven.

REAR WHEEL

Removal and Installation

1. Park the machine on level ground and block the front wheels.

2. Loosen the lug nuts (A, **Figure 1**).

3. Raise and support the machine. The rear wheels must be off the ground.

4. Remove the lug nuts and washers from the studs, then remove the wheel from the hub. If more than one wheel will be removed, mark each wheel so it can be installed in its original location.

5. If tire repair is required, make the repair as described in Chapter Eleven.

6. Clean the lug nuts, washers and studs. If studs are broken or damaged, replace the studs.

7. Install the wheel onto the studs, with the valve stem facing out.

WARNING
If more than one wheel has been removed from the machine, check that the tire direction arrow (on the tire sidewall, if applicable) is pointing forward, when the wheel is mounted. The arrow must point forward to prevent the possibility of tire ply failure during operation.

8. Install the washers and finger-tighten the lug nuts.

9. Lower the machine to the ground, then equally tighten the lug nuts in a crossing pattern. Make several passes when tightening and torque the nuts to 45 N•m (33 ft.-lb.).

10. Lower the machine to the ground.

REAR WHEEL HUB

Removal and Installation

1. Remove the rear wheel as described in this chapter.

2. Remove the cotter pin, nut and washer from the axle (B, **Figure 1**).

3. Pull the wheel hub from the axle splines. If the opposite hub will be removed, mark the hubs so they can be reinstalled in their original positions on the axle.

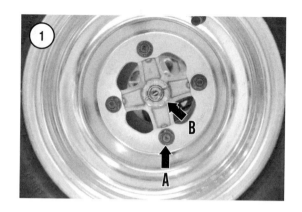

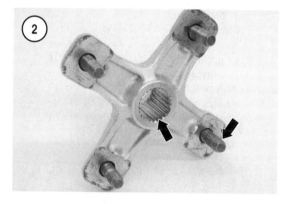

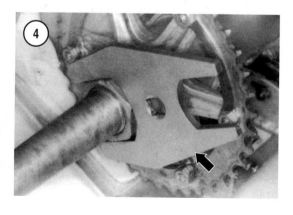

NOTE
If the hub is seized to the splines, apply penetrating oil and lightly tap the back of the hub, near the center. If light tapping does not loosen the hub, use a puller to ease the hub from the axle.

4. Inspect the hub for cracks, damaged splines and broken studs (**Figure 2**).

5. Reverse this procedure to install the hub. Note the following:

    a. Apply grease to the hub splines.

    b. Torque the hub nut to 120 N•m (88 ft.-lb.).

    c. Install a new cotter pin.

REAR AXLE

Removal

This section details the complete removal, inspection and installation of the rear axle. Before starting removal, read the removal and installation procedures and have the required tools on hand.

1. Park the machine on level ground and set the parking brake.

2. Remove the rear wheels and hubs as described in this chapter.

3. Loosen and remove the axle locknuts (A, **Figure 3**).

    a. For 2002-on models, first loosen the set screws (B, **Figure 3**) in the outer locknut.

    b. The nuts are highly torqued to one another and should be turned in opposite directions to loosen. Threadlocking compound is also used on the axle threads.

NOTE
*Preferably, use the Yamaha 50 mm axle nut wrench (part No. YM-37132, 90890-01419) (**Figure 4**) with a breaker bar to loosen and separate the locknuts. This tool can also be used with a torque wrench when installing the nuts.*

4. Pull the axle out the left side of the swing arm.

5. Inspect the axle as described in this section.

6. Inspect the seals and bearings as described in the *Rear Axle Hub* section of this chapter.

12

Inspection

1. Clean the axle and fasteners. All splines must be clean for inspection.

2. At each end of the axle (**Figure 5**), inspect the following:

    a. Check for cracks or fractures around the cotter pin holes. Replace the axle if damage is evident.

    b Check for uniform and symmetrical axle nut threads. Screw the axle nut onto the threads and check for roughness and play. If damage is detected, try restoring the threads with a thread die.

    c. Check for worn, distorted and broken wheel hub splines. Inspect the splines in each wheel hub for damage. Fit each hub onto its respective end of the axle and feel for play. If play or wear is detected, replace the parts.

3. Inspect the axle where it contacts the bearings in the axle hub. Check for scoring, galling and other damage. If damage is evident, inspect the bearings in the axle hub, as described in this chapter.

4. Check the axle for straightness using a dial indicator and V-blocks as shown in **Figure 6**. Replace the axle if runout exceeds 1.5 mm (0.06 in.).

Installation

1. Apply waterproof grease to the splines of the sprocket and brake disc hubs.

2. Apply waterproof grease to the axle splines and axle bearing surfaces.

3. If removed, install the chain on the sprocket.

4. Insert the axle into the axle hub from the left side of the swing arm. Check that the axle turns freely and runs true.

5. Install the axle locknuts as follows:

    a. Apply a medium-strength threadlocking compound to the axle threads.

    b. Install and finger-tighten the inner locknut. On 2002-on models, install the nut with the wide side facing in.

    c. Install the outer locknut. On 2002-on models, install the nut with the wide side facing out. The outer locknut also has the set screws.

NOTE
Depending on how the special wrenches are mounted on the torque wrench, when torquing the axle nuts

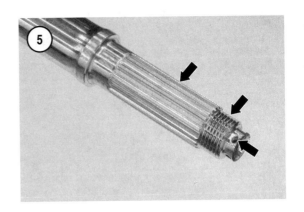

*in the following steps, the torque wrench readings may need to be calculated to reflect the actual torque being applied. When a special wrench is installed inline on the torque wrench (**Figure 7**), the overall length and leverage of the torque wrench is increased. refer to **Torque Adapters** in Chapter One*

    d. Torque the inner locknut against the brake disc hub. Torque the nut to 55 N•m 41 ft.-lbs.

    e. Hold the inner locknut in place and torque the outer locknut against the inner locknut. Torque the nut to 190 N•m 140 ft.-lbs.

    f. Draw a straight reference line across both nuts (**Figure 8**).

    g. Hold the outer locknut in place and torque the inner locknut against the outer locknut. Torque the nut to 240 N•m 177 ft.-lbs.

    h. Measure the distance between the two halves of the reference line (**Figure 9**). For the 2001 model, the distance should be at least 15 mm (0.6 in.). For 2002-on models, the distance should be at least 3 mm (0.12 in.). If necessary, continue to tighten the inner locknut against the outer locknut until the correct distance is achieved.

    i. For 2002-on models, torque the set screws to 6 N•m (53 in.-lb.).

6. Install the rear hubs and wheels as described in this chapter.

7. Adjust the chain (Chapter Three). After adjustment, torque the axle hub bolts to 90 N•m (66 ft.-lb.).

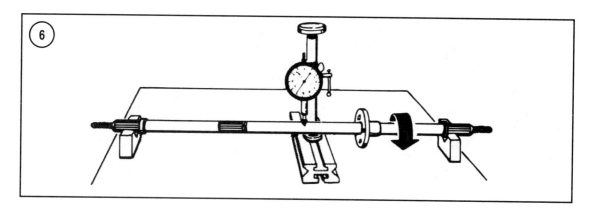

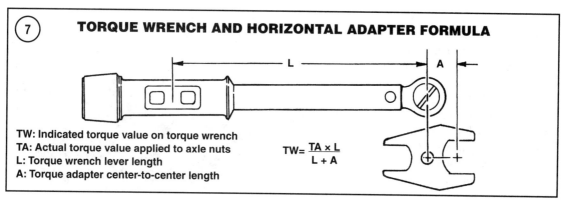

TORQUE WRENCH AND HORIZONTAL ADAPTER FORMULA

TW: Indicated torque value on torque wrench
TA: Actual torque value applied to axle nuts
L: Torque wrench lever length
A: Torque adapter center-to-center length

$$TW = \frac{TA \times L}{L + A}$$

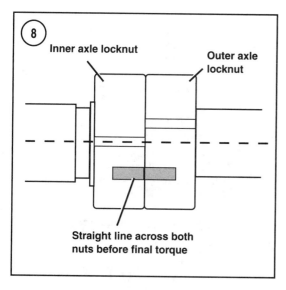

Inner axle locknut

Outer axle locknut

Straight line across both nuts before final torque

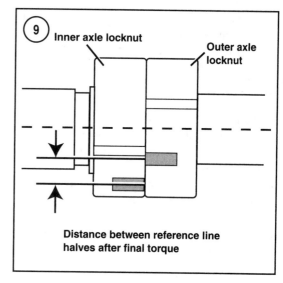

Inner axle locknut

Outer axle locknut

Distance between reference line halves after final torque

12

REAR AXLE HUB

Removal and Installation

The rear axle hub passes through the swing arm and contains the seals and axle bearings that support the axle. The hubs for the sprocket and brake disc are located to the left and right side of the axle hub respectively. This section details the complete removal, inspection and installation of the rear axle hub assembly.

1. Remove the rear axle as described in this chapter.

2. Remove the brake caliper (Chapter Thirteen).

3. Remove the brake disc hub (**Figure 10**).

4. Remove the driven sprocket hub (**Figure 11**).

5. Remove the two axle hub bolts from the brake caliper bracket (**Figure 12**). Apply penetrating oil and use a wood block to evenly tap the bracket off the hub (**Figure 13**).

6. Inspect the axle hub assembly, brake hub and sprocket hub as described in this section.

7. Reverse this procedure to install the hub assemblies. Note the following:

   a. Lubricate all splines and seals with waterproof grease.

   b. Install the rear axle hub and brake caliper bracket with the chain alignment marks facing up (**Figure 14**).

   c. Install the chain on the sprocket.

Disassembly and Inspection

1. Wipe the axle hub assembly clean (**Figure 15**). Do not immerse the hub assembly in solvent unless the bearings and seals will be replaced.

2. Inspect the dust seals for tears, distortion or other damage. If rust, dirt or moisture is evident behind the seals, leakage is occurring at the seals. Replace the seals as described in this section. For components that are not routinely disassembled, it is common practice to replace the seals whenever the part is disassembled.

3. Inspect the bearings as follows:

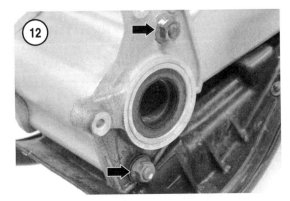

NOTE
When checking the bearings, keep the axle hub vertical. This will prevent the hub spacer from contacting the bearing being checked. If necessary, clean the space between the spacer and bearing to achieve the clearance.

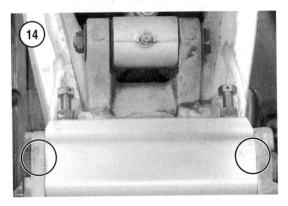

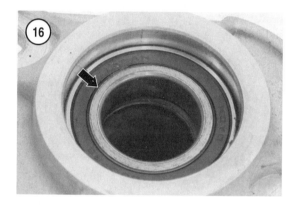

a. Turn each bearing inner race (**Figure 16**). Feel for roughness, noise or binding. The bearings should turn smoothly and quietly.

b. Check for axial and radial (**Figure 17**) play. Replace the bearings if worn or damaged. Remove and install the bearings as described in this section.

NOTE
Always replace bearings as a pair.

4. After the bearings and seals have been inspected/replaced, coat the surface of the bearing holder (that fits inside the swing arm) with a film of waterproof grease.

5. Inspect the brake caliper bracket and bore. If the bracket was seized to the axle hub, polish the interior of the bore with emery cloth to remove corrosion. Apply a film of waterproof grease to the cleaned bore.

6. Inspect the bolts, washers and nuts for corrosion and damage.

7. Inspect the sprocket and brake disc hubs.

a. Inspect the splines for corrosion and damage (**Figure 18**). Clean and lubricate all splines with waterproof grease.

b. Inspect the seal contact area on the hubs (**Figure 18**). Polish off corrosion and lubricate with waterproof grease.

c. Check that the sprocket/disc bolts are secure.

Seal Replacement

Seals are used to prevent the entry of moisture and dirt into the hub and bearings. Always install new seals whenever the axle hub is being reconditioned.

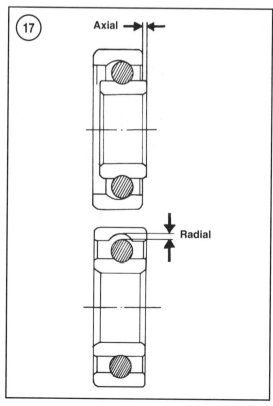

1. Pry the old seals out of their recesses (**Figure 19**). Place a shop cloth under the tool to prevent damage to the part.

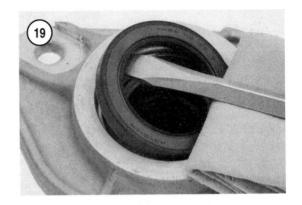

> *NOTE*
> *Identify the location of the seals in the axle hub. Although the seals appear identical, they are different part numbers.*

2. Apply waterproof grease to the new seal, packing it into the inner lip.
3. Clean and lubricate the bores.
4. Place the seal *squarely* over the bore, with the manufacturer's marks facing out (**Figure 20**).
5. Place a suitably-sized driver or socket over the seal. The driver should seat against the outside diameter of the seal.
6. Press the seal into the bore.

Bearing Replacement

1. Remove the seals as described in this section.
2. Insert a drift into one side of the axle hub and push the spacer (between the bearings) to one side (**Figure 21**).
3. Place the drift on the edge of the inner bearing race and tap it with a hammer. Work around the perimeter of the race, moving it in small increments until it is removed. Apply penetrating lubricant, as necessary.

> *NOTE*
> *Striking the drift hard can cause the bearing to jam against the wall of the bearing holder.*

4. Remove the spacer from the axle hub.
5. Remove the remaining bearing, driving it out with a bearing driver or socket that fits on the outer race of the bearing.
6. Clean and dry the axle hub and spacer.
7. Before installing the new bearings and seals, note the following:
   a. Install the new bearings with the manufacturer's marks facing out. If the replacement bearings are shielded on one side, the shield faces out.
   b. If necessary, apply waterproof grease to bearings that are not lubricated by the manufacturer. Work the grease into the cavities between the balls and races.
8. Place a bearing *squarely* over the bearing bore.

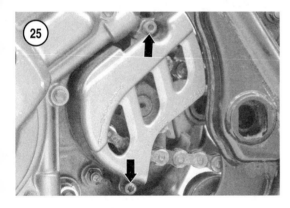

12. Press in the remaining bearing, seating it in the holder.

13. Install the seals as described in this section.

SPROCKETS

Check the condition of both sprockets and the drive chain, as described in Chapter Three. If either the chain or sprockets are worn, replace all drive components. Using new sprockets with a worn chain, or a new chain on worn sprockets will shorten the life of the new part.

Drive Sprocket and Guard Removal and Installation

1. Put the transmission in gear and set the parking brake.

2. Remove the bolts securing the left footpeg to the footguard.

3. Remove the bolts securing the footpeg to the frame (**Figure 23**). Pivot and secure the assembly away from the sprocket guard.

> *NOTE*
> *If desired, remove the complete assembly by removing the linkage bolt (**Figure 24**). Inspect, lubricate and install the assembly as described in Chapter Six.*

4. Remove the sprocket guard (**Figure 25**). For 2002-on models, also remove the chain guide.

> *NOTE*
> *The chain can now be removed from the drive sprocket without removing the sprocket. If the drive sprocket must be removed, leave the chain on the sprocket until the sprocket nut is loosened.*

5. Bend the lockwasher tabs away from the sprocket nut, then remove the nut, washer and sprocket from the shaft (**Figure 26**). Mark the outside face of the sprocket. If reused, install the sprocket in its original direction.

6. Clean and inspect the sprocket and chain (Chapter Three).

7. Twist and remove the output shaft spacer and shaft O-ring (**Figure 27**). A small amount of oil will drip from the engine when the spacer is removed.

9. Place a suitably-sized driver or socket over the bearing. The driver should seat against the outside diameter of the bearing.

10. Press the bearing into place, seating it in the hub (**Figure 22**).

> *CAUTION*
> *Do not press or strike the bearing directly. Bearing damage will occur.*

11. Turn the hub over and install the spacer.

a. Clean and inspect the output shaft spacer (**Figure 28**). Inspect the inner and outer surfaces that contact the O-ring and crankcase seal. The surfaces should be smooth and free of corrosion or damage.

b. If leakage is evident at the crankcase seal (**Figure 29**), remove the seal retainer and replace the seal as described in *Seal Replacement* (Chapter Five). Torque the seal retainer bolts to 10 N•m (88 in.-lb.).

8. Reverse this procedure to install the drive sprocket. Note the following:

a. Install a new, lubricated O-ring onto the countershaft. The O-ring must seat in the shaft groove.

b. Install the output shaft spacer with the notched edge facing in.

c. If reusing the sprocket, check that the sprocket is installed in its original direction.

d. Install a new lockwasher.

e. Torque the sprocket nut to 70 N•m (52 ft.-lb.).

f. Torque the sprocket guard bolts to 10 N•m (88 in.-lb.).

g. Adjust the chain (Chapter Three).

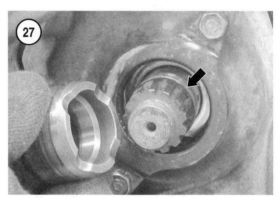

Driven Sprocket
Removal and Installation

If the drive sprocket will be replaced, loosen the drive sprocket shaft nut before raising the swing arm to remove the driven sprocket. The resistance of the machine sitting on the ground will aid in loosening the nut.

1. Put the transmission in gear and set the parking brake.

2. Bend the lockwasher tabs away from the sprocket hub nuts, then remove the nuts (**Figure 30**).

3. Remove the left rear wheel as described in this chapter.

4. Remove the sprocket from the hub.

5. Clean and inspect the sprocket and nuts. Inspect the sprocket and chain (Chapter Three).

6. Reverse this procedure to install the driven sprocket. Note the following:

a. If necessary, loosen the axle hub and chain adjusters, then move the axle forward to mount the chain.

b. Install new lockwashers on the studs.

c. Torque the sprocket nuts to 24 N•m (18 ft.-lb.).

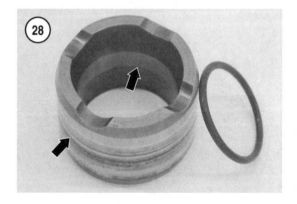

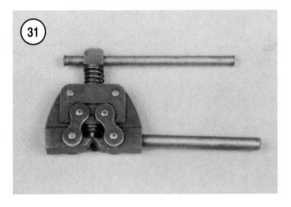

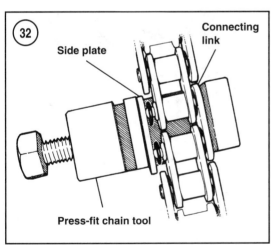

Connecting link

Side plate

Press-fit chain tool

d. Adjust the chain (Chapter Three).

DRIVE CHAIN

Refer to Chapter Three for drive chain cleaning, lubrication, adjustment and measurement. Refer to **Table 1** in this chapter for chain specifications.

When checking the condition of the chain, also check the condition of the sprockets (Chapter Three). If either the chain or sprockets are worn, replace all drive components. Using new sprockets with a worn chain, or a new chain on worn sprockets will shorten the life of the new part.

When new, the machine is equipped with an endless O-ring type chain. This type of chain is recommended since it is internally lubricated and requires minimal maintenance. Since it is permanently assembled, this increases the reliability of the chain. To remove the chain, the swing arm must be partially disassembled so the chain can pass out of the swing arm pivot.

The use of chains with a clip-type master link is not recommended. However, chains that can be assembled, using a permanent, press-fit master link are acceptable. If a chain breaker tool (**Figure 31**) and link riveting tool (**Figure 32**) are available, this can be a more convenient way to replace the chain, rather than disassembling the swing arm.

Read both procedures and understand the equipment and skill required.

Chain With No Master Link Removal and Installation

1. Remove the rear wheels as described in this chapter.
2. Remove the drive sprocket guard as described in this chapter.
3. Remove the shock absorber as described in this chapter.
4. Loosen the axle hub nuts and chain adjusters, then push the axle forward and lift the chain off the sprockets.

> *WARNING*
> *If necessary, get assistance in removing and handling the swing arm.*

> *NOTE*
> *With the swing arm disconnected from the shock absorber and linkage, it is recommended to check the condition of the swing arm bearings, as described in **Swing Arm Bearing Inspection** in this chapter.*

5. Remove the swing arm bolt (**Figure 33**) and pull the swing arm back.
6. Lower the swing arm and remove the chain.

12

7. Reverse this procedure to install the chain. Note the following:

    a. Clean and inspect the bores in the swing arm, engine case and frame.

    b. Apply waterproof grease to the parts and bores.

    c. Torque the swing arm bolt to 95 N•m (70 ft.-lb.).

    d. Adjust the chain (Chapter Three).

Chain With Press-Fit Master Link
Removal and Installation

1. Park the machine on level ground and block the front wheels.

2. Loosen the axle hub nuts and chain adjusters.

3. Raise the machine so the rear wheels are off the ground, then push the axle forward to create maximum slack in the chain.

4. Choose a convenient location along the drive chain for attaching a chain breaker tool (**Figure 31**).

5. Attach the tool to the drive chain and drive a link pin from the chain. Remove the chain.

6. Install the new chain and route it over the sprockets.

    a. Put the transmission in neutral.

    b. If necessary, attach a wire to the end of the chain to route it behind the sprocket guard and over the drive sprocket.

    c. After the chain is routed over the sprockets, remove the chain slack and position the ends together. Put the transmission in gear to prevent the drive sprocket from rotating.

7. Secure the chain ends with the master link. Check that the O-rings are on the master link pins. Insert the link from the back side of the chain.

8. Place the chain link sideplate on the master link. The identification marks must face out.

9. Stake the link pins using a chain riveting tool (**Figure 32**).

10. Adjust the chain (Chapter Three).

SHOCK ABSORBER

The single shock absorber is a spring-loaded, hydraulically-damped unit with an oil/nitrogen reservoir. For the 2001 model, the reservoir is connected to the shock absorber by a hose, while later models have the reservoir mounted on the shock absorber.

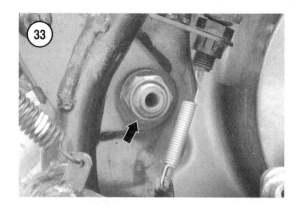

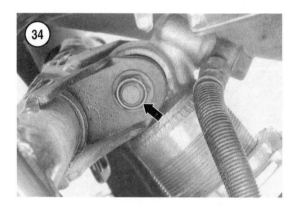

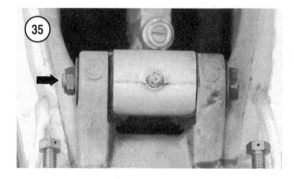

For the original equipment shock, only the spring, dust seals and mounting hardware are available as replacement parts. Parts for rebuilding the shock internally are not available. Refer to *Rear Suspension Adjustment* in this chapter for a description of the shock adjusters and their affect on the performance of the shock absorber.

Shock Absorber
Removal and Installation

The shock absorber is easiest to remove if the rear wheels are removed and the machine is supported

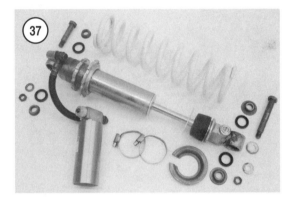

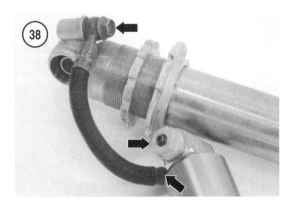

4. Support the swing arm, then remove the upper mounting bolt from the shock absorber (**Figure 34**).

    a. For the 2002-on models, a washer is used at both ends of the bolt. The 2001 model uses a washer only with the nut.

    b. For the 2001 model, also remove the reservoir and clamps.

5. Disconnect the relay arm at the upper bolt (**Figure 35**). Lower the relay arm and shock absorber away from the swing arm.

6. Remove the lower mounting bolt from the shock absorber (**Figure 36**).

    a. For the 2001 model, a washer is used at both ends of the bolt.

    b. The 2002-on models use a washer only with the nut.

7. Inspect the shock absorber as described in this section.

8. Reverse these steps to install the shock absorber. Note the following:

    a. Install the mounting bolts from the right side of the frame.

    b. Torque the bolts to 32 N•m (24 ft.-lb.).

Shock Absorber
Inspection

The following procedure shows the shock absorber spring removed for inspection (**Figure 37**). It is not necessary to remove the spring for many of the inspections, however, removal is not difficult and a complete inspection can be performed.

1. If desired, remove and inspect the spring as described in this section.

2. Inspect the reservoir, adjuster and fittings for leakage or damage (**Figure 38**).

3. Inspect the damper rod for leakage, bending, rust or other damage (**Figure 39**).

4. Inspect the bumper and adjuster for leakage or damage (**Figure 40**).

5. Inspect the condition of the seals and pivots as described in this section.

Seals and Pivots
Inspection

This procedure applies to the seals and pivot at the top and bottom of the shock absorber.

1. Remove the collars and seals from the each side of the pivot (**Figure 41**).

12

by a jack, placed at the rear of the engine. The jack allows the swing arm to be free to move and access to the shock absorber is improved. Before starting the procedure, have enough jacks/supports available to support the machine and the swing arm.

1. Support the machine with a jack placed at the rear of the engine.

2. Remove the rear wheels as described in this chapter.

3. Remove the swing arm skid plate (Chapter Fourteen).

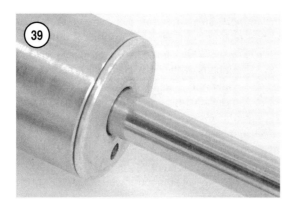

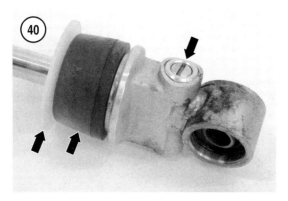

2. Clean the seals, collars and pivot bolt (**Figure 42**). Inspect the parts for cracks, wear or other damage.

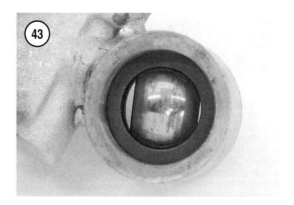

3. Inspect the pivot for corrosion, wear and looseness (**Figure 43**).

   a. If the pivots are worn, a replacement part is not available from Yamaha, however, a replacement part may be available from an aftermarket supplier.

   b. To remove the original pivot, remove the circlip from one side of the bore (**Figure 44**). Press the pivot out of the bore. Press the new pivot into place and install a new circlip.

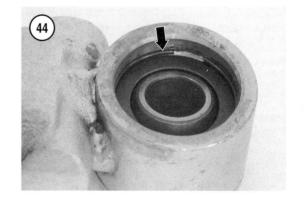

4. Pack waterproof grease into the pivot race and into the seals.

5. Install and seat the seals (**Figure 45**) by hand so the manufacturer's marks face out.

6. Apply grease to the collars and insert them into the pivot.

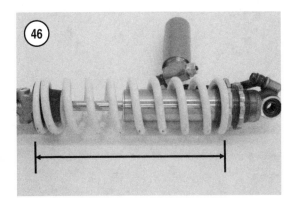

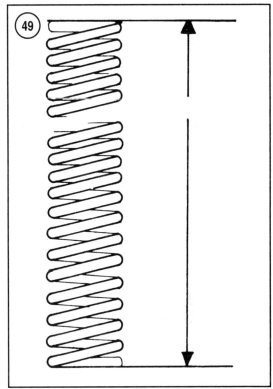

Spring
Removal, Inspection and Installation

1. Measure the spring preload adjustment prior to disassembling the shock. This is achieved by measuring the length of the spring (**Figure 46**). Record the measurement.

2. Clean the threads on the shock.

3. Mount the bottom pivot of the shock absorber in a vise with soft jaws. Check that the vise jaws grip the sides of the pivot and not the cylinder.

4. Loosen the locknut (A, **Figure 47**) and back it away from the adjuster nut (B).

5. Loosen the adjuster nut until the spring is no longer preloaded. If desired, remove the shock from the vise and twist the spring to loosen the adjuster nut.

6. Remove the spring seat at the bottom of the shock (**Figure 48**), then remove the spring.

7. Inspect the spring.

    a. Inspect the spring and seat for damage.

    b. Measure the free length of the spring (**Figure 49**).

8. Reverse Steps 3-6 to install the spring. Note the following:

12

a. Check that the spring seat is against the spring.

b. Check that the bottom adjuster is oriented correctly with the top of the shock (**Figure 50**). When installed, the bottom adjuster must face up.

c. Set the spring preload to the measurement recorded in Step 1 or to the specification in **Table 1**.

REAR SUSPENSION ADJUSTMENT

This section describes the function of the adjusters on the shock absorber. Specific settings cannot be made since these depend on the weight of the rider, riding conditions and riding habits. The rider should understand the function of the adjusters, then set the adjusters to a *neutral* position and make test rides until the desired ride is achieved. Always record the initial settings and the subsequent settings. By doing so, a record can be kept of the preferred setting for a specific riding condition.

Spring Preload

Preload determines the initial force of the spring when reacting to a bump. Preload is set with the locknut (A, **Figure 51**) and adjuster (B) at the top of the shock. Preload is the amount the spring is compressed from its free length. By tightening the adjuster, spring preload is increased and the ride becomes harsher. By loosening the adjuster, spring preload is decreased and the ride becomes softer. Preload does not change the *rate* of spring compression, only the initial reaction of the spring. The quality of the spring (soft or hard) cannot be changed by preload. Refer to **Table 1** for the recommended installed spring lengths.

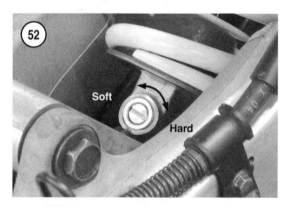

Rebound Damper

Rebound damping controls the rate of extension of the shock absorber after hitting a bump. The rebound damping adjuster is located at the bottom of the shock (**Figure 52**). This setting has no affect on the compression rate of the shock. If rebound damping is set too slow (hard), the rear wheels may bottom on subsequent bumps. To decrease (soften) damping, turn the valve adjuster counterclockwise. To increase (harden) damping, turn the valve ad-

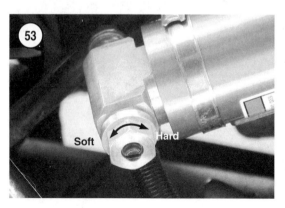

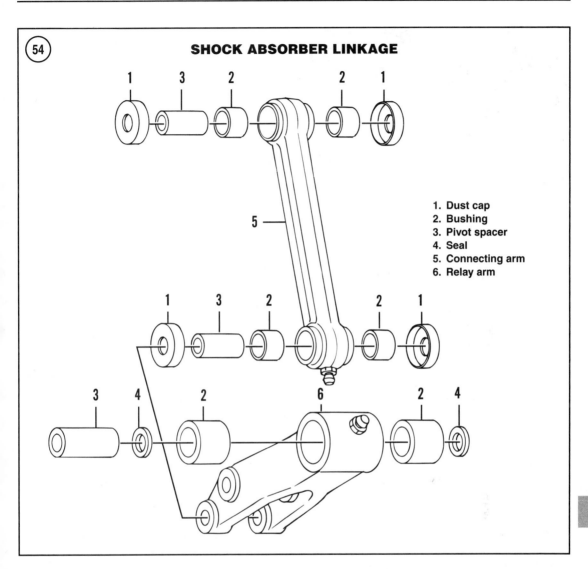

SHOCK ABSORBER LINKAGE

1. Dust cap
2. Bushing
3. Pivot spacer
4. Seal
5. Connecting arm
6. Relay arm

juster clockwise. Refer to **Table 3** for the recommended settings.

Compression Damper

Compression damping controls the shock absorber compression rate, after hitting a bump. The compression damper adjuster is located at the top of the shock (**Figure 53**). This setting has no affect on the rebound rate of the shock. If compression damping is set too slow (soft), the rear wheels may bottom on bumps. To increase (harden) damping, turn the valve adjuster clockwise. To decrease (soften) damping, turn the valve adjuster counterclockwise.

SHOCK LINKAGE

The shock linkage consists of the relay arm, connecting arm, pivot bolts, dust caps, seals, pivot spacers and bushings. Since the linkage is often subjected to harsh riding conditions, the linkage should be disassembled and lubricated at the interval indicated in the maintenance and lubrication schedule (Chapter Three). Although the relay arm for 2002-on models appears slightly different than the relay arm shown in these procedures, all servicing procedures are identical.

Connecting Arm and Relay Arm
Removal and Installation

Refer to **Figure 54** as needed.

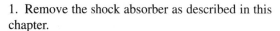

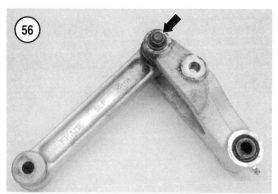

1. Remove the shock absorber as described in this chapter.

2. Remove the connecting arm bolt from the frame (**Figure 55**).

    a. For the 2002-on models, a washer is used at both ends of the bolt.

    b. For the 2001 model, no washers are used.

3. Inspect the linkage as described in this section.

4. Reverse these steps to install the shock absorber linkage. Note the following:

    a. Lubricate all bushings, seals and pivot spacers with waterproof grease.

    b. Install the mounting bolts from the right side of the frame.

    c. Torque all bolts to 32 N•m (24 ft.-lb.).

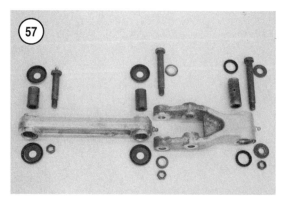

Inspection and Repair

During inspection and repair, keep all parts identified so they may be inspected and reinstalled in their original locations. Refer to **Figure 54** as needed.

1. Remove the bolt joining the connecting arm to the relay arm (**Figure 56**).

    a. For the 2001 model, a washer is used at both ends of the bolt. The 2002-on models use a washer only with the nut.

    b. Note that the connecting arm is marked FRAME and UP. When assembling the connecting arm and relay arm, check that these marks are properly oriented. Also, check that the relay arm is oriented correctly, as shown in **Figure 56**.

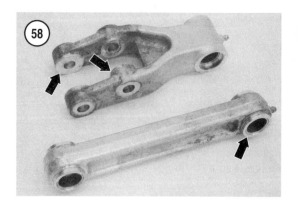

2. Remove the dust caps and pivot spacers, then pry out the seals. Clean the sets of parts (**Figure 57**).

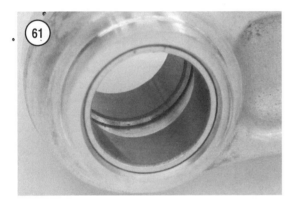

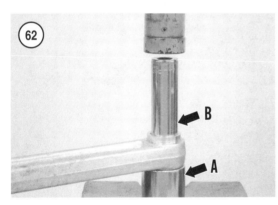

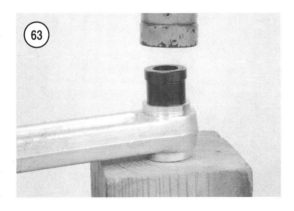

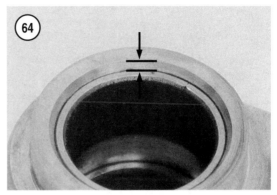

3. Inspect the relay arm and connecting arm (**Figure 58**) for cracks and other damage, particularly around bores and bosses.

4. Inspect the pivot bolts, spacers and dust caps (**Figure 59**) for corrosion, wear and other damage.

5. Check the fit of all bolts in their respective mating parts. Bolts should pass straight through the parts with no binding or difficulty to install.

6. Check the fit of all pivot spacers in their bushings (**Figure 60**). The spacers should turn freely and smoothly with no play. If play or roughness exists, replace the pivot spacer and bushings.

7. Inspect the bushings (**Figure 61**) for wear and damage. The bushings are treated with an antifriction coating. If the coating is worn through or scored, replace the bushings and pivot spacer. If necessary, replace bushings in the relay arm or connecting arm as follows:

   a. Support the part in a press so the bushings can fall from the bore. A short length of tubing or a large socket, placed with the open-end up, works well (A, **Figure 62**).

   b. Place a driver or socket that fits on the edge of the bushing (B, **Figure 62**), then press both bushings out of the bore.

   c. Clean and lubricate the bore.

   d. Place a bushing *squarely* over the bearing bore.

   e. Place a driver or socket over the bushing. The driver should seat against the edge of the bushing, but still be capable of entering the bore (**Figure 63**).

   f. Drive each bushing into place, from its respective side of the bore. For the connecting arm, drive each bushing 1 mm (0.04 in.) beyond the edge of the bore (**Figure 64**). For the

12

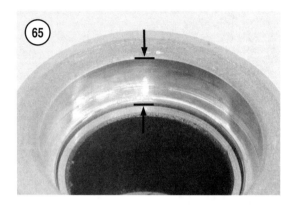

relay arm, drive each bushing 6.5 mm (0.26 in.) beyond the edge of the bore (**Figure 65**).

8. Pack the seals and bushings with grease.

9. Install and seat the seals in the bores. Install the seals so the manufacturer's marks face out (**Figure 66**).

10. Apply grease to the pivot spacers and insert them into the bushings.

SWING ARM

Bearing Inspection

The general condition of the swing arm bearings can be inspected with the swing arm mounted on the machine. Periodically check the bearings for play, roughness or damage. If the swing arm will be removed from the frame, make the check prior to removing the swing arm pivot bolt. If the swing arm will not be removed from the frame, perform the following steps before making the inspection.

1. Remove the rear wheels as described in this chapter.

2. Remove the shock absorber as described in this chapter.

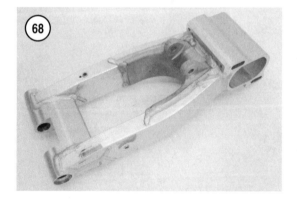

3. Loosen the axle hub nuts and drive chain adjusters, then push the axle forward and lift the chain off the rear sprocket.

4. Check the bearings as follows:

   a. Grasp the ends of the swing arm and leverage it from side to side (**Figure 67**). There should be no detectable play in the bearings.

   b. Pivot the swing arm up and down. The bearings must pivot smoothly.

   c. If there is play or roughness in the bearings, remove the swing arm and inspect the bearing and pivot assembly for wear.

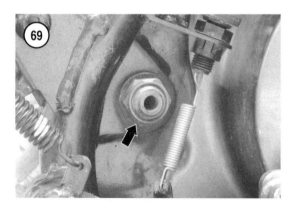

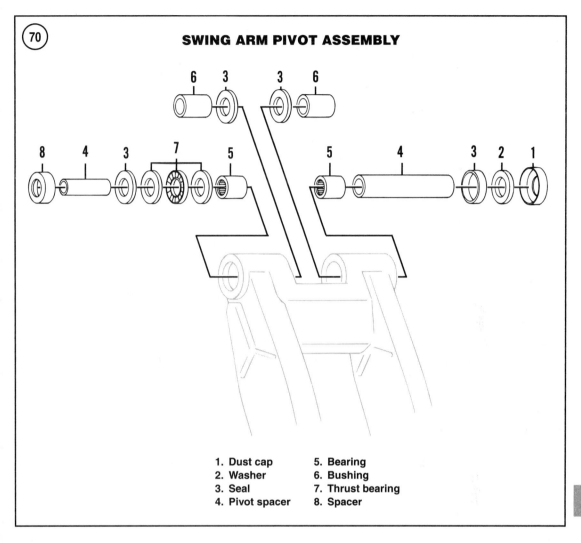

70

SWING ARM PIVOT ASSEMBLY

1. Dust cap
2. Washer
3. Seal
4. Pivot spacer
5. Bearing
6. Bushing
7. Thrust bearing
8. Spacer

12

5. Install the shock absorber and wheels as described in this chapter.

6. Adjust the chain (Chapter Three).

Removal and Installation

This procedure assumes the swing arm is being removed for service or replacement. Therefore, major assemblies attached to the swing arm are completely removed. When all assemblies are removed, the swing arm will appear as in **Figure 68**.

1. Remove the rear wheels, hubs, axle, axle hub and shock absorber as described in this chapter.

2. Remove the parking brake cable and brake hose guides from the swing arm.

3. Remove the swing arm pivot bolt/nut (**Figure 69**).

4. Inspect and service the swing arm as described in this section.

5. Reverse these steps to install the swing arm assembly. Note the following:

　a. Check that the chain is routed above and below the swing arm before inserting and torquing the swing arm pivot bolt.

　b. Torque the swing arm bolt to 95 N•m (70 ft.-lb.).

　c. Adjust the chain (Chapter Three).

Inspection and Repair

During inspection and repair, keep all parts identified so they may be inspected and reinstalled in their original locations. Refer to **Figure 70** as needed.

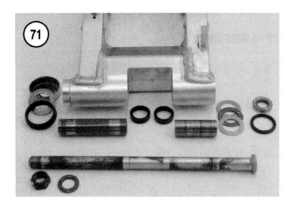

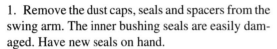

1. Remove the dust caps, seals and spacers from the swing arm. The inner bushing seals are easily damaged. Have new seals on hand.

2. Clean the sets of parts (**Figure 71**). Inspect the swing arm casting. Check for fractures and other damage. If damage is detected, replace the swing arm, or have a dealership or machine shop determine if it can be repaired.

3. Inspect the thrust bearing for corrosion and damage (**Figure 72**). The rollers can be loose in the race, but should not fall from the race.

4. Inspect the needle bearings (**Figure 73**) for wear, play, flat spots, rust or discoloration.

   a. If the rollers are blue, overheating has occurred.

   b. Inspect the bearing cages for cracks, rust or other damage.

   c. Lubricate the bearing and pivot spacer, then insert the pivot into the bearing (**Figure 74**). The pivot should turn freely and smoothly with no play. If play or roughness exists, replace the bearings as described in this section.

5. Inspect the bushings (**Figure 75**) for wear, play and deterioration. The bushings are a synthetic material and may not show obvious wear.

   a. Lubricate the pivot spacer and insert it into the bushing. The pivot should turn freely and smoothly with no play.

   b. If play or roughness exists, replace the bushings as described in this section.

6. Inspect the dust cap assembly, seals, spacer and pivot bolt assembly (**Figure 76**).

   a. Inspect the seals for cracks, wear or deterioration.

   b. Inspect pivot bolt for straightness. The bolt should roll with no indication of a bend.

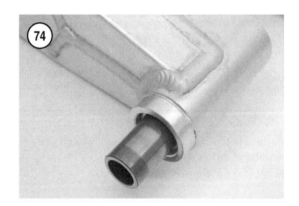

c. The dust cap assembly should seal firmly over the bearing bore.

7. Inspect the chain adjustment bolts (**Figure 77**) for corrosion, wear or damage.

8. Inspect the chain slider (**Figure 78**). Replace the slider if it is worn. Severe damage can occur to the swing arm if the chain wears through the slider.

9. Clean and inspect the chain rollers, attached to the frame (**Figure 79**). Replace the rollers if worn or seized.

10. Clean and inspect the pivot at the rear of the engine (**Figure 80**). Lubricate the pivot with waterproof grease.

11. Assemble the swing arm as follows:

a. If necessary, replace the bearings and bushings as described in this section.

b. Apply waterproof grease to the parts as they are assembled.

c. Install and seat the inner seals, with the manufacturer's marks facing out. Drive the seals by assembling a driver and extension as shown in **Figure 81**. The driver should seat against the outer edge of the seal.

12

d. At the right swing arm pivot, install the pivot spacer and dust cap assembly (**Figure 82**). Place the washer in the cap with the curved edge facing up. Install the seal so the inner sealing ribs face up.

e. At the left swing arm pivot, install the pivot spacer, thrust bearing assembly, seal and spacer (**Figure 83**). Install the seal with the manufacturer's marks facing out. The seal can be seated using the fingers.

f. Install the chain slider (**Figure 84**).

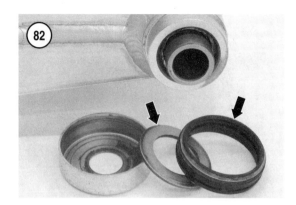

Bearing and Bushing Replacement

Replace the bearings and bushings after disassembling, cleaning and inspecting the parts as described in this section. Replace bearings and bushings as a set.

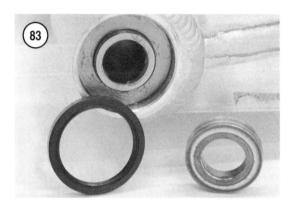

> *NOTE*
> *In the following steps the bearing must be driven to the outside of the swing arm. This requires a long driver that will pass through one pivot and to the inside of the other pivot, as shown by A, **Figure 85**. A socket and long extension works well for this procedure.*

1. Support the swing arm in a press so the bearing can fall from the bore. A short length of tubing or a large socket, placed with the open-end up, works well (B, **Figure 85**). The support should fit as close as possible around the bearing bore.

> *CAUTION*
> *The swing arm casting is brittle and must be supported properly. Failure to provide adequate support around the bearing bore can result in cracking of the casting. If in doubt, have a dealership remove and replace the parts. If the parts are severely seized in the bore, use lots of penetrating oil and work slowly.*

2. Place a driver or socket that fits on the edge of the bushing (C, **Figure 85**), then press the bearing and bushing out of the bore.

3. Clean and lubricate the bores.

4. Install the bushings as follows:

a. Use the removal method to install the bushings into their respective side of the bore.

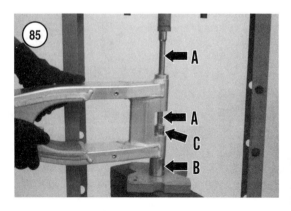

d. Drive each bushing 8 mm (0.31 in.) beyond the edge of the bore (**Figure 86**).

5. Install the bearings as follows:

a. Support the swing arm as shown in **Figure 87**. The new bearings can be driven from their respective sides of the swing arm.

b. Fit the new bearing *squarely* over the bore, with the manufacturer's marks facing up.

c. Place a driver or socket over the bearing. The driver should seat against the edge of the bearing, but still be capable of entering the bore.

d. Drive the bearing into the bore. Drive the right bearing 4 mm (0.16 in.) beyond the edge of the bore (**Figure 88**). Drive the left bearing until it is flush with the edge of the bore.

6. Insert the pivots into their respective bores and check for fit and smooth operation.

b. Place a bushing *squarely* over the bearing bore.

c. Place a driver or socket over the bushing. The driver should seat against the edge of the bushing, but still be capable of entering the bore.

12

Table 1 REAR SUSPENSION AND CHAIN SPECIFICATIONS

Drive chain free play	30-45 mm (1.18-1.77 in.)
Drive chain size	520, O-ring, endless type
Drive chain length, 11-pin span	150.1 mm (5.91 in.) maximum length
Rear suspension	Link-type swing arm
Rear shock absorber	
Type	Coil spring/gas-oil damper
Travel	100 mm (3.94 in.)
Spring free length	273 mm (10.75 in.)
Spring installed length	
2001	
Standard	253 mm (9.96 in.)
Minimum	245 mm (9.65 in.)
Maximum	260 mm (10.24 in.)
2002-on	
Standard	240 mm (9.45 in.)
Minimum	232 mm (9.13 in.)
Maximum	247 mm (9.72 in.)
(continued)	

Table 1 REAR SUSPENSION AND CHAIN SPECIFICATIONS (continued)

2002-on	
Standard	240 mm (9.45 in.)
Minimum	232 mm (9.13 in.)
Maximum	247 mm (9.72 in.)
Spring rate	55 N/mm (314.05 lb./in.)
Stroke	0-100 mm (0-3.94 in.)
Rear wheel travel	220 mm (8.66 in.)
Swing arm free play (end and side play)	1 mm (0.04 in.)

Table 2 TIRE AND WHEEL SPECIFICATIONS

Tires	
Type	Tubeless radial
Sizes	
Front	AT21 × 7-10 Dunlop KT331
Rear	AT20 × 10-9 Dunlop KT335
Recommended cold pressure	
Standard	27.5 kPa (4.0 psi) for maximum 100 kg (220 lb.) load
Mimimum	24.5 kPa (3.5 psi)
Bead seating pressure	250 kPa (36 psi) maximum
Wheels	
Rim sizes	
Front	10 × 5.5 AT
Rear	9 × 8.5 AT
Runout (radial and lateral)	2 mm (0.08 in.)

Table 3 REAR SHOCK ABSORBER SETTINGS

	Standard	Minimum	Maximum
Rebound damping [1]	10	3	20
Compression damping [2]	7	1	12

1. The numbers shown are the number of clicks *out* after the adjuster has been fully turned in (maximum damping force). Turning the adjuster out decreases damping force. Do not force the adjuster beyond its normal travel. Damage to the adjuster can occur.
2. The numbers shown are the number of clicks *in* after the adjuster has been fully turned out (minimum damping force). Turning the adjuster in increases damping force. Do not force the adjuster beyond its normal travel. Damage to the adjuster can occur.

Table 4 REAR SUSPENSION TORQUE SPECIFICATIONS

	N•m	in.-lb.	ft.-lb.
Axle hub bolt	90	–	66
Front sprocket nut	70	–	52
Inner and outer axle locknuts	Refer to text		
Rear hub nut	120	–	88
Rear sprocket nuts	24	–	18
Rear wheel lug nuts	45	–	33
Seal retainer bolts	10	88	–
Set screws	6	53	–
Shock absorber			
linkage bolts	32	–	24
mounting bolts	32	–	24
Sprocket guard bolts	10	88	–
Swing arm bolt	95	–	70

CHAPTER THIRTEEN

BRAKES

This chapter provides service procedures for the front and rear brake systems. This includes brake pads, master cylinders, calipers and discs. Refer to the tables at the end of this chapter for specifications.

Refer to Chapter Three for brake fluid level inspection, brake pad/disc inspection, parking brake adjustment, brake light adjustment and brake pedal adjustment.

DISC BRAKE FUNDAMENTALS

The front and rear brakes are hydraulically actuated and therefore do not require cables and mechanical linkages to operate. The calipers *float* on pins that allow the caliper and brake pads to automatically remain centered over the disc. When pressure is applied to the brake pedal or lever, the brake fluid compresses in the brake line and pushes the caliper piston and inner brake pad toward the brake disc. As pad pressure against the disc rises, the caliper slides and pulls the outer brake pad into contact with the disc. When pressure is relieved, the piston, inner pad and caliper assembly slightly retract from the disc, allowing the wheel to spin freely. As the pads wear, the piston in the caliper extends, automatically keeping the pads adjusted and centered around the disc. It is important to not only ensure

the piston can extend and retract, but that the caliper is free to move on its mounting bracket.

A hydraulic brake system is not maintenance-free, nor indestructible. Observe the following practices when maintaining or working on a hydraulic brake system:

1. Keep brake fluid off painted surfaces, plastic and decals. The fluid will damage these surfaces. If fluid does contact these surfaces, flush the surface thoroughly with clean water.

2. Keep the fluid reservoirs closed except when changing the fluid.

3. Replace brake fluid often. The fluid absorbs moisture from the air and will cause internal corrosion of the brake system. Fresh fluid is clear to slightly yellow. If the fluid is obviously colored, it is contaminated.

4. Do not reuse brake fluid, or use new fluid that has been in a partially-used container for any length of time.

5. When rebuilding brake system components, lubricate new parts with fresh fluid before assembly. Do not use petroleum-based solvents. These can swell and damage rubber components.

6. Bleed the brake system whenever a banjo bolt or other connector in the brake line has been loosened. Air will be in the system and brake action will be spongy.

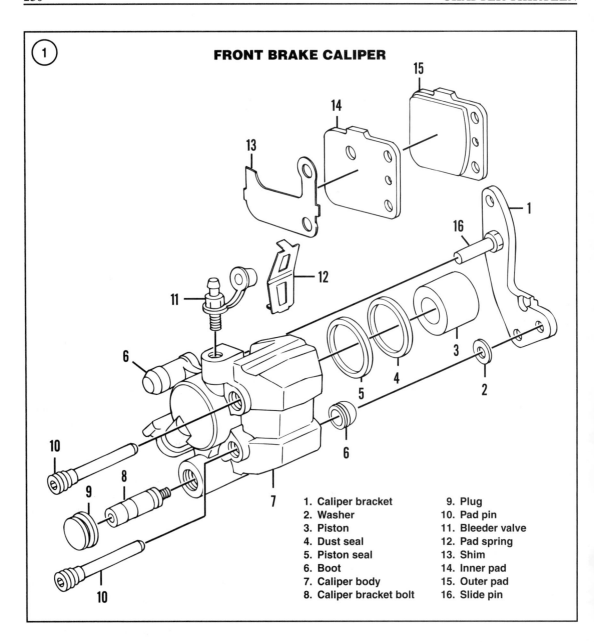

FRONT BRAKE CALIPER

1. Caliper bracket
2. Washer
3. Piston
4. Dust seal
5. Piston seal
6. Boot
7. Caliper body
8. Caliper bracket bolt
9. Plug
10. Pad pin
11. Bleeder valve
12. Pad spring
13. Shim
14. Inner pad
15. Outer pad
16. Slide pin

FRONT BRAKE PADS

Brake pad life depends on the riding habits of the rider and the type of material used to manufacture the brake pads. Replace the pads when they are worn to within 1 mm (0.040 in.) of the backing plate, or have been contaminated with oil or other chemicals.

Removal and Installation

The brake pads can only be replaced by removing the caliper from the steering knuckle. The brake hose does not have to be removed from the caliper. Keep the caliper supported and do not allow it to hang by the brake hose. When replacing brake pads, it is common practice to replace both sets of pads on the front wheels.

If the caliper will be rebuilt, or, if other damage is detected during this procedure, the pads can be removed when the caliper is at the workbench. Refer to *Front Brake Caliper* in this chapter for complete removal, repair and installation. Refer to **Figure 1**.

1. Remove the front wheel, outer disc guard and hub hardware (Chapter Eleven).

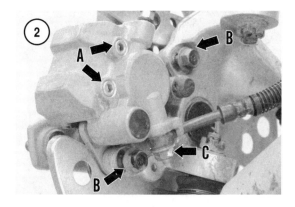

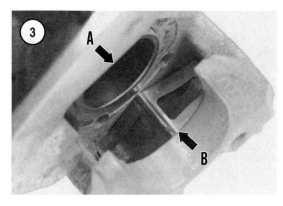

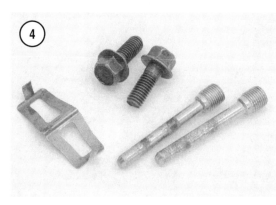

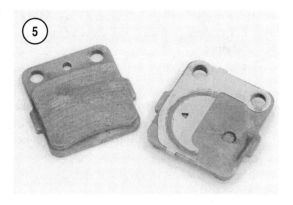

2. Loosen the pad pins (A, **Figure 2**).

3. Remove the caliper mounting bolts (B, **Figure 2**), then slide the hub, disc and caliper out of the inner disc guard. Remove the caliper from the disc. Avoid kinking the brake hose.

4. Press down on the pads to relieve the pressure on the pad pins, then remove the pins.

5. Remove the pads.

CAUTION
In the following step, monitor the level of fluid in the master cylinder reservoir. Brake fluid will back flow to the reservoir when the caliper piston is pressed into the bore. Do not allow brake fluid to spill from the reservoir, or damage can occur to painted and plastic surfaces. Immediately clean up any spills, flooding the area with water.

NOTE
Do not operate the brake lever with the pads removed. The caliper piston can come out of the bore.

6. Grasp the caliper and press the caliper piston down into the bore, creating room for the new pads (A, **Figure 3**).

7. Remove the pad spring (B, **Figure 3**).

8. Clean the interior of the caliper and inspect for the following:

   a. Leakage or damage around the piston, bleeder valve and hose connection.

   b. Damaged or missing boots.

   c. Excessive drag of the caliper bracket when it is moved in and out of the caliper. If corrosion or water is detected around the rubber boots, the parts should be cleaned and lubricated with silicone brake grease.

9. Inspect the pad pins, pad spring and mounting bolts (**Figure 4**). The pins and spring must be in good condition to allow the inner pad to slightly move when installed. Check that both small tabs on the spring are not corroded or missing.

10. Inspect the pads and shim (on back of inner pad) for wear and damage (**Figure 5**).

   a. Replace the pads when they are worn to within 1 mm (0.040 in.) of the backing plate, as shown by the wear indicator (**Figure 6**). Always replace pads contaminated with oil or other chemicals.

13

b. If the pads are worn unevenly, the caliper is probably not sliding correctly on the caliper bracket. The caliper must be free to *float* on the slide pin and retainer bolt. Buildup or corrosion on the parts can hold the caliper in one position, causing brake drag and excessive pad wear.

11. Install the pad spring with the small tabs pointing out.

12. Install the inner pad and shim, seating the pad under the caliper bracket and against the piston.

13. Install the outer pad.

14. Press down on the pads, then align and install the pad pins. Torque the pins after the caliper is installed.

15. Spread the pads so there is clearance to fit the caliper over the brake disc (**Figure 7**).

16. Position the caliper over the brake disc and hub assembly, then slide the caliper into the inner disc guard.

17. Install and torque the caliper mounting bolts to 28 N•m (21 ft.-lb.).

18. Torque the pad pins to 18 N•m (13 ft.-lb.).

19. Install the hub hardware (Chapter Eleven).

20. Operate the brake lever several times to seat the pads.

21. Check the brake fluid reservoir and replenish or remove fluid as necessary.

22. With the front hub raised, check that the hub spins freely and the brake operates properly.

23. Install the outer disc guard and front wheel (Chapter Eleven).

FRONT BRAKE CALIPER

Removal and Installation

Use the following procedure to remove the caliper from the steering knuckle:

1. Remove the front wheel, outer disc guard and hub hardware (Chapter Eleven).

2. If the caliper will be disassembled, drain the system as described in this chapter. After draining, loosen the brake hose banjo bolt (C, **Figure 2**) while the caliper is mounted. Leave the bolt finger-tight. It will be removed in a later step.

3. Remove the caliper mounting bolts (B, **Figure 2**), then slide the hub, disc and caliper out of the inner disc guard. Remove the caliper from the disc. Avoid kinking the brake hose.

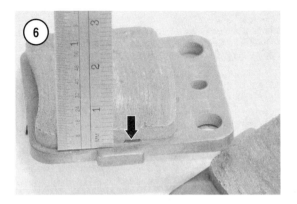

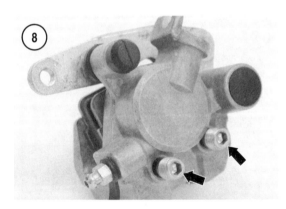

4A. If the caliper will be left attached to the brake hose, but not disassembled and serviced, perform the following:

a. Suspend the caliper with a length of wire. Do not let the caliper hang by the brake hose.

b. Insert a small wood block between the brake pads. This will prevent the caliper piston from extending out of the caliper, if the brake lever is operated.

4B. If the caliper will be disassembled, do the following:

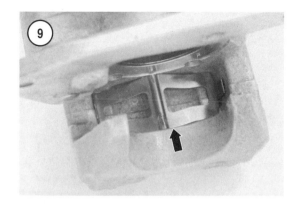

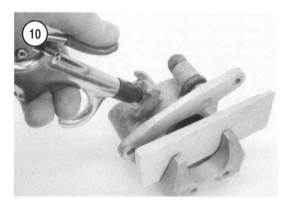

a. Remove the banjo bolt and seal washers from the brake hose. Have a shop cloth ready to absorb excess brake fluid that drips from the hose.

b. Wrap the hose end to prevent brake fluid from damaging other surfaces.

c. Drain excess brake fluid from the caliper.

d. Repair the caliper as described in this section.

5. Reverse this procedure to install the caliper. Note the following:

a. Install and torque the caliper mounting bolts to 28 N•m (21 ft.-lb.).

b. Install new seal washers on the banjo bolt. Seat the brake hose in the guide on the caliper, then torque the banjo bolt to 27 N•m (20 ft.-lb.).

6. Install the hub hardware (Chapter Eleven).

7. If the caliper was rebuilt, or the brake hose disconnected from the caliper, fill and bleed the brake system as described in this chapter.

8. Operate the brake lever several times to seat the pads.

9. Check the brake fluid reservoir and replenish or remove fluid, as necessary.

10. With the front hub raised, check that the hub spins freely and the brake operates properly.

11. Install the outer disc guard, and front wheel (Chapter Eleven).

Repair

Use the following procedure to disassemble, inspect and assemble the brake caliper, using new seals. Refer to **Figure 1**.

1. Remove the caliper as described in this section.

2. Remove the pad pins (**Figure 8**). Press down on the pads to relieve the pressure on the pad pins as they are removed.

3. Remove the brake pads and pad spring (**Figure 9**).

4. Remove the piston from the caliper bore using compressed air (**Figure 10**). To perform this technique, an air nozzle is tightly held in the brake hose fitting and air pressure ejects the piston. Do not attempt to pry the piston out of the caliper. Read the following procedure entirely before beginning removal.

a. Place the caliper on a padded work surface.

b. Close the bleeder valve on the caliper so air cannot escape.

c. Place a strip of wood, or similar pad, in the caliper. The pad will cushion the piston when it comes out of the caliper.

WARNING
Wear eye protection when using compressed air to remove the piston. Keep fingers away from the piston discharge area. Personal injury can occur if an attempt is made to stop the piston by hand.

d. Lay the caliper so the piston will discharge downward.

e. Insert an air nozzle into the brake hose fitting. If the nozzle does not have a rubber tip, wrap the nozzle with tape. This will allow the nozzle to seal tightly and prevent thread damage.

f. Place a shop cloth over the entire caliper to catch any spray that may discharge from the caliper.

g. Apply pressure and listen for the piston to *pop* from the caliper (**Figure 11**).

13

5. Remove the plug, caliper bracket bolt and boot (A, **Figure 12**). Remove the boot from the bolt before pulling it out of the caliper.

6. Remove the caliper bracket and washer (B, **Figure 12**).

7. Remove the slide pin boot (C, **Figure 12**).

8. Remove the bleeder valve and cap (D, **Figure 12**).

9. Remove the dust seal and piston seal (**Figure 13**).

10. Inspect the caliper assembly.

  a. Clean all parts that will be reused with fresh brake fluid or isopropyl (rubbing) alcohol. Use a wood or plastic-tipped tool to clean the seal and boot grooves. Use clean brake fluid to aid in cleaning the piston, bore and seal grooves.

  b. Inspect the caliper bore for wear, pitting or corrosion.

  c. Measure the inside diameter of the caliper bore (**Figure 14**). Refer to **Table 1** for specifications.

  d. Inspect the pad pins, pad spring and mounting bolts (**Figure 4**). The pins and spring must be in good condition to allow the inner pad to slightly move when installed. Check that both small tabs on the spring are not corroded or missing.

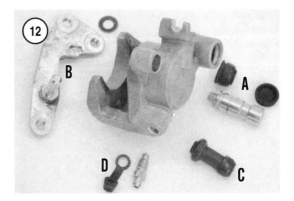

  e. Inspect the caliper bracket and slide pin for wear, pitting or corrosion.

  f. Inspect the boots for deterioration.

  g. Inspect the bleeder valve for clogging and damage.

  h. Inspect the shim on the back of the inner brake pad (**Figure 5**) Replace the shim if corroded or damaged. Always replace the shim when installing new brake pads.

  i. Inspect the brake pads. Replace the pads when they are worn to within 1 mm (0.040 in.) of the backing plate, as shown by the wear indicator (**Figure 6**). Always replace pads that have been contaminated with oil or other chemicals. If the pads are worn unevenly, the caliper is probably not sliding correctly on the caliper bracket. The caliper must be free to *float* on the slide pin and retainer bolt. Buildup or corrosion on the parts can hold the caliper in one position, causing brake drag and excessive pad wear.

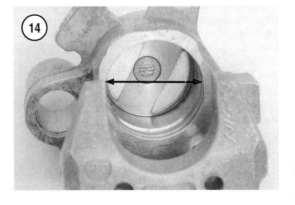

NOTE
Use new brake fluid (rated DOT 4) to lubricate the parts in the following steps.

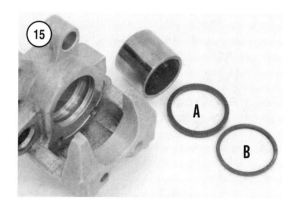

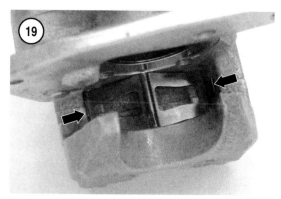

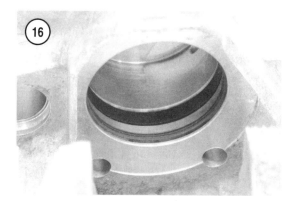

11. Install the new piston seal (A, **Figure 15**) and dust seal (B) as follows:

    a. Soak the seals in brake fluid for 15 minutes.

    b. Coat the caliper bore and piston with brake fluid.

    c. Seat the piston seal, then the dust seal (**Figure 16**) in the caliper grooves. The piston seal goes in the back groove.

    d. Install the piston, with the open side facing out (A, **Figure 17**). Twist the piston past the seals, then press the piston to the bottom of the bore.

12. Install the boots and caliper bracket bolt as follows:

    a. Apply silicone brake grease to the interior of the boots and to the bracket bolt.

    b. Install the slide pin boot onto the caliper (B, **Figure 17**). If necessary, apply a light coat of grease on the exterior of the large boot to aid in passing it through the caliper.

    c. Pass the bracket bolt through the caliper, then install the boot over the end of the bolt (C, **Figure 17**).

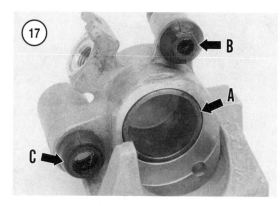

13. Install the caliper bracket as follows:

    a. Lubricate the slide pin on the bracket, then install it onto the caliper.

    b. Align the bracket with the caliper bracket bolt. Place the washer over the bolt, then tighten the bracket bolt (**Figure 18**).

    c. Torque the bracket bolt to 23 N•m (17 ft.-lb.) and install the rubber plug.

14. Install the bleeder valve and cap.

15. Install the pad spring with the small tabs pointing out (**Figure 19**).

16. Install the inner pad and shim, seating the pad under the caliper bracket and against the piston.

17. Install the outer pad.

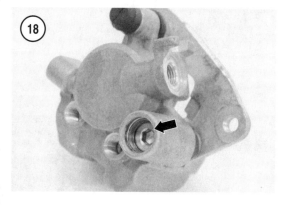

13

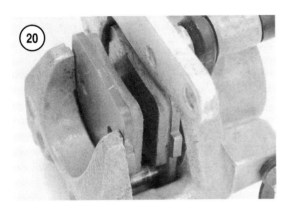

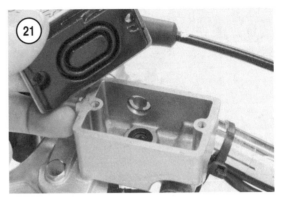

18. Press down on the pads, then align and install the pad pins (**Figure 8**). Torque the pins to 18 N•m (13 ft.-lb.).

19. Spread the pads so there is clearance to fit the caliper over the brake disc (**Figure 20**).

20. Install the caliper as described in this section.

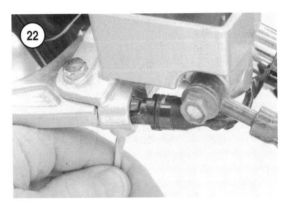

FRONT MASTER CYLINDER

Removal and Installation

Use the following procedure to remove the front master cylinder/brake fluid reservoir from the machine. Refer to *Repair* in this section to make internal repairs to the master cylinder:

1. Cover and protect the bodywork and area surrounding the master cylinder.

> *CAUTION*
> *Do not allow brake fluid to splash from the reservoir or hose. Brake fluid can damage painted and plastic surfaces. Immediately clean up any spills, flooding the area with water.*

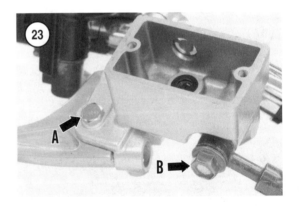

2. Drain the brake system as described in this chapter.

3. Remove the cap and diaphragm and verify that the master cylinder is empty (**Figure 21**). Wipe the interior of the reservoir to absorb all remaining fluid.

4. Remove the brake light switch. Use a small tool to press on the barb that locks the switch to the master cylinder (**Figure 22**).

5. If the master cylinder will be rebuilt, remove the brake lever pivot bolt (A, **Figure 23**) while the master cylinder remains stable.

6. Remove the brake hose banjo bolt (B, **Figure 23**) from the master cylinder as follows:

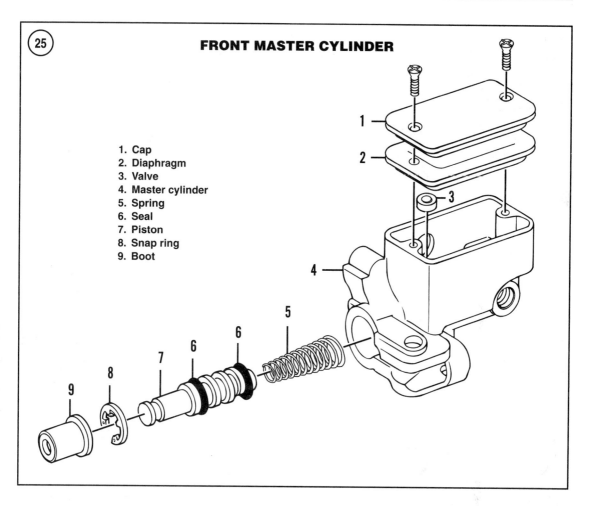

(25) **FRONT MASTER CYLINDER**

1. Cap
2. Diaphragm
3. Valve
4. Master cylinder
5. Spring
6. Seal
7. Piston
8. Snap ring
9. Boot

a. Remove the banjo bolt and seal washers from the brake hose. Have a shop cloth ready to absorb excess brake fluid that drips from the hose.

b. Wrap the hose end to prevent brake fluid from damaging other surfaces.

7. Remove the bolts (**Figure 24**) securing the master cylinder to the handlebar, then remove the master cylinder.

8. Repair the master cylinder as described in this chapter.

9. Reverse this procedure to install the master cylinder. Note the following:

a. Check that the indentations on the handlebar collar are engaged with the throttle assembly and master cylinder.

b. The mounting bracket must be installed so UP and the arrow (**Figure 24**), are facing up. Tighten the upper bolt first, then the bottom bolt. Torque the bolts to 7 N•m (62 in.-lb.).

c. Position the brake hose fitting so it slightly angled downward, keeping the hose straight.

d. Install new seal washers on the banjo bolt. Torque the bolt to 27 N•m (20 ft.-lb.).

e. Check that the brake light operates when the lever is operated.

10. Fill the brake fluid reservoir and bleed the brake system as described in this chapter.

NOTE
Brake lever adjustment is not required. If properly bled, the brake lever will automatically adjust.

Repair

Refer to **Figure 25**.

Use the following procedure to disassemble, inspect and assemble the master cylinder, using new

13

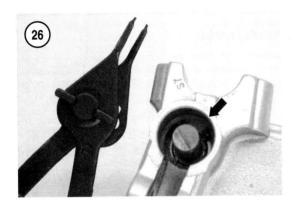

parts. The piston, seals and spring are only available as a complete assembly.

1. Remove the master cylinder as described in this section.

2. Remove the boot from the piston. The boot is a friction fit. To avoid damaging the boot on removal, apply penetrating lubricant around the perimeter of the boot. Carefully pull the bottom edge back so the lubricant can loosen the boot.

3. Remove the snap ring from the master cylinder (**Figure 26**) as follows:

    a. Press down on the piston to relieve pressure on the snap ring, then remove the snap ring.

    b. Slowly relieve the pressure on the piston.

4. Remove the piston assembly from the bore (**Figure 27**).

5. Remove the valve from the bottom of the reservoir (**Figure 28**).

6. Inspect the master cylinder assembly.

    a. Clean all parts that will be reused with fresh brake fluid or isopropyl (rubbing) alcohol.

    b. Inspect the cylinder bore for wear, pitting or corrosion.

    c. Measure the inside diameter of the cylinder bore (**Figure 29**). Refer to **Table 1** for specifications.

    d. Inspect and clean the threads and orifices in the reservoir (**Figure 30**). Clean with compressed air.

    e. Inspect the brake lever bore and pivot bolt for wear (**Figure 31**).

    f. Inspect the valve for cleanliness (**Figure 32**).

    g. Inspect the diaphragm and reservoir cap for damage (**Figure 33**).

    h. Inspect the mounting hardware and banjo bolt (**Figure 34**) for corrosion and damage. Install new seal washers on the banjo bolt.

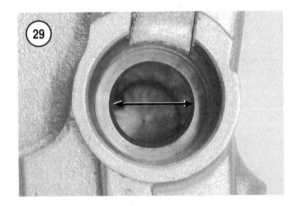

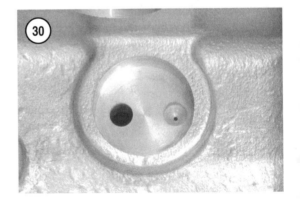

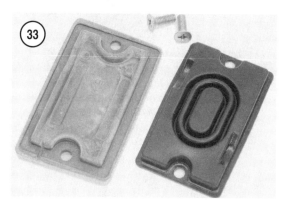

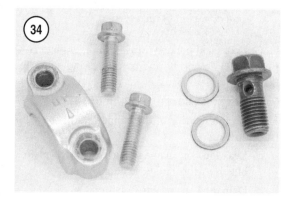

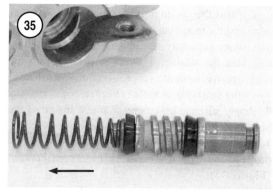

7. Assemble the piston, seals and spring (**Figure 35**) as follows:

    a. Soak the seals in fresh brake fluid (rated DOT 4) for 15 minutes. This will soften and lubricate the seals.

    b. Apply brake fluid to the piston so the seals can slide over the ends.

    c. Mount the seals on the piston. Identify the wide (open) side of both seals. When installed, the wide side of the seals *must* face in the direction of the arrow (**Figure 35**). Mount the seal with the small hole nearest the spring.

    d. Install and seat the spring onto the piston.

8. Install the piston and snap ring into the master cylinder as follows:

    a. Lock the cylinder in a vise with soft jaws. Do not overtighten the vise or cylinder damage could occur.

    b. Lubricate the cylinder bore and piston assembly with brake fluid.

    c. Rest the piston assembly in the cylinder.

    d. Place the snap ring over the end of the piston, resting it on the edge of the bore. The flat side of the snap ring must face out.

    e. Place a screwdriver over the end of the piston and compress the snap ring with snap ring pliers.

NOTE
In the following step, after the piston cups have entered the cylinder, the piston should be held in place until the snap ring is installed. Anytime the cups come out of the cylinder there is a chance of damaging the cup lips during the reinsertion process. This should be avoided.

13

f. Press the piston into the cylinder while guiding the snap ring into position. If the snap ring does not easily seat, release the snap ring and use the tip of the pliers to press it into the groove. Keep the screwdriver in position until the snap ring is seated (**Figure 36**).

9. Apply silicone brake grease to the inside of the boot. Seat the boot into the cylinder.

10. Install the lever and pivot bolt. Apply waterproof grease to the pivot bolt and lever contact point (**Figure 37**).

11. Install the valve in the bottom of the reservoir. Install the valve with the concave side down.

12. Loosely screw the diaphragm and cap onto the reservoir.

13. Install the master cylinder as described in this section.

REAR BRAKE PADS

Brake pad life depends on the riding habits of the rider and the type of material used to manufacture the brake pads. Replace the pads when they are worn to within 1 mm (0.040 in.) of the backing plate, or have been contaminated with oil or other chemicals.

The brake pads can only be replaced by removing the caliper **Figure 38** from the swing arm. The brake hose does not have to be removed from the caliper. Keep the caliper supported and do not allow it to hang by the brake hose.

If the caliper will be rebuilt, or, if other damage is detected during this procedure, the pads can be removed when the caliper is at the workbench. Refer to *Rear Brake Caliper* in this chapter for complete removal, repair and installation.

Replacement

1. Bend the tabs on the lockwasher away from the pad pins, then loosen the pad pins (**Figure 39**).

2. Remove the caliper mounting bolts (**Figure 40**). Avoid kinking the brake hose.

3. Press down on the pads to relieve the pressure on the pad pins, then remove the pins (**Figure 41**).

4. Remove the pads.

CAUTION
In the following step, monitor the level of fluid in the master cylinder

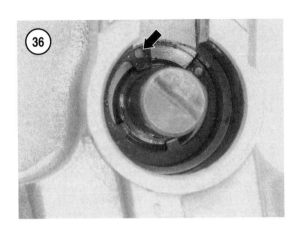

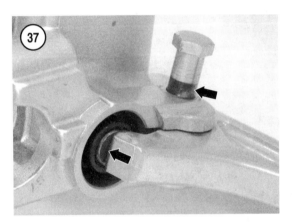

reservoir. Brake fluid will back flow to the reservoir when the caliper piston is pressed into the bore. Do not allow brake fluid to spill from the reservoir, or damage can occur to painted and plastic surfaces. Immediately clean up any spills, flooding the area with water.

NOTE
Do not operate the brake pedal with the pads removed. The caliper piston can come out of the bore.

5. Grasp the caliper and press the caliper piston (A, **Figure 42**) down into the bore, creating room for the new pads .

6. Remove the pad spring (B, **Figure 42**).

7. Clean the interior of the caliper and inspect for the following:

    a. Leakage or damage around the piston, bleeder valve and hose connection.

    b. Damaged or missing boots.

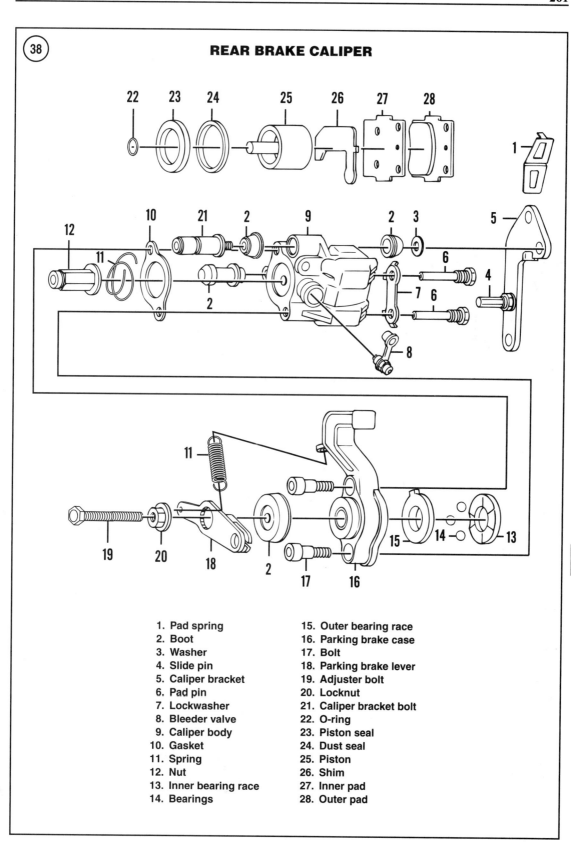

REAR BRAKE CALIPER

1. Pad spring
2. Boot
3. Washer
4. Slide pin
5. Caliper bracket
6. Pad pin
7. Lockwasher
8. Bleeder valve
9. Caliper body
10. Gasket
11. Spring
12. Nut
13. Inner bearing race
14. Bearings
15. Outer bearing race
16. Parking brake case
17. Bolt
18. Parking brake lever
19. Adjuster bolt
20. Locknut
21. Caliper bracket bolt
22. O-ring
23. Piston seal
24. Dust seal
25. Piston
26. Shim
27. Inner pad
28. Outer pad

13

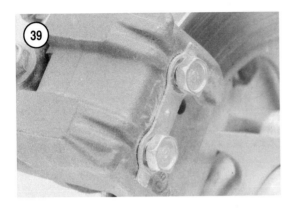

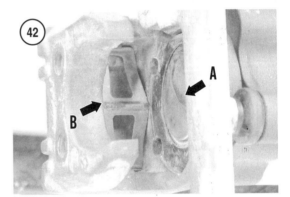

c. Excessive drag of the caliper bracket when it is moved in and out of the caliper. If corrosion or water is detected around the rubber boots, the parts should be cleaned and lubricated with silicone brake grease.

8. Inspect the pad pins, pad spring and mounting bolts (**Figure 43**). The pins and spring must be in good condition to allow the inner pad to slightly move when installed. Check that both small tabs on the spring are not corroded or missing.

9. Inspect the pads and shim (on back of inner pad) for wear and damage (**Figure 44**).

a. Replace the pads when they are worn to within 1 mm (0.040 in.) of the backing plate, as shown by the wear indicator (**Figure 45**). Always replace pads that have been contaminated with oil or other chemicals.

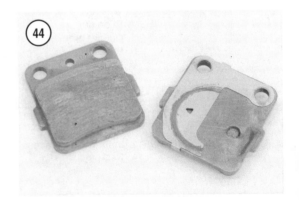

b. If the pads are worn unevenly, the caliper is probably not sliding correctly on the caliper bracket. The caliper must be free to *float* on the slide pin and retainer bolt. Buildup or corrosion on the parts can hold the caliper in one position, causing brake drag and excessive pad wear.

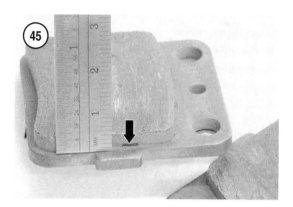

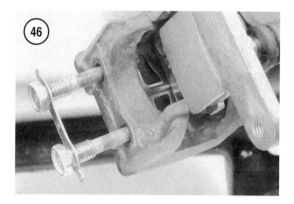

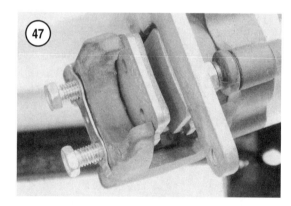

10. Install the pad spring with the small tabs point-ing out.

11. Install the inner pad and shim, seating the pad under the caliper bracket and against the piston (**Figure 46**).

12. Install the outer pad.

13. Press down on the pads, then align and install the pad pins and a new lockwasher. Torque the pins after the caliper is installed.

14. Spread the pads so there is clearance to fit the caliper over the brake disc (**Figure 47**).

15. Position the caliper over the brake disc, then in-stall and torque the caliper mounting bolts to 28 N•m (21 ft.-lb.).

16. Torque the pad pins to 18 N•m (13 ft.-lb.).

17. Bend the lockwasher tabs against the mounting bolts (**Figure 48**).

18. Operate the brake lever several times to seat the pads.

19. Check the brake fluid reservoir and replenish or remove fluid, as necessary.

20. With the rear axle raised, check that the axle spins freely and the brake operates properly.

13

REAR BRAKE CALIPER

Removal and Installation

Use the following procedure to remove the cali-per from the swing arm.

1. If the caliper will be disassembled, do the fol-lowing:

   a. Drain the system as described in this chapter. After draining, loosen the brake hose banjo bolt (A, **Figure 49**) while the caliper is mounted. Leave the bolt finger-tight. It will be removed in a later step.

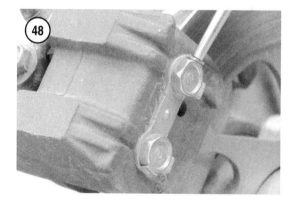

b. At the handlebar, loosen the locknut (A, **Figure 50**) and turn the cable adjuster (B) until there is enough slack in the cable to remove it from the parking brake lever (B, **Figure 49**).

2. Remove the caliper mounting bolts (C, **Figure 49**). Remove the caliper from the disc. Avoid kinking the brake hose.

3A. If the caliper will be left attached to the brake hose, but not disassembled and serviced do the following:

a. Suspend the caliper with a length of wire. Do not let the caliper hang by the brake hose.

b. Insert a small wood block between the brake pads. This will prevent the caliper piston from extending out of the caliper, if the brake lever is operated.

3B. If the caliper will be disassembled, do the following:

a. Remove the banjo bolt and seal washers from the brake hose. Have a shop cloth ready to absorb excess brake fluid that drips from the hose.

b. Wrap the hose end to prevent brake fluid from damaging other surfaces.

c. Drain excess brake fluid from the caliper.

d. Repair the caliper as described in this section.

4. Reverse this procedure to install the caliper. Note the following:

a. Install and torque the caliper mounting bolts to 28 N•m (21 ft.-lb.).

b. If removed, install new seal washers on the banjo bolt. Seat the brake hose against the guide on the caliper (**Figure 51**), then torque the banjo bolt to 30 N•m (22 ft.-lb.).

c. If the caliper was rebuilt, or the brake hose disconnected from the caliper, fill and bleed the brake system as described in this chapter.

5. Operate the brake lever several times to seat the pads.

6. Check the brake fluid reservoir and replenish or remove fluid as necessary.

7. If necessary, adjust the parking brake (Chapter Three).

8. With the rear wheels raised, check that the disc spins freely and the brake operates properly.

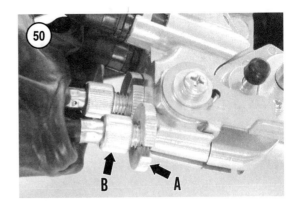

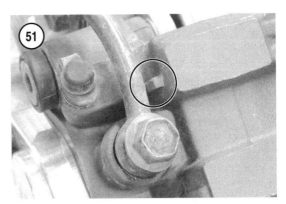

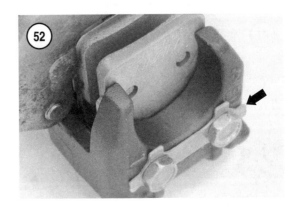

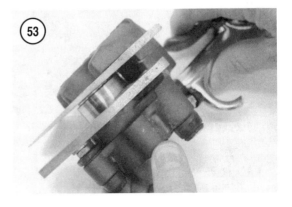

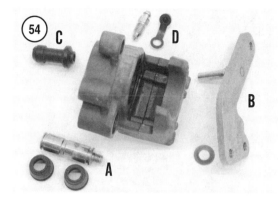

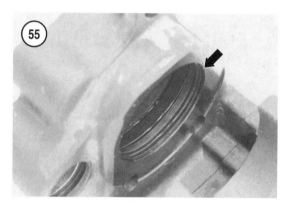

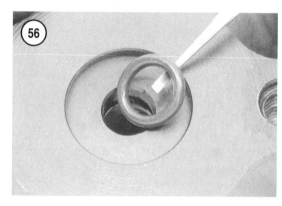

Repair

Use the following procedure to disassemble, inspect and assemble the brake caliper, using new seals. Refer to **Figure 38**.

1. Remove the caliper as described in this section.
2. Remove the two bolts securing the parking brake assembly to the caliper.
3. Bend the tabs on the lockwasher (**Figure 52**) away from the pad pins, then loosen the pins.
4. Press down on the pads to relieve the pressure on the pad pins, then remove the pins.

5. Remove the pads and pad spring.
6. Remove the piston from the caliper bore using compressed air (**Figure 53**). To perform this technique, an air nozzle is tightly held in the brake hose fitting and air pressure ejects the piston. Do not attempt to pry the piston out of the caliper. Read the following procedure entirely before beginning removal:

   a. Place the caliper on a padded work surface.
   b. Close the bleeder valve on the caliper so air cannot escape.
   c. Place a strip of wood, or similar pad, in the caliper. The pad will cushion the piston when it comes out of the caliper.

> *WARNING*
> *Wear eye protection when using compressed air to remove the piston. Keep fingers away from the piston discharge area. Personal injury can occur if an attempt is made to stop the piston by hand.*

   d. Lay the caliper so the piston will discharge downward.
   e. Insert an air nozzle into the brake hose fitting. If the nozzle does not have a rubber tip, wrap the nozzle with tape. This will allow the nozzle to seal tightly and prevent thread damage.
   f. Place a shop cloth over the entire caliper to catch any spray that may discharge from the caliper.
   g. Apply pressure and listen for the piston to *pop* from the caliper.

7. Remove the caliper bracket bolt and boots (A, **Figure 54**). Carefully remove the bolt to prevent tearing or pinching the boots.
8. Remove the caliper bracket and washer (B, **Figure 54**).
9. Remove the slide pin boot (C, **Figure 54**).
10. Remove the bleeder valve and cap (D, **Figure 54**).
11. Remove the dust seal and piston seal (**Figure 55**).
12. Remove the O-ring from the back side of the piston bore (**Figure 56**).
13. Inspect the caliper assembly.

   a. Clean all parts that will be reused with fresh brake fluid or isopropyl (rubbing) alcohol. Use a wood or plastic-tipped tool to clean the seal and boot grooves. Use clean brake fluid to aid in cleaning the piston, bore and seal grooves.

b. Inspect the caliper bore for wear, pitting or corrosion.

c. Measure the inside diameter of the caliper bore (**Figure 57**). Refer to **Table 1** for specifications.

d. Inspect the pad pins, pad spring and mounting bolts (**Figure 43**). The pins and spring must be in good condition to allow the inner pad to slightly move when installed. Check that both small tabs on the spring are not corroded or missing.

e. Inspect the caliper bracket and slide pin for wear, pitting or corrosion.

f. Inspect the boots for deterioration.

g. Inspect the bleeder valve for clogging and damage.

h. Inspect the shim on the back of the inner brake pad (**Figure 44**) Replace the shim if corroded or damaged. Always replace the shim when installing new brake pads.

i. Inspect the brake pads. Replace the pads when they are worn to within 1 mm (0.040 in.) of the backing plate, as shown by the wear indicator (**Figure 45**). Always replace pads that have been contaminated with oil or other chemicals. If the pads are worn unevenly, the caliper is probably not sliding correctly on the caliper bracket. The caliper must be free to *float* on the slide pin and retainer bolt. Buildup or corrosion on the parts can hold the caliper in one position, causing brake drag and excessive pad wear.

j. Inspect the parking brake assembly for obvious wear or damage.

NOTE
Use new brake fluid (rated DOT 4) to lubricate the parts in the following steps.

14. Install a new O-ring into the back side of the piston bore (**Figure 56**).

15. Install the new piston seal (A, **Figure 58**) and dust seal (B) as follows:

a. Soak the seals in brake fluid for 15 minutes.

b. Coat the caliper bore and piston with brake fluid.

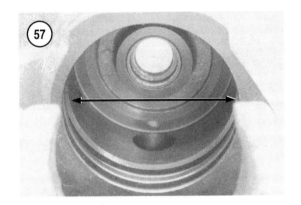

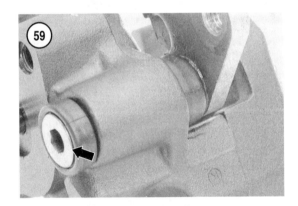

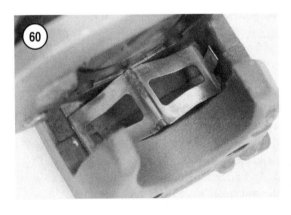

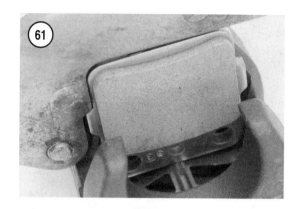

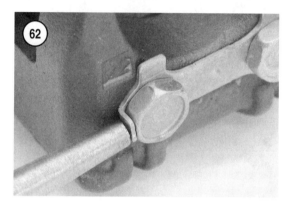

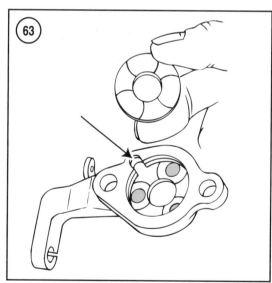

16. Install the boots and caliper bracket bolt as follows:

    a. Apply silicone brake grease to the interior of the boots and to the bracket bolt.

    b. Seat the bracket bolt boots in the caliper grooves and pass the slide pin boot through its bore. If necessary, apply a light coat of grease on the exterior of the boot, to aid in passing it through the caliper.

    c. Carefully twist the bracket bolt through the caliper, then install the boot over the end of the bolt.

17. Install the caliper bracket as follows:

    a. Lubricate the slide pin on the bracket, then install it onto the caliper.

    b. Align the bracket with the caliper bracket bolt. Place the washer over the bolt, then tighten the bracket bolt (**Figure 59**).

    c. Torque the bracket bolt to 23 N•m (17 ft.-lb.).

18. Install the bleeder valve and cap.

19. Install the pad spring with the small tabs pointing out (**Figure 60**).

20. Install the inner pad and shim, seating the pad under the caliper bracket and against the piston (**Figure 61**).

21. Install the outer pad.

22. Press down on the pads, then align and install the pad pins. Torque the pins to 18 N•m (13 ft.-lb.).

23. Bend the lockwasher tabs against the mounting bolts (**Figure 62**).

24. Assemble the parking brake assembly as shown in **Figure 38**.

    a. Apply waterproof grease to the balls and bearing races.

    b. Engage the tab on the outer race with the notch in the brake case (**Figure 63**).

    c. Apply threadlocking compound to the threads of the two mounting bolts.

25. Spread the pads so their is clearance to fit the caliper over the brake disc.

26. Install the caliper as described in this section.

REAR MASTER CYLINDER

Removal and Installation

Use the following procedure to remove the rear master cylinder and brake fluid reservoir from the machine. Refer to *Repair* in this section to make internal repairs to the master cylinder.

    c. Seat the piston seal, then the dust seal in the caliper grooves. The piston seal goes in the back groove.

    d. Install the piston with the flat side facing out. Twist the piston past the seals then press the piston to the bottom of the bore.

13

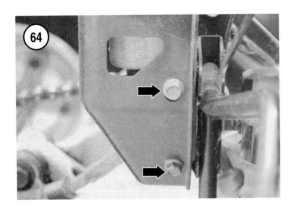

1. Drain the brake system as described in this chapter.

2. Remove the reservoir cover (**Figure 64**).

3. Remove the cap and diaphragm and verify that the reservoir is empty. Wipe the interior of the reservoir dry, then remove the bolt securing the reservoir to the frame (**Figure 65**).

4. Remove the right footguard and frame (Chapter Fourteen).

5. Remove the banjo bolt and seal washers from the brake hose (**Figure 66**). Have a shop cloth ready to absorb excess brake fluid that drips from the hose. Wrap the hose end to prevent brake fluid from damaging other surfaces.

6. Remove the cotter pin, washer and clevis pin (A, **Figure 67**), that secure the master cylinder clevis to the brake pedal.

7. Remove the master cylinder mounting bolts (B, **Figure 67**).

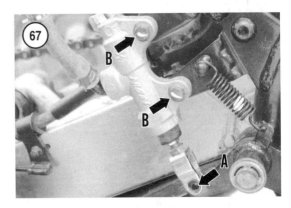

8. Repair the master cylinder as described in this section.

9. Reverse this procedure to install the master cylinder and reservoir. Note the following:

    a. Torque the master cylinder mounting bolts to 20 N•m (15 ft.-lb.).

    b. Install new seal washers on the banjo bolt. The upper washer is also a hose guide and must be installed as shown in **Figure 68**. Torque the bolt to 30 N•m (22 ft.-lb.).

    c. Install a new cotter pin on the clevis pin.

10. Fill the brake fluid reservoir and bleed the brake system as described in this chapter.

Repair

Refer to **Figure 69**.

Use the following procedure to disassemble, inspect and assemble the master cylinder, using new

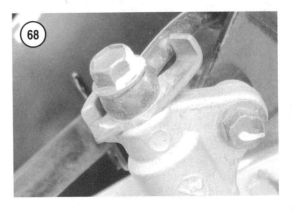

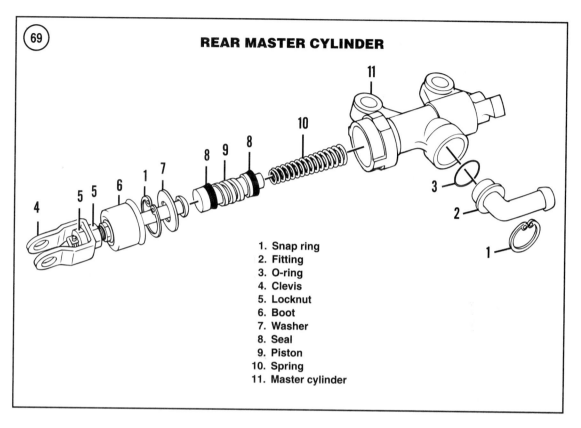

REAR MASTER CYLINDER

1. Snap ring
2. Fitting
3. O-ring
4. Clevis
5. Locknut
6. Boot
7. Washer
8. Seal
9. Piston
10. Spring
11. Master cylinder

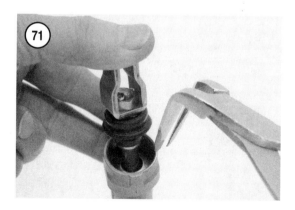

parts. The piston, seals and spring are only available as a complete assembly.

1. Remove the master cylinder and reservoir as described in this section.

2. Remove the clamp and reservoir hose from the hose fitting.

3. Remove the snap ring that retains the hose fitting against the master cylinder, then remove the fitting and internal O-ring (**Figure 70**).

4. Remove the snap ring from the master cylinder (**Figure 71**) as follows:

    a. Unseat the boot from the cylinder bore and fold it toward the clevis. The boot is a friction fit. To avoid damaging the boot on removal, apply penetrating lubricant around the perimeter of the boot. Carefully pull the bottom edge back so the lubricant can loosen the boot.

    b. If desired, lock the cylinder in a vise with soft jaws.

    c. Press and tilt the pushrod to relieve pressure on the snap ring, then remove the snap ring with snap ring pliers.

    d. Slowly relieve the pressure on the piston.

13

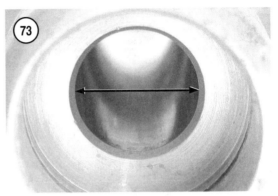

5. Remove the piston and pushrod assembly from the bore (**Figure 72**).

6. Inspect the master cylinder assembly.

    a. Clean all parts that will be reused with fresh brake fluid or isopropyl (rubbing) alcohol.

    b. Inspect the cylinder bore for wear, pitting or corrosion.

    c. Measure the inside diameter of the cylinder bore (**Figure 73**). Refer to **Table 1** for specifications.

    d. Inspect and clean the threads and orifices in the master cylinder (**Figure 74**). Clean with compressed air.

    e. Inspect the pushrod assembly (**Figure 75**). Check the parts for corrosion and wear. Install a new snap ring on the pushrod, with the sharp edge of the snap ring facing out. Remove/install the old/new snap ring by passing it by the washer as shown in **Figure 76**. Do not expand the new snap ring when installing it on the pushrod.

    f. Inspect the clevis pin, banjo bolt and mounting hardware (**Figure 77**) for wear or damage.

    g. Inspect the reservoir, diaphragm, diaphragm holder and reservoir cap for damage (**Figure 78**).

7. Assemble the piston, seals and spring (**Figure 79**) as follows:

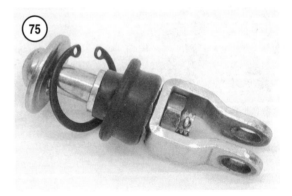

    a. Soak the seals in fresh brake fluid (rated DOT 4) for 15 minutes. This will soften and lubricate the seals.

    b. Apply brake fluid to the piston so the seals can slide over the ends.

    c. Mount the seals on the piston. Identify the wide (open) side of both seals. When installed, the wide side of the seals *must* face in

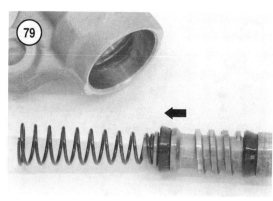

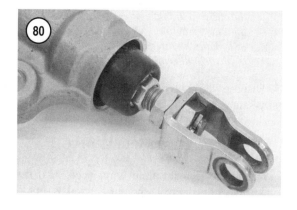

the direction of the arrow (**Figure 79**). Mount the seal with the small hole nearest the spring.

   d. Install and seat the spring onto the piston.

8. Install the piston and pushrod assembly into the master cylinder as follows:

   a. Lubricate the cylinder bore and piston assembly with brake fluid.

   b. Apply a small amount of silicone brake grease to the contact area of the pushrod.

   c. Insert the piston into the cylinder.

   d. If desired, lock the cylinder in a vise with soft jaws. Do not overtighten the vise or cylinder damage could occur.

   e. Compress the snap ring with snap ring pliers.

   f. Press and tilt the pushrod in the cylinder while guiding the snap ring into position. If the snap ring does not easily seat, release the snap ring and use the tip of the pliers to press it into the groove. Keep the pushrod compressed until the snap ring is seated.

9. Apply silicone brake grease to the inside of the boot. Seat the boot into the cylinder (**Figure 80**).

10. Install a new, lubricated O-ring into the master cylinder (**Figure 81**), then lock the hose fitting into the O-ring. Install a new snap ring with the flat side facing out.

11. Attach the reservoir and hose to the fitting, then clamp into place.

12. Install the diaphragm, diaphragm holder and cap onto the reservoir.

13. Install the master cylinder (**Figure 82**) as described in this section.

13

REAR BRAKE PEDAL

Removal and Installation

1. Remove the right footguard and frame (Chapter Fourteen).
2. Remove the following parts to remove the brake pedal (**Figure 83**):
   a. Brake light switch spring (A).
   b Pedal return spring (B).
   c. Master cylinder clevis pin (C).
   d. E-clip and washer (D).
3. Remove the pedal from the shaft.
4. Clean and inspect the parts for wear and damage.
5. Reverse this procedure to install the pedal. Note the following:
   a. Apply waterproof grease to the bore and pedal shaft.
   b. Install a new cotter pin in the clevis pin.
   c. Check brake operation.
   d. Check pedal height. If necessary, adjust the pedal (Chapter Three).
   e. Check brake light operation. If necessary, adjust the switch (Chapter Three).

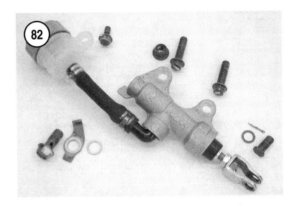

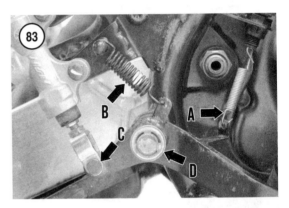

BRAKE SYSTEM DRAINING

To drain the brake fluid from the system, have an 8 mm wrench, tip-resistant container and a length of clear tubing that fits snugly on the bleeder valve. Use the following procedure to drain either the front or rear brakes:

> *CAUTION*
> *Brake fluid can damage painted and finished surfaces. Use water to immediately wash any surface that becomes contaminated with brake fluid.*

1. Attach one end of the tubing to the bleeder valve and place the other end into the container (**Figure 84**).
2. Open the bleeder valve so fluid can pass into the tubing.
3. Pump the brake lever/pedal to force the fluid from the system.
4. When the system no longer drips fluid, close the bleeder valve.

> *NOTE*
> *Before disconnecting any brake hose(s) on the front brakes, remove*

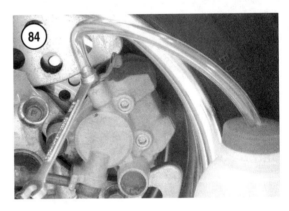

*the cap and diaphragm and verify that the master cylinder is empty (**Figure 85**). Wipe the interior of the reservoir to absorb all remaining fluid.*

5. Dispose the brake fluid in an environmentally-safe manner.

BRAKE SYSTEM BLEEDING

Whenever the brake fluid is replaced, or if the brake lever or pedal feels spongy, the brakes should

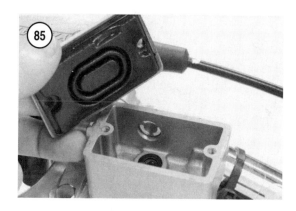

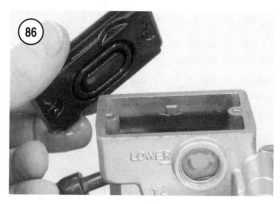

will minimize the chance of spilled fluid from an open reservoir.

Brake Fluid Reservoirs

Regardless of the bleeding method used, the reservoir cap of the master cylinder being bled must be removed so the reservoir can be filled with brake fluid. The reservoirs must not be over or under filled. Note the following when working with each reservoir:

1. Front brake reservoir.
   a. Remove the reservoir cap and diaphragm.
   b. Keep the reservoir filled between the top of the sight glass and the lower mark on the reservoir (**Figure 86**) during the bleeding procedure.
   c. After bleeding, replenish the reservoir to the upper mark, then install the diaphragm and cap.
2. Rear brake reservoir.
   a. Remove the reservoir guard, cap, diaphragm holder and diaphragm.
   b. Keep the reservoir filled between the upper and lower marks on the reservoir during the bleeding procedure (**Figure 87**).
   c. After bleeding, replenish the reservoir to the upper mark, then install the diaphragm, diaphragm holder and cap.
   d. Install the reservoir guard.

Manual Bleeding

To manually bleed the brake system, have an 8 mm wrench, tip-resistant container and a length of clear tubing that fits snugly on the brake bleeder. Bleeding the system is much easier if two people are available to perform the procedure. One person can open and close the bleeder valve while the other person operates the brake lever or pedal. Use the following procedure to bleed either the front or rear brake:

CAUTION
Brake fluid can damage painted and finished surfaces. Use water and immediately wash any surface that becomes contaminated with brake fluid.

be bled to purge all air from the system. Before bleeding the brakes, determine where the air is entering the system. Check all brake components for leakage, and fittings and hoses for deterioration, damage or looseness. The brake system can be bled manually or by using a vacuum pump. Both methods are described in this section.

CAUTION
Before bleeding brakes, always secure the bike so it is stable and locked in place, particularly the fork. This

13

1. Attach one end of the tubing to the bleeder valve and place the other end into the container (**Figure 84**).

2. Fill the reservoir to the upper level with DOT 4 brake fluid.

> *CAUTION*
> *Do not use brake fluid from an un-sealed container. It will have absorbed moisture from the air and already be contaminated. Use DOT 4 brake fluid from a sealed container.*

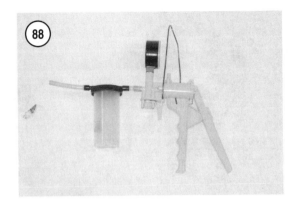

3. Apply pressure (do not pump) to the brake lever or pedal, then open the bleeder valve. As the fluid is forced from the system, the lever/pedal will travel its full length of operation. When the lever/pedal can move no farther, hold the lever/pedal in the *down* position and close the bleeder valve. Do not allow the lever or pedal to return to its *up* position before the bleeder valve is closed. Air will be drawn into the system.

> *NOTE*
> *In the following step, release the lever/pedal slowly. This will minimize the chance of fluid splashing out of the reservoir, as excess fluid in the brake line is returned to the reservoir.*

4. When the bleeder valve is closed, release the lever/pedal so it returns to its *up* position. Check the fluid level in the reservoir and replenish, if necessary.

> *NOTE*
> *During the bleeding process, the reservoir must contain fluid during the entire procedure. If the reservoir is allowed to become empty, air will be in the system and the bleeding process will have to be repeated.*

5. Repeat Step 3 and Step 4 until clear fluid (minimal air bubbles) is seen passing out of the bleeder valve. Unless the bleeder valve threads are wrapped with Teflon tape, or coated with silicone brake grease, a small amount of air will enter the system when the bleeder valve is opened.

> *NOTE*
> *If small bubbles (foam) remain in the system after several bleeding attempts, close the reservoir and allow the system to stand undisturbed for a few hours. The system will stabilize and the air can be purged as large bubbles.*

6. The bleeding procedure is completed when the feel of the lever/pedal is firm.

7. Check the brake fluid reservoir and fill the reservoir to the upper level, if necessary.

8. Torque the bleeder valve to 6 N•m (53 in.-lb.).

9. Dispose the waste brake fluid in an environmentally-safe manner.

Vacuum Bleeding

To vacuum-bleed the brake system, have an 8 mm wrench and a vacuum pump, such as the Mityvac pump shown in (**Figure 88**). Use the following procedure to bleed either the front or rear brake:

CAUTION
Brake fluid can damage painted and
finished surfaces. Use water and im-
mediately wash any surface that be-
comes contaminated with brake fluid.

1. Check that the banjo bolts are tight at the master cylinder and caliper.

2. Attach the vacuum pump to the bleeder valve. Suspend the tool with wire. This will allow the tool to be released when the fluid reservoir needs to be refilled.

3. Fill the reservoir to the upper level with DOT 4 brake fluid.

CAUTION
Do not use brake fluid from an un-
sealed container. It will have ab-
sorbed moisture from the air and
already be contaminated. Use DOT
4 brake fluid from a sealed con-
tainer.

NOTE
During the bleeding process, the res-
ervoir must contain fluid during the
entire procedure. If the reservoir is al-
lowed to become empty, air will be in
the system and the bleeding process
will have to be repeated.

4. Pump the handle on the brake bleeder to create a vacuum.

5. Open the bleeder valve and draw the air and fluid from the system. Close the valve *before* the fluid stops moving. If the vacuum pump is equipped with a gauge, close the bleeder before the gauge reads 0 in. Hg. Replenish the fluid level in the reservoir.

6. Repeat Step 4 and Step 5 until clear fluid (minimal air bubbles) is seen passing out of the bleeder. Unless the bleeder valve threads are wrapped with Teflon tape, or coated with silicone brake grease, a small amount of air will enter the system when the bleeder valve is opened. The bleeding procedure is completed when the feel of the lever/pedal is firm.

7. Check the brake fluid reservoir and fill the reservoir to the upper level, if necessary.

8. Torque the bleeder valve to 6 N•m (53 in.-lb.).

9. Dispose the waste brake fluid in an environmentally-safe manner.

BRAKE DISC

The condition of the brake discs and pads are often a reflection of one another. If disc scoring is evident, inspect the pads and disc as soon as possible. If damage is detected, perform the inspections described in this section.

NOTE
Do not true a deeply scored or warped
disc. The removal of disc material will
cause the disc to overheat rapidly and
warp. Maintain the discs by keeping
them clean and corrosion-free. Use a
solvent, that is not oil-based, to wipe
grit that accumulates on the discs and
at the edge of the pads.

Thickness and Runout Inspection

1. Measure the thickness of each disc at several locations around its perimeter (**Figure 89**). Refer to **Table 1** for the service limit. Replace the disc if it is out of specification.

2. Measure disc runout as follows:
   a. Mount a dial indicator on a stable surface and in contact with the brake pad surface of the disc (**Figure 90**).
   b. Zero the gauge.
   c. Turn the wheel and watch the amount of runout measured on the gauge.
   d. Refer to **Table 1** for the service limit. Replace the disc if it is out of specification.

NOTE
If the disc runout is out of specifica-
tion, check the condition of the hub

13

bearings before replacing the disc. If the bearings are not in good condition, the bearings should be replaced before disc runout is determined.

Removal and Installation

The discs are mounted to the hubs with bolts. Remove and install the discs as follows:

1. Remove the brake hub from the machine (Chapter Eleven or Chapter Twelve).
2. Remove the bolts (**Figure 91**) that secure the disc to the hub.
3. Clean the bolts and mounting holes.
4. Reverse this procedure to install the discs. Note the following:

    a. Apply nonpermanent threadlocking compound to the bolt threads.

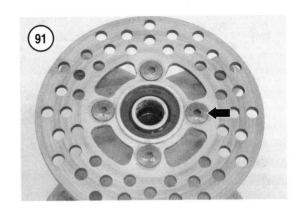

    b. Tighten the bolts in several passes and in a crossing pattern.
    c. Torque the bolts to 28 N•m (21 ft.-lb.).
    d. Check the disc for runout as described in this section.

Table 1 BRAKE SPECIFICATIONS

	New mm (in.)	Service limit mm (in.)
Brake disc thickness		
Front	3.5 (0.137)	3.0 (0.12)
Rear	3.6 (0.141)	3.0 (0.12)
Brake disc runout	–	0.15 (0.006)
Brake pad thickness		
Front	4.2 (0.17)	1.0 (0.04)
Rear	4.5 (0.18)	1.0 (0.04)
Caliper cylinder diameter		
Front	32.03 (1.26)	–
Rear	33.96 (1.34)	–
Master cylinder diameter (front and rear)	12.7 (0.50)	–
Recommended brake fluid	DOT 4	

Table 2 BRAKE TORQUE SPECIFICATIONS

	N•m	in.-lb.	ft.-lb.
Bleeder valve	6	53	–
Brake hose banjo bolts			
Front	27	–	20
Rear	30	–	22
Caliper bracket bolt	23	–	17
Caliper mounting bolts	28	–	21
Disc bolts	28	–	21
Front master cylinder mounting bolts	7	62	–
Pad pins	18	–	13
Parking brake case mounting bolts	25	–	18
Parking brake adjuster locknut	16	–	12
Rear master cylinder mounting bolts	20	–	15

CHAPTER FOURTEEN

BODY

This chapter contains removal and installation procedures for the seat, front panel, headlights, fuel tank top panel, front fender, rear fender, fuel tank, fuel tank protectors, footguard assembly and skid plate.

SEAT

Removal and Installation

The seat release is located behind the taillight.
1. Pull out on the seat release and raise the rear of the seat (**Figure 1**).
2. Pull back on the seat to disengage the prongs from the front mount (**Figure 2**).
3. To install the seat, align and lock the prongs around the front mount.
4. Slide the seat forward and lock the rear of the seat into place.
5. Lightly lift the rear of the seat to ensure it is locked.

FRONT PANEL

Removal and Installation

1. Remove the two screws located at the top of the front panel (**Figure 3**).
2. Lift the panel from the bodywork.
3. Reverse these steps to install the front panel.

HEADLIGHT ASSEMBLY

Removal and Installation

1. Disconnect the electrical connector leading to the headlight.
2. Remove the two bolts, washers and spacers that secure the headlight (**Figure 4**).
3. Reverse these steps to install the headlight.

FUEL TANK TOP PANEL

Removal and Installation

1. Turn the four slotted rivets counterclockwise to disengage them for removal. The rivets are not threaded and only require about one-half turn to disengage.
2. Lift each rivet up to unlock it from the front fender (**Figure 5**).
3. Remove the fuel cap and remove the top panel.
4. Reverse these steps to install the top panel.

FRONT FENDER

Removal and Installation

1. Remove the seat, front panel, headlights and fuel tank top panel as described in this chapter.

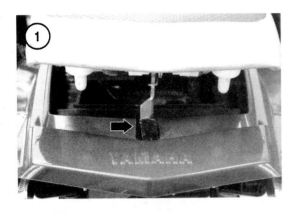

2. Remove the bolt at the rear of the fender, on each side (**Figure 6**).

3. Remove the two bolts at the rear of the fuel tank (**Figure 7**).

4. Remove the bolt at the front of the fender, near the base of the radiator (**Figure 8**).

5. Raise and slide the fender forward and away from the machine.

6. Reverse these steps to install the fender. Align and finger-tighten all bolts before tightening.

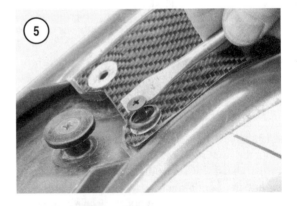

REAR FENDER

Removal and Installation

1. Remove the seat as described in this chapter.

2. Remove the two bolts at the rear of the fuel tank (**Figure 7**).

3. Remove the battery hold down bracket (A, **Figure 9**).

4. Remove the battery leads (B, **Figure 9**).

5. Remove the CDI unit and starter relay (**Figure 10**).

6. Remove the bolt at the rear of the battery compartment, near the seat latch.

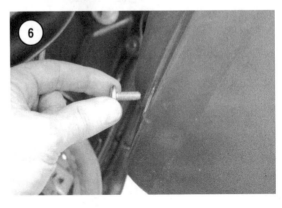

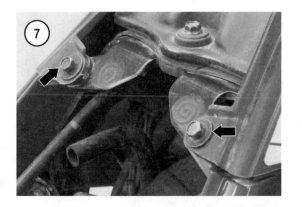

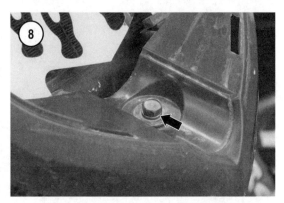

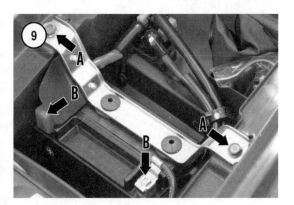

7. Remove the bolt at the front of the fender, on each side (**Figure 11**).

8. Remove the bolt at the rear of the fender, on each side (**Figure 12**).

9. Check that all wiring is clear of the fender, then raise and slide the fender back and away from the machine.

10. Reverse these steps to install the fender. Align and finger-tighten all bolts before tightening.

FUEL TANK

Removal and Installation

CAUTION
After the fuel tank is removed, store it away from sources that could cause an explosion. Store the tank where it cannot be disturbed until reinstallation.

1. Remove the seat, front panel, headlights, fuel tank top panel and front fender as described in this chapter.

2. Turn the fuel valve off (A, **Figure 13**).

3. Remove the fuel line from the fuel valve (B, **Figure 13**). Plug the fuel line and keep it in an upright position.

4. Remove the mounting bolt at the front of the tank, on each side (**Figure 14**).

5. Remove the mounting bolt at the rear of the tank (**Figure 15**).

6. Remove the fuel tank breather tube from the handlebar cover.

7. Check that the fuel cap is tight, then lift the tank from the machine.

8. Reverse these steps to install the fuel tank. Note the following:

    a. Check the condition of the fuel line clamp. Replace if necessary.

    b. Check that the fuel tank breather tube is routed correctly.

    c. Turn on the fuel valve and check for leaks.

FUEL TANK PROTECTORS

Removal and Installation

1. Remove the fuel tank as described in this chapter.

2. Remove the rear protector as follows:

    a. Remove the mounting screw on each side of the rear protector (**Figure 16**). Note that each screw is threaded into a carburetor vent hose clamp.

    b. Remove the rear protector.

3. Remove the front protector (**Figure 17**) as follows:

    a. Remove the two straps from the front of the protector.

    b. Remove the front protector.

4. Reverse these steps to install the protectors. Check that both protectors are properly seated and secured.

FOOTGUARD ASSEMBLY

Removal and Installation

1. Remove the three bolts securing the footguard assembly to the footpeg and frame (**Figure 18**).

2. If removing the right footguard assembly, remove the rear brake reservoir before removing the bolts.

3. Remove the footguard assembly from the machine.

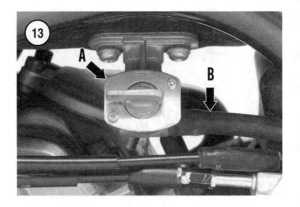

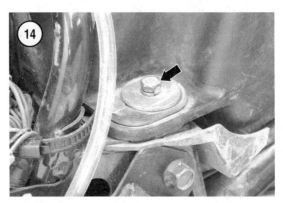

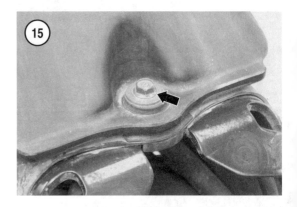

4. Reverse these steps to install the footguard assembly.

SKID PLATES

Engine Skid Plate
Removal and Installation

1. Remove the six bolts securing the skid plate to the frame (**Figure 19**).

2. Remove the skid plate from the machine.
3. Reverse these steps to install the skid plate.

Swing Arm Skid Plate
Removal and Installation

1. Remove the four bolts securing the skid plate to the swing arm (**Figure 20**).
2. Remove the skid plate from the machine.
3. Reverse these steps to install the skid plate.

INDEX

15

15

WIRING
DIAGRAMS

YFM660R

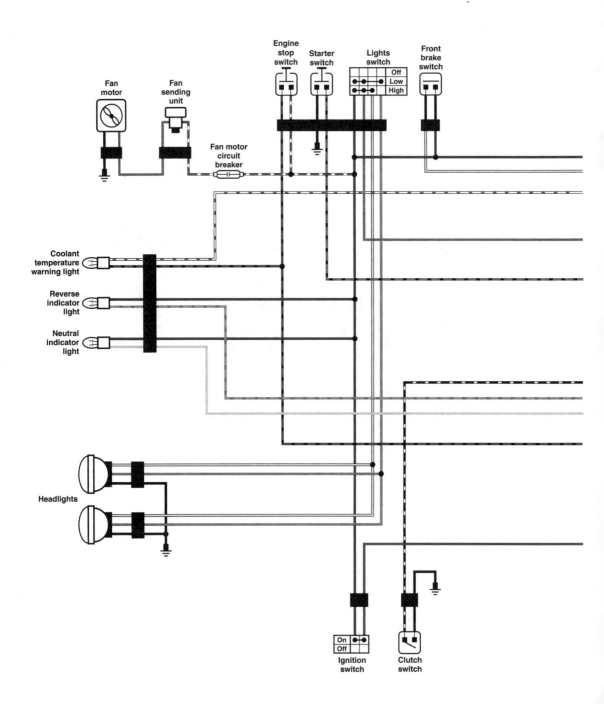

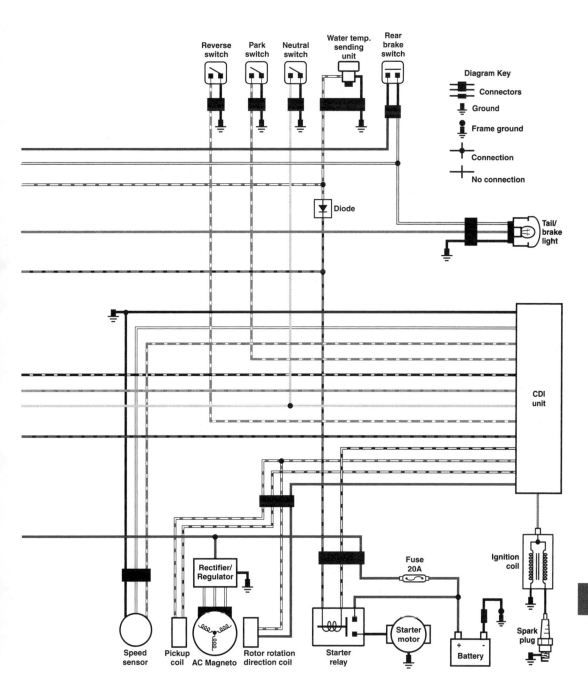

NOTES

NOTES

NOTES

MAINTENANCE LOG

Date	Hours	Type of Service

Check out *clymer.com* for our full line of powersport repair manuals.

BMW

M308	500 & 600cc Twins, 55-69
M502-3	BMW R50/5-R100GS PD, 70-96
M500-3	BMW K-Series, 85-97
M501-3	K1200RS, GT & LT, 98-10
M503-3	R850, R1100, R1150 & R1200C, 93-05
M309	F650, 1994-2000

HARLEY-DAVIDSON

M419	Sportsters, 59-85
M429-5	XL/XLH Sportster, 86-03
M427-3	XL Sportster, 04-11
M418	Panheads, 48-65
M420	Shovelheads,66-84
M421-3	FLS/FXS Evolution,84-99
M423-2	FLS/FXS Twin Cam, 00-05
M250	FLS/FXS/FXC Softail, 06-09
M422-3	FLH/FLT/FXR Evolution, 84-98
M430-4	FLH/FLT Twin Cam, 99-05
M252	FLH/FLT, 06-09
M426	VRSC Series, 02-07
M424-2	FXD Evolution, 91-98
M425-3	FXD Twin Cam, 99-05

HONDA

ATVs

M316	Odyssey FL250, 77-84
M311	ATC, TRX & Fourtrax 70-125, 70-87
M433	Fourtrax 90, 93-00
M326	ATC185 & 200, 80-86
M347	ATC200X & Fourtrax 200SX, 86-88
M455	ATC250 & Fourtrax 200/250, 84-87
M342	ATC250R, 81-84
M348	TRX250R/Fourtrax 250R & ATC250R, 85-89
M456-4	TRX250X 87-92; TRX300EX 93-06
M446-3	TRX250 Recon & Recon ES, 97-07
M215	TRX250EX, 01-05
M346-3	TRX300/Fourtrax 300 & TRX300FW/Fourtrax 4x4, 88-00
M200-2	TRX350 Rancher, 00-06
M459-3	TRX400 Foreman 95-03
M454-2	TRX400EX 99-07
M201	TRX450R & TRX450ER, 04-09
M205	TRX450 Foreman, 98-04
M210	TRX500 Rubicon, 01-04
M206	TRX500 Foreman, 05-11

Singles

M310-13	50-110cc OHC Singles, 65-99
M315	100-350cc OHC, 69-82
M317	125-250cc Elsinore, 73-80
M442	CR60-125R Pro-Link, 81-88
M431-2	CR80R, 89-95, CR125R, 89-91
M435	CR80R &CR80RB, 96-02
M457-2	CR125R, 92-97; CR250R, 92-96
M464	CR125R, 1998-2002
M443	CR250R-500R Pro-Link, 81-87
M432-3	CR250R, 88-91 & CR500R, 88-01
M437	CR250R, 97-01
M352	CRF250R, CRF250X, CRF450R & CRF450X, 02-05
M319-3	XR50R, CRF50F, XR70R & CRF70F, 97-09
M312-14	XL/XR75-100, 75-91
M222	XR80R, CRF80F, XR100R, & CRF100F, 92-09
M318-4	XL/XR/TLR 125-200, 79-03
M328-4	XL/XR250, 78-00; XL/XR350R 83-85; XR200R, 84-85; XR250L, 91-96
M320-2	XR400R, 96-04
M221	XR600R, 91-07; XR650L, 93-07
M339-8	XL/XR 500-600, 79-90
M225	XR650R, 00-07

Twins

M321	125-200cc Twins, 65-78
M322	250-350cc Twins, 64-74
M323	250-360cc Twins, 74-77
M324-5	Twinstar, Rebel 250 & Nighthawk 250, 78-03
M334	400-450cc Twins, 78-87
M333	450 & 500cc Twins, 65-76
M335	CX & GL500/650, 78-83
M344	VT500, 83-88
M313	VT700 & 750, 83-87
M314-3	VT750 Shadow Chain Drive, 98-06
M440	VT1100C Shadow, 85-96
M460-4	VT1100 Series, 95-07
M230	VTX1800 Series, 02-08
M231	VTX1300 Series, 03-09

Fours

M332	CB350-550, SOHC, 71-78
M345	CB550 & 650, 83-85
M336	CB650,79-82
M341	CB750 SOHC, 69-78
M337	CB750 DOHC, 79-82
M436	CB750 Nighthawk, 91-93 & 95-99
M325	CB900, 1000 & 1100, 80-83
M439	600 Hurricane, 87-90
M441-2	CBR600F2 & F3, 91-98
M445-2	CBR600F4, 99-06
M220	CBR600RR, 03-06
M434-2	CBR900RR Fireblade, 93-99
M329	500cc V-Fours, 84-86
M349	700-1000cc Interceptor, 83-85
M458-2	VFR700F-750F, 86-97
M438	VFR800FI Interceptor, 98-00
M327	700-1100cc V-Fours, 82-88
M508	ST1100/Pan European, 90-02
M340	GL1000 & 1100, 75-83
M504	GL1200, 84-87

Sixes

M505	GL1500 Gold Wing, 88-92
M506-2	GL1500 Gold Wing, 93-00
M507-3	GL1800 Gold Wing, 01-10
M462-2	GL1500C Valkyrie, 97-03

KAWASAKI

ATVs

M465-3	Bayou KLF220 & KLF250, 88-10
M466-4	Bayou KLF300, 86-04
M467	Bayou KLF400, 93-99
M470	Lakota KEF300, 95-99
M385-2	Mojave KSF250, 87-04

Singles

M350-9	80-350cc Rotary Valve, 66-01
M444-2	KX60, 83-02; KX80 83-90
M448-2	KX80, 91-00; KX85, 01-10 & KX100, 89-09
M351	KDX200, 83-88
M447-3	KX125 & KX250, 82-91; KX500, 83-04
M472-2	KX125, 92-00
M473-2	KX250, 92-00
M474-3	KLR650, 87-07
M240-2	KLR650, 08-12

Twins

M355	KZ400, KZ/Z440, EN450 & EN500, 74-95
M360-3	EX500, GPZ500S, & Ninja 500R, 87-02
M356-5	Vulcan 700 & 750, 85-06
M354-3	Vulcan 800 & Vulcan 800 Classic, 95-05
M357-2	Vulcan 1500, 87-99
M471-3	Vulcan 1500 Series, 96-08
M245	Vulcan 1600 Series, 03-08

Fours

M449	KZ500/550 & ZX550, 79-85
M450	KZ, Z & ZX750, 80-85
M358	KZ650, 77-83
M359-3	Z & KZ 900-1000cc, 73-81
M451-3	KZ, ZX & ZN 1000 &1100cc, 81-02
M452-3	ZX500 & Ninja ZX600, 85-97
M468-2	Ninja ZX-6, 90-04
M469	Ninja ZX-7, ZX7R & ZX7RR, 91-98
M453-3	Ninja ZX900, ZX1000 & ZX1100, 84-01
M409	Concours, 86-04

POLARIS

ATVs

M496	3-, 4- and 6-Wheel Models w/250-425cc Engines, 85-95
M362-2	Magnum & Big Boss, 96-99
M363	Scrambler 500 4X4, 97-00
M365-4	Sportsman/Xplorer, 96-10
M366	Sportsman 600/700/800 Twins, 02-10
M367	Predator 500, 03-07

SUZUKI

ATVs

M381	ALT/LT 125 & 185, 83-87
M475	LT230 & LT250, 85-90
M380-2	LT250R Quad Racer, 85-92
M483-2	LT-4WD, LT-F4WDX & LT-F250, 87-98
M270-2	LT-Z400, 03-08
M343-2	LT-F500F Quadrunner, 98-02

Singles

M369	125-400cc, 64-81
M371	RM50-400 Twin Shock, 75-81
M379	RM125-500 Single Shock, 81-88
M386	RM80-250, 89-95
M400	RM125, 96-00
M401	RM250, 96-02
M476	DR250-350, 90-94
M477-3	DR-Z400E, S & SM, 00-09
M384-4	LS650 Savage/S40, 86-07

Twins

M372	GS400-450 Chain Drive, 77-87
M484-3	GS500E Twins, 89-02
M361	SV650, 1999-2002
M481-5	VS700-800 Intruder/S50, 85-07
M261-2	1500 Intruder/C90, 98-09
M260-2	Volusia/Boulevard C50, 01-08
M482-3	VS1400 Intruder/S83, 87-07

Triple

M368	GT380, 550 & 750, 72-77

Fours

M373	GS550, 77-86
M364	GS650, 81-83
M370	GS750, 77-82
M376	GS850-1100 Shaft Drive, 79-84
M378	GS1100 Chain Drive, 80-81
M383-3	Katana 600, 88-96 GSX-R750-1100, 86-87
M331	GSX-R600, 97-00
M264	GSX-R600, 01-05
M478-2	GSX-R750, 88-92; GSX750F Katana, 89-96
M485	GSX-R750, 96-99
M377	GSX-R1000, 01-04
M266	GSX-R1000, 05-06
M265	GSX1300R Hayabusa, 99-07
M338	Bandit 600, 95-00
M353	GSF1200 Bandit, 96-03

YAMAHA

ATVs

M499-2	YFM80 Moto-4, Badger & Raptor, 85-08
M394	YTM200, 225 & YFM200, 83-86
M488-5	Blaster, 88-05
M489-2	Timberwolf, 89-00
M487-5	Warrior, 87-04
M486-6	Banshee, 87-06
M490-3	Moto-4 & Big Bear, 87-04
M493	Kodiak, 93-98
M287	YFZ450, 04-09
M285-2	Grizzly 660, 02-08
M280-2	Raptor 660R, 01-05
M290	Raptor 700R, 06-09

Singles

M492-2	PW50 & 80 Y-Zinger & BW80 Big Wheel 80, 81-02
M410	80-175 Piston Port, 68-76
M415	250-400 Piston Port, 68-76
M412	DT & MX Series, 77-83
M414	IT125-490, 76-86
M393	YZ50-80 Monoshock, 78-90
M413	YZ100-490 Monoshock, 76-84
M390	YZ125-250, 85-87 YZ490, 85-90
M391	YZ125-250, 88-93 & WR250Z, 91-93
M497-2	YZ125, 94-01
M498	YZ250, 94-98; WR250Z, 94-97
M406	YZ250F & WR250F, 01-03
M491-2	YZ400F, 98-99 & 426F, 00-02; WR400F, 98-00 & 426F, 00-01
M417	XT125-250, 80-84
M480-3	XT350, 85-00; TT350, 86-87
M405	XT/TT 500, 76-81
M416	XT/TT 600, 83-89

Twins

M403	650cc Twins, 70-82
M395-10	XV535-1100 Virago, 81-03
M495-6	V-Star 650, 98-09
M281-4	V-Star 1100, 99-09
M283	V-Star 1300, 07-10
M282-2	Road Star, 99-07

Triple

M404	XS750 & XS850, 77-81

Fours

M387	XJ550, XJ600 & FJ600, 81-92
M494	XJ600 Seca II/Diversion, 92-98
M388	YX600 Radian & FZ600, 86-90
M396	FZR600, 89-93
M392	FZ700-750 & Fazer, 85-87
M411	XS1100, 78-81
M461	YZF-R6, 99-04
M398	YZF-R1, 98-03
M399	FZ1, 01-05
M397	FJ1100 & 1200, 84-93
M375	V-Max, 85-03
M374-2	Royal Star, 96-10

VINTAGE MOTORCYCLES

Clymer® Collection Series

M330	Vintage British Street Bikes, BSA 500–650cc Unit Twins; Norton 750 & 850cc Commandos; Triumph 500-750cc Twins
M300	Vintage Dirt Bikes, V. 1 Bultaco, 125-370cc Singles; Montesa, 123-360cc Singles; Ossa, 125-250cc Singles
M305	Vintage Japanese Street Bikes Honda, 250 & 305cc Twins; Kawasaki, 250-750cc Triples; Kawasaki, 900 & 1000cc Fours